SUPERVISORY
BEHAVIOR
IN EDUCATION

Third Edition

SUPERVISORY
BEHAVIOR
IN EDUCATION

e2.
061619

BEN M. HARRIS
Professor of Educational Administration
The University of Texas at Austin

Prentice-Hall, Inc., Englewood Cliffs, New Jersey 07632

Library of Congress Cataloging in Publication Data

Harris, Ben M.
  Supervisory behavior in education.

  Includes bibliographies and index.
  1. School supervision. I. Title.
LB2806.H34 1985   371.2'013   84-3354
ISBN 0-13-877101-4

Editorial/production supervision and
  interior design: Kate Kelly
Cover design: Ben Santora
Manufacturing buyer: Ron Chapman

Printed in the United States of America

10 9 8 7 6 5 4 3 2 1

ISBN 0-13-877101-4   01

Prentice-Hall International, Inc., *London*
Prentice-Hall of Australia Pty. Limited, *Sydney*
Editora Prentice-Hall do Brasil, Ltda., *Rio de Janeiro*
Prentice-Hall Canada Inc., *Toronto*
Prentice-Hall of India Private Limited, *New Delhi*
Prentice-Hall of Japan, Inc., *Tokyo*
Prentice-hall of Southeast Asia Pte. Ltd., *Singapore*
Whitehall Books Limited, *Wellington, New Zealand*

To Children
All Over the World

CONTENTS

List of Figures and Tables   xi

Preface   xv

PART I
The Nature of Instructional Supervision

Chapter One
THE INSTRUCTIONAL SUPERVISION FUNCTION   1

Defining the School Operation, 1
Supervisory Operations, 10
Supervision for Continuity and Change, 20
Summary, 23
Suggested Readings, 24

Chapter Two
DYNAMICS OF SUPERVISORY BEHAVIOR   26

Improving Teaching, 27
Interest, Leadership, and Implementation, 31

Resistance to Educational Change, 35
The Wisdom of Conservation, 40
Summary, 41
Suggested Readings, 41

Chapter Three
SYSTEMS FOR OPERATIONALIZING
SUPERVISION PROGRAMS   43

Systems Models, 44
A System for Developmental Tasks of Supervision, 49
Change Strategies, 52
Diffusion of Innovations, 55
Summary, 60
Suggested Readings, 61

Chapter Four
ACTIVITIES FOR SUPERVISION   63

A Review of Critical Tasks, 63
Motivation for Change, 65
Activities for Change, 68
Distinctive Activities, 70
Summary, 87
Suggested Readings, 87

Chapter Five
PROGRAM IMPLEMENTATION STRATEGIES   90

Strategies, 91
Designing for Training, 92
Basic Approaches, 98
Other Strategies, 103
Quality Control Circles, 104
Summary, 107
Suggested Reading, 107

Chapter Six
ORGANIZING AND STAFFING FOR SUPERVISION   110

Current Staffing Patterns, 110
Functional Criteria, 120

Staffing Considerations, 124
Staffing by Competencies, 128
Numeral Adequacy of Staff, 130
Approaches to Team Supervision, 134
Summary, 144
Suggested Readings, 144

Chapter Seven
OBSERVING AND ANALYZING INSTRUCTION
146

The Uses of Observations, 147
Systematic Procedures, 152
Types of Instruments, 164
Analysis and Diagnosis, 176
Qualitative Analysis, 182
Summary, 185
Suggested Readings, 186

Chapter Eight
EVALUATION OF INSTRUCTIONAL PROGRAMS
189

The Nature of Evaluation, 190
Purposes to be Served, 191
Systems Analysis, 195
Multifactor Evaluation, 200
Summary, 209
Suggested Readings, 210

PART II
Reports on Supervisors in Action

Chapter Nine
SUPERVISORS AT WORK
213

Life and Problems as a New Supervisor, 214
Elementary Supervisor—A Typical Day, 217
Curriculum Planning in a Boom Town, 219
Visiting Consultant for Bilingual Education, 221
Job-Description Analysis:
    Director of Secondary Education, 223

Chapter Ten
OBSERVATION APPLICATIONS   227

The Case of John Carroll, 228
Contrasting Ways of Working, 234
Observation Record—World History, 236
Supervisory Strategy Case: A Matter of Values, 243
Not-So-Eager Helen Beaver, 246
A Survey for Curriculum Revision
    and In-service Planning, 252
Suggestions for Dealing with the Unobservable, 257
Passive Resistance? 258

Chapter Eleven
PROGRAMS IN ACTION   262

Supervisor Interview with New Teacher, 263
Disseminating Research on Classroom Management, 267
The Consultant Task Force in Intensive Team Supervision, 269
In-service Plan for Training in Reading Disability, 274
Human Relations Workshop, 277
Diagnostic Evaluation of a Staff Development Workshop, 279
The Professional Development Center, 285

Appendix A
COMPETENCY STATEMENTS
FOR SUPERVISORY PERFORMANCE   289

A. Developing Curriculum, 289
B. Providing Materials, 290
C. Providing Staff for Instruction, 290
D. Organizing for Instruction, 291
E. Relating Special Pupil Services, 291
F. Arranging for In-service Education, 292
G. Developing Public Relations, 294
H. Providing Facilities for Instruction, 294
I. Evaluating Instruction, 295

Appendix B
SPECIFIC PERFORMANCES BY COMPETENCY
FOR THE IN–SERVICE TASK AREA   296

References   299
Index   216

LIST OF FIGURES
AND TABLES

Figure 1.1   Major Functions of the School Operation.   4
Figure 1.2   Major Functions Related to Teaching and Learning.   7
Table 1.1   Illustrative Series of Endeavors: Functional
              Relationships in Improving Materials Utilization.   8
Figure 1.3   Ten Task Areas of Instructional Supervision.   13
Table 1.2   Abbreviated List of Professional Supervisory
              Competencies: Developmental Supervisory
              Competency Assessment System.   18
Table 1.3   Illustrations of Specific Performances for Selected
              Competencies and Tasks.   19
Figure 1.4   Six Orientations to Supervision along a Tractive-
              Dynamic Continuum.   23
Figure 2.1   Planning Alternatives for Instructional Change.   29
Figure 2.2   Interest, Leadership, and Progress in Program
              Implementation.   32
Figure 3.1   Simple Illustration of Systems Diagram.   45
Figure 3.2   A Clinical Supervision Linkage System.   46
Figure 3.3   Planning Model for Illustrative In-service Education
              Problem.   47
Figure 3.4   The DeTEK Ten-Step Sequence.   48

Figure 3.5	A Model for Relating Instructional Operations and Development Systems.	50
Figure 3.6	A Three-stage Change Strategy.	58
Figure 4.1	Relating Objectives, Impact, and Group Size to Selected Activities.	69
Table 4.1	List of Activities of Supervision.	72
Table 5.1	Types of Training Designs in Current Practice.	95
Figure 5.1	A Three-loop Clinical Cycle for Changing Teaching Practices.	100
Table 6.1	An Illustration of a Supervisory Competency Profile.	130
Table 6.2	A Scale for Analyzing Number of Supervisors Needed for Adequacy.	132
Table 6.3	Estimates of Adequate Supervisor Staffs for Five School Districts.	133
Table 6.4	Characteristics of Amplified Project Teams and Requirements for Change.	137
Table 6.5	A Process Sequence to Guide Amplification of a Project Core Group.	140
Figure 7.1	Pupil Enthusiasm Inventory.	170
Figure 7.2	Performance Area # 2—Friendly.	173
Table 7.1	Illustration of a Ten Minute Classroom Sequence: Dual Focus.	174
Table 7.2	Illustration of Alternate Focus Effects.	176
Figure 7.3	Work Matrix.	178
Figure 7.4	Analytical Summary of Teacher Question–Pupil Response Inventory.	180
Figure 7.5	DeTEK Instrument V: Data Analysis Worksheet.	181
Table 8.1	Basic Data and Branching Analysis Diagram for Relating Process to Outcome.	201
Figure 8.1	Branching Diagram for 15 Elementary School Teachers, Relating Input, Process, and Outcome Measure.	202
Figure 8.2	Relationships between Departmentalization, Individualization, and Pupil Enthusiasm.	204
Table 8.2	Branching Diagram Analysis for Selected Relationships in an In-Service Training Program.	205
Table 8.3	A Simple Two-Product Branching Analysis.	206
Figure 8.3	DEA Efficiency Diagram for Third-grade Reading.	208
Figure 10.1	A DeTEK Instrument: Comprehensive Observation of Performance.	231
Figure 10.2	Work Matrix.	233
Figure 10.3	DeTEK Instrument I: Teacher Performance Screening Inventory.	249

Figure 10.4   A DeTEK Instrument: Comprehensive Observation
                of Performance.   250
Table 11.1   Distribution of Participants by Interest
                and Learning.   283
Table 11.2   Participant Positions by Interest-Learning
                Categories.   284
Table 11.3   Participant Task-Group Assignments by Interest-
                Learning Categories.   284
Table 11.4   Six Work Centers of the PDC.   288

PREFACE

This volume, like its predecessors published in 1963 and 1975, deals with the theory, research, and evolving concepts of supervision of instruction. This edition is concerned in some depth with strategies and practices for promoting instructional change as well as responding to the persistent issues surrounding public education in most countries. The research base for defining and guiding supervisory behavior is now substantial. The theory building of earlier years in human relations, organizations, communications, power and influence, leadership, and teaching now provide a skeleton on which modest, but useful, models for supervision can be built. This volume attempts to move supervision of instruction from the stage of a craft to that of a professional specialization.

The writer sees supervision as one of the essential functions of the school operation. The supervision function has assumed unprecedented importance in recent decades. A 30-year epoch of educational change has produced only modest results. Gradually it is coming to be seen that systems that are permitted to change themselves in unplanned or erratic ways spawn many unfortunate side effects. Human organizations require human agents of change. Complex school organizations require a cadre of highly skilled personnel designing and implementing sophisticated programs of instructional improvement. The part-time amateur supervisor is being replaced by demands for full-time expert change agent teams.

Part I (Chapters 1-8) is the heart and core of this book, as it attempts to view supervision of instruction as a major unique function of the school operation, defines terms, analyzes strategies, and presents alternative approaches. In each chapter the current literature is heavily drawn upon; but the intent is synthesis, not a cataloging of ideas. The writer has endeavored in these eight chapters to provide a comprehensive way of viewing, analyzing, and conceptualizing supervisory behavior in educational organizations.

Part II (Chapter 9-11) is supplementary as well as complementary to the basic presentations in earlier chapters. The case material in the final three chapters illustrates a variety of practices—some new, some old, some innovative, some routine. The reader may find the cases useful as aids in translating theory into practice.

This book was written with several kinds of readers in mind. Uppermost in the writer's consciousness was the instructional supervisor (of whatever job title or position). The book is also addressed to superintendents, deans, college presidents, and school principals. These administrators are all engaged in supervision of instruction in various ways. The administrators are addressed by this writer for still another reason. Their success in administering instructional organizations in these changing times will depend substantially on their understanding of the supervision function and their ability to facilitate the more dynamic forms of supervisory behavior.

ACKNOWLEDGMENTS

Most of the substance of this book has been filtered from the writer's many experiences with administrators, supervisors, and teachers over the years. The extensive bibliographical listings cited are a bit misleading in suggesting the importance of the literature. The people and programs this writer has been involved with range from Bank Street College in New York to Punaho School, Hawaii; to Iran and Puerto Rico and Cordova, Spain, and Caracas, Venezuela; to schools in the Rio Grande Valley, to Houston, Corpus Christi, New Iberia, Enterprise, Montgomery, and Atlanta through the South; and, of course, to Lufkin, Temple, Dripping Springs, Post, Fort Worth, Baytown, and so many other exciting Texas schools. In each of these places and many more, the writer has been privileged to work with people, share ideas, and see programs for improving instruction in action. There is no practical way to acknowledge each of these individuals and institutions, but the debt is enormous nonetheless.

My many graduate students in seminar, laboratory, and internship are always a major source of ideas. Most of the case material in this volume involves a student, past or present, as narrator, player, scriptwriter, or director. A few of the citations are based on student dissertations. Many student contributions to this book are given specific acknowledgment in the text; others are given the advantages of anonymity.

One's family always makes a contribution to the professional endeavors of an educator. Mine has been no exception. My wife, Mary Lee Harris, has served as both proofreader and critic of the manuscript for this book. My daughter's contributions have been both clerical and spirituelle. To my son, Kim, I owe a special debt as one who learned to balance that special burden of having a professor-father and still remain supportive.

The University of Texas at Austin   BEN M. HARRIS

CHAPTER ONE
THE INSTRUCTIONAL SUPERVISION FUNCTION

Supervision is one of the essential functions for the operation of good schools. This chapter defines instructional supervision in broad perspective. An effort is made to present a realistic yet theoretically sound structure for viewing the professional tasks of supervision. The place of instructional supervision within the larger framework of the total school operation is analyzed with emphasis upon functional interrelationships. Supervisory behavior is described as a special form of leadership, closely related to but distinct from administrative leadership. Further distinctions are made between supervision for change and supervision for maintenance. The roles of various school personnel in the supervision of instruction are differentiated.

DEFINING THE SCHOOL OPERATION

Theoretical Perspectives

Supervision, like any complex part of an even more complex enterprise, can be viewed in various ways and inevitably is. The diversity of perceptions stems not only from organizational complexity but also from lack of information and absence of perspective. To provide perspective, at least, the total school operation must be the point of departure for analyzing instructional supervision as a major function.

Certain theoretical frames of reference have been employed in various writings about instructional supervision. Social-psychological theory has been drawn upon quite heavily to form the "human relations" view of supervisory behavior as reflected in the work of Lovell and Wiles (1983). Social systems theory has been drawn upon to form the basis for a contrasting view (Feyereisen et al., 1970). Communication theory has offered still another way of viewing supervisory behavior, with emphasis on self-analysis and feedback techniques promoted by Flanders (1970). Psychiatric theories, especially those of Carl Rogers (1959), offer still other ways of thinking about instructional supervision. All of these frames of reference seem to offer promise for improving instruction through more efficient supervision. However, most views of supervision by theory-oriented writers are more prescriptive than descriptive (Sullivan, 1982) and tend to be narrow rather than broad-gauged.

The need for objective descriptions of complex human affairs in advance of schemes for change should be obvious. Current practice in supervision of instruction is at best vaguely understood in the absence of research in either depth or scope. Case studies are few and fragmentary. Even a simple history is yet to be written.

Without waiting for these many gaps to be filled, this book attempts to piece together from various sources a description of the instructional realities, analyze the current practice, project needs, and draw upon both research and theory to suggest new and better practices in supervision. At the very least, it is to be hoped, practitioners can abandon the naive notions still common in much that is being written about "supervision made simple" (Goldstein, 1982).

Supervision in the Total Operation

Supervision must be conceptualized as a set of reasonably distinctive endeavors within the total context of the school operation. Obviously, no realm of human behavior is entirely distinctive. To categorize certain endeavors as *supervisory*, however, requires that they have certain distinguishing characteristics.

There has been a tendency to label certain arrays of behaviors as *instructional supervision* without relating them to the whole educational system of which they are a part. Hence, stereotypes have developed that lead to confusion and conflict in thought. Properly conceptualized, instructional supervision is seen as one part of a total operation geared to producing certain outcomes. More specifically, we can think of the educational system as a learning-producing enterprise with instruction as the basic set of production techniques.

A view of instructional supervision as part of a total operation is given clarity by recognizing other "parts" and showing their relationship to supervision. But the nature of supervision of instruction must also be clearly understood.

A Two-Dimensional Framework

When one focuses on learning as product and instruction as productive process, the pupil becomes the obvious counterpart which might be termed "raw material." The two critical dimensions for viewing the educational operation at its central core are pupils and instruction.* Therefore, *instruction-relatedness* and *pupil-relatedness* can be regarded as major dimensions for analyzing the operation of the school and hence for distinguishing instructional supervision from other endeavors.

Figure 1.1 presents a grid with these two dimensions. Through use of such a grid five functional areas of the educational operation are defined and differentiated. Each major functional area is characterized by the degree to which endeavors are pupil-related and instruction-related.

Illustrative Endeavors

Any endeavor of one or more school personnel can be associated with a portion of the grid shown in Figure 1.1. By estimating the degree of pupil-relatedness and instruction-relatedness of any endeavor, a point on the grid is determined. Each point designating a given endeavor can be compared with other endeavors. Similarly, the array of endeavors of a staff member can be plotted to represent a graphic job description.

Endeavors that are characterized as directly instruction-related and also directly pupil-related include classroom presentations, educational counseling, and assisting children in selecting a library book. These are only illustrative, of course. The administration of achievement tests to pupils involves behaviors that are directly pupil-related but perhaps are not as directly instruction-related as is educational counseling involving the use of such test data.

At the other extreme are endeavors that are remotely pupil-related and only indirectly instruction-related. Such endeavors include auditing accounts, collecting taxes, and changing tires on the school bus. These are all important and even essential to the efficient operation of the educational system. They are characterized, however, by behaviors that are neither pupil-related nor instruction-related in direct ways.

Still other endeavors are directly instruction-related but *not* directly pupil-related. Such endeavors include observing in a classroom, selecting new instructional materials, and conducting an in-service session. All of these are directed toward influencing instruction in rather direct ways, but they are not carried on with pupils. Their impact on pupils is indirect.

*Obviously, this analogy is overly simple. It is a dangerous oversimplification if we forget the large differences among pupils *not* found in inert raw material, or if we fail to recognize the essentially human, interactive nature of the pupil as the object of instruction.

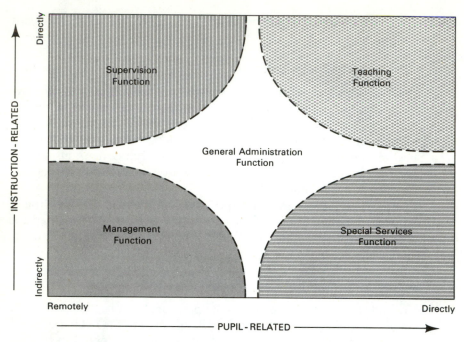

FIGURE 1.1   Major functions of the school operation.

Endeavors that are directly pupil-related but indirectly instruction-related are still different. The checking of pupil vision, tying shoelaces in kindergarten, and applying a bandage to a scraped knee are necessary and desirable endeavors that influence pupils' lives but relate only indirectly to instruction.

Many endeavors tend to be neither directly pupil-related nor directly instruction-related. The distribution of materials of instruction, conferences with parents, and rescheduling of classes are endeavors that have some relationship to pupils and to instruction but are not highly related. The materials, for instance, cannot influence pupils' lives or the instructional process until the teacher or the pupil puts them to use. Distributing such materials to classrooms has no such impact by itself. On the other hand, this endeavor is certainly *more* directly pupil-related and instruction-related than budgeting for such materials or purchasing them.

Any given endeavor, taken in isolation, can be located at some point on the school operations grid shown in Figure 1.1. As such, various endeavors can be systematically classified as falling into one functional area of the school operation rather than another. Ideally, of course, each endeavor is one of a series contributing to pupils' learning. Hence, the setting of a tax rate leads to the collection of funds, which may in turn lead to budget planning, purchasing of materials (for instance), delivery of materials, and revised lesson planning using the new and old materials. The implementation of the lesson in which teacher and pupil use the materials for the production of new learning completes a series of events ranging from those only indirectly pupil-related and instruction-related to those that are highly related to both and thus to learning. The *repeated* realization of such series of events, each carefully timed and expertly accomplished, is the essence of organization in school affairs.

Five Major Functions Distinguished

The school operations grid in Figure 1.1 uses broken lines to designate functional areas of the school operation to suggest boundaries that are less than precise. One cannot determine precisely where supervision of instruction as a functional area ends and general administration begins. In this sense, the framework is very realistic. However, fairly distinctive endeavors can be specified for each of the five areas shown.

Teaching.   This function is central to the primary purpose of the total school operation. Teaching endeavors are directly instruction-related and also directly pupil-related. As such, teaching behaviors are clearly defined and functionally realistic regardless of the person involved in the teaching act. Hence, librarians, counselors, principals, aides, and others may engage in teaching along with teachers. Teaching becomes simply *working with pupils toward instructional objectives.* As such, it is a much more limited set of endeavors than is often implied by the term. For instance, the six teaching roles defined by the California Teachers Association (1964) include a variety of endeavors that greatly overlap with other functions. This definition, however, is more broadly defined in terms of staff participation.

Special pupil services.   This function includes endeavors that are highly pupil-related but only indirectly instruction-related. A whole host of important services provided by nurses, clerks, counselors, psychologists, bus drivers, doctors, and aides—as well as classroom teachers—are rationally a part of this functional area. That these endeavors are not directly instruction-related clearly designates them as supportive services (Harris et al., 1979, pp. 23–24).

Management.   This functional area is characterized by endeavors that are *indirectly* related to instruction and also remotely related to the pupil. These endeavors occupy the time of business managers, principals, clerks, custodians, school board members, and superintendents—as well as classroom teachers. *Management* in this sense (not to be confused with the term as used in business circles) becomes simply the function of supporting other services.

Supervision.   This functional area includes those highly instruction-related but only remotely pupil-related endeavors. The work of supervisors, coordinators, consultants, curriculum specialists, principals, and classroom teachers as they influence instruction is included. These endeavors are distinguished from teaching by their indirect impact on pupil learning. Supervision provides supporting services to the teaching function of highly instruction-related kinds.

Administration.   The general administration area on the school operations grid is unique. It is characterized by endeavors that fall short of being highly instruction-related or highly pupil-related. These are the coordinating, facilitating, controlling endeavors so characteristic of the work of principals, directors, superintendents, and others. The central location of the administration area in the grid is predictive of the power and influence that these endeavors can and do exert over instruction. Administration endeavors tend to give unity to the entire operation by being *somewhat* related to all functional areas; yet these endeavors are not highly instruction-related or pupil-related.

Teaching and Supporting Functions

Figure 1.2 shows the five functional areas of the school operation in relation to teaching and learning as ultimate purposes. This diagram emphasizes, in a way that the "grid" does not, the centrality of *teaching* as the directly productive function of the operation. Supervision services and pupil services are seen as directly supportive of teaching, while management services tend to be less direct. The relationships depicted in the school operations grid provide the basis for clearly differentiating and defining endeavors necessary to an operating school.

The use of two crucial dimensions—instruction-relatedness and pupil-relatedness—to define all the major functions of the school operation is appealing in its simplicity and reassuring in its objectivity. The definitions do not rest upon philosophical points of view of professionals with vested interests. They derive instead from the implicit logic of the notion that pupils are what the schools aim to transform, and instruction is the collective set of processes that distinguishes the school from other educative institutions and influences.

Shared Functions

The growth and proliferation of specialized, differentiated educational endeavors within the modern school defy basic one-to-one relationships between a staff member, a position, and a set of functional endeavors. It is not possible to think or act as though teachers teach, counselors counsel, and supervisors supervise. Life is not so simple! On the other hand, a return to

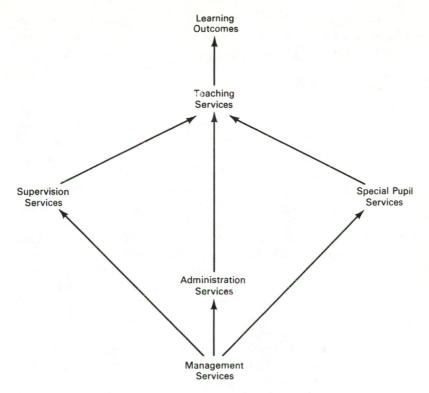

FIGURE 1.2   Major functions related to teaching and learning.

the days of "the little red schoolhouse" when the teacher was virtually all things is not possible either. Perhaps the greatest inherent weakness of most concepts of differentiated staffing is the tendency to oversimplify and hence poorly define these functions of the school operation. All too often, staffing innovations are merely a reincarnation of the little red schoolhouse with four or five teachers called a "team" substituting for the one or two teachers of old.

Technological developments in instruction in recent years, along with improvements in methods for individualizing instruction, have tended to blur the meaning of such terms as *supervision, teaching,* and *learning.* In developing certain instructional materials, the notion of "teacher-proof" programming implies a greatly reduced or more highly structured teaching role. This may also imply that the student is both teaching and learning. On the other hand, those working with computer-assisted learning studies are inclined to equate teaching with supervision and program design. Certainly each new development in education demands some rethinking of our terms and definitions. Those presented here are still applicable to nearly all instructional programs in formal or semiformal settings, but close working relationships are inevitably required among people as they relate to common tasks in functionally differentiated ways. Table 1.1 illustrates in a limited way some endeavors shared among the functional areas of the school operation.

The Shadow Functions

Behind the scenes in the operation of every school are functions assigned high priorities in fact, but not fully recognized as *legitimate*—the custodial and entertainment functions, for instance. There may be others, but these are most influential, perhaps, in shaping practices and diverting resources from the major functions related to pupil learning.

The *custodial function* is not instruction-related in either a direct or an indirect way. It may even be negatively related to instruction, as it impedes or detracts from those tasks that facilitate instruction.

The supporting society imposes custodial responsibilities on the school in many ways. The legal principle of in loco parentis, while rapidly changing, has been upheld in the courts for many years, constantly reminding the school staff of its parentlike obligations to students. Some schools are so concerned with safety, for instance, that swings, jungle gyms, horizontal bars, and other instructionally important equipment items are systematically prohibited. "Hall duty" is often assigned to teachers, with the result that scarce, valuable instructional planning time is nearly eliminated. Field trips may be infrequently scheduled and planned as look-see-but-don't-touch trips under the pressure of custodial responsibilities felt by teachers.

TABLE 1.1 Illustrative Series of Endeavors: Functional Relationships in Improving Materials Utilization

SEQUENCE OF ENDEAVORS	FUNCTIONAL AREA INVOLVED
1. Tax-rate setting	Management
2. Budget planning*	Administration
3. Tax collecting	Management
4. Selecting materials for instruction	Supervision
5. Purchasing materials	Management
6. Distributing materials	Administration
7. Exhibiting materials	Supervision
8. Demonstrating instructional uses	Supervision
9. Revising lesson and unit plans	Supervision
10. Using materials with pupils	Teaching
11. Evaluating materials in use	Supervision
12. Revising specifications for future purchases	Supervision
13. Planning further in-service training	Supervision

*Budget planning presumes the availability of instructional materials specifications to guide selecting and purchasing endeavors.

Compulsory attendance laws, special education classes, drug-sniffing dogs, and acceptance of high dropout rates are all related to the strong preoccupation with the protection of the student. Support for compulsory attendance of students at post-elementary age levels has come from many sources, including organized labor (control the supply of labor), law enforcement agencies (keep the youth off the streets), and parents (know where the children are while at work). High dropout rates, in contradistinction to high attendance rates, have been accepted, even promoted, through various school policies—to ensure a "safe" social environment for other students. Even special education classes have their acceptance, in part, conditioned by the fact that segregation of the retarded, the physically handicapped, and the disturbed may offer protection to the "normal" pupils. Resistance to "mainstreaming" may stem from a similar source.

It is not really necessary to dwell on racial segregation, homogeneous grouping, tracking, or fraternities and sororities as further examples of educational practices based substantially on the desire to offer custodial services of protection and control rather than to instruct the student.

The *entertainment function* is *not* instruction-related. Like the custodial function, entertainment is sometimes negatively related to instruction. The entertainment tasks are generally of two varieties: (1) those aimed at diverting the students themselves and (2) those aimed at serving the entertainment demands of the community, including the students. The interscholastic athletic programs in senior high schools and colleges are the more striking examples of the latter form of entertainment. The school clubs, sponsored organizations, intramural sports, dances, and declared holidays are examples of the former.

Like custodial practices described above, these various forms of entertainment often impede instructional improvements and almost always divert resources from instruction. They are usually defended in the name of instruction but resist adaptations that might make them more nearly instruction-related. For instance, athletics on an interscholastic basis or on an intramural basis might be highly instruction-related. If the goals and objectives of such programs were clearly accepted as the development of physical stamina or recreational skills, then widespread participation, use of school hours, a broad variety of activities, maximum involvement for the least "athletic" students, and free admissions practices would logically follow. Instruction and learning would be facilitated, while entertainment would be a by-product. The contrary conditions, of course, generally prevail in a school system. The goals are those of entertainment rather than learning.

The importance of shadow functions is not to be found so much in their existence as in their disguise. Every organization learns to live with its informal organizational structures, with its precariously valued functions, and with its illegitimate offspring. It is when these portions of the school operations disguise themselves as instructional-related tasks and then become large

domains of practice overshadowing the major functions of the school operations that they turn into serious liabilities. They impede, under such circumstances, the improvement of instruction. They siphon off resources—
money, time, staff, and student energy—which might otherwise be allocated
to either the maintenance or the improvement of teaching. Masquerading
as highly instruction-related, custodial and entertainment tasks gain dispro-
portionately high priorities and seriously distort the operation of the instructional program. Study halls and in-school suspension centers may be the most
interesting recent forms of this charade.

Supervision Defined

Supervision of instruction is what school personnel do with *adults* and
things to maintain or change the school operation in ways that *directly* influence the teaching processes employed to promote pupil learning. Supervision is highly instruction-related but not highly pupil-related. Supervision is
a major function of the school operation, not a task or a specific job or a set
of techniques. Supervision of instruction is directed toward both maintaining
and improving the teaching-learning processes of the school.

SUPERVISORY OPERATIONS

Now that the unique nature of supervision as one of the major functions of
the school operations has been emphasized, it is necessary to operationalize
supervision by specifying its goals (tasks), its processes (activities), and its pre-
requisites (competencies). This reflects a very simple rationale, namely, if
instructional supervision services are to influence teaching, certain instruction-related tasks must be accomplished as a result of certain supervisory activities, implemented by competent people—instructional leaders.

The Tasks of Supervision

Every kind of professional task in the school setting has some implications for instruction and may therefore be a supervisory task. The tasks of
supervision need to be specified operationally as those that either are predominantly instruction-related or are instruction-related in certain critical
ways. The following 10 task areas seem to qualify as being supervisory.

Task 1. Developing curriculum.   Designing or redesigning that which
is to be taught, by whom, when, where, and in what pattern. Developing
curriculum guides, establishing standards, planning instructional units, and
instituting new courses are examples of this task area (Rubin, 1977; Lewey,
1977).

Task 2. Organizing for instruction.   Making arrangements whereby pupils, staff, space, and materials are related to time and instructional objectives in coordinate and efficient ways. Grouping of students, planning class schedules, assigning spaces, allocating time for instruction, scheduling, planning events, and arranging for teaching teams are examples of the endeavors associated with this task area (Trump and Vars, 1976).

Task 3. Providing staff.   Assuring the availability of instructional staff members in adequate numbers and with appropriate competencies for facilitating instruction. Recruiting, screening, selecting, assigning, and transferring staff are endeavors included in this task area (Bottom, 1973; Harris et al., 1979).

Task 4. Providing facilities.   Designing or redesigning and equipping facilities for instruction. The development of space and equipment specifications is included in this task area.

Task 5. Providing materials.   Selecting and obtaining appropriate materials for use in implementing curricular designs. Previewing, evaluating, designing, and otherwise finding ways to provide appropriate materials are included in this task area.

Task 6. Arranging for in-service education.   Planning and implementing learning experiences that will improve the performance of the staff in instruction-related ways. This involves workshops, consultations, field trips, and training sessions, as well as formal education.

Task 7. Orienting staff members.   Providing staff members with basic information necessary to carry out assigned responsibilities. This includes getting new staff members acquainted with facilities, staff, and community, but it also involves keeping the staff informed of organizational developments.

Task 8. Relating special pupil services.   Arranging for careful coordination of services to children to ensure optimum support for the teaching process. This involves developing policies, assigning priorities, and defining relationships among service personnel to maximize the consistency between services offered and the instructional goals of the school.

Task 9. Developing public relations.   Providing for a free flow of information on matters of instruction to and from the public while securing optimum levels of involvement in the promotion of better instruction.

Task 10. Evaluating instruction.   Planning, organizing, and implementing procedures for data gathering, analysis, and interpretation, and decision making for improvement of instruction.

It is important to recognize that these task areas—broad as they are—provide a framework for planning, guiding, directing, and evaluating supervisory services. These are only a portion of the many tasks undertaken in the total school operation. These 10 tasks are distinguished by their high level of instruction-relatedness. Hence, they are appropriate to the supervision function.

Certain of the tasks specified above are obviously so broad that they cannot be viewed as exclusively supervisory. Perhaps no task is pure in the sense of its falling entirely within a single functional area. However, some are crucial while others are distinctly not. For instance, the task area of providing facilities includes such highly instruction-related tasks as *writing educational specifications* and such noninstruction-related tasks as *specifying bidding procedures.* The task area of developing public relations can be highly instruction-related when the planning of parent education programs is involved, but the task of getting support for a new bond issue may or may not be instruction-related.

The real core of a program of supervisory services is usually found in five task areas: evaluation, curriculum development, in-service education, materials development, and staffing. These tasks become the operational fabric of a well-balanced program of supervision, especially when improvement of, as distinguished from maintenance of, instructional practices is to be emphasized.

Tasks in a Developmental Sequence

The 10 tasks of supervision shown in Figure 1.3 are categorized as *preliminary, operational,* and *developmental.* These terms refer to the sequence in which the tasks are often employed to facilitate teaching. Developing curriculum, providing facilities, and providing staff are essential tasks prior to the conducting of any instructional activity. On the other hand, organizing for instruction, orienting staff, providing materials, relating services, and developing public relations are all part of the ongoing operation of the program. These tasks tend to be continous, with or without *changes* in the program. The final task areas of evaluation and in-service education are uniquely developmental. They can be ignored completely, and the instructional program will still operate. However, it is these tasks that provide critical new inputs for changing the instructional program.

Leadership Processes for Supervision

The exercise of leadership processes in maintaining and changing operations has been the subject of extensive study in several fields. Much of what is known seems to apply reasonably well to supervision of instruction.

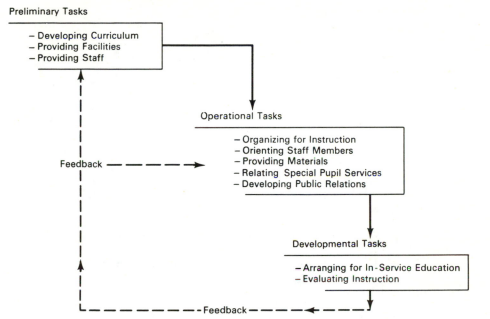

FIGURE 1.3   **Ten task areas of instructional supervision.**

Regardless of the specific nature of the task, assessing, prioritizing, designing, allocating resources, coordinating, and directing processes are demanded for changing and maintaining the operation. Consequently, the task of selecting a new set of materials for use with a group of children involves assessing the needs of the children, assigning priorities to those needs to ensure attention to those that are most urgent, designing a selective sequence of activities, allocating people, time, and money to the sequence, coordinating the selective activities, and directing all actions toward priority needs. This cycle of processes would end with a return to the initial process of assessing the accomplishments as a basis for improved planning in future efforts to select new materials.

Operationally, these six processes employed by leadership personnel are made more vivid and explicit when defined by action terms such as the following:

a. ASSESSING

The process of studying the status quo to secure data for use in determining needs for change.

Analyzing—studying or determining the nature and relationship of the parts through analysis
Observing—seeing through carefully directed analytic attention
Reviewing—going over or examining critically or deliberately

Measuring performances
Comparing performances

b. PRIORITIZING

The process of arranging goals, objectives, and activities in order of importance.

Setting goals
Specifying objectives
Selecting alternatives
Assigning priorities

c. DESIGNING

The process of planning or outlining a system for effecting change.

Organizing—arranging elements into a whole of interdependent parts
Devising—forming in the mind by new combinations or applications of ideas or principles
Preparing—arranging things in readiness
Systematizing—making into a system; arranging methodically
Programming

d. ALLOCATING RESOURCES

The process of allotting and assigning resources for the most efficient use.

Allotting (resources)—assigning resources by need to persons or programs
Distributing (resources)—dividing resources among personnel or programs
Apportioning (resources)—making a proportionate division of resources
Designating (resources)—indicating and setting apart resources for a specific purpose
Assigning personnel to specific programs or purposes

e. COORDINATING

The process of relating people, time, materials, and facilities to form a functional unit for accomplishing change.

Coordinating—bringing into common action so as to act together in a smooth, concerted way
Harmonizing—bringing into consonance or accord
Adjusting—bringing the parts to a true or more effective relative position
Scheduling—assigning time periods and sequencing events
Defining relationships

f. DIRECTING

The process of influencing practices to conform with those essential and appropriate to accomplishing change.

Appointing—fixing or setting officially
Prescribing—laying down as a guide, direction, or rule of action
Regulating—fixing or adjusting the time, amount, degree, or rate of
Guiding—regulating and prescribing
Specifying procedures
Deciding on alternatives

These process terms and their definitions as applied to instructional supervision were developed by the author and his colleagues in connection with the work of the Special Education Supervisor Training Project (King, 1976). They reflect, however, the scholarship of Louis Allen, Charles P. Loomis, Dan E. Griffiths, and many others.

Some of these processes fit common notions about supervision of instruction better than others. Designing and coordinating are more widely accepted as legitimate processes of supervision than are directing and assessing. Given the natural sequence suggested by these six processes in promoting change, it seems wise not to exclude any from our thinking about instructional supervision operations, even though they are not unique.

As important as the identification of these processes may be to an understanding of supervisory behavior, they not only fail to distinguish supervisory behavior from other forms of leadership but also fail to distinguish one supervisory position or task from another.

Leadership processes tend to be employed in all the task areas of supervision, as well as in the tasks of the other major functions of the school operation. These processes characterize the leadership style of the supervisor, teacher, or administrator only in the broadest sense.

Competencies in Supervision

There is a continuing need to view human behavior of task-oriented kinds in terms of competencies (McCleary, 1971). Administrator and supervisor preparation programs (King, 1976) along with those for teachers are being developed with the hope of defining behavior in terms of professional competencies rather than in terms of knowledge, grades, credits, and certificates (Enos, 1976).

This effort is highly consistent with this book's emphasis upon supervisory behavior in education as distinguished from principles and concepts, as important as these may be. Defining *competency* has continued to be a problem that has frustrated all systematic efforts to define professional practice in such terms. If one defines competencies for teachers as "how to categorize questions" and "knowing intellectual developmental stages" and "sequencing instruction," they represent a rather diverse range of performances. They seem to lack the common characteristics that justify classification under a single term.

Whether the concern is for planning training programs or for evaluating in-service performance, the problem is always one of moving from general classes of learning toward designating the character of the competencies in performance terms.

An important distinction needs to be made, perhaps, in characterizing a competency as a task-relevant capacity to act, while viewing supervisory activity as any distinctive endeavor directed toward task implementation. In the former instance, we are concerned with the personal *potential* for behaving in certain task-relevant ways. In the latter, we are concerned with the relations among people, problems, and situations as they are actually faced in school or college settings.

Competencies of supervisory personnel might be best defined, then, as any combination of knowledge and skill that is adequate for accomplishing some specified outcome, even though insufficient for the completion of an entire task (Harris and Lightsey, 1975; King, 1976, pp. 33–35). For instance, the task of evaluating a teacher's performance in the classroom might require a substantial variety of competencies. One competency might be defined as that knowledge and those skills required for producing a completed matrix, reporting on a sample of observed verbal interaction in the classroom. The elements of such a competency include (1) knowledge of an interaction analysis category system, (2) skill in listening to and categorizing verbal behavior with reliability, (3) skill in transferring categorized events to a matrix, and (4) skill in computing certain ratios and percentages.

Such a competency would be incompletely defined if we were concerned only with knowledge of categories or even skill in categorizing verbal behavior, because such endeavors would not, in themselves, lead to a useful result. Similarly, computational skills in deriving ratios and percentages would be inadequate for contributing in a professionally relevant way to teacher evaluation in the absence of the other specified knowledge and skills.

Obviously, the complexity and variety of knowledge and skills included in various competencies will vary depending on the task involved. Since different configurations of similar knowledge and skill will form competencies that are relevant to the accomplishment of different tasks, it seems economical to think about and train for supervisory competencies that are as simple as possible while being genuinely functional in task accomplishment.

To illustrate this latter point, let us compare the competency described above with another concerned with the in-service education task. The competency necessary for guiding the work of role-playing T-groups as they learn to conduct parent-teacher conferences may require (1) knowledge of T-group techniques, (2) skill in organizing large groups into three-person T-groups, (3) knowledge of materials needed to guide the activity, (4) knowledge of analytical category systems useful in observing verbal interaction patterns, and (5) skill in observing and reinforcing T-group activities.

In this list of knowledge and skill elements, number 4 could be identical with number 1 in the teacher evaluation competency described previously. Hence, the one competency, when acquired, makes the acquisition of the other a bit easier. However, it is important to keep clearly in mind that the presence of even a single unique element in a competency distinguishes it in an important way. If we assume that each competency is composed of all elements *essential to* but not exceeding those needed to accomplish some outcome, then the absence of any skill or knowledge element is a critical deficiency.

An array of 36 supervisory competencies is presented in Table 1.2. These competencies suggest, at least, the kinds of professional behaviors that supervision programs require. Their definition as configurations of closely interrelated knowledge and skill elements is illustrated in Table 1.3 for a few of these competencies. Their testing for internal consistency, uniqueness, and applicability has only just begun. Sullivan (1982) reported that an interview study with Atlanta area supervisors gave only limited support for these competencies in current practices. Hence, either theory or practice must be somewhat lacking. Perhaps both need further refinement. (See Appendix A for a complete set of competency statements for supervisory performance.)

Supervisory Activities

In viewing supervisory competencies as capacities for applying certain skill and knowledge complexes to the accomplishment of supervisory tasks, we have a way of thinking more operationally about supervision of instruction. Obviously, we are drawing heavily upon the *processes* and the *tasks* of leadership that have previously been delineated.

Activities of supervision are basic units of behavior in action as directed toward one or more tasks. Since tasks as operational goals have many variations from situation to situation and from time to time, it is not possible to generalize on the array of activities needed for task accomplishment. Supervisory planning therefore involves, in large part, the designing of activity sequences suitable for task accomplishment in each particular situation.

Specific illustrations of the supervisory planning suggested here will be found in subsequent chapters. At this point it is most important, however, to recognize the relationships among competencies, activities, and tasks. When a task, a relevant goal, or a target is defined and appropriate activity sequences are planned, supervisory competencies of various kinds are called upon to carry out the activities themselves.

Supervisory activities are not unique to supervision program endeavors. However, given some task-relevant goal or purpose, *supervisory activity* can

TABLE 1.2 Abbreviated List of Professional Supervisory Competencies: Developmental Supervisory Competency Assessment System

A. DEVELOPING CURRICULUM
  A-1 Setting instructional goals
  A-2 Designing instructional units
  A-3 Developing and adapting curricula

B. PROVIDING MATERIALS
  B-1 Evaluating and selecting learning materials
  B-2 Producing learning materials
  B-3 Evaluating the utilization of learning resources

C. PROVIDING STAFF FOR INSTRUCTION
  C-1 Developing a staffing plan
  C-2 Recruiting and selecting personnel
  C-3 Assigning personnel

D. ORGANIZING FOR INSTRUCTION
  D-1 Revising existing structures
  D-2 Assimilating programs
  D-3 Monitoring new arrangements

E. RELATING SPECIAL PUPIL SERVICES
  E-1 Analyzing and securing services
  E-2 Orienting and utilizing special personnel
  E-3 Scheduling services
  E-4 Evaluating the utilization of services

F. ARRANGING FOR IN-SERVICE EDUCATION
  F-1 Supervising in a clinical mode
  F-2 Planning for individual growth
  F-3 Designing in-service training sessions
  F-4 Conducting in-service training sessions
  F-5 Training for leadership roles
  F-6 Assessing needs for in-service education
  F-7 Developing a master plan
  F-8 Writing a project proposal
  F-9 Designing a self-instructional packet
  F-10 Designing a training program series

G. DEVELOPING PUBLIC RELATIONS
  G-1 Informing the public
  G-2 Involving the public
  G-3 Utilizing public opinion

H. PROVIDING FACILITIES FOR INSTRUCTION
  H-1 Developing educational specifications
  H-2 Planning for remodeling
  H-3 Outfitting a facility

I. EVALUATING INSTRUCTION
  I-1 Observing and analyzing teaching
  I-2 Designing a questionnaire
  I-3 Interviewing in-depth
  I-4 Analyzing and interpreting data

Source: Ben M. Harris, *Developmental Supervisory Competency Assessment System* (Round Rock, Tex.: Ben M. Harris Associates, 1980).

TABLE 1.3   Illustrations of Specific Performances for Selected Competencies and Tasks*

A. CURRICULUM DEVELOPMENT
      A-1   SETTING INSTRUCTIONAL GOALS
          (a)   Leads groups . . . for goal setting . . .
          (m)   Identifies criteria . . . to determine if goals have been attained.
      A-3   DEVELOPING AND ADAPTING CURRICULA
          (h)   Conducts a needs assessment . . .
          (s)   Analyzes the scope, sequence and content in a curriculum guide . . .

B. PROVIDING MATERIALS
      B-2   PRODUCING LEARNING MATERIALS
          (i)   Designs audiovisual materials for use in an instructional unit . . .
          (l)   Arranges for and monitors the commercial production of a set of materials . . .

F. ARRANGING FOR IN-SERVICE EDUCATION
      F-3   DESIGNING IN-SERVICE TRAINING SESSIONS
          (f)   Specifies objectives for a training session . . .
      F-7   DEVELOPING A MASTER PLAN
          (x)   Designates strategies for use . . . matching strategies to needs and constraints . . .

I. EVALUATING INSTRUCTION
      I-3   INTERVIEWING IN-DEPTH
          (h)   Designs interview procedures and materials . . .

Source: Harris, *Developmental Supervisory Competency Assessment System.*
*See Appendix B for details on specific performance statements.

be defined as one or more competencies *purposefully* applied to the accomplishment of some specific task-relevant outcome. Twenty-three fairly distinctive supervisory activities are listed, analyzed, and described in Chapter 4.

A specific illustration of these relationships follows:

TASK AREA: STAFFING

Specific Task: To balance teaching staffs in individual schools with respect to racial, interpersonal, and instructional criteria

TASK OBJECTIVES:

1. To rank teaching personnel on three sets of criteria
2. To recommend staff assignments based on "balance"
3. To obtain voluntary acceptance of assignments recommended
4. To distribute staff assignments as planned while maximizing "balance" and "voluntary acceptance"

ACTIVITIES:

1. *Observing* in classrooms
2. *Administering* individualization of instruction inventories
3. *Interviewing* teachers, using "focused" technique
4. *Analyzing* observation and interview data
5. *Writing* balanced staffing plans and recommending needed changes
6. *Illustrating* balance achieved in graphic forms (other activities)

COMPETENCIES NEEDED:

1a To assess verbal interaction processes in the classroom, using Flanders or other appropriate systems
  b. To assess practices for individualizing instruction in the classroom, using the Individualization of Instruction Inventory or other systems
2. To test a group, using a standardized set of procedures
3a. To score and prepare profiles and matrices based on observation, test, and inventory data secured from activities 1 and 2 above
  b. To prepare tabular and graphic displays showing means, medians, ranges, and other comparisons among individuals and groups of individuals in various staff groupings
4. To plan focused interviews, make appropriate arrangements, and conduct the interviews in such ways as to present and elicit all necessary information
5. To write an analytical report, presenting recommendations for staff assignments and showing objective support for and limitations associated with each recommendation
6. (See 3b above for competency related to this activity)

(See Appendix B for a detailed list of specific performance statements associated with professional supervisory competencies.)

SUPERVISION FOR CONTINUITY AND CHANGE

Activities of supervision are many and varied. They are brought into operation through various competency configurations. They apply differentially to the diverse tasks of supervision. Supervisory personnel holding quite different positions share in giving direction to these many activities of supervision. However, it is the orientation toward continuity versus the orientation toward change that makes a truly unique distinction in the outcome of supervision.

The importance of continuity in the school operation has long been recognized. A major responsibility of virtually all administrative personnel—principals, directors, superintendents, and such—is to maintain a smooth, efficiently running organization in which program continuity is safeguarded. Less clearly seen is the conflict between activities oriented toward change and those oriented toward continuity of operations. One of the major needs in schools, as in other institutions, is for change. The program of supervision of instruction should stimulate and facilitate change in instructional processes through curriculum development, in-service education, and other task areas. However, each of the tasks of supervision can be pursued in ways that maintain present practice and promote continuity rather than change.

Change is, of course, inevitable. Time changes everything. However, change per se is neither desirable nor undesirable. The value assigned to a change tends to be determined by the *directions, quality, rate,* and *side effects* that characterize the change. The dynamics of supervision for change will be treated more systematically in Chapter 2. However, at this point in our overview of supervisory behavior, it seems important to describe both *tractive* and *dynamic* orientations to supervision.

Tractive Supervision

Certain supervisory endeavors geared to continuity are those that are intended simply to maintain the existing level of instruction, to accept only minor changes in program, to enforce or support existing relationships, and to resist pressures for change. We call this *tractive* supervision. This is not to suggest that such activities are undesirable. On the contrary, continuity is essential to any enterprise that has responsibility for producing something according to the standards and expectations of some segment of society. To destroy all continuity would be to terminate production in any systematic sense of the word.

Tractive supervision is illustrated by many endeavors that engage the time and attention of administrators, supervisors, and teachers. Orientation programs for new teachers are essentially tractive in most instances. They strive to indoctrinate the new staff members—to get them to accept and comply with the ongoing ways of doing things. Policy development is often geared more to maintenance than to change when it seeks to promote uniformity of practice. Faculty meetings are similarly a part of tractive supervision when they deal primarily with smoothing out minor difficulties, informing everyone of approved procedures, and giving directions regarding standard operating procedures.

Dynamic Supervision

Supervisory endeavors that are directed toward changing instructional practices may be thought of as *dynamic.* Here the emphasis is on discontinuity, the disruption of existing practices and the substitution of others.

Dynamic supervision is exemplified by many endeavors of administrative, supervisory, and teaching personnel. A new program addition to a school or a system is dynamic in the changes demanded in the "old" program as it accommodates the new. When new materials are selected for use, they imply changes in both pupil and teacher behavior. When certain courses or units are added, discontinued, or moved to a new place in the program, changes are demanded by all directly involved.

Perhaps the most striking examples of dynamic supervision are to be found in those schools in which extensive individualization of instructional programs has been initiated. In these instances, content, materials, schedules, teaching practices, group arrangements, and evaluation endeavors have all undergone change. Every person associated with the school, from pupil and parent to school board president, has been called upon to change in some ways.

Orientations of Supervision

The deceptively simple notion of dynamic versus tractive supervision is dangerous. It is more accurate to view these as ends of a continuum ranging from one extreme to the other. Whether the efforts at change are massive or minute, they entail at one extreme radical departures from existing practices with unknown elements and concomitant risks. At the other extreme, tractiveness involves not only maintenance of current practice but active efforts to prevent change by opposing forces for change.

Figure 1.4 suggests six descriptive terms representing different points along a continuum—from most tractive to most dynamic. Presumably, much supervision is characterized by the terms that are at neither extreme. A supervisory endeavor might also include efforts to change or maintain practices at different points along the continuum simultaneously.

A faculty meeting could serve almost any orientation. In-service training* activities tend to serve a broad array of orientations as well. On the other hand, course-writing, policy-developing, and materials-selecting activities tend to be largely tractive at the codifying level.

A supervision program should be expected to promote *both* continuity and change. The special challenge to planning and staffing for supervision of instruction is to ensure appropriate emphasis on both!

Recent staffing patterns remain in a state of flux, with little clear emphasis on assuring a full array of competencies needed to maintain instructional improvement efforts. Clinical supervision has been widely accepted for its promising effects on teachers' classroom performance, but such approaches seem likely to be limited to only moderately dynamic change. Increasingly, the pressures for accountability emphasize supervisory practices that promote control and predictability rather than change. Bureaucratization of school staffs also seems to restrict rather than enhance the dynamic efforts of supervisory staff (Firth and Eiken, 1982).

A movement in education toward clearly distinguishing between su-

---

*Designs for in-service education programs are characterized, for example, by Harris (1980, p. 101) as more or less dynamic. Four types of designs—"stereotyped," "standard," "redesigns," and "creative"—are considered.

Tractive _____ Dynamic

1	2	3	4	5	6

1. Resisting – actively preventing change

    2. Enforcing – seeking uniformity or conformity

        3. Codifying – formalizing practices

            4. Upgrading – making minor changes
               without altering related practices

                5. Restructuring – changing
                  several practices, including
                  the way they relate to
                  each other

                      6. Redesigning –
                        changing many
                        if not all
                        practices
                        associated with
                        a particular
                        operation

FIGURE 1.4   Six orientations to supervision along a tractive-dynamic continuum.

pervision for change and that concerned with the routine of tractive endeavors is long overdue. Such a movement seemed to be forming in the 1960s and 1970s as project centers, service centers, and development labs were organized across the country. Much of that effort was less than fully productive for various reasons. But the direction is clear and necessary if dynamic supervision is to prevail or even survive.

SUMMARY

Supervision is what school personnel do with adults and things to maintain or change the instructional operation of the school in order to facilitate the learning process.

Five central functions of the school operation can be differentiated by using two dimensions of the operation, instruction-relatedness and pupil-relatedness. The endeavors of all staff members fall into one of four quadrants of Harris's school operations grid except for an array of endeavors that may be considered "general administration."

Ten tasks of supervision can be described as essential in guiding the goal-setting process for a program of instructional supervision. These task areas are (1) developing curriculum, (2) organizing for instruction, (3) providing instructional staff, (4) providing instructional facilities, (5) providing materials, (6) arranging for in-service education, (7) orienting staff members, (8) relating other services to instruction, (9) developing public relations, and (10) evaluating instruction.

A supervisory competency is any combination of knowledge and skill that is adequate for accomplishing some specified outcome related to a supervisory task. Competence is the capacity to perform. Diverse problems and situations may alter the effectiveness with which a supervisor accomplishes tasks. Essential competencies for supervisory staffs can be identified as a basis for both staffing and training.

Supervisory endeavors are oriented toward both continuity and change. Tractive supervision can be characterized as resisting enforcing, and codifying. Dynamic supervision can be characterized as upgrading, restructuring, and redesigning.

Leadership for supervision involves nearly all professional personnel. Administrators are inevitably involved in supervision of instruction, as are classroom teachers in significant ways. Supervisors are distinguished as those professional personnel responsible for maintaining a full array of supervisory endeavors, attending to all tasks of supervision, and giving special emphasis to dynamic supervision. (See Chapter 9 case reports on "Supervisors at Work" for examples of tasks and competencies in operation with *both* tractive and dynamic effects.)

SUGGESTED READINGS

CUNNINGHAM, WILLIAM G.,   *Systematic Planning for Educational Change.* Palo Alto, Calif.: Mayfield Publishing Co., 1982.

A systematic overview of various problems and approaches related to dynamic supervision of instruction. Planning is given heavy emphasis.

GRIMSLEY, EDITH E., and RAY E. BRUCE (1982),   *Readings in Readings in Educational Supervision.* Alexandria, Va.: Association for Supervision and Curriculum Development, 1982.

Carefully selected articles drawn from recent issues of *Educational Leadership* are presented under nine topical headings. Nearly all aspects of supervision of instruction are given some attention in this volume. Virtually all the major scholars in the field are included, with many perspectives represented. The reader gets a quick introduction to supervision issues and ideas in 200 pages. The editors provide a fascinating "Readers' Guide" at the end relating the readings to 14 well-known major works.

KERR, DONNA H .,   "The Structure of Quality in Teaching," in *Philosophy and Education*, 80th Yearbook, Part I, ed. Jonas F. Solti. Chicago: National Society for the Study of Education, 1981.

A carefully developed discussion of the distinctions between learning, teaching, and schooling.

LUCIO, WILLIAM E., and JOHN D. McNEIL,   *Supervision in Thought and Action,*
3rd ed. New York: McGraw-Hill, 1979.

A classic in the field, this book is most useful for giving the reader some perspective on a variety of viewpoints about supervisory practice.

NETZER, LANORE A., GLEN G. EYE, DWIGHT M. STEVENS, and WAYNE
W. BENSON,   *Strategies for Instructional Management.* Boston: Allyn & Bacon, 1979.

A nontraditional view of supervision as an aspect of management is presented.
This book is unique in taking many of the concerns and tasks of administration
and relating them to supervisory purposes.

SERGIOVANNI, THOMAS J., ed.,   *Supervision of Teaching.* Alexandria, Va.: Association for Supervision and Curriculum Development, 1982.

An ASCD yearbook with carefully crafted statements by many leaders in the
field of supervision of instruction. Chapters by Firth and Eiken, McNeil, and
Sergiovanni present thought-provoking ideas of wide-ranging interest.

CHAPTER TWO
DYNAMICS
OF SUPERVISORY
BEHAVIOR*

Supervisory behavior in its most dynamic applications is among the most complex and demanding forms of educational leadership. The improvement of teaching through supervision poses problems that involve fundamental changes in the individual teacher and changes in the organizational context within which the entire staff works, as well as changes in goals and objectives. When supervisory endeavors involve long-range goals and many people, the need for leadership that can stimulate and guide a complex array of changes becomes essential. Perhaps nothing challenges the supervisor more than those programs seeking fundamental changes which inevitably generate much resistance.

The term *dynamic orientation* to supervision of instruction was defined in the preceding chapter to distinguish supervision for change from the important but less demanding supervision for maintenance (Burton and Petrie, 1980). Change engineering has become an important way of thinking about supervision. Its dynamic orientation, while more difficult and challenging, is essential to meeting modern society's demands for educational changes (Sarason, 1971).

*Revised with the assistance of Mrs. Kathi Heinz.

IMPROVING TEACHING

Improving the effectiveness of teaching in the school operation is central to almost all supervisory endeavors. Knowledge is limited concerning the effectiveness of various activities for improving learning by improving instruction. Kerr (1981) has suggested that some of our lack of knowledge stems from reliance on learning theory to guide practice without proper attention to theories of teaching. True as this may be, there is much yet to be known that goes far beyond most concepts of teaching. Enormous are the uncertainties about the relationships between in-service programs (Rubin, 1970), curriculum development efforts, organization climate, change processes, and improved pupil learning (Hering, 1972).

There is little room for doubt, however, about the importance of assuming a relationship between teacher behavior and promotion of pupil learning. Consequently, dynamic supervision must be essentially oriented to changing teaching in ways that are perceived as improving. The effectiveness of many efforts in this direction in the past is open to question. Programs directed toward instructional change have been unrealistic about both the nature and the magnitude of the job at hand, (Owens and Steinhoff, 1976). Much emphasis has and is being given to new curriculum writing, materials development, and retraining of teachers in both subject matter and teaching methods. The results from most of these instructional change efforts have been either limited or disappointing. Even rather elaborate, highly funded, nationally sponsored "movements" have fallen short of realistic expectations.

There are those, of course, who claim successes (Stallings, 1981), and the picture is far from completely disappointing. Nonetheless, much still has to be learned about the kinds of actions that will suffice.

Basic Problems: Strategic, Not Tactical

The record of modest success and much failure in bringing about major improvements in teaching during a 20-year period of instructional ferment (1960–1980) can be very instructive. It has become painfully obvious that instructional change does not come about easily. It is not produced simply by changing the fund of knowledge, teaching techniques, materials, or organization of class groups. Changes in teacher behavior are needed if pupil learning is to be enhanced, but they are much more complex and fundamental changes than most school officials recognize. Furthermore, changes in behavior must extend to the entire school operation (Bandura, 1977), including the ways of relating to local communities and organized professional associations.

Three sets of factors have been described as being important in viewing the problem of change:

1. *The problem factors*—those factors that relate to the nature of classroom events and stimulate the teacher to behave in one way or another.
2. *The situational factors*—those factors in the situation that include classroom, school, and community and do not relate to teaching specifically but do set limits and influences teaching behavior.
3. *The personal factors*—those factors within the individual teacher that include knowledge, skill, attitudes, values, beliefs, and habits and are reflected in classroom behavior.

Many studies relating to the dynamics of planned change are now available to guide supervisory endeavors for improving instruction (Katz et al., 1980; Smith, 1980; Argyris, 1982; Rogers and Shoemaker, 1971). The adoption of new practices often involves the identification and use of early adopters who can "afford" to take chances. Change agents are needed, both internal and external, who have time, energy, commitment, skill, and a supporting administration. The wide gap between what is known as possible, even promising, and our capacity to put such practices into successful operation continues to perplex both administrators and supervisors. But many of the more obvious steps are often neglected. There must be supervisors competent to lead diffusion and adoption activities. Linkages between research, development, and implementation must be strengthened (Havelock, 1971). Leadership personnel must secure clear policy mandates for selected change efforts and follow through by building the climate and the incentives necessary to sustain long, complicated, sometimes painful change processes.

There are a few emerging consistencies about change process that research, theory, and practice all reflect. These consistencies provide "handles" for getting a grasp on the problem in schools.

1. Change processes are often in conflict with processes for maintaining the status quo.
2. Change always affects people, and in human organizations like schools people are always crucially involved in the process.
3. Change in one person or in any part of the organization influences others.
4. Change processes in schools necessarily involve both organization structure and behaviors of teachers as well as other staff members.
5. Change processes require a special kind of leadership combining conceptual, technical, and human skills.

Change toward the improvement of teaching cannot be a piece-by-piece affair if these points regarding change process have validity. Fragmented efforts to change the mathematics curriculum were certain to generate difficulties. Television programs that dictated new roles for classroom teachers were bound to meet resistance. Foreign language programs requiring mechanical aids dictated training the scheduling changes that could not easily be accommodated by traditional secondary schools. Supervision for dynamic change in teaching must be planned strategically. Tactical approaches with narrow objectives and little concern for related portions of the instructional program will not be effective or efficient.

Approaches to Change

The problem of improving teaching is difficult but not impossible. Considerable progress is made in just recognizing the magnitude and uniqueness of the problem of basic changes in behavior in complex school organizations. Equally important, however, is recognition of the various alternatives at hand.

Figure 2.1 suggests a simple decision-making sequence for analyzing a problem. Change will inevitably occur, but it may or may not be planned. Normally, planned change is preferred, since it provides some sense of control over the quality, direction, and rate of change. Any plan for change is confronted with alternatives or combinations of options. Physical, rule, and organizational changes can best be associated with the situational factors previously discussed. Functional changes are problem-oriented and involve changes in ways of relating to the problems. Personnel changes most directly affect the teacher or other staff members.

FIGURE 2.1   Planning alternatives for instructional change. Source: Adapted from Ben M. Harris and E. Wailand Bessent, *In-Service Education: A Guide to Better Practice* (Englewood Cliffs, N.J.: Prentice-Hall, 1969), p. 16.

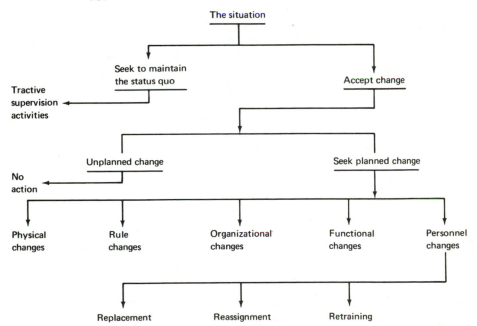

The arguments for strategic planning in efforts to improve teaching still hold in considering these decision alternatives. Once planned change is selected as a course of action, plans must include consideration of all options for change. Rare indeed is the improvement in teaching of real significance that can be accomplished with only retraining or reassignment or physical changes. The engineering feature of supervision of instruction seeks to design a strategy for affecting instruction by using a carefully orchestrated array of change options.

Physical changes involve changes in facilities, material, and equipment as they relate to instruction. Open-classroom designs, closed-circuit television, videotape recording equipment, games, visual aids, programmed materials, and other hardware and software can contribute to a plan for instructional change. These elements in a program plan demand long- and intermediate-range planning, control of funds, and logistical support personnel. They rarely suffice to generate predictable or significant amounts of change. Overreliance on physical change elements in a program design can have negative effects as people become dependent upon these matériel and expect too much, too quickly, too easily. When the results are less than fully effective, a convenient scapegoat is provided by software as teachers decide to "go back to the old way." On the other hand, the long-run influence of technology on behavior should not be underestimated.

Rules changes involve changes in laws, regulations, policies, goals, and objectives as they relate to instructional practices. The development of new curriculum guides is often a process of rule changing, but new laws, regulations, or board policy decisions are more clearly influential as sources of rule change. Increasingly, supervisors are finding it necessary to seek legal or regulatory changes to accommodate and support instructional improvement efforts. Legal mandates may, of course, initiate instructional changes, which in turn must be guided by interpretations, implementing regulations, and procedural guidelines. Laws, policies, and regulations may be in conflict with one another or pose obstacles to instructional improvement efforts. In such instances supervisors must be proactive in securing rule changes in support of good practice.

Organizational changes are traditionally the most widely used options. Graded systems, grouping arrangements, special classes, and scheduling arrangements are but a few of the classic efforts to improve instruction. Most simple restructuring of time, space, and people relationships has not been effective in promoting change in instructional practices. Again, simple approaches relied upon too heavily have been unproductive. Currently, flexible modular scheduling, demand scheduling, independent study, team teaching, and ungraded programs are a few uses of organizational change that have promise as parts of larger designs.

Functional changes involve teacher aides, peer tutoring, self-paced instructional devices, and team differentiation of function. In the past, departmentalization of instruction was the most common effort to improve teaching. It too has been ineffective because of the simplistic character of the approach and the failure to recognize negative side effects, such as time and content fragmentation. Current use of functional change options holds less substantial promise, as these options are part of designs that call for closely coordinated, shared, flexible allocation of teaching and nonteaching responsibilities. Of critical importance in making functional change elements serve to improve teaching is the inclusion of retraining and reassignment elements in the overall plan for change.

Personnel changes include retraining of personnel, reassignment, and replacement. None of these change options has been as widely or persistently employed as the others. In all probability these change options have the greatest promise. Retraining involves a vast array of arrangements and endeavors which will be discussed later. Replacement of personnel is not often used, even though widespread agreement can be obtained regarding the need to eliminate incompetent persons from teaching and other staff positions. Reassignment tends to be a substitute for replacement; those who might well be replaced are often reassigned to another grade or another school, or are even recommended to another unsuspecting school district. The demand for greater attention to and more rigorous use of each of these personnel change options will undoubtedly be required for both effective change and accountability purposes.

INTEREST, LEADERSHIP, AND IMPLEMENTATION

Change involves people, and much of this involvement is necessarily in group situations. Group activities take many forms—meetings, demonstrations, discussions, and so forth. Each activity has unique characteristics which distinguish it from others. The people, the task, and the situation all prescribe additional conditions which influence the group. Despite these difficulties, certain common elements are found in all group endeavors. First, group activities have a *time dimension*. Second, the activities are presumably task-oriented and hence have *goal specificity*. Third, all group activities involve people, which makes *interest* or motivation a crucial dimension. Finally, there is the element of *leadership*. These four elements give us a partial basis for analyzing group activities as dynamic efforts toward planned change in instruction.

Phases of Program Implementation

Regardless of the length of time, a supervisory program can be thought of as that period during which certain activities are consciously pursued to accomplish some specific goal or goals. A program generally has a beginning

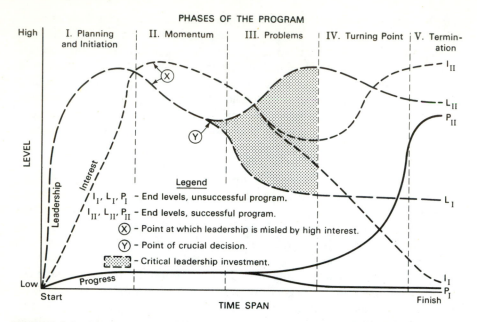

PHASES OF THE PROGRAM

FIGURE 2.2   Interest, leadership, and progress in program implementation.

with the recognition of a problem and a decision to allocate resources to it. A program may be focused on a given task or may cut across several tasks. Groups are generally involved, although it is conceivable that the group will include only the supervisor and a teacher. (See Figure 2.2.)

The analysis of many experiences with supervisory programs suggests that several phases are frequently involved. Typically, these phases come in the following order, but they often overlap each other.

Phase 1—Planning and Initiation.   The purpose of the program is considered. The goals to be sought are given some degree of clarity. Ways of working are explored. Initial activities are selected. Resources available or needed are considered. Interest mounts as individuals involved sense the relationships between the program and its goals and their needs.

Phase 2—Momentum.   Goal-directed activities get under way. Resources close at hand begin to be used. Interest continues to be relatively high and mounts still higher. Feelings of involvement and personal worth grow. The activities are recognized as potentially satisfying. Leading and organizing processes are most heavily employed in this phase.

Phase 3—Problems.   The activities lead to unexpected problems. The plans become increasingly complex. Initial activities lead to the proliferation of still more activities. Certain resources are not readily available. Differences in goal perception among group members become apparent. The demands of other responsibilities produce conflicts. The goal seems more remote and more difficult to attain than before. Some participants fail to live up to expectations. Interest levels out and begins a steep decline.

Phase 4 — Turning Point. At this point the problem trends described in Phase 3 either continue to grow *or* are overcome and minimized. The momentum the program has gained, the effectiveness of initial planning, and the individuals in the operation are all quite important at this point. Above all, however, the amount and quality of leadership become crucial.

Phase 5 — Termination. If unexpected problems, the complexity of the task, the lack of resources, the pressure of other responsibilities, and the lack of goal consensus persist, they tend to be compounded by lack of interest; and goal-directed activities may rapidly deteriorate and come to a halt. If, on the other hand, problems are dealt with promptly, the task is analyzed and simplified, new resources are made available, and goals are clarified, then interest gradually mounts again and goal-directed activities proceed at an increasing pace. Interest is now based on a sense of anticipated accomplishment and personal worth.

Although this sequence of events undoubtedly has variations and exceptions, it appears to be a reasonably accurate description for most programs that require extended periods of time and a variety of activities and participants.

Dynamics of the Change Process

Certainly there are many forces that enhance or retard the goal-directed activities of a supervisory program. Critical to the flow of events described above are three variables shown graphically in Figure 2.2. The interest of participants, the leadership exercised, and the perceived progress toward goals over time are all variables that can account for either success or failure.

Interaction of interest and leadership is shown as being closely associated in Phase 1 as a program is in the planning and initiation stage. As the activities proceed into phase 2 the level of progress remains low, since even the preliminary accomplishments are not yet clearly recognized. The leaders, however, may be influenced by the keen interest of participants and may become complacent. The level of leadership may even be reduced somewhat. As activities continue, much work and few accomplishments cause interest to decline. Problems (Phase 3) grow, and dissatisfactions and expressions of uncertainty regarding goals result (Heller, 1982). The goal seems so far away that the problems seem to multiply; grumbling and critical questioning about the worth of it all mount.

A *turning point* (Phase 4) has now been reached. Two main alternatives are available:

1. Leaders may choose to retreat at this point. Sensing a morale problem represented by increasing resistance, leaders often reduce the pace of scheduled activities to "take the pressure off." Goals may be modified for easy attainment.
2. Leaders may choose to become more dynamic and active. Activities are rescheduled, new resources are secured, more personal involvement increases communications, and goals are clarified.

Each of these alternatives seems to produce dramatically different consequences. A decision to retreat is perceived as a signal to relax efforts; the validity of the goal is called into question, especially by those not fully committed in the first place; other concerns of participants get the time, interest, and energy being released. The consequences are declining interest, unresolved problems, reduced thrust, and little progress toward goals.

Alternatively, the renewed commitment and thrust represented by the second choise is likely to result in problem solutions, new interest, and consequent progress toward goals.

The *components of leadership* are important to specify, as the term *leadership* is used to describe the critical variable operating to make a program successful. This term means many things to many people. It is a fashionable term in government, school, and business alike. As used here it refers to active, purposeful, skilled influencing of people to facilitate change.

Two dimensions of leadership that have had longtime recognition are *consideration* and *initiation*. Supervisors giving leadership to instructional change process need to be perceived as friendly, kindly, sympathetic, and concerned for people. However, they must also be seen as *doers*—people who take risks, take initiative, and make things happen. Much supervisory talent is wasted when the individual supervisors or their supporting administrations insist on a low-key, "laid back" approach to instructional improvement. A difficult balance is needed between contemplation and action. Hersey and Blanchard (1977) argue for great versatility in combining these leadership dimensions in responding to different situations.

Leadership as applied specifically to change process in schools can be thought of as change agentry. The importance of expertness and competence in the person perceived as a leader is clearly needed (Harris, 1982). Still another dimension of leadership appears to be related to the concept of *charisma*. Leaders are dynamic, positive, and supportive, and are easy to relate to (Korda, 1981).

Leadership is not entirely determined by personal factors. Situations vary in ways that influence leader behavior. Furthermore, successful leaders in one context may face failure in others (Caldwell and O'Reilly, 1982). Cuthbertson's (1982) study clearly reflects the strong influence of uncertainty in the work environment on the leadership style employed. Argyris (1982) stresses the effects of established traditions and patterns of thinking in an organization as special conditions requiring an "interventionists'" approach.

The incentives available (or not available) to leaders may clearly influence what they can accomplish.

RESISTANCE TO EDUCATIONAL CHANGE

Supervision may be defined so as to recognize both tractive and dynamic endeavors. However, much emphasis is placed on dynamic supervision because of its special importance on two counts: (1) Dynamic supervisory endeavors require more skill and sophistication. (2) Instructional change is more urgent in a dynamic society than is the maintenance of a set of standards.

The importance of dynamic forms of instructional supervision gives special significance to the problem of resistance to change. Change in education may be analogous to certain physical changes, and it may be governed by similar laws. If we regard an ongoing program, with its staff, procedures, customs, values, satisfactions, and outputs, as the human equivalent of a moving object in space, certain laws of motion may apply in a similar way to both.

A moving object tends to remain in motion, resisting all efforts to change its direction or rate of movement. The consequence of efforts to change the state or condition of the physical object is friction, generating light or heat. Similarly, an object that is not in motion resists all efforts to place it into motion. This is known as inertia. The larger the mass of the object, the greater the resistance to a change in its state or condition.

If physical laws have any merit in thinking about education, we can substitute the word *program* or *practice* or *staff* for the word *object,* and the implications for supervisory practice become apparent and follow three laws:

1. Instructional practices tend to persist in the forms generally practiced in a given situation (motion).
2. Efforts to change instructional practices will be resisted in a variety of ways regardless of the merits of the change contemplated (inertia).
3. Resistance to change efforts will produce nonfunctional effects, such as rationalization, hostility, avoidance, and passivity (friction).

Several alternatives for dealing with resistance to change in instruction can be recognized. One alternative is to leave the program alone, allowing it to maintain a steady state almost certain to collide with and be shattered by some more powerful forces in a changing society. A second alternative is to amass great forces for change and apply them directly to the whole system and related subsystems of instruction to force changes regardless of the smoke, fire, and wear and tear likely to ensue. A third alternative is to apply forces here and there, steering a zigzag course, avoiding collisions but hardly providing for steady progress. A fourth alternative involves applying forces to the system in amounts carefully calculated to influence direction, rate, and quality of change. In the physical realm, lubricants, insulating materials, carefully fitted parts, efficient designs, and a cooling system may be required to reduce friction and guard against the damaging effects of heat and vibration. The changing instructional system likewise must have its path smoothed, its directions guided, and protection offered against excessive resistance.

The Fallacy of Peaceful Change

An array of fallacies and misconceptions persists in the minds and habit patterns of educators as they approach tasks of change.

The administrative fallacy is a serious problem identified by Wright (1960). This refers to the assumption "that when affairs are working without apparent friction and through proper channels, they are working well . . ." (p. 113). Quite a contrary view would be more realistic. In a changing society, peace and calm without friction are likely to mean that what is transpiring is removed from the significant events of life.

The white-hat fallacy is still another that creates problems for those leading change-oriented activities. This fallacy is based on the belief that if the operation is producing some "positive" results, it must be successful. Hence, the undesirable side effects or inefficiencies of the operation are ignored. This has been referred to as the "boomerang effect," when side effects are so great that they virtually cancel out desirable effects. In reality, virtually every effort at change involves both main effects and side effects. The side effects may be both desirable and undesirable, and the latter require special consideration because they can corrupt or complicate the change process.

The morale-building fallacy is a point of view based on a misconception that greatly hinders efforts to promote change. This view is widely held in educational circles and has been reinforced by the human relations emphasis in the supervision literature over the years. The misconception is that morale must be either steady or improving and that any downward fluctuations are highly undesirable. Associated with these notions is the one that high morale and high efficiency are very nearly inseparable. In reality, morale is more likely to be a function of various factors, including one's sense of belonging, achievement, and expectations of self and others.

When change efforts are initiated, both achievement and a person's sense of belongingness may suffer temporarily, and a decline in morale is almost inevitable. Similarly, high-morale situations may be those in which achievement is low, belongingness is high, but both personal and situational expectations are low, so the difference between these expectations approximates zero. If such a set of relationships exists in practice, fluctuation in morale will be inevitable in changing situations. However, problems of morale are manageable by adjusting situational expectations, building belongingness through involvement in planning for change, and ensuring a sense of achievement through skillful implementation of new programs and projects.

Resistance as Normal

Friction in the form of conflict and resistance to change must be seen as inescapable—a reality with which we learn to live and work rather than something to be avoided at all costs as a sign of failure. Role conflicts and competing pressures on staff members are sources of conflict. Sources of resistance to change involve fear of the unknown, disorganization, vested interests, and conflicts of interest.

Resistance to change in education can be seen in each of these and other forms. The teacher who refuses a suggestion to relax control over "behavior problems" may be reacting to pressures from parents, fellow teachers, or the principal to maintain order. A principal's antagonism to a new independent study program may be rooted in his fear of disorganization when a flexible schedule is adopted. The lack of cooperation between the school social worker and the school counselor in dealing with parents may be based on vested interests of each and the resulting conflict of interests. Even more fundamental conflicts may arise when a new girls' athletic program begins to compete with already established athletics for time, money, staff, publicity, and space.

The dynamics of resistance are offered in the ideas developed by Kurt Lewin concerning a "quasi-stationary equilibrium" between "driving" and "restraining" forces. In force-field analysis, driving forces toward change are resisted by restraining forces, so that equilibrium tends to be established. Change is brought about, given equilibrium, either by strengthening or increasing driving forces or by weakening or eliminating restraining forces.

However we view the change process, the existence of resistance must be anticipated. Supervision for instructional change will not be peaceful and smooth. Instructional leadership under such conditions must be concerned less with avoiding resistance and more with dealing with it effectively (Drucker, 1980).

Dealing with Resistance

If the importance of change is accepted along with the inevitability of resistance to it, the engineering or design problem for the instructional supervisor–change agent is that of planning and guiding change processes that include provisions for dealing with resistance (Zander, 1982). This involves need assessments that provide clear evidence to support changes. Priorities must be carefully assigned to various change efforts to be sure that the values and interests of those concerned are well represented. Goal setting must be realistic in terms of resources available and restraining forces to be overcome.

Change-oriented activities must be carefully planned, sequenced, and implemented with resources realistically reallocated.

Securing the fullest possible participation in the activities of change is a useful approach to reducing resistance. Close working relationships between instructional leadership personnel and others who are concerned can promote attitudes of acceptance of change. Participation in implementing as well as in planning while avoiding the use of regulatory and persuasive approaches makes the change target and the vehicle for change essentially the same in many ways, and resistance is reduced.

Still another approach involves increasing driving forces by securing active support from opinion leaders, assigning high-status staff members to the project or program, and allocating funds to facilitate action. Reducing restraining forces is also possible by reassigning personnel and providing monetary rewards for participation.

Change as a Precarious Value

Perhaps the most important consideration for staff members working toward educational change is the priority given to change in the value hierarchy of the school operation. Both individuals and organizations hold values that are arranged in some hierarchical order. Some goals, activities, and processes are valued highly; others are not. Certain activities are precarious in the sense that they do not have a clearly designated place in the hierarchy of values—people are uncertain about them. Most new programs are precariously valued by the school initially. This has been true of special education classes. Desegregation activities generally fall into this category.

Most activities involving changes in instruction are evidently given low levels of value and are held in precarious position. The general predisposition to highly value traditional programs combines with the pressures for change and innovation to give new instructional efforts a very uncertain position in the value hierarchy of most schools. Traditional organizational structure, academic subjects, control, and routine are all highly valued. The current enthusiasm for educational technology, new curricula, and innovations of various kinds is often in conflict with strongly ingrained traditional practices. The result of such inconsistently held values is to make programs of change relatively precarious undertakings.

In promoting precariously valued programs, supervisory personnel tend to be tolerated but not thoroughly embraced by the organization they serve. They are likely to be viewed as intruders in an otherwise peaceful and well-managed situation. The strong allegiance of most school boards to stability and little change as both a valued condition and the essential source of their power to control makes supervision in its dynamic forms inevitably precarious.

The recognition of this precariousness provides supervisors with the opportunity to seriously consider alternative courses of action:

1. They may adapt to the value system of the larger organization and adopt a relatively tractive, service-oriented posture.
2. They may seek relative autonomy and isolate themselves from organization life insofar as necessary to avoid conflict.
3. They may seek to become an elite group recognized and supported by the powerful, high-status segments of the organization.

Because educational change is likely to be precariously valued in most school operations, a careful assessment of the situation should be made by all leadership personnel. If change is truly desired, the realities of the situation cannot be ignored. A staff can cope only with resistance patterns that have been carefully assessed.

Tolerance for Turbulence

The inevitability of change and the conflicts, cross-pressures, and dislocations that follow have been described here as problems of dynamic supervision. The approaches for dealing with these problems of resistance to change all assume some tolerance for turbulence by staff members, and most of all by leadership personnel. Tolerance for turbulence is essential at all levels of the organization. It is especially critical in those who make policy decisions, but it is also important in classroom teachers, custodians, parents, and even pupils. The great danger in too little tolerance for turbulence is that decisions will be made to cut short efforts toward change, that balance will be reestablished and strain reduced before the action potential can become change in reality.

A healthy attitude toward change needs to be cultivated within self and community alike by leadership personnel. Such attitudes enhance supervisors' opportunities to pursue programs for educational change. With such attitudes, supervisors can provide both freedom and challenge to try things even though their efforts may produce difficulties, get reactions, and run risks. Some confusion, some disorder, some anxiety can be carefully arranged to encourage creative efforts at problem solving as distinguished from avoidance reactions.

The conflict-prone nature of the school grows increasingly obvious as social, economic, political, and moral issues are debated in public but acted out within the school setting. The school has again become the primary vehicle for acculturation in our society. Bilingual education, career education, competency testing, Bible reading, and creationism are only the more obvious programmatic manifestations of a society convulsed by uncontrolled change rates and seeking resolution of conflicts through education. As an ideological organization promoting an array of selected learnings, the school faces conflicts in values and lack of goal consensus. As schools have become giant bureaucracies, they suffer from conflicts that arise from overspecialization, poor communications, conflicting interests and limited participation by clients. As a purely local operation at the neighborhood elementary school level, conflicts arise from constant direct pressures of community groups and influential individuals against an increasingly unionized "professional" staff group.

It is hardly surprising that the school, so conflict-prone from both within and without, is reluctant to accept, let alone promote, dynamic supervision for improving instruction. The challenge to leadership personnel of all kinds is to utilize pressures and conflict to fuel changes in instruction while assisting the staff in reducing conflicts that are less productive.

Deploying supervisors to give nearly undivided attention to change process is an important aspect of developing tolerance for turbulence. Change management, planning for change, and staffing for change agentry need the attention of policy makers and chief administrators as well as supervisors. The important distinction between staffing and organizing for change versus maintenance activities needs full recognition. Gresham's law of planning warns that "routine drives out planning, routine drives out thinking." The implications are all clear that supervisors must be deployed so as to plan and implement change process and be relieved of most obligations for the routine of maintenance activities.

THE WIDSOM OF CONSERVATION

The emphasis on change should not blind the reader to the importance of *tractive* supervisory endeavors. Selective effort to conserve the best of past practices is an essential part of *planning* for change. Much of the change-oriented activity in education is ill conceived. Massive efforts to utilize educational television to replace educated classroom teachers (U.S. government efforts in the Samoan Islands, for instance) were based on ignorance and expediency. Transitional bilingual programs directed toward eliminating the second language from the classroom as quickly as possible will likely be very ineffective with children in greatest need. These are only two examples of new developments in instructional design that are not well founded in terms of well-established past practices. But, a more significant form of conservatism calls for greater recognition of the accumulated wisdom of the profession.

Educational practices have emerged with painful trial-and-error processes over centuries. It is commonplace to note the slowness with which new practices are accepted in schools and colleges. Yet that very recalcitrance has some virtue. Those practices which have been accepted in preference to others that were previously well established cannot be dismissed too lightly. Yet the dazzle and the glamour of the "latest technique" often blind us.

Change is not advocated by this writer for its own sake alone. In some conservative economic circles, change is equated with "growth" and growth is "good." Change is not necessarily desirable nor is it undesirable, but it is inevitable. Supervision for change is essential because the schools and their instructional programs are part of a larger, changing society. Furthermore, teaching and schooling are still in their infancy. Most of what can be done in promoting student learning is as yet unknown or untested, or both.

Supervision for change must be concerned with *direction* and *quality*. Change that represents a return to old and inappropriate practices is to be avoided. Changes that involve poorly designed or shoddily implemented instructional practices are also undesirable.

Supervision for change must conserve the best of established practice and build on it in promoting change. Teaching is both art and science (Gage, 1978). It is also a craft with a long history of development. The professional wisdom embodied in the best work of outstanding teachers needs clear recognition and protection from overly eager efforts at innovation.

Consensus is not an absolute assurance of virtue. But there is a body of practice more clearly recognized, like any fine art, in its rarity than in its commonness. Every change effort should stand multiple tests and *one* of those tests must be the wisdom of *best* practices.

SUMMARY

Dynamic supervisory behavior is concerned with the difficult tasks of *improving* rather than maintaining teaching practices that promote pupil learning. A variety of approaches to improvement in teaching are possible, including changes in any and all aspects of the environment in which the school operates.

Basic to change is leadership. In teaching, instructional leadership is faced not only with the problems of implementing appropriate change processes but also with the problems of dealing with resistance to change. Resistances to change are real, normal, and substantial. They can be dealt with by recognizing fallacies, accepting the natural character of resistance, resolving to cope with them systematically, and developing tolerance for the turbulence that is inevitably a concomitant of change.

SUGGESTED READINGS

ALPERT, JUDITH L., et al., *Psychological Consultation in Educational Settings.* San Francisco: Jossey-Bass, 1982.

The author presents a four-phase model for educational consultation and illustrates the operational problems of working in schools in various ways. Several cases are especially insightful. The model deserves serious attention.

ARGYRIS, CHRIS, *Reasoning, Learning and Action*. San Francisco: Jossey-Bass, 1982.

An organizational management theorist attends to the problems of ineffectiveness of people in organizations. Case studies are utilized to illustrate basic concepts of the theory of reasoning. Faults in organizational effectiveness are traced to faulty reasoning, deciding, and acting on the part of individuals. A double-loop learning concept is presented as the solution of an "interventionist."

BANDURA, ALBERT, *Social Learning Theory*. Englewood Cliffs, N.J.: Prentice-Hall, 1977.

A classic in the applications of systems analysis to concepts of social theory and learning.

CRANE, A. R., "Anxiety in Organizations: Explorations of an Idea." *The Journal of Educational Administration, 18*, no. 2 (October 1980): 202–212.

Analyzes the sources of anxiety and the ways anxieties manifest themselves to affect organizations.

CUBAN, LARRY, "Persistent Instruction: The High School Classroom, 1900–1980," *Phi Delta Kappan, 64* (October 1982): 113–18.

A carefully crafted report of 80 years of stability in secondary teaching. The author suggests possible causes of secondary school rigidities and proposes approaches to change.

GOODMAN, PAUL S., et al., *Change in Organizations*. San Francisco: Jossey-Bass, 1982.

A comprehensive review of current thought on organizational change. Various authors stress planned change and adaptation. Chapters on "counterforces" to change, participatory work structures, increasing worker involvement, and managing change are especially relevant to instructional supervisors.

KATZ, DANIEL, et al., (eds.), *The Study of Organizations*. San Francisco: Jossey-Bass, 1980.

A compendium of articles on organizations. A basic source book with many fascinating reports on change process.

NETZER, LANORA, et al., *Strategies for Instructional Management*. Boston: Allyn & Bacon, 1979.

A rather nontraditional view of instructional supervision, as "management" is presented by these authors. As such, some unique ways of dealing with change process are presented.

SARASON, SEYMOUR B., *The Culture of the School and the Problem of Change*. Boston: Allyn & Bacon, 1971.

A penetrating analysis of the schools of the country from a cultural perspective. A focus on federal programs and their failures is most enlightening. He points to the tendency to exercise control as frustrating to change processes.

CHAPTER THREE
SYSTEMS
FOR
OPERATIONALIZING
SUPERVISION
PROGRAMS*

Viewing supervision of instruction as change-oriented and focused by a set of tasks still leaves the problems of organizing, staffing, goal setting, designing, and implementing programs for task-effective action. In Chapter 1 the basic character of supervision for instructional change was presented. Chapter 2 described the context, pressures, and problems within which supervisors must function. In this chapter the emphasis is on conceptualizing ways of organizing for optimum thrusts toward improvement of instruction.

Certain assumptions are made in this chapter regarding the change process in school organizations. It is assumed that: (1) the crucial tasks of supervision are curriculum development, materials development, staffing, in-service education, and evaluation; (2) these are tasks that must be recognized as distinctive, one from another, yet to be accomplished in a systematic, interrelated manner; and (3) planned, systematic change is a complex, difficult set of processes substantially distinct from the routine ongoing processes of maintaining teaching and learning.

*Revision of this chapter was accomplished with the assistance of Susan Monds.

SYSTEMS MODELS

The operation of a mature program of instructional supervision can be understood as a whole only if we can grasp concepts of behavior and organization, and their relationships to instructional improvement. We need a method of systematic viewing. This suggests the use of a conceptual model. There are few models to guide the design of supervision programs that are comprehensive in nature. Clinical models offered by Cogan (1973), Snyder (1981), Boyan and Copeland (1978), and others are all limited to specific training strategies. They fail to give attention to many essential tasks or to alternative training strategies. Obviously models can be created only to the extent that agreements can be reached on what the jobs of supervisors are all about (Sullivan, 1982). A comprehensive model of school improvement with emphasis upon instruction is essential, given an age of rapid change and an immature profession. Without such a comprehensive view, educators' ability to stay in tune with the times will continue to be limited.

A Systems View

An operating system is a "synthetic organism" composed of interrelated and functionally supporting components that produce specified outcomes (Banathy, 1968, 1973). Operations can be viewed and analyzed using models built on the systems concept of organizations. Basic concepts included in this view of organizations are inputs, processes, or products. It is this way of thinking about and analyzing an operation as an entity without isolating it from a larger context of related events that gives it great utility.

The concept of system is a creation of the industrial world. It is essentially a mechanical model as distinguished from models derived from astronomy, psychiatry, or communications, which also have great utility in some circumstances.

Illustrating Model Utility

A specific illustration may be in order here to make these systems concepts more intelligible. Suppose we face the problem of improving learning by individualization of instruction. Assuming that evaluation of existing practices provides a fairly clear definition of the problem, we can begin thinking about the plans for dealing with this problem in systems analysis terms as follows:

WHAT ARE THE INPUTS REQUIRED TO RESOLVE THIS PROBLEM?

1. *Objectives* clearly specified in terms of kinds and amounts of individualizing practices desired.
2. *People* clearly identified as needing assistance with individualization.

3. *Personnel* clearly identified in terms of anticipated supervisory tasks to be employed.
4. *Time* allocated for involving people (clients and others) in processes anticipated.
5. *Materials* allocated for use in processes anticipated.

WHAT ARE THE PROCESSES REQUIRED?

1. *Training experiences* regarded as essential to develop skill in, understanding of, and acceptance of specified objectives.
2. *Reallocation* or rescheduling of responsibilities to allow for training interventions.
3. *Production, distribution, or purchase* of materials needed to facilitate application of new understandings.

WHAT ARE THE PRODUCTS ANTICIPATED?

1. *Increased frequency of use of practices* specified in objectives.
2. *Increased quality of practices* specified.
3. *Increased variety of practices* as specified.

In simple schematic form this system is depicted in Figure 3.1. A slightly more elaborate model is required to provide for measuring products, comparing them with stated objectives, and hence evaluating the effectiveness of the system. Obviously, the operating system can be planned and implemented without the evaluation components; however, once operating, success can be objectively determined only by some kind of measurement and analysis process. Again, the systems concept serves to guide not only planning and implementation but evaluation as well.

The problem described above could, of course, be viewed employing quite a different model. For instance, a model drawing on Maslow's hierarchy of needs theory might identify needs, analyze the need-satisfying potential in various individualizing practices, and then proceed to arrange for the easy

FIGURE 3.1   Simple illustration of systems diagram.

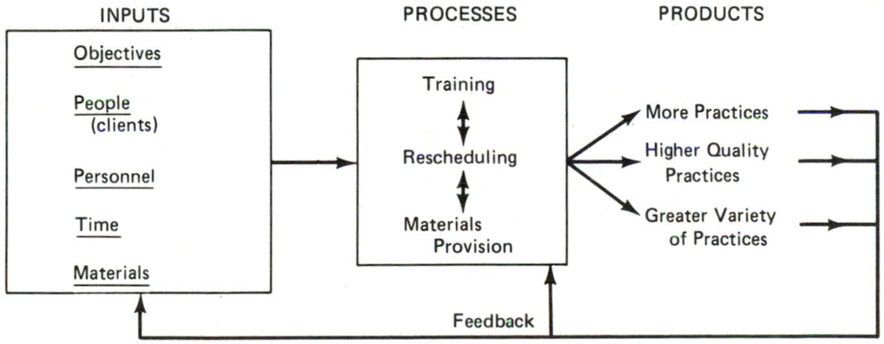

adoption of those practices, relying on awareness and opportunity to motivate for change on an individual self-actualizing basis. Obviously, this model can be useful too. Its adoption by supervisors facing the problem described above will lead to a quite different plan of action. Needs assessment of individuals will be undertaken. Highly individual arrangements for making clients aware of practices for individualizing and their potential for meeting needs will be planned. Evaluation of results will encounter difficulties, since criteria of success will be highly individual.

Snyder (1981, p. 39) uses a simplified systems model to illustrate the broader context of clinical supervision within a program of instructional improvement. In Figure 3.2 inputs are shown as various aspects of planning. Clinical procedures are the heart of the operating system, while performance outcomes represent products of the system. This, too, is an extremely simple illustration of a systems diagram. Even so, it contributes a broader conception of the operation of a clinical supervision program than other authors provide.

Flowcharting for Systems Analysis and Planning

The basic concepts of "a system" and the acceptance of these ways of viewing operations have led to the development of rather elaborate flowcharts to represent plans for organizing or ways of analyzing an ongoing operation. Banathy (1968, p. 83) is among those who have developed rather elaborate models to guide the planning of instructional systems. Curriculum development projects have likewise been guided by elaborate flowcharts (Feyereisen et al., 1970, p. 134) that not only show steps from problem identification and diagnosis through trial, adoption, and evaluations but also detail numerous alternatives and decision points within each step. These flowcharts, while based on the basic systems model, become fairly detailed, showing sequences and interrelationships among various classes of events. As such, they provide more specific guidelines for planning.

The problem of individualizing instruction described above could have

FIGURE 3.2   A clinical supervision linkage system. Used with the permission of Texas Association for Supervision and Curriculum Development.

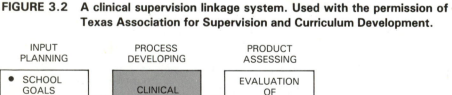

been analyzed in greater detail in the actual operating situation by using the techniques adapted from Feyereisen and associates (1970). Figure 3.3 shows such a flowchart developed to guide the planning process, from diagnosing the problems, through a variety of alternative approaches, to evaluation of outcomes. This model lacks specific details that will be required to make a plan fully operational. However, it serves as the broad framework for planning and, more importantly, offers fairly concrete guides to action. Hence, very complex supervisory practices are represented in a simple form.

Flowcharting that guides both evaluation and in-service education procedures has been utilized in the *Developmental Teacher Evaluation Kit* by Harris and Hill (1982). In Figure 3.4 each step in a sequence of activities is specified along with alternative courses of action. In such a flowchart a continuous cycle of data gathering, analysis, decision making, and planning activities is shown. While this model is much more complex than most clinical models, it can nonetheless serve to both inform and guide the actions of those engaged in the improvement operations.

More complex systems diagrams like the one illustrated in Figure 3.4 do not retain the simple input → process → product sequence. Instead, these three components of any systems are sequenced operationally. Data gathered

FIGURE 3.3   Planning model for illustrative in-service education problem.

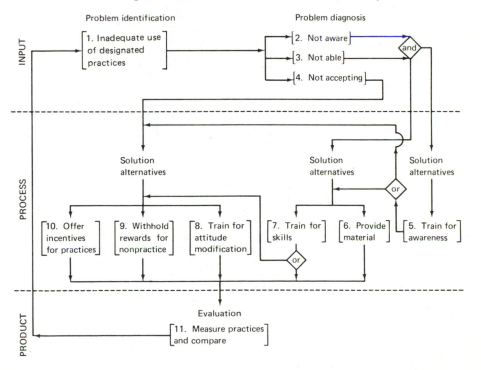

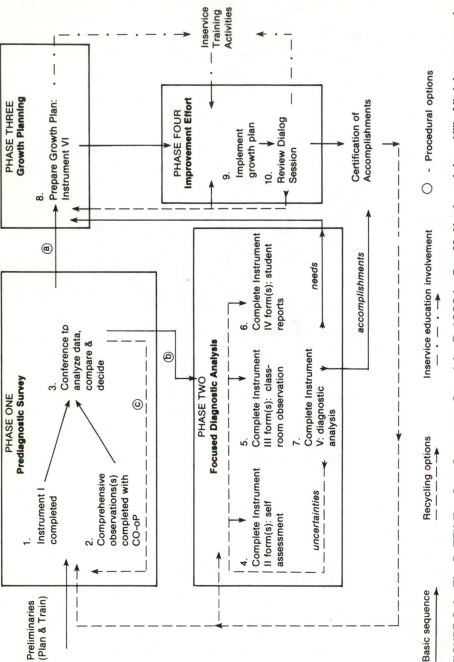

FIGURE 3.4 The DeTEK Ten-Step Sequence. Copyright © 1982 by Ben M. Harris and Jane Hill. All rights reserved. Reprinted by permission of National Educational Laboratory Publishers, Inc., Austin, Texas.

48

in steps 1 and 2 are inputs in the DeTEK system. At step 3 processes involve analyzing input data, while action decisions, also made at this time, become the products. Curiously, the decisions from step 3 (products) become the inputs for step 8.

A SYSTEM FOR DEVELOPMENTAL TASKS
OF SUPERVISION

The developmental tasks—evaluation and in-service education—share with curriculum development, materials development, and staffing a high potential for stimulating and directing change in instruction. These tasks can, of course, be pursued in tractive orientations. Likewise, other tasks of supervision, public relations for instance, might be highly dynamic. For various reasons, however, only five tasks are included in the systems view of a supervision program presented below. The purpose is to provide a conceptual model showing the essential components and their interrelationships for a dynamic program of supervision of instruction.

Operating and Development Systems Distinguished

The operating system of a school or other unit of organization consists of inputs necessary for daily routine operations, processes dominated by whatever teaching practices and organizational arrangements have evolved, and products of various kinds—ideally, basic knowledge and skills plus others not so clearly specified. These are the more or less standard components of the school operation. They vary in detail from school to school and from town to town but are very similar in kind. *Inputs* almost always include students, materials, classroom space, teachers, schedules, and goals and objectives, general or specific. *Processes* too are fairly routine and predictable and include lecturing, reading, reciting, writing, constructing, listening, talking, viewing, and so forth. *Outputs* or *products* too may well be quite similar, at least when students as inputs are similar.

This basic operating system is maintained by an array of supporting subsystems for transportation, building maintenance, purchasing, paying obligations, controlling intrusions, communicating within and outside the system, and so forth. There are also auxiliary subsystems that relate only indirectly or not at all to the main operating system. These include systems with such goals as athletics, recreation, baby-sitting, and crime prevention (Harris et al., 1979).

The vast majority of personnel, funds, and time are allocated to these systems that are all essentially *operational*. They are expected to produce *direct* service products on a fairly routine basis. By contrast, *development* systems exist, which are focused on indirect services as outputs.

This developmental activity is directed toward producing changes in the various components of the operational system, even changing its structure in fundamental ways. These developmental activities, if present at all, are generally carried on within the other systems and are difficult to identify as distinct subsystems. In fact, they may well be almost nonexistent in many school situations because of their precariousness and the operation of Gresham's law of planning, previously mentioned.

The conceptual model for a dynamic program of supervision of instruction as shown in Figure 3.5 does not reflect common practice for the reasons mentioned. This model suggests a system for designing, staffing, and implementing supervision for instructional change. A sharp distinction is made between the instructional operations system and the instructional development subsystems of the supervision program. It is assumed that they must be closely interrelated but functionally identifiable and distinct. Drucker (1980) speaks to this in advising that "they set up their innovations as major distinct businesses." Spady (1982a) cautions about the "illusion of school improvement," suggesting that small changes are appropriate but not sufficient. He argues for improvement efforts that are more imaginative and far-reaching than most.

The Instructional Development System

Five major task areas suggest the goals and define the operational characteristics of the several subsystems for instructional development. The eval-

FIGURE 3.5   A model for relating instructional operations and development systems.

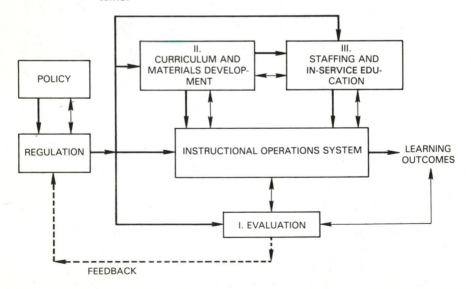

uation subsystem is concerned with the assessment of products, processes, and inputs of the operational system. The interpretations and conclusions derived from the analysis of data by the evaluation subsystems provide the basis for decisions at policy or administrative levels regarding the need for change in the operation system. Such decisions, when change-oriented, provide authorization for staffing, in-service education, and curriculum and materials development activities aimed at changing the operational system in appropriate directions.

The *evaluation subsystem* (I) in Figure 3.5 is shown separated from the others. This is intentional but may be misleading. The whole set of processes and procedures for evaluation of instruction is reviewed in later chapters of this book. The separation of the evaluation subsystem in this schematic is meant to emphasize the rather distinctive, specialized, complex, and demanding activities required for effective evaluation of instruction. The feedback provided via evaluation provides the basis for revisions in policy or regulations. These policies and decisions can initiate new evaluation efforts and changes in the routine operations of the instructional program, as well as initiating curriculum development, materials development, staffing, and in-service activities. Evaluation involves organized, systematic ways of gathering data regarding selected but critical elements in the operating system and analyzing these data so as to generate interpretations about the effectiveness of the system. Reports (in various forms) communicate these analyses and interpretations to the systems requiring such information.

The *staffing and in-service education subsystem* (III) is shown combined, even though the two functions are not generally closely related tasks in current practice. When evaluation reports suggest problems in personnel as distinguished from materials, objectives, and design of program, a variety of actions may be indicated. An insufficient number of staff members may require recruitment and selection activities. Inappropriateness of staff may require reassignment activities. New complications may require specialized competencies to be secured by a combination of recruitment, selection, and reassignment activities; and dismissal or early retirement may also be involved. Training activities are called for whenever problems can be met by modification of behaviors of staff members. The inclusion of both staffing and in-service education tasks in the same subsystem implies the obvious: significant changes in personnel for improving instruction often require recruitment, selection, assignment, reassignment, and training of various kinds.

The *curriculum and materials development subsystem* (II) is shown as a combination of the two task areas. This emphasizes differences in the forms of these tasks under tractive as opposed to dynamic conditions. In change-oriented endeavors, cirriculum and materials design become virtually inseparable; selection of materials becomes less important than production and testing. Change-oriented curriculum development deals with all input and process elements as variables subject to modification in the design process.

The essential activities of this subsystem are all directed toward improving the design of the inputs in ways that make for more efficient teacher-pupil-material interaction. Hence, curriculum materials development involves the tasks of: redefining goals and objectives in terms of pupil and societal needs and school capabilities; redesigning the guidelines for using materials, facilities, space, time, and people to create planned learning experiences; and producing materials for communicating about and facilitating the use of the redesigned experiences. Obviously, such activity must be closely related to the operating program. Staffing and in-service activities are almost always associated with curriculum and materials development of dynamic kinds.

The *policy-regulatory subsystem* is shown as directly related to both the *operational* system and the *developmental* system. Within this subsystem school boards, administrative cabinets, and curriculum councils, as well as individual officials, act to generate decisions affecting the *operational* and *developmental* systems. Often, in practice, decision making occurs on the basis of little information, fragments of data, poorly analyzed and of doubtful reliability. This model would give a unique place to the evaluation subsystem as the stimulator of decision making. This model also clearly provides for decisions that not only direct the routine modifications in the operating system but also direct the focus of attention for each of the *developmental subsystems.*

Unifying the operation of the developmental subsystems is given considerable attention in the chapter on staffing and organizing for instructional supervision. In interpreting this model, it is essential to recognize the close relationships needed among the staffs of the developmental subsystems. Sharing of staffs would be the rule rather than the exception. Developmental plans would result from collaborative efforts in large measure and be closely coordinated in any event. Only the main *feedback* channel is shown in Figure 3.5, but many other channels of information flow would, of course, be essential in relating these systems to one another. Finally, wherever the arrows in this model have double arrowheads, they represent closely coordinated relationships that can give unity to the whole with identity for each major system.

CHANGE STRATEGIES

The discussion of the problems of resistance to change in Chapter 2 emphasized the need for realistic planning and strategic deployment of staff. The use of systems models analyzed in this chapter has emphasized conceptualizing systems for planning and organizing dynamic supervision. The strategies selected are no less important than the character of the instructional development system in ensuring the successful operation of the supervision program. A curriculum development project that adopts a school-by-school diffusion strategy may find innovations outmoded before extensive change is produced. An in-service education project that relies on a mass communications strategy may result in more awareness than capability to perform, with morale problems added.

Each problem may be viewed as strategically unique. In some respects each one is. However, some strategies are generally adaptable to various kinds of problems of instructional change. Three fairly distinctive strategies might be labeled as follows:

1. Information processing and feedback
2. Diffusion of innovations
3. Local development

Each of these will be described. Each has to do with changing people directly. Structural change strategies, so popular in educational circles, are not included here because of their severe limitations when instructional practices are the change targets. Similarly, targeted funding, legalistic, or charismatic strategies are not discussed because of their limited availability to most instructional leaders.

Information Processing and Feedback

The provision of a communications and feedback system that provides a steady flow of essential information about instruction to all subsystems of the school is an essential in any change process. However, when adopted as the essential strategy, the information flow is expected to stimulate change in a variety of ways. (1) Information about what *is* in contrast with what *should be* is used to stimulate decisions for changes. (2) Information processing and analysis techniques employed identify specific changes needed in the operation. (3) Information provided reinforces best practices while discouraging least-desirable practices. (4) Information is widely shared by various subgroups, and competitiveness and cross-pressures stimulate change.

This strategy is essentially the one employed by journalists as they study an institution, program, or person and write a series of "exposés." It is the strategy that underlies most school surveys and regional accreditation programs as the data gathered about a school or district or program are presented to staff and other officials with recommendations calculated to stimulate changes. This is the strategy involved in clinical supervision as well as organizational development (Schmuck et al., 1975) and quality circle programs (Ouchi, 1981).

Clinical supervision as it has evolved under Boyan and Copeland (1978), Goldhammer, Anderson, and Krajewski (1981), Cogan (1973), and others is a highly personalized strategy for improving instruction. Other personalized approaches closely associated with clinical supervision are depicted by Glickman (1980), Redfern (1980), and Harris and Hill (1982). All of these can be expected to have only limited effects in the absence of other more dynamic efforts to change the total school operation. The questions about personalized strategies that need to be answered relate to both their effectiveness and the economy of use. There can be little doubt that clinical experiences can promote individual growth of the kind that upgrades common practices. They may even lead to innovations. However, the former are more probable outcomes. Furthermore, change efforts that rely heavily on one-on-one relationships for information processing and feedback are very costly and may be prohibitively so unless made a part of a larger strategic effort.

Quality circles (Zenke, 1982) are being widely discussed as still another approach of the information processing and feedback type. This strategy has strength, like clinical supervision, in being closely related, even inbedded in the context of the work site. The use of the reality of the job and the regularized interaction with others who are associated with that same reality give quality circles a lot of promise. Unlike personalized strategies, these quality circle efforts are somewhat more economical in terms of staff time.

CBAM stands for "concerns based adoption model." This strategy for personalizing change process has been developed by Hall and Loucks (1978). Unlike the other information processing approaches mentioned, this one gives only passing attention to the job context. The model assumes that the individual is the essential unit of change but also assumes the existence of fairly regularized "stages of concern" (Hall, 1982) that guide individual decisions and other actions toward innovative teaching alternatives. Such assumptions seem certain to restrict the utility of this strategy.

Organizational development (OD) can be thought of as still another information processing change strategy. Its focus is on improving the operational functioning of the organization and the interactions of members within it. OD seeks to develop the organization by developing the individuals within the organization. OD seeks planned change that improves the operations on an interpersonal basis by altering perceptions, attitudes, and values, and hence improving interactions (Cunningham, 1982, pp. 195–99). Blake and Mouton (1979, pp. 54–64) have established principles of OD that seem to apply to industry. Some of these may be applicable to the field of education:

1. The unit of change is an organization that is autonomous and responsible for itself. The OD unit must contain within itself those persons with authority essential for setting new directions.
2. The top leadership must be actively involved in the decision making to bring about needed changes.
3. The entire human system of the organization must be involved, not just representatives or officials.
4. Those responsible for managing change need to be given opportunities to learn sound concepts of leader behavior and to test their skills in working with people.

Organizational development practices, of course, have much in common with the techniques of quality circles.

Weaknesses in these information processing strategies become most striking when the changes needed are rather complex and call for retraining, new staffing arrangements, and new curricula. The persistent feedback signaling the need for changes when the capability to effect them is absent or limited can lead to frustrations. Perhaps the greatest weakness in this strategy is sometimes found in the requirement that feedback be so specific that reinforcement is on target and needed changes are apparent; such precise information is hard to get. However, more general information with nonspecific feedback can lead to serious errors.

DIFFUSION OF INNOVATIONS

The diffusion of innovations strategy has been used widely in business and industry when changes are directed by or encapsulated in a specific invention or other innovation. This strategy has much in common with the information-feedback strategy in that it relies heavily upon information sources, usually supported by research or field tests of relative advantage (Rogers and Shoemaker, 1971). Unlike the preceding strategy, this one (1) concentrates upon the promotion of a specific change, (2) involves an active change agent (by implication at least), and (3) emphasizes trial and evaluation by the adopter.

Rogers and Shoemaker's (1971) theoretical model describes the change process under innovation adoption conditions. A sequence of steps in the adoption process is described as typical: (1) knowledge, (2) persuasion, and (3) decision. Information sources are viewed in this model as facilitating evaluation at the knowledge stage, permitting the potential adopter to consider the innovation in terms of social system variables—system norms, support structures, and so forth. Information sources are also employed at the persuasion stage to assist potential adopters in assessing the characteristics of the innovation—relative advantage, compatibility, complexity, and so forth.

This view was developed from studies of the adoption of innovations in agriculture, where the Agriculture Extension Service and its agents were unusually successful in the industrialization of U.S. agriculture. Rogers and Shoemaker (1971) recognized that "important and fundamental differences exist between agricultural and educational diffusion." They point out that schools are not like farmers and that the relative advantage of adoption tends to be small or uncertain in educational innovations. Littleton's study (1971) of elementary school principals offered little support for Rogers's theory in public school settings.

Owens and Steinhoff (1976) have compared strategies for changing farmers' behavior and strategies for changing that of school personnel. Both groups are generally conservative and tradition-bound. Strategies for changing an individual farmer may be applied to a school superintendent, for such a person may be able to influence many others in the organization (Owens and Steinhoff, 1976, pp. 9–10).

Social interaction models are usually based on diffusion of innovations strategies in that they focus on the implementation of a specific innovation. Paul (1977) discusses such a strategy emphasizing communication channels and messages for diffusing innovations, interpersonal influence patterns leading to adoption of innovations, and stimuli for adoption originating outside of the adoption system (pp. 21–22).

The diffusion of innovations strategy has been widely used by regional laboratories, state departments of education, and commercial firms in efforts to secure quick, widespread adoption of new equipment, materials, and practices in classrooms. Mixed results have been reported. For relatively simple, highly compatible, clearly advantageous innovative programs, materials, and techniques the strategy seems useful; thus, overhead projectors, spelling kits, and movable furniture have been widely adopted.

By contrast, however, more complex changes have not been responsive to diffusion strategies. The 16mm sound film remains little used after more than fifty years of ready availability. Individually Prescribed Instruction (IPI) died in very early life. Team teaching and flexible scheduling arrangements have only rarely survived.

Local Development

The two major weaknesses of the preceding two strategies, team teaching and flexible scheduling, are (1) too little facilitating support from one and (2) too much imposition from the other. Those who advocate local program development borrow ideas from any and all sources but rely primarily on the ideas, needs, and resources of local staff personnel to produce changes as needed and uniquely suited to local situations. Ideally, action research and curriculum development are closely integrated so that curricular changes evolve. In-service training becomes a by-product of a systematic problem-solving endeavor.

This strategy is widely used to develop revised courses of study as a product of faculty committee study. Many schools become aware of innovations of complex kinds and adopt this strategy for building their own version of the original. Some of the truly exciting innovations to become widely recognized have originated in this local development mode.

Change strategies that are locally developed can take into account the changes that occur between needs assessment, goal formulations, and implementation. As the project takes shape, the staff and participants become better aware of the problems and their objectives, and therefore the goals change. Similarly, as the innovation or intervention activities develop, considerable adjustments—mutual adaptations—must take place. Success depends on updating or altering the techniques and methods at regular intervals (Foster and Easton, 1980, pp. 15–18).

The strengths of this strategy are obvious. Involvement can be very high and creative. Changes can be tailored to local circumstances. Skills developed in learning to design changes in instruction are readily available for continuing efforts to change instruction in still other areas.

Weaknesses of this strategy are numerous. Without an objective independent evaluation system, problems selected for local development efforts may be superficial. Local traditions may restrict the variety of alternatives considered. Most of all, usually neither time nor talent is available in sufficient quantity to generate changes of major kinds when local staff members have these responsibilities added to others.

Those who can recall decade after decade of efforts by local "inventors" find it difficult to view such change strategies with high levels of optimism. Report cards and teacher evaluation instruments are regularly "revised" in hundreds of U.S. school systems with little meaningful change in most instances. Homogeneous grouping systems for instruction have been "reinvented" throughout the land for at least 100 years with little added creativity or improvement. Local invention often amounts to primitive and uninformed copying of past practices. As such, it illustrates change process that is clearly not synonymous with improvement.

A Three-Stage Strategy

The strategies discussed briefly here might well be regarded as parts of a grand strategy. This grand strategy would initially be concerned with (1) the *creating* of perceived alternatives to present practices, (2) the *adopting* of an alternative, and (3) the implementing of *installing* of these practices so they become an established part of the operating system. Rogers and Shoemaker (1971) assumed the creation of alternatives through research and development. In education, these may be sources of alternatives, but they are often inadequate or incomplete. Local production strategies rely heavily on integrating creation, adoption, and installation stages, when in fact they may be so inefficient or limited in scope as to fall short of meeting needs for change. The information processing strategy fails to address itself to the need for *creating alternatives* but also seriously oversimplifies the installing process.

The grand strategy being suggested here is presented schematically in Figure 3.6. Alternatives to current practices are derived from a variety of sources, and the awareness of these alternatives combines in creating a *new perception* or perceptions of possible alternatives. Study activities combined with trial and evaluation activities in Stage II produce a decision to adopt or not. Stage III involves producing changes of various kinds within the operating structure and within the staff to implement the decision to adopt. The last events in this stage call for evaluation of the new operation, leading to modifications or abandonment. This model also suggests the possibility of *corruption in practice.*

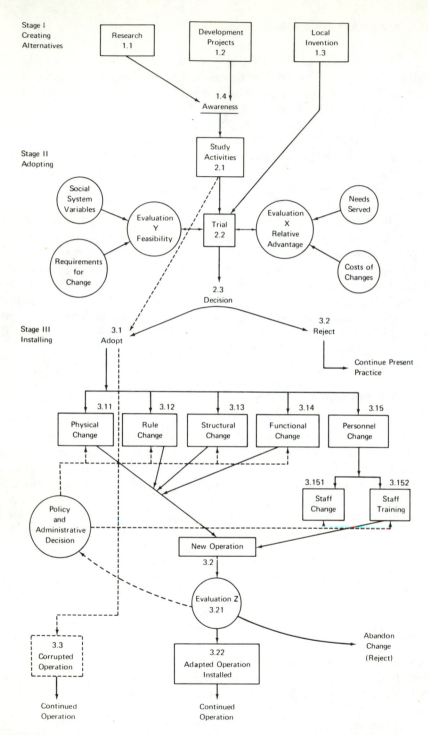

FIGURE 3.6   A three-stage change strategy.

Creating alternative perceptions of what might be is an essential stage in the change process. At its simplest, an invention by someone is perceived as potentially useful. More complex creation of alternatives may involve research and development combinations. The invention of television, combined with studies of the effectiveness of television viewing compared with live lectures, led to opportunities to consider instructional television as an innovation in practice. Local inventions or locally developed new practices may, of course, be related to research and development projects outside the local adopting and installing situation. To the extent that alternatives are locally created, the *awareness* is an integral part of local creation, and study activities are not even needed by those involved in the creative process.

Adopting an alternative set of practices is essentially a process of trial, evaluation, and decision making. When a single individual is the adopter, this is a relatively simple stage; with groups or entire organizations doing the adopting, a much more complex set of events needs to be facilitated. In this strategy, study activities are provided to assist adopters (individual or group) to understand the features and implications of the alternative practices; trial use of alternative practices provides the basis for comparing new and old practices in terms of both *feasibility* and *relative advantage* criteria. This process of evaluating trial practices in terms of several sets of variables is crucial to adoption decisions. Social systems variables need to be accurately assessed regarding the support that can be expected for the new practices from various sources. Similarly, trial experiences need to be assessed with full recognition of the characteristics of divisibility, compatibility, and complexity that relate to the commitment to adopt. Evaluation of trial practices also involves consideration of their relative advantages over prior practice. The needs served—both personal and institutional—can be assessed. The relative costs—economic, institutional, and personal—can be assessed. Decisions to adopt or to reject the new alternative practices when thoroughly tried and carefully evaluated in trial are most likely to be sound and firm.

Installing a newly adopted practice or practices is, of course, a complex sequence of events. Changes in the total operating system are required for any but the simplest innovations. Staff development is critical in nearly any instructional change, with extensive retraining often required. As new practices become operational even on a pilot program basis, evaluation efforts are required to alert staff to modification of practices and further changes in related subsystems.

Under ideal conditions these three stages of change lead to an installed, improved instructional innovation in continuing operation. Sometimes this strategic approach results in the abandonment of the projected change or in its corruption. Rejection of alternative practices or abandonment after installation efforts are both signs of failure of the change strategy. More serious, however, is the matter of *corruption*.

Corruption of Instructional Innovations

When a set of changes in practice is characterized or labeled as an innovation, the "bandwagon" effect is often observed. Decisions to adopt may be made without the systematic processes depicted in Stage II. Trials with the alternative practices may be omitted or only superficially evaluated. Decisions may be imposed rather than fully participatory. Any or all of these flaws in the use of this strategy for change may contribute to corruption of the practices.

Even when adoption decisions are carefully made, Stage III processes may be faulty and hence lead to corruption. Training programs planned for installing new practices may be superficial. Staff changes required may be insufficient or inadequate. Physical and rule changes may be adopted without personnel changes also being implemented. Any failure to install by making all necessary changes will contribute to the danger of corruption of practices.

Complex changes in instruction are more susceptible to corruption than those that are so simple as to require few changes in the installation process. Complex changes are likely to be frustrating to early adopters and require patient evaluation and adaptation. Initially, new operations are likely to be less than fully successful because skill is lacking in the adopting staff. Intensive or extensive retraining may be required.

Complex changes may not be fully supported by various interest groups. New interests may have to be cultivated before successful installing is possible.

One of the many needs for research in instructional change process is in this area of cause of corruption. The phenomenon can readily be described; its causes need further study. Corruption is evident when "ungraded" programs have all kinds of new "levels" that violate the very concept of ungradedness. Corruption is evident when "team teaching" looks more like departmentalization than anything else. Corruption is evident when the report card is replaced by a reporting system that keeps parents and pupils still uninformed. In essence, corruption exists whenever one or more essential features of the original design have been eliminated. However, corruption is also characterized by extremely low-quality implementation of essential features.

SUMMARY

The need for ways of conceptualizing dynamic supervision has been the concern of this chapter. Conceptual models, especially systems models, were discussed as having much utility, despite their having limiting characteristics. The system models, mechanized as they are, seem especially adaptable to developing detailed plans.

A systems model is presented here in an effort to depict and guide plans for a distinctive and separate developmental system for supervision of instruction. The distinctiveness and close interrelatedness of instructional supervision to the operating instructional system is shown in this model.

Strategies for change within any operating framework continue to be a concern here. In earlier chapters problems in producing change were emphasized. In this chapter change strategies generally in vogue are critiqued. An attempt to synthesize various strategies into a single grand strategy is made with an appeal for research to test some of the assumptions being made.

Refer to Chapter 11 case reports for a few illustrations of supervisory efforts encountering resistance of various kinds. Chapter 10 case reports on the use of observational activities to promote individual and program changes may also be useful at this point.

SUGGESTED READINGS

ARENDS, RICHARD I., and JANE H. ARENDS,   *Systems Change Strategies in Educational Settings.* New York: Human Science Press, 1977.

Even though this book is directed toward counselors and school psychologists, it provides some practical and realistic ideas of change as well as strategies and techniques for implementing change.

CUNNINGHAM, WILLIAM G.,   *Systematic Planning for Educational Change.* Palo Alto, Calif.: Mayfield Publishing Co., 1982.

This book describes and discusses important perspectives for viewing and understanding planning. These perspectives include theoretical models, various approaches to the processes of planning, and the influence of important contextual realities. A wide range of techniques and procedures for implementing planning are presented. These techniques represent concepts of the human dimension of the organization and the use of organizational development.

GLICKMAN, CARL D.,   *Developmental Supervision.* Alexandria, Va.: Association for Supervision and Curriculum Development, 1981.

The author recommends a developmental approach to supervision that allows a supervisor to draw from behavioral, cognitive, and humanistic supervisory approaches in order to develop an approach that takes into account a teacher's unique characteristics and stages of development.

LIEBERMAN, ANN,   "Practice Makes Policy: The Tensions of School Improvement," in *Policy Making in Education,* eds. Ann Lieberman and Milbrey W. McLaughlin. Eighty-first Yearbook of the National Society for the Study of Education. Part I. Chicago: The University of Chicago Press, 1982.

In this essay the author examines the implications of school improvement from a local perspective. The ways in which a teacher views his/her job are important in order to understand the full impact of change. The results of many studies and actual experience indicate that effective change is dependent upon a setting that is supportive.

PAUL, DOUGLAS,   "Change Processes at the Elementary, Secondary, and Post-Secondary Levels of Educational Administration," in *Linking Processes in Educational Improvement: Concepts and Applications,* eds. Nicholas Nash and Jack Culbertson. Columbus, Ohio: University Council for Educational Administration, 1977.

This book is a collection of papers that describe the roles of linking agents, the obstacles likely to be encountered by linking agents, and information for developing new plans as well as procedures to secure better cooperation between producers and users of resources. The essay by Paul presents the dimensions of change, change strategies, and research to support generalizations about change processes.

SCHMUCK, RICHARD A., DONALD MURRAY, MARY ANN SMITH, MITCHELL SCHWARTZ, and MARGARET RUNKEL,   *Consultation for Innovative Schools: OD for Multi-unit Structure.* Eugene: University of Oregon Press, 1975.

This monograph describes a research project that tested the efficacy of consultation in organizational development with whole staffs compared to group development consultation for a part of the staff in an effort to implement team teaching in elementary schools. The project was successful in some schools and not in others. A summary of the research offers implications and recommendations for the future. This research project offers some practical procedures and techniques for an administrator to use in implementing an innovation in a school system.

CHAPTER FOUR
ACTIVITIES
FOR SUPERVISION*

Earlier chapters have defined the functional domain of supervision of instruction, analyzed the special concern for change-oriented leadership, and described systems models for operationalization. This chapter is concerned with the building blocks of the program in contrast with the earlier emphasis on concept and design. The *activity* is described here as the basic unit of operation for accomplishing the tasks of supervision. These are the "tools of the trade"; their skillful use in appropriate situations and sequences is the hallmark of the professional instructional leader.

A REVIEW OF CRITICAL TASKS

Five of the ten tasks of supervision as defined in Chapter 1 have already been identified as especially important to the more dynamic aspects of supervision of instruction. These tasks may be called "critical" in the sense that they are the unique vehicles for dynamic efforts, but they are also most distinctively and directly concerned with the instructional program. The five

*Revised with the assistance of Safia Duwaigher of Bahrain.

critical tasks are those of developing curriculum, providing staff, providing materials, arranging for in-service education, and evaluating instruction. Two of these are primarily concerned with *people*—who they are and how they perform. Two of these tasks are primarily concerned with *things*—the curricular guidelines and the materials for teaching. The fifth task is primarily concerned with relationships among people, things, and resultant effects.

Of all the tasks of supervision, *evaluating instruction* and arranging for *in-service education* are most unique and, perhaps, most important. They can easily be neglected, because they are *not* essential to the routine operation of the instructional program. They become important primarily as the supervision orientation shifts from the tractive to the dynamic. Conversely, staffing, curriculum, and materials are essential tasks for both tractive maintenance-oriented supervision *and* dynamic change-oriented endeavors.

While evaluating instruction is the most widely neglected of all tasks, its importance in guiding the change process needs little discussion. It is precisely because of the importance of evaluation activities in change-oriented situations that growing interest and attention have been given to this task area in recent years (Bloom et al., 1971). However, supervisors' lack of sophistication in employing evaluation activities has seriously retarded instructional improvement activities.

In-service education is perhaps the most important of all the tasks. It is essential to the change process in nearly all instances. However, its unique place in the improvement of instruction derives from the uniquely human character of the teaching-learning process. In-service education is the task that specifically seeks to improve instruction by changing the performance of people. The words *in-service education* mean different things to different people. When we try to give the term special meaning, we face a dilemma. On the one hand, if we adopt some of the timeworn stereotypes of in-service education, the term becomes inconsequential and is likely to evoke even negative connotations. On the other hand, a newer, more vital view of in-service education runs the risk of embracing a broad range of goals and objectives that are unrealistic.

Reports of programs and practices in in-service education are numerous, as are opinions and rave notices about their effectiveness. Carefully evaluated programs are much more limited in number but are becoming increasingly common (Almanza, 1980; Lawrence, 1974; Hagen, 1981). Some people think that in-service education is little more than isolated faculty meetings or a workshop or a visiting lecturer. Other think that in-service education involves selecting a "course" from a list offered by a nearby college. "Curriculum study" is frequently used as a term synonymous with in-service education. Some writers, especially those emphasizing clinical approaches to supervision, tend to equate supervision with in-service education.

In-service education is distinctive in its exclusive concern for the way *people* perform in relation to the instructional program. Other curriculum and materials development tasks are concerned with *things* that guide or facilitate instruction-related performance.

This distinction is difficult to maintain operationally. People and things are inevitably interrelated. We cannot assist a teacher in the development of a new learning packet for use in a particular school situation without influencing that teacher's performance in some way. We cannot hope to engage in such evaluation activities as systematic classroom observation without affecting classroom events including teacher behavior. Nonetheless, it makes for some clarity of thought and enhances planning if we conceive of the in-service education task as having as its purpose the *changing of the behavior of personnel in ways that improve instruction* (Harris et al., 1969, p. 2). Other activities aimed at evaluating instruction or developing materials may do likewise, incidentally or accidentally. Conversely, in-service education activities may generate other outcomes.

The distinction between in-service education and other tasks on the basis of purpose—changing people—will not suffice to differentiate between in-service education, staffing, and public relations tasks. These are also concerned with people. Staffing and in-service education are often amalgamated under the term *staff development*. This term is confusing unless we clearly understand the differences between changes *within* people and changing the people occupying positions or roles. Staffing is concerned with recruitment, selection, assignment, reassignment, dismissal, and retirement of personnel. As such, the capacity to perform is a most important consideration in all staffing activities. However, the staffing task aims to improve instruction by *moving* people rather than changing their capacity to perform as in in-service education.

Public relations is the other people-oriented task that must be distinguished from in-service education. Obviously, it tends to be distinguished on the basis of the different *client group* being served. Many in-service activities are quite appropriately employed with people outside the staff of the school when engaged in public relations activities.

MOTIVATION FOR CHANGE

Most of us tend to regard the status quo as normal. The individual teacher, principal, supervisor, or parent tends to perceive what *is* as more or less what *ought to be,* with minor flaws deserving change. The problem, given this tendency, is to selectively develop new perceptions of the state of things as they relate to instruction. Dissonance needs to exist if change is to gain any acceptance or support.

Five approaches to shifting perceptions in the direction of creating cognitive dissonance seem available:

1. *Incentives* can be offered for alternative events or actions.
2. *Fear* can be produced regarding continuation of the status quo.
3. *New needs* that are not currently being satisfied can be cultivated.
4. *Reality structure* can be modified so that old needs are met better in alternative ways.
5. *New concepts* of superior ways of meeting needs can be developed.

There may well be other ways of creating cognitive dissonance, but these five approaches are certainly all in common use. They are presumed to operate on the basis of a needs satisfaction model of behaviors that are habitual. These habits are perceived as being adequate for meeting at least minimal levels of need satisfaction.

The use of incentives, reality restructuring, and models makes no attempt to change the values or life-style of the individual or the group but does promote behavior change that will improve need satisfaction. Fear is essentially a device for reducing need satisfaction by making it too costly. Cultivating new needs is the only one of these five approaches that promotes fundamental change in the person.

Use of *fear* and *need cultivation* requires special consideration because of ethical and practical considerations alike. Any approach that actually restricts a person's opportunities for need fulfillment demands strong justification on humanistic grounds. Negative side effects are also likely to be associated with this approach, giving pause in its use from a purely practical point of view. *Need cultivation,* on the other hand, raises essentially ethical questions associated with propaganda techniques, brainwashing, and thought control.

Incentives

Incentives can be influential as external forces for change (Cooper et al., 1980). The teacher who achieved recognition from influential parents for her rigorous teaching of the rules of English grammar might be inclined to change her behavior in this or another community if she could gain recognition as chairman of the committee to develop a "fused" English program, or she might gain more recognition promoting dramatic creative activities. Financial incentives have been used to induce teachers to emphasize certain behaviors while minimizing others in connection with coaching and performance contracting alike. We see this in athletics and in instrumental music programs. Similarly, teachers who attend summer institutes with fellowships, scholarships, or other stipends might not otherwise be interested in summer study.

On the other hand, certain existing incentives can be removed so as to influence behavior. The employment of full-time bus drivers might make it easier to get male teachers involved in faculty affairs after school. Eliminating "free periods" in a departmentalized program might stimulate acceptance of team relationships in using assigned team-planning periods.

Fear

Fears and anxieties can influence behavior. Just let a lawsuit develop involving a pupil injured while tumbling in the gymnasium and watch the physical education teacher change his or her approach to teaching. Let an influential member of the community express antagonism toward the school for failing to emphasize the teaching of phonics in the primary grades, and superintendent, principal, and teacher are likely to react (Floden et al., 1981). Study of the impact of investigations of the McCarthy era established the powerful influence of fear on classroom behaviors even among highly autonomous college professors.

On the other hand, fears can be eliminated or reduced, and this too can influence behavior patterns. Fear of criticism when dealing with controversial social or economic issues can be reduced by virtue of cooperative planning with influential citizens and distinguished scholars.

New Needs

New needs and priorities can influence behavior. The teacher who had no great need for recognition or extrinsic rewards might enjoy the insularity of the self-contained classroom. However, a sense of enjoyment, exhilaration, and prestige, once gained in a public demonstration or film-making situation, could lead to new acceptance of team-teaching roles. Even more striking are cases of recently widowed or divorced women teachers, or young men with a new baby on the way, who begin to perceive their professional responsibilities with new seriousness as the need for promotion, recognition, and security develops.

Reality Structure

Reality structure can influence behavior. Policy changes, for instance, do not ensure behavior changes, but they do encourage them. Existing policies set limits. Similarly, a teacher who enters a new classroom with ample floor space, bulletin boards, and facilities for use of visual aids may be stimulated to do more creative teaching, but this same teacher in another physical environment would find the use of such teaching procedures frustrating and not worth the effort.

New Concepts

For the classroom teacher, former teachers have provided the models for patterning teaching behavior. Ryans's studies (1960), as well as those of Flanders (1970) and others, suggest that most of us operate in relatively stable patterns. We are more creatures of habit than we like to believe. Once we begin to teach, we have little opportunity to see other teachers in action. Our behavior patterns tend to crystallize. When new concepts can be provided, change can be fostered (Adams, 1970). On the other hand, we cannot adopt new practices without some concept of the character of such practice.

ACTIVITIES FOR CHANGE

Activities for the promotion of change are the essential tools of supervision of instruction. Activities are means to ends and must be selected on the basis of purposes and objectives and situational realities including group size and available resources. A useful framework for guiding the selection and application of activities to in-service training and other supervisory tasks must specify rational, logical relationships between the objectives and the experience impact required to foster change.

Objectives

Since in-service activities are primarily concerned with producing change in people, objectives can be designated as learning outcomes—knowledge, understanding, skill, attitude. If instructional change demands new knowledge, certain activities—attending lectures, reading, viewing films—are readily available and seem appropriate. Skill in constructing a useful test item, on the other hand, demands activities of quite a different type (Davies, 1976, pp. 130–33).

Group Size

Activities accommodate participant groups of various sizes with greater or lesser ease. The interview, for instance, is essentially an activity that calls for a one-to-one, face-to-face relationship for greatest effectiveness. Discussion activity requires small groups of eight to twelve participants. The formal lecture, on the other hand, has its greatest advantage in being suitable for use with large groups. Still other activities, such as the field trip, are almost equally effective with individuals, small groups, and large groups.

Experience Impact

Activities are differentially useful for accomplishing certain objectives because of the impact they are likely to have on participants. The *experience impact characteristics* of each activity can be estimated, at least, and used to guide activity selection.

Experience impact is estimated as the sum total of (Harris, 1980, p. 75) (1) the senses, (2) the interactions, and (3) the reality orientation involved.

These will vary depending upon the nature of the activity and the quality of the experience. Ideally, perhaps, an activity could be created in which all characteristics were equally and fully included. In contrast, it would be easy to imagine an activity that would have few of these characteristics.

Harris (1980) identifies the characteristics of activities that make them different in potential experience impact as follows: (1) senses involved; (2) multiple interactions; (3) control of experience; (4) focus; (5) activeness; (6) originality; and (7) reality. In practice, the fullest possible impact is not often realized, but the potential is there nonetheless.

We can estimate the experience impact potential of each activity. In doing so, activities can be arranged in hierarchical order by impact to be anticipated. This serves as a guide in planning for supervisory programs, avoiding the use of either ineffective or inefficient activities for given purposes.

Objective, Impact, Size Relationships

The relationships among objectives, group size, and experience impact can at least be hypothesized. Figure 4.1 shows these relationships as they might apply to selected activities.

FIGURE 4.1   Relating objectives, impact, and group size to selected activities.

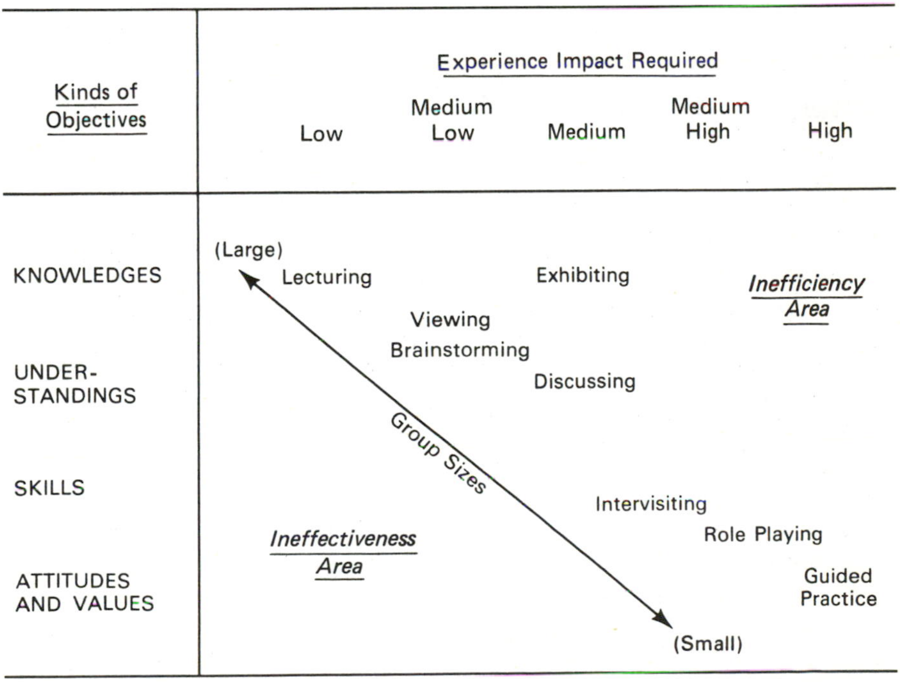

When the various kinds of objectives are placed in logical order, from knowledge at the top to values at the bottom, appropriate activities tend to fall into a pattern. Large-group activities tend to be appropriate for trans-mission of knowledge. Small-group, high-experience-impact activities tend to be appropriate for objectives involving skill development and value change. Perhaps one of the valuable ideas derived from this analysis is that of an inappropriate or ineffectiveness area indicated by the use of large-group and low-experience-impact activities for higher-level objectives. Such activities are appropriate for neither skill development nor changes in values and attitudes.

An *inefficiency* area is also defined in this figure. Small-group, high-experience-impact activities can be employed for simple cognitive objectives, but the costs involved in staff time are likely to be higher than necessary.

Selecting and employing appropriate activities for accomplishing spec-ified goals and objectives is a key planning problem the supervisor faces in promoting instructional change. The *ineffectiveness area* must be avoided, or results will not be forthcoming. The *inefficiency area* must also be avoided, or scarce resources of the staff will be wasted.

Of course, the proper selection of activities does not ensure a coherent program that moves toward the accomplishment of important long-range goals. Specific short-term objectives and activities must be planned as parts of programs with larger, more complex goals in view. Such planning involves careful designs for in-service education that effectively and efficiently em-ploy a variety of activities over time.

DISTINCTIVE ACTIVITIES

Earlier in this chapter the characteristics of supervisory activities were iden-tified in terms of objectives, group size, and experience impact. Based on these essential guidelines for planning supervisory undertakings, an array of activities, each bearing its own individual characteristics and applications, is presented here. The skillful supervisor will not only become familiar with these activities but develop expertise in utilizing them to produce the great-est effect in a particular situation for accomplishing specific objectives.

Before the supervisor is able to select the most suitable approach to a given task, he or she should carefully select the basic components of a plan. In the creation of this unique design, the ability to select from all the avail-able activities those that are most likely to result in the desired outcomes will be important to efficient use of resources. By identifying needs and speci-fying objectives, the selection of appropriate activities clearly follows as log-ical decisions. Poorly defined objectives will produce ineffective and undesirable results, since poor activity selection often results.

Every educational change program plan is at least two-dimensional. This is usually expressed as means and ends, process and product, input and output. For the program planner the more appropriate terms would be the *objective*—the immediate outcome of the program—and the *activity*—the means of achieving and producing the desired objective. The use of these two terms has a utilitarian or pragmatic value, as they define the results to be produced and the means to bring about the desired change in the staff or institution.

In the formulation of specific objectives, the supervisor must be concerned with both *behavioral goals*—(changes desired in individual or group behaviors) and *organizational goals* (changes desired within the organization). Generally speaking, behavioral and organizational objectives specify the anticipated change, the conditions under which this change is to take place, and a standard of minimum acceptable performance. Performance specifications are expressed in terms of the action to be performed. This form of expression of behavioral or performance objectives is an improvement over the sweeping generalized objectives used in educational undertakings for years, because of the precision and clarity of intent provided by such written statements (Davies, 1976).

Once the supervisor has established the behavioral and organizational objectives expressed in direct relationship to the identified needs and problems, then the selecting of appropriate activities to be employed can easily be determined by those who understand the unique characteristics of a variety of activities.

The analysis of activities and the selection from the broad array of those available must be made to determine the one approach or combination of approaches that will provide the best vehicle for attaining specified outcomes.

Activities listed and described here are organized in order of experience impact potential as best that can be estimated for each activity. Table 4.1 lists all 23 activities in this same order.

1. Lecturing.   This activity is one of the oldest involved in in-service education, public relations, and teacher-orientation tasks. In its simplest form it is purely an aural-oral activity. As the lecture requires no interaction, it has low experience impact and is primarily suitable for the transmission of knowledge. It can be used with groups of all sizes. Lecturing is most commonly associated with the formal conference, institute, or course in in-service and orientation programs. It is also used in public meetings for public relations purposes. The more dramatic the delivery or the more extensive the use of visual materials to underscore the oral message, the greater the experience impact. This activity may have fallen into disrepute in recent years principally because of ill-fated attempts to use the lecture to change attitudes, behaviors, and values, for which it is unsuitable.

2. Visualized lecturing.   This is an essentially oral-aural presentation supported by visual materials. The lecturer may use slides, transparencies,

TABLE 4.1   List of Activities of Supervision

ACTIVITY	ESTIMATED LEVEL OF EXPERIENCE IMPACT
1. Lecturing	Low
2. Visualized lecturing	Low
3. Panel presenting	Low
4. Viewing film or television	Low
5. Listening to tape, radio, or recordings	Low
6. Exhibiting materials and equipment	Medium-low
7. Observing in classrooms	Medium-low
8. Demonstrating	Medium
9. Interviewing, structured	Medium
10. Interviewing, focused	Medium
11. Interviewing, nondirective	Medium-high
12. Discussing	Medium
13. Reading	Medium
14. Analyzing and calculating	Medium
15. Brainstorming	Medium
16. Videotaping and photographing	Medium
17. Instrumenting and testing	Medium
18. Buzz session	Medium
19. Field trip	Medium-high
20. Intervisiting	Medium-high
21. Role playing	Medium-high
22. Writing	High
23. Guided practice	High

chalkboard drawings, charts, or other visual media. This activity involves the participant in seeing as well as in listening, and forms of attention can be sharpened; hence, experience impact is not so low as in the simple lecture. Knowledge transmission objectives are still most appropriate to this activity, but somewhat higher levels of cognitive outcomes are possible.

Multimedia presentations have become increasingly common. These generally include visualized lecture activity as well as film clips, recordings, and so forth. To the extent that the human lecturer is eliminated from these presentations, the activity may well lose more experience impact than is gained.

3. Panel presenting.   A large-group presentation may have its impact value increased by modifying the formal lecture using a panel mode. This may be done in several ways. The *informal panel* is composed of several speakers who interact with one another on a given topic with a substantial amount of spontaneity. This may include formal presentations of papers by each speaker first, followed by the interplay of positions by the panel members. Again the panel may be a group of "reactors" who informally present their reactions to the formal lecture or paper presentations. The *symposium* is a highly structured panel in which the individual members make formal presentations usually approaching a central theme or question from several perspectives or from cross-disciplinary viewpoints. The debate is still another adaptation of the panel, which has been elaborately developed in collegiate and legal circles but is rarely employed for educational supervision purposes.

All of these activities place the emphasis on the presentation of facts, or ideas, to large groups—frequently at conferences, institutes, or workshops—with limited experience impact. The participant's involvement is predominantly restricted to an aural one. The degree of experience impact may be increased by following the formal panel presentation with small-group discussions, buzz sessions, brainstorming, or testing so as to secure interaction with the issues and factual presentations of the formal setting. The debate format may also enhance experience impact by focusing interest on issues and arousing emotions.

4. Viewing film or television. The uses of visual presentations through the media of film, television, or videotape are increasingly important to in-service education, public relations, and evaluation tasks. Whatever the specific form this activity takes, it is a kind of visualized lecture by mechanical means. It has most of the characteristics of visualized lecture—low experience impact and appropriate for large groups with low-level objectives. The adaptability of film and videotape to small-group or even individual use offers possibilities for somewhat higher experience impact. This is especially true when videotapes are used by an individual and observation and analysis activities are combined with viewing.

The 16-mm film has a special virtue in that the supervisor can select any part of the total production, rerun segments, and stop the film at will. This feature makes it effective for use along with role-playing and discussion activities. Film cases are available depicting teaching problem situations to produce the focus for group discussions.

Broadcast or closed-circuit television continues to serve in limited ways for in-service education, but more widely for public relations. The lack of control and flexibility in broadcast television restricts its use with higher levels of experience impact. The development of two-way closed circuits is gradually offering opportunities in connection with demonstrations, directed practice, panels, and discussions for higher levels of impact.

5. Listening to tape, radio, or recordings. This activity involves using sound recordings to present ideas to one or more listeners in such ways as to help develop understanding or skills. Sound recordings are often associated with group discussion, group therapy, role playing, and directed-practice activities. Radio is not as popular as it was before the advent of television.

Tape recordings of selected portions of a class meeting have been successful in stimulating group discussions. The tape recorder is used as an activity along with nondirective interviews for helping a teacher gain understanding of her behavior in the classroom.

Tape-recorded interviews may be quite useful for training teachers, administrators, and supervisors in interview techniques. Role-played interviews can be recorded to help the players analyze techniques. This device can be helpful in a public relations program geared to stimulating and improving parent-teacher interviews.

Group-discussion or group-therapy sessions will find the tape recorder helpful in analyzing patterns of events and the work of the leader. Playback of recordings in relation to role-playing activities is suggested for presenting information about the situation and for "action continuation." The last few minutes of a discussion session may be played to the group when it meets again as a stimulus to renewed activity with assurance of continuity.

Microteaching and self-analysis techniques have generally stressed the use of videotaping (Borg, 1968); however, verbal behavior can be analyzed quite adequately with ordinary sound-tape recordings.

6. Exhibiting materials and equipment.   This activity is of considerable help in in-service education and materials development task areas. The exhibit generally takes form at professional association meetings and under the direction and control of commercial firms. Perhaps it is this association with commercialism that discourages the use of exhibits for professional supervisory purposes. However, the exhibiting of library book collections has been widely used as a way of familiarizing teachers with new library materials and improving the quality of books selected for purchase. "Public Schools Week" and "Back-to-School Night" exhibits of pupils' works have apparently been successful in improving school-parent relations.

The exhibit has its greatest value when related to other activities calling for more activity involvement of exhibit viewers. A book exhibit has more meaning when teachers have been allocated money to spend or have been asked to serve on a selection committee. An exhibit of new media is a worthwhile preview to a demonstration using such media. An exhibit of students' work in science or art or home economics takes on more meaning for parents or teachers when associated with discussions of curriculum and teaching ideas involved.

7. Observing in classrooms.   This activity involves the systematic live observing of a staff member for analyzing his or her practice. Observation techniques are similar to those employed in viewing demonstrations and intervisitations except that they are more rigorous. Observations are primarily made for evaluation purposes, although they are generally closely associated with in-service education as well.

The observation involves a skilled (trained) observer with some kind of observation instrument to facilitate systematic, objective recording of events. There are now many instruments available for observing classroom events. Some focus on the teacher primarily, while others are more concerned with interactions. They all have in common some prestructured set of categories to guide the observer and a set of clearly specified procedures for recording observable events.

The casual "drop-in" visit to a teacher's classroom is still a common procedure. It has a place as a social amenity or as a part of the routine of communicating one's presence in the building. It should *not* be confused with classroom observation activity, however.

Observations serve to inform supervisors not only of the problems teachers are encountering but also of the outstanding practices in effect. They serve to help supervisors make decisions about needs for in-service education or curriculum development programs: When classroom observations are an integral part of an in-service effort with a single teacher, they are, of course, heavily dependent upon preplanning and feedback sessions.

In a later chapter various observation instruments are presented and utilization procedures are discussed in detail. In one form or another, observation and analysis of instruction have become essential feature of nearly all supervisory programs and models. This activity continues, despite its rebirth of rigor and objectivity, to be very anxiety-producing for both observer and observed.

8. Demonstrating.   The activity involves the presentation of a prearranged series of events to a group for their viewing. The demonstration is planned to be realistic, but by its very nature it emphasizes those elements that are of greatest importance in the operation being demonstrated. Since viewers of a demonstration are involved in only a limited way and interaction with the demonstrator is not readily available, the experience impact is not very high. Group size can range widely for demonstrations, with small groups being uneconomical and large groups losing opportunities to see and hear details.

Physical arrangements are important to an effective demonstration. Ideally, the demonstration is planned in great detail and rehearsed to ensure presenting details needed to accomplish objectives. Artificiality is to be avoided, however, since viewer acceptance depends in part upon the illusion of reality.

Demonstrations are most effective when involvement is enhanced by viewers using systematic observation procedures. Also, follow-up activities such as discussion, videotape replays, and directed practice intensify their impact.

9. Structured interviewing.   This activity involves a one-to-one relationship that is primarily used in obtaining or imparting information. It is a helpful activity for selecting staff, communicating with public groups, and securing evaluation data. Various terms are used to describe the highly structured or focused interview in which the supervisor is imparting his impression or his perceptions to the teacher. Others suggest the term *investigate* to describe a similar type of interview. The "personal selection" interview is essentially investigative and does not differ in its basic form (Molyneaux and Lane, 1982).

Because of its structure under interviewer control, this activity has little value when attitude changes are desired. For imparting information on a personal basis, the structured procedure is effective. It is also effective in the systematic collection of ideas, opinions, instructional descriptions, and attitudes. Although the validity of the interview as the primary source of information for staff selection is questionable, it still is widely used. Certainly, interviewing prospective staff members to gain supplementary information for screening and selection is a most desirable application of this activity.

The structured interview involves a predetermined set of questions. An interview schedule is desirable to ensure coverage of all questions, proper sequencing, and systematic recording of the information elicited. The interviewer in this activity is concerned only with answers to the predetermined questions. Other responses and supplementary information are usually ignored.

10. Focused interviewing.   This activity is only semistructured. It is described by Merton and Kendell (1946) as having the following characteristics:

1.   The person interviewed has been involved in a known situation.
2.   The significant elements of the situation have been analyzed by the interviewer.
3.   An interview guide has been developed.
4.   The interview is focused on the subjective experience of the interviewee.

This approach is quite compatible with many supervisory situations that follow classroom observations. By employing systematic observation procedures, the supervisor can analyze the classroom situation, develop an interview guide, and focus the teacher's thinking on his or her individual classroom experiences. This activity has important values in developing understandings about significant elements in the classroom behavior of the teacher. As this activity is concerned with subjective as well as objective data, the teacher's perceptions are elicited by the questions posed by the interviewer.

Evaluations that probe for feelings and needs that lie below the surface of the consciousness of the individual may require the semistructure of the focused interview. Usually, as the teacher perceives the supervisor probing in a given direction, there is a tendency to become defensive, to feel threatened, to be resistive to real penetration of the underlying causes of the observable phenomena.

The focused interview offers sufficient flexibility for the interviewer and interviewee alike to react in ways that reduce tensions and threat.

Public relations programs profit greatly from the understanding gained in analyzing public opinion through the process of the focused interview. To know what people think and feel, one must ask them. The answers obtained will generally be no more or no less superficial than the type of interview technique employed and the degree of the investigator's skill in involving the interviewee in a commitment to the process.

Many times this focuses attention on concerns of the supervisor while totally missing the needs awareness of the teacher. Because of the structured nature, the teacher frequently does not feel free to interject those areas of greatest concern to him as an individual or to divert the direction of the interview.

11. Nondirective interviewing.   Perceiving the concerns under discussion from the perspective of the concerns of the teacher or other clients and expressing ideas and feelings from their frames of reference are basic to this activity.

Various symbolic elements are important facets of the nondirective approach (Kindsvatter and Wilen, 1981). The nondirective interview process involves guiding the individual in rehearsing his past and canvasing his present and future with emphasis on self-assessment and self-determination. The professional relationship between the teacher and the supervisor is one that helps the teacher to gain maximum autonomy through self-understanding.

The nondirective approach provides a face-to-face interaction of the teacher and the supervisor as its greatest depth. The interview is highly "teacher-centered," and the teacher's problems, interests, and concerns provide the focus of the interview. The supervisor creates an environment of permissiveness as he attempts to reflect both the ideas and the feelings accurately. He continually encourages a full verbalization of the teacher's concerns, frustrations, and anxieties. This procedure is most useful when attitude and value changes are of the utmost importance for in-service purposes. When a situation is charged with emotion, the nondirective interview also provides catharsis for the staff member. Once feelings have been expressed, and attitudes and values have been analyzed in a nonthreatening interview setting, new understandings and perceptions can be developed.

Nondirective interviews tend to be prolonged and less logically sequential than other interview forms. Tape recordings of these interviews are sometimes helpful as an accurate, confidential record to refresh the supervisor's and the teacher's memory from one session to another. A recording enables the interviewer to dispense with distracting note taking and, thus, to concentrate on the feelings being expressed. Obviously, strong rapport is required if recordings of interviews are made, and appropriate safeguards must be taken to ensure proper disposal of these confidential tapes. When recordings are not feasible, handwritten notes may be helpful in providing continuity from one session to another.

The nondirective interview tends to develop (*a*) as the teacher's perceptions develop and skills of self-analysis increase, and (*b*) the interventions of the supervisor decrease until such time that (*c*) the teacher feels that he can carry on independently.

Sometimes the supervisor-counselor senses that the more the individual delves into his feelings in a particular area of concern, the more uncomfortable he or she will become. In this situation it is the supervisor's task to redirect by simply changing the subject to something less intense yet still relevant. The supervisor should assure the teacher that he is free to return to the subject at a later date when the teacher feels that it will be of benefit. Some react to the client-centered approach, feeling that it is a formal denial of a real relationship. Fortunately for the supervisor, active participation with the teacher in real situations of school life, as well as in the interview activity, give him or her the opportunity to make nondirectiveness more than just verbal interaction.

12. Discussing.   This activity involves task-oriented small groups engaged in active verbal interaction. It tends to have medium-level experience impact because of the in-depth involvement in both verbal and nonverbal interactions. Discussions are distinguished from social activities by their task orientation; from interviews, by their small-group characteristics; and from meetings, by their informality and looseness of structure. Discussion activity is also distinguished from group dynamics and encounter group activities to the extent that the latter employ a variety of activities other than discussion. Buzz sessions and group discussion activities have many similarities. The buzz session, however, uses a short time frame of 10–30 minutes, while the larger group's goals and objectives establish its purpose, with maximum interaction desired as distinguished from a developmental process. Discussion groups tend to have longer lives, often continuing for several sessions, and group members are guided in specifying the objectives and developing the procedures for arriving at these objectives (Mills, 1967; Pino and Emory, 1976; Smith, 1980; Zander, 1982).

Discussion groups make their major contribution in stimulating the improvement of understanding. Organized courses are increasingly making use of discussion as well as other interaction activities.

In recent years discussion-leading techniques have been developed to the level of a fine art. Cantor in 1951 developed many ideas about discussion-leading techniques; he thought of discussion-leading as a professional endeavor. The dynamics of the interaction of group members have also been rigorously studied by Bales (1950), among others, with the result that discussion-leading has become both an art and a science (Tropman, 1980).

The question of efficiency of group discussion in solving problems often arises. Participants and leaders sometimes grow apprehensive that the discussion "isn't getting us anywhere." Small groups can effectively tackle even rather specific game-type problems (Moxley, 1977). Individual solutions to problems take less time, but groups have fewer failures in solving these problems than do individuals. Accordingly, group discussion offers much promise in curriculum development, evaluation, and public relations areas where problem solving as well as training outcomes is desired.

When group discussion activities have purposes involving complex problems, they are often used in connection with role playing, films, readings, research, intervisitations, demonstrations, and lectures. The so-called case method (Ostlund, 1968; Herriott and Gross, 1979) has become widely used. This involves the reading of case studies by small groups followed by a guided discussion using the case materials for the stimulation of thought. "Analytic" discussion activities with teacher groups rely on closely parallel, if not common, group experiences to provide the raw materials for discussion. A "fishbowl" adaptation of group discussion activity has become popular in counseling circles.

13. Reading.   Reading as an activity of supervision is almost universally recognized. Professional libraries have been widely developed in schools to encourage reading among the staff. Curiously enough, the use of reading materials seems most common in highly structured formal courses. Efforts to make systematic use of reading activities in connection with discussion, in-service workshops, or interviews have not been very promising. Motivation for reading broadly and intensively seems lacking and difficult to develop. On the other hand, when readings are introduced into a faculty meeting or an in-service session, their introduction tends to be an afterthought.

Some interesting ways of combining reading activities with in-service education sessions have been developed. Cases used in connection with group discussions have been included in administrator training programs in ways that make the reading activity an integral part of the partiticpants' involvement. Similarly, "in-baskets" have been developed for simulating problem situations that require substantial reading activity as a central part of the training experience (Greenblatt and Duke, 1981). Harris has developed "lesson protocols" for analyzing teaching. These are typescripts of actual classroom situations that are used as basic readings for in-service sessions (Harris et al., 1969).

14. Analyzing and calculating.   This activity is more important for supervisors than ever before because of federal demands for systematic evaluation of special projects and the growing concern for "accountability" in education. The action research movement of several decades ago helped many supervisors gain an appreciation of the use of data in stimulating and guiding instructional practices. Testing programs demand some analytical skills on the part of those guiding teachers, administrators, and policy makers in interpreting test results. Systematic classroom observation practices have emerged that require data analysis and simple calculations for effective interpretation (Harris and Hill, 1982).

As the roles of the supervisor become increasingly defined in the areas of program evaluation and public relations, skills in analyzing data in ways that yield more useful information will be demanded. Analyzing and calculating need not be complicated mathematical or computer-related activities. Simple graphic analyses, simple tabulations, and simple indices often suffice to make raw data helpful in planning, training, and public relations pursuits.

15. Brainstorming.   This activity involves the production of basic ideas, alternatives, and creative suggestions. The general procedures are usually credited to A. F. Osborne. Although brainstorming has been characterized as "freewheeling," it is only in the sense that there is a concerted effort to generate many ideas representing various points of view in a relatively short span of time. It is highly structured in the sense that the problem area is defined and the responses are restricted accordingly. Even though highly structured and restrictive, it is capable of producing the greatest number of ideas on a given topic in the shortest possible time.

Brainstorming is a group activity in which ideas held by the individual participants are orally expressed without discussion, criticism, or analysis. As the brainstorming ground rules prohibit discussion, criticism, and analysis, the base distinction between the *buzz session* and *brainstorming* is evident. Basically, brainstorming is a group effort to generate an oral inventory of interrelated ideas associated with a particular area of concern.

Four basic structural rules follow: (1) It is the quantity of ideas that is desired—the production of a large number of different ideas is the object. (2) All adverse criticizing and evaluating of ideas is discouraged; "killer-phrases" are excluded. (3) Freewheeling, visionary, and even "wild" ideas are encouraged. (4) Combinations and improvements of ideas are sought: "hitch-hiking" on another's idea frequently occurs while various notions are combined and expanded. Although highly creative responses are sought in this activity, the problems presented must be simple and specific.

A unique quality of brainstorming is the permissive atmosphere toward all ideas. The suspension of criticism or analysis of ideas and the willingness to adapt and borrow ideas of others enrich the process of generating alternatives.

That brainstorming is productive of new ideas is evidenced by the sheer number of ideas produced by the group in a relatively short span of time.

Both the quality of ideas and the number of unique ideas are high for brainstorming groups. As the analysis, evaluation, and synthesis of ideas are important, follow-up activities—discussion, buzz sessions, panels, and the like—are essential in taking advantage of brainstormed ideas. This follow-up reduction process becomes the essence of decision making.

Participants enjoy brainstorming, but, at the same time, they expect something to be done with the generated ideas and embryonic concepts. Concurrently, participants must be cautioned that not all ideas can be implemented and that only those ideas that survive the critical analysis process will be utilized.

Brainstorming is an activity for the stimulation of ideas expression and production. It can be used in the school setting to inform, stimulate, and develop understanding and attitudes relating to a problem. Precautions should be exercised that brainstorming be selected only for appropriate purposes in which a large variety of alternatives is needed for comparison and study.

16. Videotaping and photographing.   These activities involve securing visual images for use with curriculum development, evaluation, in-service education, or public relations tasks. Photographic work with 8-mm film or slide reproduction has been overshadowed in recent years by the introduction of portable videotape recorders. Nonetheless, both media have well-established uses in supervisory programs.

Videotaping has tremendous advantages when live events are to be analyzed, including both visual and auditory information. Most classroom events fall into this category. Additionally, videotape has the advantages of immediacy of playback, erasability, and reusability. Hence, microteaching and self-analysis endeavors are greatly facilitated by the videotape recorder (Authier and Gustafson, 1982). Similarly, public relations needs often call for immediate responses, which this electronic equipment can provide.

Photographic activity has its special contributions to make, nonetheless. When vivid true color is important, film is hard to beat. When the editing and organizing of visual display material is important, photographic activities are demanded.

Various creative ways of using video and photographic activities have been described. Their uses seem limited only by the imagination and skill of the supervisor. Caution must be exercised to keep this technology from being used beyond its true limits. These devices are in no sense adequate replacements for the live observer in the classroom, for instance.

17. Instrumenting and testing.   This kind of activity involves use of tests, inventories, reactionnaires, rating scales, and other ways of securing data in social situations. The use of tests and questionnaires is often combined with discussions, role playing, interviews, and observations. The development of new observation instruments and their widespread application to classroom observations, in-service education, and evaluation purposes has been one of the striking changes of the 1960s. The tests of teacher knowledge and attitude have had only limited value for staffing purposes, even though "teacher competency" tests are experiencing a new wave of popularity at the preservice training level. However, new interest in the "assessment center" approach to selecting administrative and supervisory personnel for schools has emerged (Harris et al., 1979, p. 161). Borich and Madden (1977) have also provided a new and useful critique of an array of instruments.

18. Buzz sessions.   This activity involves small groups that are temporarily formed to discuss a specific topic with minimum structure, maximum emphasis upon interaction, and full opportunity to express ideas related to a specific topic (Hare, 1982). An optimum amount of critical analysis of ideas related to the topic is encouraged in a permissive, topic-centered, face-to-face situation.

This technique was first described by J. D. Phillips in 1948. Since that time the techniques have undergone many refining processes. Before the buzz groups are actually formed, the total group is briefed on the question, issue, or topic to be discussed. The charge to the small buzz groups should be simply worded and clear to all concerned. In many situations, this charge to the groups follows a formal presentation—lecture, film, or panel discussion. At other times the topic may arise out of a well-known common concern of the group. A "chairman" is responsible for getting things going and then for passing leadership to the group and permitting independent verbal interaction to take place.

A buzz session appears to have at least two values: (1) it determines what the group is thinking, and (2) it gives the individual an opportunity to "blow off steam," and the group to question what has been said. Keen involvement and interest are often generated within the group. The group participates vigorously—discussing and arguing. In preparing their end-of-session reports and in later comments, participants often use the pronoun *we.* Individuals often express pride in their specific list of group concerns in the concluding report session.

Different assignments could be given to various groups. One group might be asked to listen for implications within the opening presentation. Another group might be asked to determine ideas that the speaker(s) should elaborate in the closing portion. A third group might be asked to determine the high points of the talk that should be reemphasized, the need for additional data, and so forth.

The buzz groups should be completely free in their interaction, with full expression of all ideas being sought. If this activity is to be successful, the participants must have an immediate concern for the problem or an interest in the topic, some knowledge about the problem or topic, and opinions, attitudes, or feelings to express. They should be encouraged to discuss, to agree or disagree, and to offer alternative suggestions. The interaction should be spirited, free-flowing, and, except for the natural restrictions of a defined topic, unstructured.

Buzz sessions, like most other activities, do not suffice without follow-up activities. At the conclusion of the allotted time, the appointed or elected recorder shall summarize the main concerns of the group and formulate questions to be presented to the speaker or panel for further consideration.

19. Field trip.   This activity is characterized by a trip away from the school, designed to allow staff members to see ongoing operations that relate to their jobs. Although this activity is popular with many teachers and school-children, it is not often used for in-service education or staffing purposes. Tours of the school community, visits to industrial plants, foreign travel, and home visits are some specific examples of field trip situations.

Unlike intervisitations, these trips do not involve visiting another teacher's classroom. They are distinct from exhibits and demonstrations by the ongoing reality of the operation being visited.

While most common for orientation purposes with new teachers, there appear to be abundant opportunities to have the field trip serve as a rich source of new experience for highly experienced teachers. Unusually obvious for in-service training of vocational, mathematics, and science teachers are trips to industrial concerns, planetariums, and research laboratories. Only a little imagination is needed, however, to come up with field trips of unusual value to teachers of social studies, business education, and fine arts.

Very little consideration has been given, apparently, to the potential value of field trips for staffing purposes. Two possibilities come to mind. Field trips could be a way of encouraging staff members to consider job opportunities other than teaching when they seem inadequate as teachers. Field trips could also help in recruiting outstanding persons from other fields of endeavor into teaching or administration.

20. Intervisiting.   In this activity, one person visits and observes another person in action. This is sometimes referred to as "teacher visitation." It is an individual activity in most instances, although small groups can visit effectively. Intervisitation is distinguished from the demonstration in that little prearranging of the teaching is provided. It is unique in that the visitor sees reality, as nearly as that is possible.

Techniques and procedures involved in intervisitation activities are very much like those for the demonstration as far as the observers are concerned. The latter are briefed beforehand on the things that they are likely to find most valuable. An observation guide is used and follow-up activities are planned. Arrangements with the person being observed include *selecting* a person who can skillfully do those things that the observer wants and needs to see, agreeing on a *time* for the visitation, and arranging for the visited and the visitor to *interact* following the observation period. Arrangements usually include providing the visitor with information in advance about the situation to be observed. Lesson plans, seating charts, long-range goals, and background of the individuals involved are almost essential if intervisitations are to be effective.

The intervisitation is most widely used to permit classroom teachers to see other teachers in action. Any staff member can be observed, however, and there is increasing interest in this activity for building improved understanding among the various staff members in a system. While skills and knowledge may be gained in intervisitations, the principal values of the activity lie in improving understanding of such things as teaching techniques, pupil-teacher relationships, room arrangements, and lesson planning (Lovell and Wiles, 1983).

Abuse of this activity has given it an undeserved reputation. Teachers persist in claiming its value to them! Intervisitations have been made on a mass scale without specific purpose, planning, or follow-up. An observation situation should be identified in terms of the specific needs of an individual to see and to hear. Staff members who without plan or purpose simply select someone to visit are not likely to profit much from the intervisitation. Follow-up is essential for best results. Supervisors must preview and analyze a situation for intervisitation purposes just as they do films, books, or field trips for school use.

21. Role playing (Milroy, 1982).   This activity is sometimes referred to as *sociodrama*. It draws upon the power of dramatization for effectiveness. The view of Hamlet reflects in part the power of role playing:

> ". . .The play's the thing
> Wherein I'll catch the conscience of the king."

In less ambitious ways, sociodrama has its value in eliciting and analyzing feelings.

Role playing has been employed to reflect variability within a culture and differences between cultures. Moreno, sometimes thought of as the father of this activity, used it as a basis for psychotherapy and research. Organizational role conflicts have been studied using the activity.

Role playing in education has its value in providing a bridge between talk and action, providing a safe learning environment, providing concrete situations against which to react, and providing for spontaneity and flexibility. The technique has been found useful in classroom settings at all academic levels, beginning with the elementary grades.

In supervisory group situations, problems of teachers are used to structure role playing. Participants are allowed to make up their own conversation, motions, gestures, and so forth. As they act out their ways of dealing with a problem, they reveal the way they feel. In some situations each player is urged to be himself; in other situations he is told to take the part of someone else, to gain insight into another's view of the problem or to see how another person views him. Thus the involved teachers act out problems in a serious attempt to understand the behavior of self and others. This technique facilitates presenting a situation in fewer words and with greater clarity than is possible through ordinary discussion methods. A variety of specialized techniques for use in role playing have been described:

1. *Role reversal*—allowing two individuals to exchange roles,
2. The *double technique*—permitting a second individual to assume the identity of the subject, allowing the merging of the two personalities as the double verbalizes the conflict feelings in a low voice as the first personality acts out his dilemma,
3. The *soliloquy*—the action of the drama is suddenly "frozen" and each participant is asked to soliloquize or to speak out what feelings are in his mind that he is not expressing,
4. The *mirror technique*—permitting the individual to see himself in action as his substitute ego is placed across from him and mimics his behavior,
5. *Periodic stimuli technique*—designed to test spontaneous adaptations to surprise elements,
6. The *hidden theme*—developing the ability of an individual to perceive behavioral themes in a social situation and to create an appropriate role to deal with it,
7. The *mute technique*—a situation to reveal nonverbal resources of communication and expression as the participants must communicate only by gestures and bodily movements.

Regardless of the specifics of purpose and context, role play is structured by a briefing of participants, the actual interaction of the "players," and follow-up discussion (Milroy, 1982, pp. 9–10). The briefing is especially important. Milroy suggests six steps: (1) choosing a simulated situation, (2) determining roles, (3) explaining the situation, (4) allocating roles, (5) assembling necessary information, and (6) explaining observer function.

At an appropriate time the role-playing action is terminated by the group leader if it does not naturally terminate. Discussion of the situation follows as the observers evaluate and analyze what they have observed. Thus role playing provides for intellectual analysis of an essentially emotional experience.

Role playing has had great value in developing skills as well as insight into complex professional situations involving person-to-person relationships. It has been used as a direct training activity for interviewing, discussion-leading, and teacher-questioning skills. Its tremendous potential as a highly flexible activity for in-service education programs is best revealed by the fact that gaming, microteaching, sensitivity and T-group training, and laboratory teaching all draw upon role-playing technique in one way or another.

22. Writing.   Although this activity is most widely associated with the supervisory bulletin and courses of study or curriculum guides, supervisors themselves are becoming increasingly involved in the writing of proposals and evaluation reports in connection with specially funded projects.

Writing activities are obviously required in nearly all tasks of supervision. This activity is central to the communications system of the school whether it takes the form of a friendly note or letter, bulletin, memo, report, or news release. Writing for publication appears to have considerable potential for in-service outcomes, as the authors are required to organize their ideas and communicate them to others. Writing for newspapers, radio, or television programs or for professional journals can have multiple value if properly guided to improve the quality of understanding of both writer and readers.

23. Guided practice.   This activity involves individualized or small-group manipulative activities. It is a counterpart of the interview in which *doing* is emphasized rather than *talking.* Although skillful supervisors have long used guided practice, it is not often referred to in the literature. Guided-practice sessions are characterized by individualization and the emphasis upon doing, but they are distinguished from firsthand-experience activities by the fact that practice activities are arranged out of context. This permits guided experience without the pressures of the real-life situation.

New interest in this skill-building activity has been generated by the development of microteaching (Authier and Gustafson, 1982), minicourse, and laboratory training activities (Harris et al., 1969). Clinical supervision advocates have emphasized interview and observation activities (Cogan, 1973; Champagne and Hogan, 1981), but guided practice may well make the difference between supervision that changes classroom performance and supervision that makes no difference or generates anxieties.

Guided-practice activities are sometimes associated with intervisitation, observation, and interview activities. Classroom observations may indicate the need for skill development. If lesson-planning skills are involved, an interview may lead to a visit to observe a teacher whose teaching reflects skillful planning. A follow-up activity may well include a guided-practice session in which the teacher develops her plans with direct, individual assistance from the supervisor.

Practice activities may be appropriate wherever skill development is required and the problem calls for individual treatment. The use of materials, equipment, and techniques can be improved by means of this activity. The disadvantage inherent in directed practice is its cost. Obviously, if practice could be provided in groups or left to the individual without guidance, the cost in supervisor's time could be reduced. Demonstrations, buzz sessions, field trips, exhibits, and even discussions are group activities that *can*—but unfortunately are unlikely to—lead to skill development. Skill development tends to be individual and to require practice under guidance. Firsthand experience, of course, can be effective, but it often lacks the opportunity to develop a minimum level of competence with sufficient guidance to control the hazards of failure.

SUMMARY

Effective action to implement change in the instructional program requires attention to the tasks of supervision, but also to the specific activities and their impact on current practice. Five of the nine task areas of supervision—curriculum development, materials development, staffing, in-service education, and evaluation—were singled out in Chapter 3 as of special relevance to supervisors in their efforts to promote instructional improvement processes in systemslike ways. In this chapter the focus is narrowed still further to consider ways of changing the behavior of personnel toward better instruction.

Motivations for change in behavior are diverse and hence must be studied carefully as they relate to both individuals and organizations. Activities selected for promoting change can be carefully selected with due regard for variety, experience impact, and objectives. Group size also plays a role in making it possible to utilize various activities with greater effeciency as well as effectiveness.

The distinctive character of over 20 supervisory activities cannot be easily ignored. Because they are both numerous and distinctive, the supervisor who can select, combine, and employ these activities with skill can have influence not otherwise possible.

Refer to case reports in chapters 9 through 11 for examples of activities in action. "Elementary Supervisor—A Typical Day" (pages 217–219) indicates the special reliance placed on classroom observing. Chapter 10 elaborates on a variety of problems associated with individualized approaches to supervision. Chapter 11 includes several case reports detailing activities in workshop settings.

SUGGESTED READINGS

BRUSEHI, PHILIP,   "Listening: The Neglected Communication Skill," *Journal of Communication Management,* 11:17–18.

> A brief article that offers an important list of benefits to be derived from active listening. The author draws upon the literature of psychotherapy and clinical psychology for data on the topic. Ideas are made clearly appropriate for use by practitioners.

CHAMPAGNE, DAVID W., and R. CRAIG HOGAN, *Consultant Supervision: Theory and Skill Development*. Wheaton, Ill.: C H Publications, 1981.

The authors go well beyond clinical supervision practice in viewing a broad range of ideas related to consultation in the field of instructional supervision.

DONOUGHUE, CAROL, ed., *In-Service: The Teacher and the School*. London: Kozan Page, Ltd., 1981.

Case studies were presented of various in-service programs of all types. Some have been initiated by teachers, some by headmasters; some were voluntary, while others were not; some were successful, while others were only adequate. Important points to note are that the who, why, what, and when questions must be answered to avoid wasting time and effort. In other words, in-service education must be carefully planned with specific objectives based on real and important data.

HARE, A. PAUL, *Creativity in Small Groups*. Beverly Hills, Calif.: Sage Publications, 1982.

Distinctive ways to promote creative thinking in small groups are presented. Content analysis, interaction analysis, dramaturgical analysis, and exchange analysis are introducted. Emphasis tends to be on social problem solving.

HARRIS, BEN M., *Improving Staff Performance Through In-service Education*. Boston: Allyn & Bacon, 1980.

A comprehensive treatment of problems and procedures for staff development in public school settings. Basic concepts, session design, program planning, and staffing for effective training are all considered in separate chapters. Case material and illustrations are provided.

HARRIS, BEN M., E. W. BESSENT, and K. E. MCINTYRE, *In-Service Education: A Guide to Better Practice*. Englewood Cliffs, N.J.: Prentice-Hall, 1969.

A unique part of a two-volume work emphasizing the use of laboratory training techniques for teacher in-service education. Actual guides for directing a variety of carefully designed sessions are provided.

MILROY, ELLICE, *Role-Play: A Practical Guide*. Aberdeen, England: Aberdeen University Press, 1982.

A practical reference book giving case illustrations, detailed procedures, and illustrations. While focusing on the use of role playing in classrooms, it still has basic information needed for developing sound practices with adults.

MOLYNEQUX, DOROTHY, and VERA W. LANE, *Effective Interviewing: Techniques and Analysis*. Boston: Allyn & Bacon, 1982.

A semitechnical guide to utilizing interview techniques in a variety of situations for various purposes. An all-around good source of ideas for practitioners.

NICHOLSON, ALEXANDER et al.,   *The Literature on Inservice Teacher Education.*
Palo Alto, Calif.: Stanford Center for Research and Development in Teaching,
1967,

Very few scientifically acceptable studies of in-service education exist; however,
in reviewing those which meet the standards of such research, the authors relate that in-service education is most effective when it is self-directed, takes
place at school, aims at changing knowledge basis and performance rather than
attitudes, is based on specific objectives, is active, is individualized to meet the
teacher's needs, involves demonstration and supervised practice, and is part of
an overall staff or program development.

SMITH, PETER B.,   *Group Processes and Personal Change.* London: Harper & Row
Ltd., 1980

This book contributes a wealth of information from research in social psychology. The author examines the impact of the small-group processes in effecting personal change emphasizing the leaders' behavior and organizational
development.

ZANDER, ALVIN,   *Making Groups Effective.* San Francisco: Jossey-Bass, 1982.

This book is written with the administrator or supervisor in mind. It is a practical book of readings designed to assist in optimizing and understanding groups.
It does not address theories but practices. It does not tell people how to do
their jobs; it does, however, suggest how one can establish conditions for effective groups.

CHAPTER FIVE
PROGRAM
IMPLEMENTATION
STRATEGIES

The supervisory activities described in the preceding chapter are in some ways analogous to the bricks used in constructing a new building: they can be utilized in an infinite array of patterns or designs to produce distinctively different structures. Activities, then, are the building blocks for design efforts to promote changes in instructional programs. The *tasks* of supervision were previously presented as the basic framework for viewing the total function that supervisors and other supervisory personnel might strive to fulfill (Sullivan, 1982).

Traditionally much supervision of instruction follows a few simple patterns. *Training* programs reflect one of these patterns, in which problems or needs for improvement are more or less automatically treated with workshops, lectures, or other training activities. Another common pattern involves *curriculum* planning. Improvements, regardless of their peculiarities, are sought using a series of curriculum planning activities, usually resulting in a new "curriculum guide." Still other patterns of improvement are purely *organizational,* as homogeneous grouping of students, or large-group instruction, team teaching, or open-space arrangements are utilized to foster improvement and change. The current interest in microcomputers in education reflects the emphasis on *facilities* for improvement.

All of these efforts have some merit when skillfully planned and implemented. They tend, however, to be *tactical* rather than *strategic* in nature (Beisser, 1981). They address only limited portions of larger, more complex problems. To the extent that they fail to utilize a full array of activities directed toward full-scale change, they may tend to be less than fully effective. To the extent that only one task area is utilized, the systemic character of the instructional program is ignored (Edelfelt and Smith, 1978). For instance, the microcomputer invasion of our schools and classrooms represents an exciting opportunity for the improvement of instruction, but tactical approaches are almost certain to be inadequate. Obviously, materials and equipment (software and hardware) selection will be required. In-service training will be crucially important. Scheduling may have to be changed in a variety of ways. New technical personnel will be needed. The evaluation and testing programs utilized to assess learning outcomes may need dramatic redesign. Such far-reaching multitasked efforts to make effective use of new instructional hardware require strategic planning rather than purely tactical efforts. "Limited vision leads to limited practice which reinforces the limited vision" (Spady, 1982b).

STRATEGIES

Strategies for improving instruction are not easily identified, nor simply described. Some efforts to think and plan in strategic ways are being reported with increasing imaginativeness by both scholars and practitioners. Common suggestions as possible strategies for change include: clarifying lines of authority; specifying teacher job descriptions; involving staff in goal setting, staff selection, and evaluation; training personnel in conflict resolution techniques; and providing for supporting services. This set of suggestions is rather loosely conceptualized but does represent a multitask approach to change process. Crawford and associates (1980) review four general strategic approaches as utilized in an urban school renewal program: (1) individual change, (2) "techno-structure" change, (3) survey feedback, and (4) organizational development. These terms, though somewhat obscure in meaning, suggest the use of four task areas—in-service training, materials development, evaluation, and organizing for instruction. It is the ways in which the four approaches are linked to one another and related to common goals for improvement or "renewal" that make for strategic planning.

A few strategies that cut across task areas and employ a variety of activities are emerging with more clarity for use in the 1980s because of the pioneering efforts at innovative programming in the preceding two decades. It seems probable that substantial improvements in instruction will emerge in response to such strategic efforts (Lieberman and Miller, 1981). Such strategies involve diverse activities and multiple tasks and offer versatility with respect to the array of specific problems that can be resolved. Several strategy types that seem promising include the following: (1) consultation (Brown, 1979), (2) networking, (3) organizational development (Schmuck et al., 1975), and (4) information processing (Rogers and Shoemaker, 1971). Undoubtedly, others will also emerge out of the innovative efforts of supervisors.

Training and education are understandably of overriding importance in any effort aimed at instructional improvement. The humane character of the school (Harris et al., 1979, pp. 99–109), combined with the changing nature of our society, makes training of personnel an overarching requirement of all strategic efforts to improve the instructional operations system (Edelfelt and Smith, 1978). In fact, nearly all strategy types can be conceptualized as training and education strategies to some degree.

DESIGNING FOR TRAINING

A design can be unique to any given program, situation, or group. With minor changes, however, designs that seem appropriate for accomplishing certain kinds of goals may well be equally appropriate in other circumstances. Some designs have been developed, tested, and publicized to the point of becoming almost standard practice. Some have suffered from faddism almost approaching religious zeal.

Assuming that goals are clearly set, what approaches seem inadequate? The visiting lecturer is not likely to make a difference in practices, no matter how persuasive his manner or provocative his ideas. The 30-minute after-school faculty meeting will not be adequate for stimulating professional growth related to practice. The preschool "workshops" or "institutes" tend to be tolerated and endured, but they rarely stimulate change. The NDEA-type institutes on college campuses were better designed to recruit graduate students than to change school practice. The inevitable curriculum revision committee continues as a useful approach for producing attractively bound documents for display in the superintendent's office, but its impact on classroom practice is probably negligible and possibly undesirable. The development of the new modular schedule, the new grouping plan, or the new teaching team all seem to result in changes that are only skin-deep. The latest mania appears to be the addition of microcomputer courses and computing laboratories, changes certain to divert and possibly to make substantial contributions as well; but such changes can have massive side effects.

Now, none of these is a bad practice. Nor are they "good." All of them undoubtedly have some potential usefulness in promoting instructional change. They represent, however, approaches that are essentially inadequate. What is usually lacking is a well-designed program, with an appropriate change target, implemented with sufficient resources. Our approaches tend to be atomistic rather than molecular, and diffused rather than focused. Teachers are persistent in reporting dissatisfaction and disappointment with simple presentational designs for in-service education. They are supportive of, and even eager for, training experiences that relate to their concerns, get them involved, and lead to new and better performance (Joyce and Showers, 1983, p. 2).

Designing for Complex Change

A design calls for a unique formulation of time, material, space, people, and activity for each goal or objective. Hence a well-designed dump truck is a dramatically different piece of machinery in operation from an equally well designed passenger car. The design of a workshop in which teachers' aides are trained to operate the duplicating equipment is quite different from the design of a workshop in which experienced teachers are given demonstrations on using role playing in the classroom. Each design may have activities, material, space, and other elements in common with, or similar to, another. But when objectives are different, designs must be modified. A simple design can be illustrated by the case of a school staff whose members decided to plan a program that would (1) inform them about recent developments in team teaching, (2) help them get a better *feeling* for team planning, and (3) improve their lesson-planning *skills*. With these kinds of objectives in mind, a guest speaker was secured to talk about team teaching. A group session was planned for role playing several hypothetical examples of team planning. Finally, a specialist was obtained to work individually with several teachers who were correlating lesson plans in separate subject fields.

A design for multiple outcomes when they are so closely interrelated that a variety of activities are selected to reinforce one another could be employed in the case described above. A series of activities—lecture, visual presentation, and recitation—all dealing with information on recent developments in team teaching would constitute such a design. Conversely, the use of a series of role-playing sessions to *inform* the faculty, help develop *feelings*, and even develop some planning *skills* would constitute still another design. All of these are relatively simple designs. A design involving a relatively complex set of objectives demands that a variety of activities be selected and employed for changing a behavior pattern. Various kinds of learning are usually essential to significant change, and a larger number and greater variety of activities are necessarily employed. This type of design would be illustrated in the case previously discussed if a major goal were specified as "to train a single teacher team representing several subject fields to work together in planning and presenting integrated lessons 20 percent of the time, so that all team members assume responsibility for planning, presenting, and evaluating outcomes for these integrated sessions." Such a hypothetical goal demands training in lesson planning. Concepts of integration of content may be developed. New teaching techniques such as small-group discussions and use of games may have to be trained for. Evaluation techniques that require new skills may have to be provided. Such a design will involve not only selection of a variety of activities but also scheduling time, arranging for space, securing consultants, sequencing activities, preparing training materials, and so forth. Table 5.1 identifies and analyzes a few features of a variety of in-service program types in current use. While these are often implemented without adequate designing for specific situations and objectives, each has some potential for effectiveness in limited ways when well implemented (McCleary and McIntrye, 1971).

Promising Practices

Many schools are now facing situations in which money, staff, time, and even facilities are available for innovating in the field of in-service education. There is no need for instructional leaders in such situations to remain with the tried and not so true! Examples of promising and exciting in-service programs exist and can be used as models to be adapted to individual situations and problems. A growing array of research and project reports provides a basis for innovative leadership. A few promising developments follow.

Observing and analyzing teaching activities have been used as the central core of a variety of programs reflecting promising designs. Real teaching, teaching demonstrations, and taped and photographed teaching, as well as role playing, have been used to provide observation opportunities for individuals or groups. Group discussions, focused interviews, clinical counseling, and a variety of analytical procedures combine with systematic observations to produce programs that are truly promising. In very simple terms these designs can be characterized as Teach—Observe—Analyze—Discuss—Interpret. The interaction analysis systems developed in recent years are being used in conjunction with sound and video recordings to produce fairly elaborate programs. The designs vary, of course. One may include taping and teacher self-analysis, followed by clinical counseling. Another employed by this writer involves the preparation of detailed typescripts of lessons from video and sound tapes (Harris et al., 1969) and are used by groups that analyze and role play alternative behavior patterns. Still another approach involves microlab teaching with videotaping, followed by group discussion, self-analysis, and directed practice in planning another lesson.

Demonstrations of classroom teaching sequences have long been crudely used for in-service purposes. New and more sophisticated programs are now being designed using closed-circuit television, videotapes, and even satellite transmission. These technologies make better viewing possible for large groups. This means that demonstrations can be carefully planned with specific in-service objectives in focus, preobservation briefings can provide orientation for viewers, and follow-up activities can be developed for maximum impact.

TABLE 5.1 Types of Training Designs in Current Practice

TYPE OF DESIGN	SIZE OF GROUP	ACTIVITIES INVOLVED	EXPERIENCE IMPACT	TYPE OF OBJECTIVE*
Clinical counseling	Individual	Interviewing, testing, listening, writing, reading	Hi	Aff
Self-analysis	Individual	Taping or photo, observing, analyzing	Hi	Cog
Observational analysis	Individual	Observing, analyzing, interviewing	mH	Cog
Tutorial	Individual	Reading, listening, analyzing, guided practice, interviewing	mH	Cog-Sk
Internship	Individual	Reading, observing, directed practice, analyzing, interviewing, writing	Hi	All
Programmed experience	Individual	Reading, viewing, analyzing, writing	M	Cog
Microteaching	Small	Writing, role playing, recording, analyzing	mH	Sk
Microlaboratory teaching	Small	Writing, role playing, recording, analyzing	mH	Sk
Clinical study	Individual or small	Instrumenting, reading, analyzing, writing, interviewing	mH	Cog
T-Group training	Small	Role playing, analyzing, discussing	M	Aff-Sk
Scenario	Small	Writing, analyzing, reading, brainstorming	M	Cog
Team practice	Small	Writing, reading, directed practice	M	Cog-Sk
Action research	Small	Testing, writing, analyzing	M	Cog
Group therapy	Small	Discussing, role playing	Hi	Aff
Sensitivity training	Small	Role playing, directed practice	M	Cog-Aff
Pilot project	Small or large	Writing, instrumenting, discussing, observing, reading, field trip, guided practice	Hi	Cog-Sk
Gaming	Small or large	Reading, analyzing, role playing	M	Cog
Laboratory training	Small or large	Viewing, reading, analyzing, testing, discussing, visual lecturing	mH	Cog
Discussion group	Small or large	Discussing, reading, listening	mLo	Cog
Analysis	Small or large	Reading, writing, discussing	M	Cog
Social	Large	Discussing, observing, listening	mLo	Aff
Survey	Large	Instrumenting, analyzing, interviewing	M	Cog

*Aff = Affective; Cog = Cognitive; Sk = Skill, H = High; mH = Medium High; M = Medium; mLo = Medium Low.

Classroom experiences are used as a major vehicle for in-service out-comes in a variety of other designs. The Harvard-Newton program developed as a rather elaborate array of in-service education activities involving class-room observation, teaching, and analysis with much group interaction. The Far West Laboratory minicourses represent still another interesting design emphasizing the reality of the classroom with teacher self-analysis. Formal clinical supervision models all depend on shared experiences in live class-rooms (Cogan, 1973; Boyan and Copeland, 1978).

These sketches of promising practices all rely heavily on activities that help participants to focus on, and interact in various ways with, real class-room events (Joyce and Showers, 1983, pp. 19–22). In this sense, they are all *reality-oriented* designs. Although any in-service experience should perhaps be reality-oriented, for many kinds of learning, direct interaction with real classroom phenomena may not be most appropriate.

Reality Simulation

Emerging programs that employ *reality simulation* as the vehicle for activities are causing much interest and excitement. To simulate reality in-volves some loss in experience impact. This may be compensated for, how-ever, by other design characteristics. Using reality also presents problems. Under certain conditions reality may be too time-consuming, as in a field trip; it may be too expensive, as in foreign travel; it may be too dangerous, as in being thrown into a pool to learn to swim; or it may be too uneconom-ical, as in certain on-the-job experience.

The *laboratory design* is one approach to using reality simulation in in-service education (Harris, 1980, pp. 251–68). A single laboratory session on communications for teachers will illustrate designs of this kind:

a. We have in mind certain objectives relating to understandings about commu-nication with a group.

b. We present to a group an oral communications problem in a highly simulated setting. We ask the participants to listen carefully to one of their peers as he describes a diagram. They are asked to draw what he describes. This diagram is described orally in a "no-feedback" situation. This means that the commu-nicator cannot see the faces of the participants and they cannot communicate with him in any way.

c. When the diagram is described to the best of the communicator's ability, he stops, records an estimate of how well he thinks he has communicated, and waits for participants to do the same so their drawings can be collected and scored.

d. The communicator is now given another diagram and asked to describe it or-ally, but this time with a "free-feedback" situation. The participants try to draw this new diagram and are encouraged to ask questions, to insist upon clarifi-cation, and let the communicator know when they do not understand.

e. When this communication period has ended, communicator and receivers re-cord their estimates of how well they have done, and all papers are collected and scored.

f. While scoring of the two sets of drawings is in progress, a group leader stimulates participants to talk about their feelings when faced with these kinds of situations. They talk about other situations that are real—a lecture, a memorandum, a message over the intercom system, a note from the central office supervisor, a set of directions for assembling a toy or making a dress, and so forth.

g. A report contrasting the two situations is presented to the group. A table summarizes in simple terms the data gathered in the two simulated situations.

h. The leader helps participants interpret the data. He calls attention to the findings related to the communications concepts he hoped would be learned:

The no-feedback situation took less *time*.

The no-feedback situation resulted in a lower level of *accuracy* of message reception.

The no-feedback situation was one of relative *overconfidence* for both communicator and receivers.

The free-feedback situation was one of *realistic confidence* level for receivers.

The free-feedback situation was one of relative *underconfidence* for communicator.

i. Now a discussion is organized to allow participants to ask questions, consider other interpretations, question the reliability and validity of this evidence, and so forth.

j. Finally, implications and applications to classroom practices are discussed. The limitations of notes, memos, written assignments on the board, textbooks, report cards, and lectures as no-feedback devices are mentioned.

The sequence of events represents a crude, quick description of a laboratory session requiring about two-and-a-half hours. It originated with the recognition that teachers have many serious problems that are based on faulty communications. It emerged as an in-service program by drawing upon research studies. It is designed as a laboratory experience by using reality simulation to simplify experiences with communications systems to ensure clear insights for learners.

Laboratory sessions are characterized by the following design features:

1. A *simulated reality* is presented to participants.
2. *Reactions* of participants are solicited.
3. *Records* of reactions are obtained.
4. *Analysis* of recorded reactions is completed.
5. *Feedback* is provided to participants, showing their own reactions.
6. *Interpretations* of the analyzed data are provided.
7. *Implications* and *applications* are considered.

Other laboratory-type programs have been designed to throw light rather than heat on the homogeneous versus heterogeneous grouping issue. A single laboratory session on evaluating pupil performance using actual samples of pupils' work seems to highlight the key concepts of educational measurement more than some college courses requiring 10 times as many hours (Harris et al., 1969). A programmed laboratory session on curriculum decision making has been developed to help teachers in using performance objectives in curriculum planning.

Still other, more elaborate kinds of simulations are coming into use. Military training programs have historically employed "war games" as simulated reality on a grand scale, and elaborate equipment, usually life-size models of the real thing, is to be seen at nearly any army, navy, or air force training center.

Pennsylvania State University's computer-assisted instruction mobile training unit is an example of elaborate hardware becoming a part of the reality of in-service education programming (Meisgeier et al., 1972). No less impressive has been the decade of leadership of the University Council on Educational Administration in developing simulated school districts using films, tapes, scenarios, in-baskets, and slides for training administrators.

The instructional game usually employs reality simulation. Games often employ rules, materials, and activities designed not just to simulate participation or competition but to simulate reality so that implications for the real worlds' problems are recognized (Greenblatt and Duke, 1981). While games have become most popular in human relations training and social and political science concept development, they are highly promising for future use with a wide variety of in-service education goals and objectives. Horn and Cleaves's guide to simulations and games is one of several sources of rather extensive listings of such material (1980). Pfeiffer and Jones (1977) have published several volumes of descriptions of "structured experiences" for training sessions.

BASIC APPROACHES

Attention to new, innovative, or technologically exciting ways of improving instruction should not overshadow very basic strategies that have demonstrated their efficacy in the hands of skilled supervisors. Some of these "tried-and-true" basic approaches include clinical supervision, developmental evaluation, group work, and consultation. The professional practice of instructional supervision is advanced by continued use and refinement of basic strategies as new approaches are developed and tested.

Clinical Approaches

The literature and practice of instructional supervision has come alive in recent years with ideas and programs for clinical approaches to in-service education (Cogan, 1973). The terms *clinical supervision* and *microteaching* (Borg, 1968) are used most widely as variations are invented, such as micro-counseling (Ivey and Moreland, 1971), microlab teaching, and clinical teaching (Olsen et al., 1971). Each has its own variation of design characteristics and activity elements. Clinical supervision is coming to mean in-service education activities of highly individualized kinds. Microteaching is frequently a way of working in clinical situations, with the supervisor and the teacher sharing in the task of analyzing videotaped microlessons. Microlab teaching was developed by Davis and his assistants to use peers as students in the microlessons. Growing interest in self-analysis has resulted from studies showing that teachers trained in analytical techniques (Perrott, 1976) can self-supervise toward improved teaching (Borg, 1968).

Clinical designs have borrowed heavily from clinical counseling in viewing the supervisor as a facilitator more and an active change agent less. The diagnostic practices of medicine are emulated in using teaching samples, real or simulated, for systematic analysis. The strengths of these designs vary, of course. To the extent that teachers are motivated to analyze their own performance, self-analysis has promise. Clinical efforts that bring a skilled supervisor and a teacher together in close collaborative efforts are likely to carry intense experience impact (Harris, 1980, pp. 217–45). The economy of simulating real teaching with microteaching or microlab conditions is certainly important.

Limitations, of course, are also obvious in clinical approaches. The one-to-one relationship is expensive in supervisor time. The equipment required for general use of videotaping can be very expensive also. Opportunities for group interaction are sacrificed in many clinical designs, with considerable loss in group morale. Perhaps the greatest danger is found in those clinical designs that focus exclusively on the "self" and prevent any looking outward for new ideas.

A Three-Loop Clinical Cycle

Individualized teacher guidance is provided by an essentially process-oriented evaluation intervention system depicted in Figure 5.1. In this system live teaching is observed, using one or another of the available systematic observation instruments. The observation data are analyzed to provide feedback to the teacher who was observed. Arrangements are made for ensuring that the observed teacher will be able to interpret the feedback information in terms of "strengths," "weaknesses," "patterns," and "possible modifications." This leads to plans for making changes, trying alternatives, and hence teaching that is essentially different—hopefully, improved.

This is a fairly standard view of a clinical teaching cycle. It can function as a self-improvement process as promoted by Far West Laboratory programs if observations are recorded mechanically (electronically) and teachers know how to analyze, interpret, and plan for change independently. However, this same cycle can be implemented with a principal or a supervisor serving as

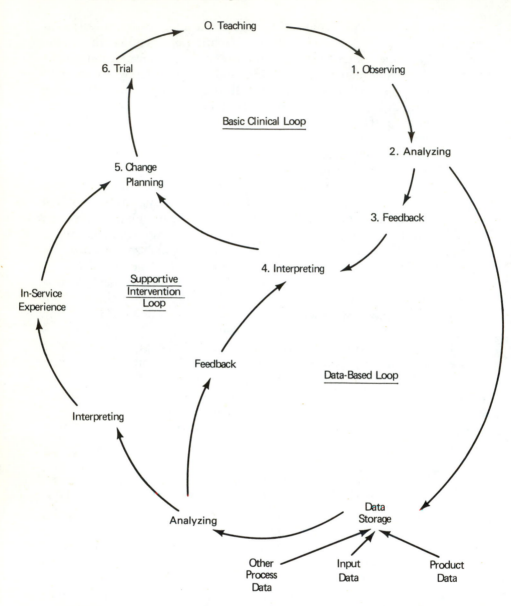

FIGURE 5.1   A three-loop clinical cycle for changing teaching practice.

observer, analyst, and feedback and interpretation agent, assisting the teacher with planning in-service activities.

This more elaborate approach to changing teaching practice by using both observation and other data in a three-loop design is an effort to over-come some of the weaknesses of clinical approaches. Greater effectiveness is sought in providing feedback in two quite unique loops to carry greater impact. Furthermore, the third loop guides in-service experiences that may be individual or small group; this is aimed at greater efficiency in the use of supervisor or principal time. It should also contribute to more effective adoption of changes by providing for new in-service learning that might not occur in a self-improvement effort.

Developmental Evaluation

The combining of training and evaluation activities to promote growth in individual staff members is a strategic approach that is gaining acceptance in current practice. The management-by-objectives (MBO) programs for personnel development advocated by Redfern (1980) have heavily influenced both scholars and practitioners. These pioneering efforts have used needs assessment or other kinds of evaluative data-gathering processes to guide highly personalized programs of staff development.

The Harris-Hill Developmental Teacher Evaluation Kit (1982), also known as DeTEK, is a very recent, highly structured version of a developmental evaluation strategy. The system is implemented through the use of a kit of materials that provides for an ongoing, objective, diagnostic evaluation process, leading to individual growth planning. Teachers, administrators, and supervisors collaborate in all phases of the program, leading to teacher improvement in classroom practices. (See the illustrations and cases in Chapters 7 and 9 illustrating this system.)

The DeTEK system is operationalized in four phases utilizing a 10-step sequence of activities. Figure 3.4 illustrates these phases and steps and shows feedback pathways that assure both an ongoing but highly flexible operation. Hence, a single structured system designed to promote improvement in teaching in all classroom teachers is still highly individualized.

Key elements in this strategic effort include the following:

Criteria of performance are carefully specified in advance.

Four phases are included in a process that leads from a survey, to diagnostic analysis, growth planning, and implementation.

Emphasis is placed on the use of objective data in all steps.

Collaboration is required between teacher and supervisor in all steps.

Responsibilities for implementing growth plans are shared.

Flexibility is provided in implementing the process to accommodate varying needs of individual teachers.

Summative decision making is clearly excluded (separated from) this development system.

Group Processes

There is an enormous body of literature reporting a variety of designs for working with groups in human relations training. These practices, procedures, and techniques range from sensitivity training (Stringer, 1970) to group therapy, T-group training (Paris, 1966), developmental counseling, and case discussion (Gall and Gall, 1976). Terminology lacks standardization, design characteristics are rarely reported explicitly, and procedures seem to vary widely with the individual leader.

While T-group and sensitivity-training activities are sometimes reported as being very much alike, sharp differences of opinion about their similarities and their effectiveness are held and expressed. It is difficult for supervisors to systematically draw upon this wealth of practice in the absence of agreement on their idiosyncratic nature. Nonetheless, the fields of psychotherapy, clinical counseling, and social psychology have developed an amazing array of designs for working with groups. It remains for supervisors to carefully select, test, and redesign for their purposes in working with teacher groups. Quality control circle techniques for group problem solving offer at least one new strategy worthy of further consideration. Harris (1980, pp. 271–94) has described and illustrated such well-known group process activities as buzz groups, brainstorming, and role playing. Pfeiffer and Jones (1977) offer a great variety of "structured experiences" in a set of publications, making reference to them only as "human relations training."

Consulting

The use of systematic consulting with both individuals and groups is hardly new. It has an extensive record of use in many fields, including mental health, government, engineering, and education. New interest in consultation strategies is reflected not only in the spread of clinical supervision practices but also in the recent works of Champagne and Hogan (1981) and Brown and associates (1979).

Consulting is much more than just conferencing, of course, but its essence is face-to-face interaction to influence practice. Some view consulting as essentially interpersonal "helping" (Marshall et al., 1982), but a broader spectrum of consultant roles and relationships are generally recognized (Hood and Cates, 1978). The consultant as *expert* is of course one category of role that implies special knowledge to be selectively drawn upon and shared in the consulting relationship.

Another role in consulting is that of *process* specialist. The consultant who has specialized skills in helping people interact, analyze, plan, or otherwise deal with their problems influences changes in people (Silverblank, 1979). This is a much more indirect way of influencing the instructional improvement process (Smith, 1980). It presumes that the expertise already exists or can be developed within the individual or group (Ruch et al., 1982).

A third role of consulting involves the *resource* specialist. This is closely related to the other two, but emphasizes assisting individuals and groups in getting access to people, ideas, materials, and other resources needed to deal with their problems.

Consultants invariably play all three roles as circumstances dictate the need. Consultants as experts are widely utilized in curriculum development as subject matter or methods specialists. Similarly, expertness operates through the in-service education and evaluation task areas, as specialized information is secured and utilized for training or other purposes. The resource consultant role may also be important in curriculum development, materials development, and in-service education as new materials and alternative methods are being considered by a study group or project team.

Alpert (1982, pp. 312–16) describes "consultative stages" involving entry, diagnosis, intervention, and evaluation. These stages have many similarities to clinical supervision but offer many more action alternatives.

OTHER STRATEGIES

Of the many other than training strategies in use for promoting change in schools, organizational development and quality control circles are of special interest. Each of these is explored further here.

Organizational Development

A variety of approaches to organizational development are being utilized and explored in school settings. Organizational development is a point of view in part but also an array of methods for influencing behavior in organizations. As a point of view, it emphasizes the interdependence of positions, roles, and responsibilities of various persons within an organization such as a school; hence, the emphasis is on group decisions, sharing of information, and clarifying goals and values. Organizational development, according to Baker (1982, p. 69), "focuses on the attitudes, values, and accepted practices of people in an organization. It recognizes that groups influence the behavior of group members and changes must occur in the organization's culture."

As a strategy to be considered by supervisors in planning for improving instruction, organizational development is both promising and perplexing. The methods and techniques of OD are rapidly changing and not yet well documented. Schmuck and associates (1975) have given emphasis to consultation as a part of the organizational development process. Blake and Mouton (1979) have outlined some principles of organizational development as they seem to apply in industrial settings. They define the organization as a somewhat autonomous unit; they emphasize the need for strong leadership; they stress involving the entire staff rather than representatives; and they emphasize diagnostic processes.

Despite critical concerns about the theoretical assumptions and the urgent need for better evaluation (Terpstra, 1981), the emerging variations on OD as a strategy for improving organizational behavior are worthy of serious attention by supervisors. In at least one form, OD has recently gained great popularity. "Theory Z" as formulated by William G. Ouchi (1981) deals with a broad array of notions about "consensual management." However, the specific techniques for working with groups (under the banner of quality circles or quality control circles) have possibilities that should be explored (pp. 261–68).

QUALITY CONTROL CIRCLES

Ouchi (p. 261) stresses the use of Q-circles as a management technique for sharing the responsibility for locating and solving problems of coordination and productivity. A variety of quality control circles (Q-C circles) are recommended in a single organization to ensure a broad base of voluntary participation but also to ensure implementation.

The Northwest Educational Cooperative has been sponsoring training for educators in the use of quality control circle techniques (1982). "Quality Circles utilize many participatory management methods. . . . The Circle method synthesizes the best practices of participatory management with established motivational theory . . . data analysis [and] problem-solving."

Characteristics of Quality Circles*

A quality circle is a group of people with related jobs who meet together regularly. Using a structured format, they identify, analyze, and solve problems in their area of job responsibility. The ideal circle has four to ten voluntary members plus a leader trained to use the quality circle techniques. The leader is usually a supervisor or administrator directly related to the participants' job.

A key requirement in establishing quality circles in a school setting is that of securing top-level support. This issue must be resolved before a circle sets its own objectives. For a while the successful circle will focus on objectives that will increase productivity in its own school or department; eventually circles expand to deal with problem prevention questions that may involve other schools, programs, or entire school districts. Circles may elect to solve problems referred to them by administrators or the school board, but that is not usual. Without a firm belief by the school administration that circles can be trusted to solve work problems in their own work areas, there can be no successful circle program (Dewar, 1982).

There are many possible objectives appropriate to a department- or grade-level circle. Such circles might wish to improve students' work habits, reduce damage to laboratory equipment, increase motivation or creativity, increase safety awareness, resolve discipline problems, improve the curricu-

*This section was developed with the assistance of Ruth Ann Hoffhines.

lum or a specific teaching technique, or increase harmony among staff members. Whatever objectives are selected, the circle, meeting one hour per week, involves all its members in using a *four-step quality circle process.*

The quality circle process consists of problem identification, problem analysis, problem solution, and a recommendation for action. The goal is to recommend specific methods for improving the way in which work is accomplished. The circle leader guides members through the application of circle techniques to the solution. There are seven specific techniques: (1) structured brainstorming and voting, (2) data gathering, (3) statistical check sheets, (4) Pareto analysis, (5) fishbone cause-effect analysis, (6) process cause-effect analysis, and (7) presentation of findings.

The heavy emphasis on data and analysis within a structure of group dynamics, the formal presentation of results, and the careful training of each member in the use of the circle techniques differentiates the quality circle from many other participatory management approaches (Monte, 1981). It has many similarities with the structured DeTEK system described earlier.

Quality Circle Techniques

The seven standard techniques are utilized in a step-by-step sequence in at least one organization (Gryna, 1981, p. 62). The steps and related techniques include:

1.	Choose a problem	Discussion and voting to be sure.
2.	Gather information about the problem	Brainstorming. Interviews. Observations. Records.
3.	Analyze for causes	Statistical check sheets. Pareto analysis. Fishbone analysis.
4.	Decide on solutions	Brainstorming. Voting. Discussion. Fishbone analysis.
5.	Plan action	Discussions.
6.	Take actions	Presentations. Graphics.
7.	Check on problem	Interviews. Observations. Records.
	Move on to next problem or recycle.	

Structured brainstorming is utilized, with only minor variations on the technique as it is commonly known. Dewar (1980) emphasizes the free flow of ideas and recording all ideas. Some recommend eliciting ideas by going around the circle, asking for a response from each individual. Those not ready to respond simply say "pass" and wait for the next time around. ·

Discussion of all ideas follows brainstorming to be sure the ideas are understood. *Voting* to establish a rank order of importance is sometimes recommended.

Voting is a technique utilized in a variety of ways to facilitate progress. Problems may be ranked by vote and solutions selected by vote.

Data gathering is utilized to verify the nature of the selected problem and to check on results. Interviews, questionnaires, and observations are utilized as well as available records to produce objective data on problems.

Statistical check sheet analysis involves some kind of tabular analysis of data to relate the facts to the various possible "causes."

Pareto analysis involves construction of simple bar graphs to visualize comparisons among possible causes. Histograms are also utilized when appropriate (Gryna, 1981, p. 61).

Fishbone cause-effect analysis is a technique for graphically portraying a variety of causes in relation to the problem. Four categories of causes are used in industrial applications. They are manpower, machinery, materials, and methods. For educational purposes, these categories might be changed to organizational, material, method, and student causes.

Process cause-effect analysis is still another method used to visualize relationships between the problem and its causes. In this technique any single high-priority cause is further analyzed as a "chain" of logical events, using available data. Hence, the problem of poor achievement by students could be caused in part by lack of homework effort. Assuming the data supported this as a strong cause, further analysis follows:

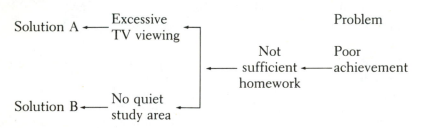

Such cause-and-effect analysis leads the circle participants toward a variety of more appropriate solutions than they might otherwise consider.

Presentation techniques draw upon all the graphics utilized in arriving at conclusions or recommendations.

Key Elements

While quality circle technique may appear simplistic, it contains several key elements. First, the members use a common method and a common vocabulary. Once the method is mastered by all, the circle has a clean, well-understood structure to use with much more difficult problems. Second, data are gathered carefully to ensure that fact, not opinion, is the basis for the decision and action. Third, the process actively involves all members of the circle; hence, all are more likely to support decisions. Fourth, the structure keeps each member focused on the task. This focus avoids personal conflict on more difficult problems and builds a teamwork attitude. In short, mastering the techniques with simple problems leads to success with tougher issues. This balance of task focus and people involvement is the core of quality circles' success.

Currently, quality circles are enjoying the popularity of a full-blown fad. Their ultimate worth is yet to be assessed (Patchin, 1980, p. 7). If quality circles prove promising as a way of improving instruction, they are likely to require many carefully designed modifications. Hopefully, the Q-C technique will not suffer the oblivion accorded so many other innovative practices.

SUMMARY

When the supervisor turns to the demanding tasks of supervision as an agent of change rather than as a mere maintenance person, the complexities, resistances, and constraints decree careful planning. But the best-laid plans are of little value until they become implemented realities. The strategies we develop are tools for implementing change.

The designing for change through training strategies is emphasized here in preference to curriculum design, materials, organizational development, or other important tasks. Not that training is everything. It is not! But nothing is more central to the change process. We know enough about designing for training to really make a difference.

Truly strategic efforts to improve instruction become indispensable as the complexities increase. Simple changes use simple means, but for complex problems strategic approaches are generally required. Hence, consultation and organizational development are often needed in addition to better designs for training. Refer to Chapter 10 case reports on observations utilized in clinical ways. Also refer to Chapter 11 case reports on various workshop efforts.

SUGGESTED READINGS

EDELFELT, ROY, and E. B. SMITH,   *Breakway and Multidimensional Approaches: Integrating Curriculum Development and Inservice Education.* Washington, D.C: Association of Teacher Educators, 1978.

Building on the old notion about institutionalizing curriculum change through in-service education, the authors make a case for more carefully integrating the two task areas.

HARRIS, BEN M,   *Improving Staff Performance Through Inservice Education.* Boston: Allyn & Bacon, 1980.

Chapter 2, "Designing Training Sessions," and Chapter 3, "Planning Programs," offer detailed and practical illustrations relating to design and strategic planning for change. Chapters 6, 7, and 8 discuss and illustrate strategies for using clinical supervision, simulations, and group techniques. Appendix E illustrates a comprehensive training plan.

HARRIS, BEN M., E. W. BESSENT, and KENNETH E. MCINTYRE,   *In-service Education: A Guide to Better Practice*. Englewood Cliffs, N.J.: Prentice-Hall, 1969

This is essentially a collection of leaders' manuals for selected laboratory training sessions. For those interested in either using or knowing about some of these old training designs, the guides are well illustrated and detailed. A companion volume, *Materials for Laboratory Training Sessions*, was also published as a paperback with reproducible handouts.

KATZ, DANIEL, ROBERT L. KAHN, and J. STACY ADAMS, eds.,   *The Study of Organizations*. London: Jossey-Bass, 1980.

An unusual compilation of reviews of organizational research and theory reflecting current thought in the field. Chapter 9 on determinants of supervisory behavior is especially useful.

KERSH, BERT Y.,   *Faculty Development for Inservice Education in the Schools*. Washington, D.C.: American Association of Colleges for Teacher Education, September 1978.

This monograph promotes the development of joint college–local district inservice training programs. The author argues that colleges can offer unique services to local school personnel and yet gain experience for professors that will enhance preservice teacher training programs.

LAWRENCE, GORDON, DENNIS BAKER, PATRICIA ELZIE, and BARBARA HANSEN,   *Patterns of Effective Inservice Education*. Gainesville, Fla.: University of Florida, College of Education, December 1974.

A report on a systematic review of nearly 100 training programs. The focus is on evidence of effectiveness. Only well-evaluated or researched programs were included in this study. Hence, the authors clearly report on the "patterns" that are effective. They find a surprising proportion that are effective in terms of teacher behavior.

LIEBERMAN, ANN, and LYNN MILLER   "Synthesis of Research on Improving Schools," *Educational Leadership*, 38 (April 1981): 583–86.

In a review of three major studies of school improvement models, these authors attempt to synthesize overarching strategies and identify common elements.

NADLER, LEONARD,   "Implications of the HRD Concept," *Training and Development Journal*, 28 (May 1974): 3–13.

One of the leaders in the field of adult education and industrial training discusses the concept of human resources development as a broader view.

NICHOLSON, ALEXANDER et al.,   *The Literature on Inservice Teacher Education.* Palo Alto, Calif.: Stanford Center for Research on Development in Teaching, 1975.

A comprehensive review of the extensive literature in this field in recent years.

OUCHI, WILLIAM G.,   *Theory Z.* Reading, Mass.: Addison-Wesley, 1981.

A major effort to analyze Japanese business management practices in search of their implications for American institutions. Appendix Two provides detailed information on quality control circle techniques.

PFEIFFER, J. WILLIAM, and JOHN E. JONES,   *Reference Guide to Handbooks and Annuals,* 2nd ed. La Jolla, Calif.: University Associates, Publishers and Consultants, 1977.

The authors review some concepts about training session design and give brief reference listings to literally hundreds of "structured experiences." these experiences are neatly classified as "ice breakers," "group process," "feedback," etc. Six volumes of the handbook plus other publications are cross-referenced for more detailed information on each experience.

SEALEY, LEONARD, and ELIZABETH DILLON,   *Staff Development: A Study of Six School Systems.* New York: The Ford Foundation, 1976.

A limited sample of school districts' programs are analyzed in this report. While the study was somewhat superficial in its procedures, on-site interviews were utilized, and it is one of the few efforts to look systematically at current practice on a school systemwide basis.

CHAPTER SIX
ORGANIZING
AND STAFFING
FOR SUPERVISION

Preceding chapters have considered various aspects of supervision, emphasizing tasks. The scope and tasks of supervision in the total school operation have been defined. The dynamics of supervisory behavior regardless of the specific staff or organizational structures have been discussed. We have conceptualized operational features of supervisory programs. This chapter now emphasizes people, organizational arrangements, and working relationships for accomplishing supervisory tasks with both effectiveness and efficiency. Current staffing patterns are reviewed. Issues surrounding supervision staffing patterns are described, and various approaches to team supervision are proposed.

CURRENT STAFFING PATTERNS

Current practice as a guide to better practice has more than enough deficiencies to caution the reader against prolonged study of the status quo. Still, to know where we are is helpful in charting a new and better course. Most of the literature on supervision of instruction makes the assumption that supervisory services will be provided by an individual, either a central office supervisor (with one of many titles) or a school principal (with many jobs but only one title). Less frequently it is suggested that supervisory services should be provided by classroom teachers without benefit of either title or status (Ban and Soudah, 1978).

These assumptions evade consideration of both issues and alternatives relating to supervisory effectiveness. Our concern is for clearly recognizing the various people involved, the organizations in which they hold positions, and their relationship to one another.

Supervisory Positions

The complexity of the educational operation combines with the crucial importance of supervision to necessitate the involvement of nearly all professional school personnel. Modern educational organizations that hope to maintain their effectiveness as institutions of learning must involve administrators, supervisors, teachers, and special service personnel in the activities of supervision of instruction.

The long-established practices associated with supervision as a *shared* function have generated many issues, conflicts, and uncertainties among staff personnel. Frequently, supervisors' identity and effectiveness are at issue. Conflicts between principals and supervisors often emerge from undifferentiated responsibilities for supervision.

Supervisors and Other Supervisory Personnel

Supervisors are part of the tradition of a developing system of professional specialists in American education. Confusion over supervisors' roles and responsibilities has been one of the striking characteristics of supervisory practice over the past few decades (Blumberg, 1980, pp. 9–17). The rise of the school principal as an instructional leader has added to the confusion already present. The new and growing involvement of school principals in supervision of instruction has made more urgent the need for clarification of roles and responsibilities among supervisory personnel (Cawelti, 1980; Cohen, 1982). State and federal funding of innovative programs of instruction has led to rapid expansion of supervisory staffs, with new specialities and assignments disrupting established operational patterns (Berman and McLaughlin, 1980).

Many, if not most, of these new developments have offered new opportunities as well as challenges to supervision as the dynamic function of instructional improvement. These changes have also created confusion and uncertainty in supervisor ranks.

Many titles have been assigned to supervisors of instruction over the years—*consultant, coordinator, specialist,* and *director* are but a few of the titles currently in general use (Dull, 1981, p. 7). A variety of titles can only add to the confusion about supervisor responsibilities when used without clearly differentiating one from another in functional terms. In practice, a new title is often selected for a supervisor in the hope that this will create a new halo of proficiency for the person involved. Obviously this is an illusory notion, guaranteed to confuse but not to resolve problems.

The supervisor as a person tends to shape the position, whatever the title may be. This has led various writers to define the roles, functions, or responsibilities of supervisors in such general terms as supporting, assisting, and sharing rather than directing. Others have hoped to use the "line and staff" dichotomy to clarify roles (Esposito et al., 1975). As helpful as such definitions may be in emphasizing modern concepts of leadership in general, they provide little help in guiding specific supervisory practice (R. C. Williams, 1982). A specialty must be carefully differentiated as well as coordinated with other positions when they are closely related to each other operationally (Kane, 1975). Hence the designations supervisor, coordinator, curriculum worker and consultant mean nothing unless they assist in differentiating performances. Burch and Danley (1980) and Sullivan (1982) are among the many expressing concern that supervisors tend to become "all things to all people" and often fail to maintain a clear focus on the improvement of instruction.

A simple set of distinctions can be made, however. First, the term *supervision* as a function of the school operation has already been defined and must not be confused with the title or equated with the work of the supervisor. Second, the term *supervisor* can be defined as a generic term and not as a title or a specific position. Third, supervisors' many titles conferred for whatever situational or personal reasons must be interpreted on the basis of functional job descriptions. Fourth, supervisory personnel can be defined as all professional personnel actively engaged in giving leadership to supervision of instruction. Fifth, supervisor can be defined as a professional person whose major responsibilities are in the supervision function area (Walker and Hamm, 1981, p. 17).

Supervisory personnel by these definitions include superintendents, principals, assistant principals, team leaders, department chairmen, and other administrative and special service personnel who are responsible for leading supervisory endeavors. The term supervisor is reserved for those professionals whose responsibilities in the administrative, teaching, management, and special pupil service function areas are limited. These supervisors, regardless of title or position in the hierarchy, are usually responsible for one or more of the tasks of supervision.

Acceptance of a few basic definitions of terms eliminates some confusion surrounding supervision and the people who lead in these task areas. However, the scope of responsibilities suggested by the 10 tasks of supervision and the great variety of organizations engaged in supervisory endeavors make for lack of clarity even when terms are defined. Of course, some might question the need for distinguishing the supervisor from the other supervisory personnel. It seems logical, however, that if responsibility is to be clearly designated, an individual or a group must be clearly identified. The fact that the supervisor does not have responsibility for the operation of a school or a classroom distinguishes him or her and makes it possible for supervision tasks to become full-time responsibilities. The assignment of the supervisor outside the classroom serving several school units makes it possible for him or her to function in ways not possible for a teacher or a building administrator.

The Local District Staff

Local school districts involve teachers, principals, assistant principals, deans, department chairmen, counselors, diagnosticians, school social workers, supervisors, directors, superintendents, and even school board members in the processes of supervising instruction. They also draw upon supervisory services from other agencies. Organizing these many resources for effective and efficient instructional change is much neglected, but very important nonetheless. The coordinated efforts of such a variety of instructional staff personnel have great potential for change. Their efforts could lead to chaos and confusion without clear understanding of individual tasks, roles, and responsibilities.

Supervisors of instruction have dramatically increased in number in the past few decades. U.S. Department of Education statistics show the following (Grant and Eiden, 1981, 1982):

Supervisors employed by local districts:

1959–60	13,775
1961–62	16,300
1968 (fall)	26,165
1970 (fall)	27,720
1975–76	35,100
1979–80	35,000 (est.)
Increase	154%

Total instructional staff employed by local districts:

1959–60	1,464,031
1968 (fall)	2,320,863
1970 (fall)	2,448,620
1975–76	2,476,487
1979–80	2,438,000
Increase	67%

Even with the employment of supervisors at a rate in excess of instructional staff growth, the ratio of classroom teachers to supervisors was still 62 to 1 in 1979. The size of supervisor staffs varies widely by region, state, and type of school district. However, the general acceptance of supervisors on local district staffs is evidenced by the fact that more than 94 percent of all school districts enrolling over 5,000 students have supervisors of instruction.

Declining enrollments and budget cutting may produce a trend reversal in supervisor staffing in the 1980s. This should, of course, be examined very carefully. Cuts in this area may seriously damage the capacity of schools to respond to needs for instructional changes. A 12-year study of staffing practices in Indiana (Walker and Hamm, 1981) shows a very inconsistent pattern in this one state. Unfortunately, the National Center for Educational Statistics recently changed its reporting classification system, creating a new category of over 100,000 "other professionals." Hence, accurate trends are being obscured.

The principal as an instructional supervisory person is widely recognized as an ideal, as reported by the Department of Elementary School Principals in past decades (1968) and more recently emphasized in studies by the California State Legislature (1978). The ideal of the principal as an "instructional leader" continues to receive growing attention in the work of Goodlad (1975), Corbett (1982), and others.

Because principals are so numerous, if for no other reason, it is reasonable to expect them to make a major contribution to the supervision function. According to recent statistical summaries (Grant and Eiden, 1981, p. 58) there are over 100,000 principals and assistant principals in the schools of this country. This is nearly three times the total force of local district supervisors (Wiens, 1970).

Department chairpersons and assistant principals or deans of instruction are widely reported to be employed for supervisory purposes. These personnel generally serve at the secondary school levels where school size and organizational complexity frustrate the efforts of most principals to engage in supervision with any intensity. The use of the assistant principal or dean of instruction to assume the principal's responsibilities seems doomed to failure at the outset. This subordinate inherits all of the principal's liabilities and rarely has special capabilities for taking on such a difficult assignment. However, team supervision arrangements whereby the principal shares responsibilities with other supervisory personnel seem to have considerable promise (Harris and Hill, 1982).

Department chairs as supervisory positions continue to be widely advocated (Sergiovanni, 1977). The Port Arthur, Texas, schools report one of the more rigorous long-standing efforts to make this kind of supervision effective by freeing the department chairpersons from teaching duties up to three periods a day and by training them in basic supervisory practices (Butler and McMillan, 1968).

It seems likely that improvement of instruction will get leadership from the departmental level within a school only if more time is allocated to supervision and more competent, better coordinated chairpersons are provided. While the weight of the evidence to date is discouraging regarding the effectiveness of both department chairpersons and assistant principals as supervisory personnel, it does seem possible to make these positions effective. Better selection, more training, and clearly defined duties as members of a supervisory team will be required. Currently these positions often constitute costly and wasteful expenditures that can be better utilized.

Lead teachers and resource teachers often assume some supervisory responsibilities. Many of the difficulties mentioned for department chairpersons are also faced by regular classroom teachers or resource teachers when they have heavy teaching loads and limited training in supervisory practices. Even so, schools and districts continue to seek ways to more fully utilize teachers in leadership roles. Such efforts need to be continued because interest is high and the potential for extending instructional improvement efforts is great.

The *superintendent* of the local school district is often overlooked as an important supervisory staff member. This person is, of course, chief of supervisory services. Unfortunately, superintendents are often too busy, too ill prepared, or too disinterested to become actively involved in supervisory tasks. The recent survey of school superintendents by Cunningham and Henges (1982) reveals interesting facts about them. Some 15,000 superintendents view the "central office staff" as the most "weighty" source of information for the school board next to themselves. Supervisory issues and challenges like "goal setting," assessing educational outcomes, staff evaluation, and special education are reported among the top seven in importance by these superintendents. Some 24 percent rely most heavily on principals, compared with only 7.2 percent who rely most heavily on supervisory personnel; but they see "curriculum and instruction" as the area most in need of still further staffing in the immediate future.

Differentiated teaching staff assignments were widely publicized in the past as having profound implications for improving education (Shaplin and Olds, 1964). Under several identical labels rather diverse concepts of differentiated staffing emerged. One organizational arrangement employed the master teacher or team leader, with only nominal supervisory responsibilities. Another arrangement proposed a hierarchy of teaching staff within the school, with virtually all supervisory responsibilities assigned to the teaching team or curriculum council within the school. Both concepts have been tried, neither has flourished.

The shortage of well-qualified personnel to give dynamic leadership to instructional improvement is so severe that the kind of staffing pattern proposed as team teaching has not been feasible except under rather special conditions. Much of the material presented in Chapters 2 and 3 speaks to the problem of trying to effect change from within an operating production-oriented organization. To the extent that differentiated staffing arrangements allocate all staff for supervision to the individual building or department, instructional change is likely to be incremental and halting, at best.

A host of problems and promising features in differentiated staffing patterns have been identified (Scobey and Fiorino, 1973; Hillson and Hyman, 1977). There is great promise for more and better involvement in supervisory tasks in any situation that reduces technically simple demands while allowing and encouraging higher-level skill and concept development among teachers. The Cooperative Teaching Program in Corpus Christi has shown great promise in organizing teacher teams that differentiate curriculum development responsibilities, foster cooperative planning, and avoid departmentalization tendencies. New and exciting arrangements for relating staff to both teaching and supervision functions are developing under such labels as "individually guided instruction" and "open classroom concept" (Hillson and Hyman, 1977, p. 373). To date, these staff arrangements have much more impact on teaching practices than supervisory staffing. The use of "resource teachers" in special education, reading, and bilingual programs is surely a promising alternative for improving instruction. Whether they can really be utilized effectively in supervisory tasks to make substantial and continuing school improvements still remains to be seen.

Intermediate Units and Service Centers

Any view of current practices in staffing for supervision of instruction would be very incomplete without at least a glance at the staffs of county offices, regional service centers, study councils, and other organizations, both old and new.

The "functions" of intermediate units have been described as articulative, coordinative, and supplementary (Marks et al., 1978, pp. 26–38). Under each term, supervision services are defined as interpreting local educational needs, improving education, providing special consultative services, developing courses of study, and promoting in-service education. The proper staffing of the intermediate unit to provide services to local schools is regarded as crucial. In experience and in qualifications, the professional staff must be comparable to those employed in similar service areas at the local district level.

Intermediate units for supervisory as well as other service purposes emerged after World War II in a number of states in the form of reorganized county superintendents' offices. California's County School Services Program illustrated this with a special state fund being allocated specifically for new staff and services, many of which were supervisory. In Texas, a series of studies led to the abandonment of the county superintendents' offices for most supervisory services, but 20 regional centers were created to provide "media and other services" for the improvement of instruction. Wisconsin eliminated the office of county superintendent and created cooperative Education Service Agencies in 1965. New York State has long had its Board of Cooperative Educational Services engaged in supervision of instruction on a regional level. Pennsylvania, Georgia, and Colorado are among the many states that now have some form of "service center" operation for in-service education, curriculum development, or other supervisor tasks. In contrast, Florida and Louisiana are states that attempted to deal with the need for supervisory services from outside the local community by making the county (in Florida) or parish (in Louisiana) into unified local school districts.

While intermediate unit organizations originally tended to be county units, a surge of interest in service centers of various sizes for many special purposes developed in the Elementary and Secondary Education Act of 1965. Grants under these acts promoted regional projects. Officials ignored, for the most part, a growing program of service center development in many states and opted for special centers to stimulate instructional change and innovation. The Southern Regional Education Board was awarded a contract for "regional cooperation in the utilization of recorded materials for educational television in the South." An Educational Curriculum Resource and Research Center was established in 1966 in Orange, Texas, with a combination of federal and state funds.

The Department of Rural Education launched PACE in response to Title III funding for "Supplementary Educational Centers and Services." These centers were directed to emphasize "innovative and exemplary" programs, with emphasis on improvement of instruction.

The Tennessee Valley Education Center (TVEC) is still another example of regionalization of supervisory services. This 24–school district northern Alabama center was initiated in 1967 to provide "professional improvement" and "curriculum development" services. Instructional Laboratory Centers as regional demonstration and in-service training organizations were created (Bailey et al., 1966). The New England School Development Council, offering supervisory services for more than a quarter of a century, created a Division of Field Studies in 1967 to emphasize consultant services to districts, employing the ad hoc team approach. The Boards of Cooperative Services were started in Colorado in 1965 (not unlike those in New York State) to offer supervisory services such as planning and in-service training as well as direct teaching services.

The development of new organizational patterns for offering supervisory services has been strikingly rapid. That many regional, yet essentially local, organizations have been formed emphasizes the need for services "close to home," yet extending in number and variety of competencies beyond those the local school district can expect to employ. Each of these intermediate service organizations has supervisors of some kind on its staff. Curiously, it is almost impossible to get accurate information as to their number, competencies, or ways of working. It seems that a relatively small supervisory staff ratio persists in these situations, as in local districts; however, Krantz's (1966) report on over a thousand "new programs," of which 85 were supervisory, with 3,667 personnel and only 37 supervisors, makes this observer wonder about the rationality of both funding and staffing patterns in this era.

Teacher Centers

In 1971 the U.S. Office of Education established Teachers' Centers, which were intended to be under the control of teachers (Wilhelms, 1973, pp. 47–49). The purpose of these centers was to provide a framework and opportunities for teacher professional development (Dull, 1981, pp. 124–32).

Teacher centers are or were consortia—joint ventures by school systems, universities, teachers' unions, and other agencies. Most usually they were created under federal funding and law with state-level sponsorship. Van Fleet and associates (1977) describe "the Florida experience" with these staffing/service delivery hybrids. In-service education and materials development were most often cited as the task areas of concern to these teacher centers. Some centers have been created as in-service/preservice training centers with joint sponsorship by a university and local districts (Klugman, 1974; Maryland University, 1975). Others created primarily for in-service training purposes in Texas were organized through the Regional Education Service Centers (Killough, 1977).

Because of their diverse forms and purposes, teacher centers added in the 1970s to the already confusing array of staffing patterns for supervision that had developed in the two preceding decades. Harris (1980, p. 145) commented that "the impression an observer is likely to get is one of unbelievable chaos."

Federal legislation sponsoring teacher centers under the 1976 amendments to the Higher Education Act had several curious provisions. The law provided that "each teacher center must operate under the supervision of a policy board, the majority of which are representative of elementary and secondary classroom teachers" (Education Amendments of 1976, p. 51551). Another provision of the Act provided, however, "for grants to local education agencies." These provisions led to conflicting and confusing regulations that produced both staffing and funding problems for many of these centers.

Other Supervising Agencies

State departments of education, regional laboratories, accrediting associations, and private groups of various kinds are all represented in supervisory endeavors in our schools and colleges. A detailed listing of these other supervising agencies is not feasible, nor would it be particularly useful. It is important, however, to recognize the variety of sources offering supervisory services and to at least contemplate the influences these supervisors might have on changing instructional practices in our schools and colleges.

State departments of education have a long tradition of control of instructional practices through curriculum prescription, text adoption or approval, teacher certification, and funds allocation (Crandall, 1977, pp. 189–274). Large federal grants have been made for strengthening and rehabilitating state departments of education, with special emphasis on their role in planning and implementation of innovations (Berman and McLaughlin, 1974). Staff members in state departments have greatly increased since 1965 under this federal stimulation. Statewide needs assessment studies have become increasingly common, demonstration networks of innovative practices have developed (Bishop, 1970; Butler and Paisley, 1978), and pilot programs of instructional improvements on a grand scale have been undertaken (Marks et al., 1978, pp. 42–71). State testing programs have multiplied rapidly in recent years, placing heavy responsibilities for evaluation of instruction on these staffs.

Regional laboratories for educational development have exercised supervisory leadership on a national basis in some instances. The Far West Laboratory has stimulated considerable interest in in-service education using microteaching techniques with specially developed "minicourse" materials. The Southwest Educational Development Laboratory has emphasized curriculum development for early childhood education, bilingual education, and social education. The laboratory activities at the University of Pittsburgh (later in Philadelphia) have provided schools all over the country with individually prescribed materials to test and evaluate. This "lab" has recently become more directly involved in training school personnel in special time-on-task analysis techniques. The Northwest Regional Educational Laboratory has emphasized helping teachers develop instructional competencies, working at larger strategies of teaching (Wilhelms, 1973, pp. 8–13).

Professional associations, including regional accrediting associations, have a long tradition of involvement in supervisory activities. Accrediting standards development, stimulation of faculty study activities, workshops and conferences, and publications are but a few examples of the contributions to in-service education and program evaluation staffed by these agencies. Professional association meetings have come to be regarded as outstanding sources of in-service training experience, even though their impact on instructional practices is open to question. On the other hand, the special seminars of the Association for Supervision and Curriculum Development, the conferences of the National Academy for School Executives, and portions of annual conventions of many professional associations illustrate efforts at in-service education of a substantial kind.

Private organizations have entered the field of supervision of instruction in amazing variety and number in recent years. Nearly every city now has its consulting firms offering to contract for curriculum development, in-service training, materials development, and program evaluation. Several large corporations have created special educational development companies with an eye to making profits from innovative instructional programming.

Of course, textbook publishers continue to provide consultants to work with staffs in selection and utilization. Film companies offer demonstrations, as do other companies selling instructional media. Supervisors employed by these businesses are often outstanding leaders with extensive school experience and professional training. The newest addition to this group are the microcomputer manufacturers and distributors.

The existence of a wide range of organized staff groups offering supervisory services is a blessing of diversity and a dilemma in complexity. A major responsibility for both administrators and supervisors at local district levels is to mediate between the needs of the staff at the classroom level and the plethora of available supervisors in the professional environs! If federal legislation can be channeled in the future toward more support to improving instruction without deciding on organizational patterns, then some reasonable variety of staffing patterns may gradually emerge. Presently, scarce human resources for improving instruction are being wasted at nearly all levels.

Federal and state politicians and bureaucrats need to be informed of the extensive array of organizations already in existence for supervision of instruction. If these authorities can refrain from creating new special-purpose organizations and assist instead with the funding and staffing of those that can respond best to local needs, real progress is possible.

FUNCTIONAL CRITERIA

Because supervision of instruction is such a highly shared function, the delineation of responsibilities becomes critically important.* Sharing of responsibilities is important in this functional area, as in teaching, administration, and other functions, because different persons have distinctive contributions to make toward the accomplishment of the essential tasks. However, the essential nature of supervision does not make a case for a staff of supervisors as equally essential. On the contrary, supervisors seeking acceptance as instructional leadership specialists must describe the substantive nature of their work and demonstrate their unique contributions. Three criteria give support to supervisory positions in the school setting: relevance, uniqueness, and efficiency.

Relevance Criterion

Are the tasks for which the supervisors assume responsibility genuinely relevant to the long-term success of the total operation? This criterion of relevance is readily met when responsibility for the tasks of supervision, especially curriculum development, staffing, in-service education, and evaluation, are properly assumed.

---

*This section draws heavily upon material previously published by the author in *Toward Professional Maturity for Supervisors and Curriculum Workers* (Wahle, 1967).

Uniqueness Criterion

Are the contributions the supervisors make to the accomplishment of the tasks unique ones? This criterion of uniqueness is met when supervisors have an array of competencies for effective use of leadership skills and processes as previously described, which are either not possessed by other personnel or are not readily available for deployment in the various task areas of supervision.

Efficiency Criterion

Are the contributions made so as to accomplish the tasks more efficiently than they would be without supervisors? The criterion of efficiency is met when a number of personal and situational factors are combined in appropriate ways. These factors include time, energy, freedom, flexibility, conferred status, and special competencies.

Time and Energy

Many supervisory endeavors require that large quantities of leadership energy be allocated to a specific problem for a prolonged period of time. These endeavors are not often successful when only intermittent attention, limited time, or limited energy is devoted to them. An experimental program in curriculum development, for example, involves activities that can be very demanding in time and energy. The preparation for, and the leading of, an intensive in-service program is similarly very demanding. Assignments that prevent such concentrated use of time and energy in pursuit of supervisory tasks will not promote efficient supervision. Conversely, specific supervisory positions need to be created and structured just because these requirements are real.

Freedom of Access

Certain supervisory endeavors require freedom of access to individuals, facilities, and other resources within and outside the school. When supervisory endeavors do not demand access outside the building, the school principal, department chairman, or team leader may be able to exercise the necessary leadership. Similarly, when resources are required from various schools, but not from other communities, the supervisor assigned to those schools may be able to exercise the necessary leadership.

Leadership responsibility is best placed with supervisors who have access to schools at various levels when articulation of subject matter from level to level is involved in curriculum development or evaluation. Similarly, a health education project requiring community agency involvement can be expedited by a health supervisor who has already established relationships with such agencies. When dramatically innovative teaching practices are being introduced, communications with the superintendent, school board, teachers in various schools, and civic leaders may be important. Leadership responsibility for such dynamic supervisory endeavors is wisely vested in a supervisor with access to these diverse groups of people.

All aspects of supervision need to be led by those who have freedom of access to the people, facilities, and other resources that may be required. All supervisory personnel have easy access to certain of these resources but not to others. For some endeavors, the principal may be the most efficient leader; for others, a supervisor may more efficiently exercise leadership; for many endeavors, only a leadership team can serve well.

Flexibility

Flexibility in the use of one's own time and available resources is still another factor to consider in assigning supervisory responsibilities. Supervisory endeavors with highly dynamic orientations tend to be periodic rather than continuous. This discontinuity requires that time, staff, and other resources be available with maximum flexibility.

A great portion of a supervisor's time may be allocated for one month to urgent requests from new, inexperienced teachers. Three months later these demands may be less urgent, and that same supervisor can launch into a project with an experienced teacher group to do educational planning for a new middle school or a new effort at individually prescribed instruction. An in-service action-research project may blossom forth and generate unexpected demands for statistical and data-processing services, which a supervisor from a regional service center or an intermediate unit can supply.

The positional expectations of various supervisory personnel tolerate different degrees of flexibility in the use of time and other resources at their disposal. The individual position holder tends to influence the time flexibility characteristics as well as the flexibility of other resources at his disposal, but to a substantial degree the role expectations of supervisors, subordinates, and clients determine utilization. Those responsible for the ongoing program of instruction and closely related aspects of the school operation are rarely permitted much flexibility in the use of their time. Time-scheduled routines, in addition to unexpected urgent demands, tend to control the time of teachers, principals, counselors, and librarians alike.

In contrast, the supervisor can be given considerable flexibility. He can avoid rigid schedules. Role expectations need not be stereotyped or crystallized. Financial resources can be allocated for supervision tasks with flexibility provided. The expectation that supervisors will assume responsibility for supervision tasks while avoiding in-depth involvement in other functions of the school operation is a mandate for flexibility. The developmental tasks approached dynamically are not to be accomplished in a routine manner.

Special Competencies

The special competencies required to lead a designated aspect of supervision to successful results are, of course, important to consider in assigning or accepting supervisory responsibilities. All supervisory personnel presumably have certain basic competencies in leadership and instruction. All personnel vary from one another in the kinds of competencies they have beyond the basic ones. They vary also in the level of sophistication at which their competencies have been developed. Supervisory responsibilities that are assigned to staff members after a careful assessment of the competencies available and needed are likely to be carried out with greatest success.

By virtue of their special training and concentrated experience in supervision task leadership, supervisors should have special competencies and more sophisticated leadership competencies of some types than do other supervisory personnel such as principals or department chairpersons. Certain aspects of supervision will, for instance, require group facilitation competencies that few department chairmen have. The development of curriculum guides often requires competencies in synthesizing and verbalizing concepts that are not readily available in teachers and may be found only in a few supervisors. Working with individual teachers under stress may require a special kind of competence in empathizing that certain supervisors have and others do not.

Many competencies of special and highly sophisticated kinds are needed for efficient pursuit of the tasks of supervision. Team *leadership* is often essential to bring these various competencies together in coordinated ways. Team supervision will most certainly be one of the striking developments in the improvement of instruction in the years ahead (Bender, 1982).

Conferred Status

The ability of supervisory personnel to lead effectively is influenced by the status each supervisor has. Status is the relative rank of a person "in a hierarchy of prestige." Efforts to lead are, of course, facilitated when supervisory personnel have prestige in the eyes of those with whom they work. Prestige is derived from various sources, such as title, salary, past accomplishments, known competencies, and position in the hierarchy.

High status may be gained by supervisors who have demonstrated competence or accomplishments over the years. However, status can be conferred. In the absence of known competence, a title may imply it. Similarly, the assignment of a person to a position with a higher salary may contribute temporarily to that person's status.

Unfortunately, conferred status is rarely lasting. Those working closely with a leader soon come to judge him or her and gain or lose respect for him or her on the basis of demonstrated competence and the ability to get things done. Even when a person is very competent by certain standards, his or her prestige may suffer if things do not go well (Sergiovanni and Starratt, 1971, pp. 48–50).

Supervisors and other supervisory personnel alike need to be prestigious people. They need to be perceived as leaders who can get things done. Conferring status may be an essential step for new supervisors or others assigned new responsibilities. The more challenging, demanding, risky, and long-range the endeavor, the more important is status from whatever source. Obviously, status conferred will not persist as prestige in the eyes of one's peers, subordinates, or superiors without the eventual demonstration of competence and results.

The importance of the status factor emphasizes a genuine dilemma in supervisory staffing and organizing for effective task accomplishment. The confusing titles and uncertain positions in the formal hierarchy of the school often work to prevent the supervisors from gaining conferred status. On the other hand, the supervisors' most important contributions result from undertaking supervisory tasks with a highly dynamic orientation, which makes quick respect or recognition unlikely.

Supervisory assignments need to be realistic in terms of the status required. But even more, the status of supervisory personnel needs to be cultivated in relation to responsibilities assigned. The clarification of titles, the clear designation of supervisory positions high in the hierarchy, and the maintenance of relatively high salaries are essential. The in-service cultivation of sophisticated supervisory competencies via in-service education is also essential.

STAFFING CONSIDERATIONS

No staffing pattern is likely to be equally effective in the wide variety of school-community settings to be found within each state and region of the United States. Staffing patterns serving well at one time will not continue to do so as problem and situation factors change. A few guidelines for supervisory staffings can be identified, however, in carefully analyzing the kinds of people employed and the number needed.

Special versus General Supervision

There has been a steady trend toward specialization in all walks of life (Firester and Firester, 1970). Instructional supervision, like other functions in education, has tended to become increasingly specialized. The larger school systems have naturally led the way, employing an array of supervisors who are subject specialists. As suburban school districts grew larger, special supervisors were added to their staffs (Bassin and Gross, 1980, pp. 114–30). As the curriculum has become diversified, special supervisors have been employed to give leadership to these new instructional programs—homemaking, family life, industrial arts, and adult education (Walker and Hamm 1981, p. 31). Older programs that have received renewed emphasis through federal legislation have been staffed with special supervisors in agriculture, foreign languages, guidance, and science. The development of supervision at the secondary school level has tended to result in further growth in the number of special subject supervisors employed. The staffs of state education agencies have expanded with the employment of special supervisors, while intermediate service units have come into being that also offer highly specialized services (Murphy, 1973; Marks et al., 1978).

Problems of overspecialization.   The need for specialization of function in large or technically complex operations cannot be denied. Specialization produces serious problems, however, for any organization. Communication between specialists tends to be difficult because of their limited range of interests and their specialized vocabularies. Conflicts tend to be produced between subunits of the organization under the influence of specialists who often find it necessary to make the operations related to their specialties as autonomous as possible. Coordination of relatively autonomous, highly specialized groups is especially difficult (Sergiovanni and Starratt, 1971, pp. 51–70).

This dilemma of supervisory staffing needs to be faced realistically. Supervisors must be specialists, but the evils that result from staffing with specialists must be eliminated or at least mitigated.

Approaches to staffing.   Several approaches to staffing with specialists that maximize their effectiveness have been developed:

1. Staffing with high-quality personnel
2. Staffing in terms of a variety of specialists rather than of traditional ones alone
3. Staffing for certain specialties on a purely temporary basis
4. Organizing staff members for maximum interaction
5. Allocating resources to specialties with planned diminution

The quality of personnel employed for supervision determines to a substantial degree the problems of overspecialization that will result. A specialist with limited intelligence, a narrow background of knowledge about the culture, a rigid personality structure, and limited interests in education is likely to be difficult to communicate with. Those supervisors of higher quality in these respects can more readily coordinate their activities. The relationships between the specialists' responsibilities and the total operation will be better understood. Conflicts will tend to be less frequent and not so serious or prolonged.

Staffing with a variety of subject matter and grade-level specialties without consideration of many other kinds of specializations has aggravated the problem of overspecialization. Every conceivable specialty cannot be adequately staffed. Choices must always be made that result in the neglect of certain important specialties (Walker and Hamm, 1981, p. 30). This implies the need to provide a staff of supervisors who can give leadership to the *main strands* of both the woof and the warp of the fabric of instruction. To provide supervisors for every subject taught in the schools would necessarily result in neglecting supervision in such specialties as the library, audiovisual materials, curriculum development, guidance, and public relations. To staff in terms of the tasks of supervision with specialist supervisors assigned exclusively to each task would result in the neglect of certain subject areas. A supervisory staff might be selected and assigned in terms of skills and processes or of their abilities to employ certain supervisory activities skillfully. This approach would also leave other specialties neglected.

Temporary assignments are one approach to the problem of necessarily neglecting certain specialties. Since all possible needs for specialists cannot be met, a larger array of specialties will be provided over a period of years if certain staff positions are filled periodically with new specialists. This has been done in some districts by using teacher-supervisors for in-service education purposes on a temporary-assignment basis. Skillful administrators sometimes fill naturally occurring vacancies so as to introduce new specialists. Still another means of providing supervisors for a specialty on a temporary basis is to utilize visiting consultants from colleges, intermediate units, commercial agencies, the state education agency, and other public and private institutions. A sabbatical-leave program also provides an approach to this problem. However accomplished, maintaining a staff of supervisors, some of whom are on temporary assignments, not only provides for a greater array of specialties over a period of time but also reduces problems of excessively autonomous subunits.

Organizing supervisors with various special competencies for maximum staff interaction is an important consideration. Communications are enhanced when specialists work, plan, and play together to some substantial extent. The use of a curriculum council on which various supervisors serve to consider policy and to plan programs in relation to the broader aspects of the instructional program can be valuable to specialists (Jackson, 1972). Action-research projects provide natural opportunities for supervisors with various specialties to work together. Curriculum development activities that depart from the course-by-course pattern and focus on large segments of the program structure can very usefully bring subject-specialist supervisors together.

The planned diminution of resources allocated to one specialty is an important approach. When special emphasis needs to be given to library developments, or science in the elementary schools, or programs for the gifted, heavy resource allocations tend to be made to staff members working in these areas. With resource allocations come power, prestige, influence, and vested interests. Long-range planning can prevent these special programs from becoming entrenched beyond the time that they serve the best interests of the total instructional program. A time limit needs to be set up on the special status of programs. Excess time and special funds allocated to such programs need to be budgeted so as to return to normal on a designated schedule. Certain responsibilities for the program need to be reassigned to the school principal following that period of protected development.

Special Services Personnel

An effective program of special services requires supervision activities. The *special services function* has been defined as those activities carried on with pupils that indirectly facilitate accomplishment of the major instructional goals of the school. As such, special services are services to instruction through pupils, in the same way that supervision activities are services to instruction through teachers and other staff members. But many services to pupils are effective only when teachers and other staff members are also involved. It is in such instances that supervision and special services are closely related.

Specialized counseling services for pupils have limited value, for instance, unless teachers also are giving consideration through instructional procedures to the guidance problems involved. Special education programs require not only special services for children but also curriculum development and in-service education for the teachers and administrators involved. The role of the school nurse as a medical technician may be no more important than her role as a public relations person building understanding about the relationships between physical health and instructional effectiveness. The school social worker can help obtain social welfare services for a family, but an equally important role is found in the in-service education of staff members that helps them understand and adapt instruction to the diverse social and cultural needs of individuals.

These are a few of the many ways in which special services personnel can and should get involved in supervision. The distinction was made between *supervisors* and *other supervisory personnel*. Special services personnel—counselors, nurses, school social workers, psychologists, and others—are inevitably engaged in supervision to some extent, just as are many other professional staff members. There is an increasing interest in, and an increasing need for, special services personnel who are essentially *supervisors*. These are staff members who devote a major portion of their time to the tasks of supervision as they relate to special services.

Special services can and should be related to instruction. Ordinarily the schools provide these services for educational rather than humane reasons.

The contributions of these services to the major goals of the school are maximized only when they influence the instructional program as well as the pupil.

Certain special services personnel should function as supervisors. However they are organized for this purpose, such specialists should be considered a part of the staff-supervisor team. Their jobs should be defined so as to permit their giving major attention to the instructional program through in-service education, curriculum development, public relations, materials, and other tasks. These specialists should be given opportunities to become intimately acquainted with the instructional staff and program. Their time should be protected to prevent direct service demands from corrupting the supervision function.

STAFFING BY COMPETENCIES

The most neglected consideration in supervisory staffing may be that of competence. What competencies do supervisors and other supervisory personnel possess? What staffing patterns, assignments, or organizational arrangements provide the best *balance* of competencies?

Competency Analysis

Supervisory staffing, like nearly all staffing in education, tends to be a person-with-a-degree-filling-a-slot process. "Slots" are titled positions, ill defined by job descriptions but rigorously constrained by a place in the hierarchy, the salary authorized, and the credentials (degrees, experience, and credits) required. As useful as these elements in staffing for supervision may be, they tend to ignore or give very low priority to competency *needs*, the competence of the supervisor, and the match between need and competence available.

Harris and associates (1979, p. 172) have proposed a three-factor model for selecting, assigning, and balancing staff personnel. They argue for considering the following:

I. *Positional Factors*
   1. What are the existing openings?
   2. What are the likely future openings?
   3. What openings might be created?
   4. What are the legal, financial, and other constraints?
II. *Competence Factors*
   5. What kinds of competence do we have?
   6. What kinds of competence do we lack?
   7. What kinds of competence can we develop?
   8. What kinds of competence can we find?

III. *Situational Factors*
  9. What are our maintenance needs?
  10. What are our improvement needs?
  11. What can we get approved?

The argument for more attention to competency analysis in staffing for instructional supervision is based in part on the recognition that instructional leadership will be shared among teachers, principals, supervisors, outside consultants, and many others. Hence it makes sense to view any staffing decision as more than just filling or eliminating a position. More urgent support for competency analysis in supervisory staffing comes from two additional considerations:

1. Supervision is a very complex function involving nine task areas and a great variety of competencies.
2. Many tasks and competencies of supervision, especially when utilized in highly dynamic forms, call for competency patterns that tend to be rare in any individual (Harris, 1980).

Balancing Staff Competencies

The concept of balance for more effective teaching and learning has been explored by Harris and associates (1979, pp. 192–200) with respect to team teaching, desegregation programs, and teacher selection and assignment practices. Supervisory staffs can profit too from analyses that focus on both competence and balance. In Table 6.1 possibilities are illustrated with 10 staff members shown by position title. The illustration refers to personnel regularly assigned to a senior high school. The specific supervisory competencies of greatest strength are shown for each person. (See Appendix A for a list of 36 supervisory competencies designated by task areas.) The two rows under "other" in Table 6.1 indicate the possibility of utilizing *outside consultants* from college, university, service center or other agencies to provide *balance*.

This competence profile illustrates a way of analyzing staff competence within an organization. The competency "strengths" shown in Table 6.1 include only those for three task areas. Such designated strengths can be derived by utilizing Harris's *Developmental Supervisory Competency Assessment System* (1982a). To the extent that any task area is well covered by individuals (one or more) who have appropriate varieties of competency strengths, the profile suggests capability for task accomplishments. When certain competency *strengths* are clearly missing in any important task area, the profile suggests potential problems of task implementation.

In this illustrative profile for a senior high school staff a serious "deficiency" in competency "F–5—Training for Leadership" is shown in the inservice education task area. This capability, if needed for any particular effort

TABLE 6.1　An Illustration of a Supervisory Competency Profile

SUPERVISORY STAFF POSITIONS	SELECTED TASK AREAS*		
	A. CURRICULUM DEVELOPMENT	B. MATERIALS DEVELOPMENT	F. PROVIDING IN-SERVICE EDUCATION
In-School			
Principal	—	B-2	F-1
Asst. Principal #1	—	—	F-1
Asst. Principal #2	—	B-1	F-2
Asst. Principal #3	A-1	—	—
Dean of Instruction	A-1, A-3	B-1, B-2	F-3, F-8
Vocational Director	A-1	—	F-8, F-9, F-10
Central Office			
Language Consultant	A-2	B-1	F-4, F-8
Science/Math Coordinator	A-1, A-2, A-3	B-2	F-1, F-3
Social Studies Specialist	A-3	B-2	F-1
Music Education Director	A-1	—	—
Other			
College	?	?	?
Education Service Center	?	?	?
Abundant Competence	A-1, A-3	B-1, B-2	F-1, F-3, F-8
Missing Competence		B-3	F-5, F-6, F-7

*See Chapter 1 and Appendices A and B for descriptions of task areas and competencies designated here.

at improving instruction, might be provided by contracting with an "outside" consultant. Similar consideration might be given to supplementing competencies B–3, F–6, and F–7.

Profiles of competence for several schools may also be useful in making decisions on the best location for pilot programs, the assignment of interns, and the scheduling of central staff supervisors. Such profiles may also be useful in making decisions about assigning and reassigning personnel for optimum balance (Harris et al., 1979, pp. 181–92).

NUMERICAL ADEQUACY OF STAFF

A staff is said to be adequate when it it just large enough to get the job done well. This is no help at all in thinking about a staff of supervisors, because their job is never *done* and we cannot say when it is done *well!* It seems inevitable that judging the adequacy of a staff of supervisors will remain an uncertain process. Guidelines are provided in terms of the tasks to be accomplished, the existing practices, and perceived inadequacies in existing practices.

Factors to consider.   Thinking only in terms of numerical adequacy for the total staff of supervisors and not in terms of the assigned responsibilities of staff members, a variety of factors should be considered. The available financial resources and the availability of qualified personnel will obviously influence staff size. Other factors of substantial importance include the following:

1.   The rate of pupil population growth in the district
2.   The competence of the school principals as instructional supervisors
3.   The quality of the teaching staff
4.   The rate of turnover in the teaching staff
5.   The amount of change desired in the instructional program
6.   The resistance to change likely to be encountered
7.   The size of the district in pupil enrollments

These seven factors provide a basis for making judgments about the number of full-time equivalent supervisors needed in a given situation. The availability of funds and qualified personnel are independent considerations.

There is no simple procedure for properly analyzing a given situation to arrive at a number. Certainly, supervisors will have to be increased in number in most, if not all, school districts in the United States if the snail's pace of past and present educational change is not to continue with suicidal results. Not only have past rates of change produced many instructional antiquities in our public schools, but the accelerating rate of developments in our society demands much more rapidly changing educational programs. All of this suggests the need for substantially larger staffs of supervisors in the immediate future than in the past.

Estimating needs for supervisors.   At the risk of seriously oversimplifying a very complex problem, Table 6.2 is presented as a scale that can be applied to a local situation to analyze the need for supervisors beyond minimum staff requirements. This author would not attempt to defend the specific procedures suggested, but the basic scheme for systematically analyzing local conditions seems fundamentally sound. The scale presented assumes a basic minimum staff of one full-time equivalent supervisor per 100 instructional staff members. The factor ratings based on suggested criteria can be used as indices for analyzing the need for supervisors *beyond* the minimum. If a rating of one were assigned to each factor, a minimum staff of supervisors might well be adequate. Higher ratings suggest the need and the reasons for more supervisors.

TABLE 6.2   A Scale for Analyzing Number of Supervisors Needed for Adequacy

RATING FACTOR	DESCRIPTION	RATINGS
1. *Pupil population growth*	Average annual increase in the number of pupils in average daily attendance for a three-year period including the current year*	1 — 0 to 4% 2 — 5% to 9% 3 — 10% to 14% 4 — 15% to 19% 5 — 20% and above
2. *Principal competencies*	The time that building principals competently spend on instructional supervision	1 — 61% or more 2 — 51% to 60% 3 — 36% to 50% 4 — 26% to 35% 5 — 25% or less
3. *Quality of the teaching staff*	The estimated level of performance of the average teacher in the district as compared with teachers throughout the state	1 — Superior to 90% or more 2 — Superior to 60% to 89% 3 — Superior to 40% to 59% 4 — Superior to 20% to 39% 5 — Superior to less than 20%
4. *Staff turnover*	The average annual replacement rate plus additions to staff for the past three years	1 — 0 to 4% 2 — 5% to 9% 3 — 10% to 14% 4 — 15% to 19% 5 — 20% or more
5. *Change desired*	The desire for supervision activities that are directed toward producing fundamental changes in the program of instruction	1 — Not desired at all 2 — Very limited 3 — Some such changes desired 4 — Substantially desired 5 — Extensively desired
6. *Probable resistance*	The estimated reluctance of influential persons and groups in the community and the school to accept and support substantial changes in the instructional program	1 — Virtually no resistance 2 — Little resistance 3 — A normal amount of resistance 4 — Substantial resistance 5 — Extreme resistance
7. *Pupil enrollments*	The average of the total pupil enrollments for a three-year period including the current year	1 — 20,000 or more 2 — 10,000 to 19,999 3 — 5,000 to 9,999 4 — 2,000 to 4,999 5 — Fewer than 2,000

*Where projected estimates of future enrollments are available, they should be included in the three-year average employed.

Computing numerical adequacy.   To translate ratings into estimated numbers of supervisors is even more difficult than to arrive at the ratings. One possible approach is illustrated in Table 6.3 using the four school districts studied and discussed earlier and another small district known to the writer. Ratings were made, squared, and totaled for each district. Total instructional

TABLE 6.3   Estimates of Adequate Supervisor Staffs for Five School Districts

	DISTRICTS				
	A	B	C	D	E
I. *Basic Data*					
Pupils in average daily attendance (est.)	6,000	21,000	12,000	10,000	1,000
Computed total instructional staff	240	840	480	400	40
II. *Factor Ratings Squared*					
1. Pupil population growth	4	4	16	16	1
2. Principal competencies	16	4	25	9	16
3. Quality of teaching staff	4	4	16	9	16
4. Staff turnover	1	4	9	4	4
5. Change desired	9	9	25	9	25
6. Probable resistance	4	4	16	9	16
7. Pupil enrollments	9	1	4	4	25
Total	47	30	111	60	103
Index of Need $\frac{\text{Total}}{100}$	0.47	0.30	1.11	0.60	1.03
III. *Computations for Adequacy*					
1. Add the Index of Need and 1.00. This is the *Adequacy Index*	1.47	1.30	2.11	1.60	2.03
2. Multiply the *Adequacy Index* by the computed total instructional staff and divide by 100 ..	3.53	10.92	10.13	6.40	.81
3. Add 20% of this total for necessary non-supervisory duties . This is total full-time equivalent staff positions for adequacy.	4.24	13.10	12.16	7.68	.97
IV. *Needs*					
1. Estimate present full-time staff equivalent positions based on at least 80% of the time devoted to the tasks of supervision	2.00	11.00	3.00	4.00	.20
2. Compute the difference between D1 and C3 above .... This is added staff positions required for adequacy.	2.24	2.10	9.16	3.68	.77

staff members were *computed* (actual figures not used) on the basis of 40 instructional staff members per 1,000 pupils in average daily attendance. Total factor ratings were converted to an *Index of Need* by dividing by 100. This index, multiplied by the number of computed instructional staff members, serves as an estimate of an *adequate* number of full-time staff equivalents to be devoted to supervision tasks. Twenty percent is added to this number to allow for certain nonsupervisory duties that are inevitably a part of a supervisor's job. This total is the estimated full-time equivalent staff positions for adequacy. The difference between this figure and existing staff suggests the need for increased staff, if any.

The computations shown for the five selected school districts are all estimates based on the writer's studies of these districts and of the jobs of their staff members. Even so, they are only estimates and are used here purely for illustrative purposes. These districts all appear to need additional supervisors. District B, the largest, is a fairly wealthy district and has one of the more competent and better-organized staffs in the state. By contrast, District C is in an impoverished area, rapidly growing, and facing many problems, among which is that of securing qualified teachers and other staff members. The financial conditions in this district have prevented the development of a well-organized staff of supervisors. District A is the wealthiest of these five but has done relatively little toward developing a staff of supervisors. District D is reasonably wealthy, has a rapidly expanding school population, has a substantially developed staff of supervisors in special services, but has done very little staff development in other task areas.

This approach to the analysis of numerical adequacy is based on the assumption of an adequate local unit of administration for providing supervisory services. Additional services of supervisors from outside sources will, of course, be required in nearly any district. For smaller districts, increasing quantities of supervision services from intermediate, state, and other sources will be required. Even if District E, for example, had approximately one full-time equivalent supervisor, this would hardly be adequate unless complemented by services from other sources. Very small districts will rely almost entirely on outside sources, and the scheme of analysis suggested here is not likely to apply.

The use of the rating scale and the computation of an *Adequacy Index* constitute only one systematic approach to the analysis of a local situation. Other approaches should be developed and tested to determine their worth. The important need is for staffing in terms of systematic analyses of local situations. The scheme presented here will certainly not produce staffs of supervisors that are numerically ideal. For most districts, the computations suggested will result in rather modestly expanded staffs.

APPROACHES TO TEAM SUPERVISION

Although supervisory staffs have undoubtedly had many people with whom to share the responsibility for supervisory tasks, past approaches have obviously been less than gloriously successful, especially where dynamic supervision is concerned.

How can a school system organize itself for instructional change? Much of the literature has emphasized the constraints, barriers, and problems nearly always encountered, but ways of conceptualizing the problem and ways of organizing to make change efforts strategic rather than purely tactical are also needed (Beisser, 1981). Such complex change efforts require careful *goal specification*, a feasible plan of implementation, and the capability for influencing each of the subsystems of the organization toward changes as required for attaining the specified goals.

The problems of divided, diffused responsibilities have already been discussed as being major contributors to supervisory ineffectiveness and inefficiency. However, it is doubtful whether even more carefully structured supervisory staffs will be very effective. The problems go much deeper and rest with the requirements for change (Duncan, 1972) versus those for maintenance of ongoing operations.

Staff members organized to maintain the status quo must concentrate heavily on their survival as individuals and on justifying themselves as a group (Giacquinta, 1973, pp. 178–202; OECD, 1974, pp. 1–62; Argyris, 1982). Staff groups organized to change educational practices must work to eliminate the need for survival—they seek to put themselves out of business by solving the problem the group is uniquely capable of dealing with. Of course, if the staff group is incompetent and hence unsuccessful in solving its assigned problems, the chances of survival are much better (Lieberman, 1980)!

Supervisory staffs, bewildered by their inability to sustain truly dynamic programs for instructional change, have resorted quite naturally (if unwisely) to well-known defensive actions. They attack what they perceive as a barrier; they embrace those who resist; or they retreat to solitary, unobstrusive activities. All of these accommodations are comforting, but ineffective in promoting change. Attacking creates more resistance; and the other two approaches simply result in goal displacement. Then the supervisory staff is forced to create a fiction about itself as the champion of instructional change, and much energy is siphoned off into image building, and guilt feelings consume still more emotional energy.

Requirements of Change Agentry

If change efforts of supervisors are frustrated because goals are not explicit enough, *then* a staff should be organized around specific goals rather than around programs, schools, grade level, and subjects (Alioto and Jungheur, 1971).

a. If change efforts fail because lone individuals cannot command the full array of competencies needed to implement complex changes, *then* a team of supervisors representing a diversity of competencies should be formed (Kane, 1975, pp. 1–86).

b. If change efforts fail because power and influence are supporting the status quo, *then* influence and power potential must be systematically organized and staffed for as change efforts are planned (Weick, 1976).

c. If change efforts fail because individuals become frustrated by patterns of resistance to change, *then* team members must share these difficult responsibilities in order to provide support for each other.

d. If change efforts fail because the vast bulk of all available resources is rigidly allocated to the maintenance of operations, *then* resources must be reallocated and flexibility in their use guaranteed.

e. If change efforts fail because the total system is not *changed* in appropriate ways, *then* access to any and all parts of the system must be ensured.

f. If change efforts fail because plans are not adequately developed to clearly offer a superior alternative, *then* those responsible for change must have sophisticated planners at their disposal (Bailey, 1980, p. 193).

g. If change efforts fail because well-designed innovations are not rigorously implemented, *then* those responsible must have a staff of sufficient numbers and competence to ensure faithful implementation.

h. If change efforts fail because evaluative feedback is not available to guide corrective action, *then* those responsible must have carefully developed evaluation plans and staff available with evaluation competencies.

i. If change efforts fail because responsibility is diffused and authority to act not clearly delegated, *then* the change agents in charge must be few in number and clearly designated.

Amplified Project Team Approach

The arrangements for change efforts of the kinds being discussed are obviously *not* going to consist of individual supervisors supporting their individual programs. Just what a task group that can succeed will be like is unknown at this time. The general characteristics of such a group are clearly sketched, however, by the failures of the past and by the research, theory, and developmental know-how at our disposal:

1. A small group organized to assume full responsibility assures initiative. This type of organization for change has been used effectively in government and industry as well as in education (Ouchi, 1981).

2. The specified project guards against goal displacement or diversionary activities.

3. A group that will have a short clearly designated *life span*. A few weeks, months, or years at most can be designated for the life of such project groups to promote rigorous planning and efficient use of time. The short work life of the group can also eliminate much expenditure of energy in image building and other life-sustaining activities. Finally, such time limits can encourage risk taking rather than caution (Schwartz et al., 1976).

4. The project group will be *amplified* by *temporary* appointments of selected people with specifically needed competencies. The term *amplified* here refers to the need to modify the project group composition from time to time to ensure the full array of competencies needed for each phase of the project.

5. The amplified project team group (APT) will be *commissioned* by the highest-level authority for each specific project. Hence, there would be minimum confusion and uncertainty about the legitimacy of the activities (Duncan, 1972; Goodson and Hagstrom, 1971).

6. The project group will be amplified with high-prestige *influentials* from both within and outside the sponsoring organization (school system or other) to ensure access to such influence when needed. Influentials should be substantial in number and variety in high-risk projects.
7. The project group will be amplified with classroom teachers, administrators, and others primarily concerned with maintenance to ensure reality orientation and facilitate permanence of implementation.

Each of the characteristics listed in Table 6.4 is an essential element in the creation of supervisor staff groups that can assume responsibility for dynamic supervision of instruction. The logic of the proposal for the Amplified Project Team approach is supported by much of the best thought and practice. The advocates of the individual school and classroom clusters as the locus of leadership for change (Bishop, 1971; Goodlad, 1975) are not being realistic about change process in complex organizations. Thompson (1967) cautions that the lower the level in the bureaucracy, the more the concerns for immediate problems in defiance of planning. Mills (1967) supports this view of limitations imposed on administrators, forcing them to be reactive rather than proactive. A strong case is easily made for the notion that those who work with structure and those who work with function have difficulty communicating, let alone functioning in the same position (Kane, 1975). It appears that different principles govern traditional organizational work and ad hoc group work. These sometimes "theoretical" concerns are made dramatically real by a flood of studies on program innovations showing no significant differences because the programs did not exist (Babb, 1969; Duncan, 1972; Murphy, 1973; and Smith, 1968) or were not effectively implemented.

TABLE 6.4   Characteristics of Amplified Project Team and Requirements for Change

CHARACTERISTICS OF GROUP	SUPPORTING REASONS
Small group	(*i*) Responsibility must be clearly designated.
	(*a*) Diversity of competencies needed.
	(*c*) Support in the face of resistance needed.
Specified project	(*f*) Sophisticated planning lacking.
Limited life span	(*h*) Evaluative feedback missing.
	(*c*) Frustrations tend to be great.
Amplification of staff	(*f*) Sophisticated planning needed.
	(*a*) Diversity of competencies needed.
Commission at highest level	(*i*) Authority must be clearly delegated.
	(*d*) Resources insufficient and inflexible.
	(*e*) Access to all parts of the system needed.
Influential participants	(*b*) High resistance to change in status quo.
Operative participants	(*g*) Implementation with more rigor needed.

This and other evidence leads to rejection of plans for effecting change within traditional organizations, using traditional staffing patterns. Alternatives somewhat like the Amplified Project Team Approach have been tested in a few places (Goodson and Hagstrom, 1971, pp. 172–84). "Strategy teams" including consultants, psychologists, counselors, supervisors, area superintendents, and others have been attempted. The use of such a team for planning purposes avoids extremes of *both* centralization and decentralization. Coughlan and Zaltman (1972) proposed the "change team concept," which was not unlike earlier proposals. Argyris (1982) builds much of his theoretical work on improving organizational effectiveness on the need for "interventionists" on teams (p. 455).

Organizing the Team

How would the Amplified Project Team (APT) be organized? Several important steps should be included:

Specify the goals for which the project is being organized.
Appoint a core group to see the project through from start to finish.
Designate a target completion date.
Relieve the core group staff members from nearly all other *responsibilities.*
Communicate with all those likely to be affected by or interested in the project or its mission.

These steps are not substantially different from those so commonly taken to launch special projects in traditional settings. However, some significant and important differences should be made explicit. The designation of a *core group* to assume full responsibility is different from the usual practice of hiring a project director or a coordinator who may or may not be clearly responsible. Furthermore, regular members of the staff should be selected for the *core group* instead of hiring supplementary personnel, as is so often done. Still another difference involves selecting and releasing high-status staff members rather than selecting low-status persons or adding project responsibilities to those already carrying heavy job loads.

It is important to note the impact of the organizing procedures suggested for an APT on the image of the project and its core group. Every one of these moves by school officials gives evidence that the goals have high priority and that the APT has an officially sanctioned and supported mission with responsibility, authority, and resources properly delegated. When special projects are organized traditionally, each official organizing act implies lack of status for the project, its goals, and its staff. This low-level image is conveyed by making the project a subunit within the bureaucracy, by failing to select a top person within the staff to direct it, by failing to relieve assigned staff of other important duties, by keeping authority and responsibility for implementation indefinite, and by allocating only *extra* resources to the project—clearly signaling that if funds get scarce the project will be abandoned. All of these events doom many special projects to failure or limited success. "By your deeds we shall know you." By the actions taken to initiate an APT, the school community will know that change is the real intent.

Amplifying the Project Core Group

Amplification involves adding staff to the *core group* as different phases of the project are undertaken. A problem-solving sequence provides a useful framework for selecting personnel for amplification of the core group. The planning phase of the project demands competence in specifying goal-related objectives, selecting alternatives with strategic considerations in mind, and assigning priorities among objectives. However, a different aspect of planning requires *design* competencies as the activities are selected and sequenced. Allocating resources and coordinating project activities become critical concerns and require still other kinds of competencies as the project moves into implementation.

Table 6.5 presents a sequence of processes for instructional change. For each sequenced process, types of activities are suggested and the kinds of personnel who might supply necessary competencies are listed. These processes are listed in clusters, or phases—evaluating, planning, implementing, and operationalizing. Evaluating is distinguished from assessing by the focus of one on the status quo while the other focuses on the change itself. The sequence suggested is a bit misleading unless we keep in mind that these are ongoing processes that overlap considerably.

The personnel types suggested for each process need further consideration. In practice it is competence that should dictate each assignment to the Amplified Project Team. The *core group* would retain membership in the APT throughout all phases of the project as far as possible. Accordingly, supervisors in the core with strong competencies as designers of programs might make it unnecessary to amplify with this kind of person in the planning phase. Similarly, a principal assigned to an APT core group might have competencies needed in the implementing phase without further amplification.

The amplification procedure is one that will require careful planning, since arranging to involve the superintendent, principals, school board members, and community leaders in substantial ways at appropriate times will be difficult. Such involvement must be *real* and substantial, not purely advisory or superficial. Funds will be required for arranging *retreat-type* work sessions involving amplifying personnel to ensure capturing their attention, interest, and capabilities.

Obviously, another kind of amplification of the core group is required. The intermediate-term reassignment of personnel to the APT will often be necessary. Classroom teachers and principals may have to be given leave from their regular assignments for a week or even for months to provide needed

TABLE 6.5   A Process Sequence to Guide Amplification of a Project Core Group

PROCESS TERM AND DEFINITION	TYPES OF PERSONNEL
EVALUATING PHASE	
a. *Assessing:* The process of studying the status quo to obtain data for use in determining needs for change	Evaluators Statisticians Board members Superintendents Community leaders Visiting experts
PLANNING PHASE	
b. *Prioritizing:* The process of arranging goals, objectives, and activities in order of importance	Board members Superintendents Program directors Principals Visiting experts
c. *Designing:* The process of planning or outlining a system for effecting change	Visiting experts Design specialists Classroom teachers (creatives)
IMPLEMENTING PHASE	
d. *Allocating Resources:* The process of allotting and assigning resources for the most efficient use	Board members Superintendents Principals Community leaders Program directors
e. *Motivating:* The process of promoting acceptance of and interest in relevant personnel to accept change	Community leaders Principals Classroom teachers (influentials)
f. *Coordinating:* The process of relating people, time, materials, and facilities to a functional unit for accomplishing change	Principals Program directors
g. *Directing:* The process of influencing practices to conform with those essential and appropriate to accomplishing change	Principals Program directors
OPERATIONALIZING PHASE	
h. *Stabilizing:* The process of overcoming tendencies toward backsliding, corruption, retrogressing, and fluctuating away from the goals of change	Principals Superintendents Program directors Classroom teachers
i. *Renovating:* The process of eliminating dysfunctional or detrimental elements to the achievement of goals for change	Board members Superintendents Principals Program directors Classroom teachers
EVALUATING PHASE	
j. *Evaluating:* The process of obtaining data regarding the change to guide implementation processes toward goals	Evaluators Statisticians Visiting experts

competencies. Visiting consultants from colleges, service centers, or private firms may have to be attached to the APT for days, weeks, or months.

A third form of amplification must also be considered. Certain types of projects will require pilot operations within a school or in a cluster of schools. Under these conditions the entire staff of a school may become attached to the APT for designated purposes and time periods. Obviously, the implementing phase may require some of this kind of amplification. The operationalizing phase will necessarily depend heavily upon this form of amplification.

Dismantling the Project Team

The Amplified Project Team will, if structured properly and operated efficiently, exercise both power and influence for change in various segments of the school operation. The changes will not be restricted to one or two small parts of the total system because the changes sought will be such that many segments of the total system will need to be affected. This organization—the Amplified Project Team—must have power, influence, resources, and competence; but it must also have a funeral. Not a sudden death of failure or termination without cause, however!

The APT should develop plans for dismantling itself. The target date for completion of the project is clearly established in the beginning and may be changed in process, but only at the highest level of administrative decision making. The operationalizing phase is one in which increasing responsibility is transferred *from* the core group of supervisors *to* the superintendent, principals, program directors, and teachers who will be expected to maintain the change in operation. The core group turns its energies increasingly to the evaluating process as others assume the operationalizing responsibilities.

As the core group withdraws from much of the activity of the operationalizing phase and essentially becomes an evaluation group, plans for members' reassignment must be initiated. The important guidelines here are the following:

1. Core group staff members should know what their new assignments will be before the end of the project itself.
2. New assignments should not harm the staff member professionally or economically.
3. Core group staff members assigned to another APT should form a new *core group*. Under only rare conditions should a *core group* be maintained, intact, for a second project.

The dangers these guidelines seek to minimize have to do with making it desirable to be a member of a core APT without creating a new bureaucracy.

Other Staffing Considerations

Several basic assumptions underlie this entire proposal for using the Amplified Project Team Approach for instructional improvements: (1) that improvements in instruction involve changes that are more than superficial, (2) that such changes are going to face resistance, (3) that these changes will be in conflict with the needs of those responsible for the maintenance operations, (4) and that the changes must be led from outside rather than from inside the operating organization. Every characteristic of the APT approach is directly related to these realities. However, the maintenance of the ongoing operations of instruction are also important. "Anything that is organized emphasizes togetherness . . . and generally promotes conformity. Without conformity, any organization would fly apart. . . . [It] allows us to do things and believe things without continuously examining them (Smith, 1966, p. 38). These too are important ideas for staffing for supervision of instruction. Maintenance needs for supervision must be met while change-oriented needs are given new priorities.

The key to this seeming dilemma is to be found in differentiated staffing of a kind quite unlike that usually associated with team teaching. Differentiating staff for focus on maintenance versus change endeavors calls for *planned insulation, good coordination, and communication, but avoidance of integration.* The conflict between maintenance and change; the irresistible tendencies for routine to drive out creativity; for conformity to stifle diversity; for security to appeal over risk—all of these are too poweful. Supervisors must make a commitment to one or the other—maintenance or change in instruction—if a sense of effectiveness, efficiency, and peace of mind are to prevail in their lives. The same choices face administrators.

The reorganization of existing supervisory staffs will be required, of course, to implement the APT approach. For small school systems, the reorganization will not be too complicated. Supervisors should have a chance for reassignment as the new change orientation of the staff is made clear. Principals and their staffs must be made responsible for the quality of instructional programs as currently designed. Essential staff needs to support the school in maintaining the current levels of instruction or making limited improvements should be provided.

The other side of the coin involves reassigning, or recruiting and selecting, a supervisory staff group for *focus on change agentry.* This should be a relatively small group (2 percent of the staff). Group members' competencies should be diverse and directly related to appropriate tasks and to the several processes described in Table 6.5. The APT core group should be paid at least as well as other top officials within the system. They should be risk-taking, emotionally stable, personally secure individuals.

When not on an APT core assignment, supervisors should become part of a staff pool serving under the direction of the superintendent or his assistant. As members of such a pool, they might engage in needs assessment, take temporary assignment as amplified personnel, return to temporary teaching and administrative assignments, take professional growth leaves, or engage in maintenance supervision.

All of these assignments out of the superintendent's pool of supervisors must be carefully controlled to ensure the continuance of a topflight staff of supervisors for APT assignments as core group members.

The Project-Program Paradox

Projects tend to have a limited life span; programs tend to persist (almost into eternity). Projects are "special"; they are created for special purposes, they tend to be insulated and separated from the mainstream of operational events in the school or district. Projects have separate funding sources, separate organizations, even separate staffs.

The many virtues of project status sometimes mask the liabilities. Their lives are always precarious! Projects are special but also expendable. When funds are tight, they are the first to go. Being separate, project staffs and their contributions are often overlooked. The very special protections conferred upon a project make it peripheral to the ongoing programs of the educational system.

What is to be done? Well, it is obvious that the project must be converted. Either it has to (1) be absorbed (integrated) into ongoing programs or (2) become a full-fledged program of its own. Either conversion is full of problems. In fact, a real paradox may exist.

If a project is to be integrated into the mainstream of operations, its "special" characteristics must be abandoned. Special funding is lost, its unique visibility and status are lost; its staff is dismissed, reassigned, or assimilated. Why should those who have nurtured the project give it all up? Why should those who have their own interests in other programs want to absorb the project without funding or special status?

But another option exists—to convert a project into a program of its own with continuing funding. This course of action, even if financially feasible, often leads to conflict, for the project usually has its origin in addressing problems of other programs. If the project remains separate and becomes a permanent program, it is seen as a threat to those operating in related areas. A threat is posed if it operates to accomplish goals other programs cannot attain, but it is also a threat in absorbing scarce resources that might be allocated to other programs.

The dilemma seems hard to resolve. In practice, decisions tend to be delayed. Projects maintain their separate structures long after their goals are accomplished. In many cases they simply fade away and tend to be forgotten.

The Amplified Project Team approach is a worthy proposal for attempting a solution to this difficult set of realities.

SUMMARY

Organizing the staff for supervision has been widely neglected by researchers and administrators as well as by supervisors themselves. Perhaps it is quite natural that supervisors as a group so overwhelmingly involved with people—children and teachers—would find no time or energy left to think or plan for their own way of organizing. Such neglect has threatened the very survival of supervisory positions in education.

This chapter describes the current status of staffing for supervision of instruction. Criteria of uniqueness of supervisors as a professional specialty group are proposed as a basis for rethinking the kinds of supervisors needed and their numbers too! However, competent and dedicated people in supervisory positions cannot continue under the illusion that the large demands for change in instruction are going to be met by isolated individuals, each pursuing his own interests and problems. The proposal for a major change in supervisory strategy toward projects rather than programs, and toward teams rather than individuals, is developed in some detail as the Amplified Project Team approach. Whether it will work remains to be seen. However, there is some consensus among writers in the field of instructional supervision that the future will give rise to many new global problems with educational implications. Thus, novel supervisory approaches will be needed (Shane and Weaver, 1976).

Refer to the case report on the "Professional Development Center" (see Chapter 10) as an illustration of one slightly different approach to staffing change processes.

SUGGESTED READINGS

DULL, LLOYD W., *Supervision: School Leadership Handbook.* Columbus, Ohio: Charles E. Merrill, 1981.

This is a reference book on supervision. It details the tasks of supervisory personnel and the competencies they must possess in a background of theory and research. The book delineates team supervision, organizational principles, governmental roles, and leadership. The functions of supervision and resources that can be used to facilitate student learning are presented.

GIAQUINTA, JOSEPH B., "The Process of Organizational Change in Schools," in *Review of Research in Education*, ed. Fred Kerlinger. Itasca, Ill.: Peacock Publishers, 1973, pp. 178–207.

Change in any school's organization and the speed with which it occurs depend upon the nature of the innovation introduced, the tactics used to introduce it, the characteristics of the individual school members, and the properties of the school structure. This book presents a review of the literature and research concerning these factors, which are outlined around the themes of knowledge and commitment, with the underlying principle of participation.

MILSTEIN, MIKE M., ed., *Schools, Conflict, and Change.* New York: Teachers College, Columbia University, 1980.

This collection of papers focuses on the growth of conflict in schools and the processes of change necessary to combat problems. The elements of conflict and change are explored presenting new strategies which can address the fiscal, declining enrollment, and organizational forces. The writers review the specific linkages between micro- and macro-strategies for change.

OUCHI, WILLIAM G., *Theory Z: How American Business Can Meet the Japanese Challenge.* Reading, Mass.: Addison-Wesley, 1981.

Ouchi points out that the success of Japanese industrial organizations has been due to the development of social institutions around trust, subtlety, and intimacy, which has produced great productivity and coordination. The development of collective decision making with the technique of Quality Control Circles has placed the responsibility in the hands of the workers. He challenges American business to investigate these ideas as the development of Theory Z organizations becomes a reality in the future.

WEICK, K., "Educational Organization as Loosely Coupled Systems," *Administrative Science Quarterly, 12,* no. 1 (1976): 1–19.

Weick proposes that, contrary to prevailing notions of school organizations being structured through tight linkages, it may be more appropriate to conceive them as "loosely coupled systems," each preserving its own identity and physical or logical separateness. This relationship between loosely coupled noninterdependent organizational systems might be an important inhibitor of change in any part of the system.

CHAPTER SEVEN
OBSERVING
AND ANALYZING
INSTRUCTION*

Much that is done by supervisors involves observing and analyzing classroom practices in some way. Observations have gained a new popularity among supervisors, principals, and others as more reliable instruments and better procedures have been developed (Lamb and Swick, 1975).

The growing popularity of new observation instruments has also generated a greater variety of alternative ways of utilizing this distinctive type of activity for improving instruction. Observations need no longer be viewed as an inspection trip involving only the crudest of procedures, a single "rating scale" (Ingils, 1970), and the dreaded judgmental feedback.

Even though new instruments and new systems for using them have been abundantly developed, their spread into common practice has been slow. As a result, much teacher anxiety continues to be associated with the possibility of "being observed." Much of the literature concerns itself with alleviating anxiety rather than dealing with its causes.

Another outcome of new observation systems has been the inevitable faddism. Well-publicized instruments or procedures have gained rapid popularity while others have been neglected or ignored. In consequence, the many technological developments associated with classroom observations are

*Revised with the assistance of Danita Hall.

only now coming to be drawn upon as tools in strategic endeavors for improving instruction.

This chapter analyzes classroom observations as a basic kind of activity useful for a variety of purposes. An array of instruments is useful if properly selected and skillfully employed. Detailed guidelines on the use of various instruments are available in other sources (Simon and Boyer, 1970). This chapter is concerned with identifying various uses of observations, specifying systematic procedures generally required, reviewing a variety of instruments, and suggesting promising diagnostic and follow-up practices.

THE USES OF OBSERVATIONS

Any view of classroom observation practice must include an awareness of its limits as well as its promise. Observational activities are essentially ways of gathering evidence. When applied to the classroom, they are ways of gathering evidence regarding life in this teaching-learning space. The focus may be on things, students, or teachers, or combinations of these. When our purpose is to gather evidence on learning, the focus is logically on the learner. When our purpose is to gather evidence about teacher behavior, the focus is on the teacher. When our purpose is to gather evidence on the teaching-learning process or instruction, the focus must be on interactions among teacher(s), pupil(s), and things.

What other ways are there to gather evidence about instruction? Several are at our disposal and should at least be noted. The teacher self-report is a commonly used source of evidence (Jones and Hayes, 1980). In a sense it is derived from observation—self-observation. Another source of evidence on instruction is the pupil report. Pupils can and do function as classroom observers and can therefore provide evidence on instructional practice. Documents may also serve as evidence regarding instructional practices. Lesson plans and syllabi are perhaps the most readily available evidence of this kind.

Each of these sources of evidence regarding instruction has some usefulness in improving instruction. Pupil reports have the greatest similarity to systematic classroom observations and have the greatest potential as a supplementary source of evidence. Teacher self-reports, while less objective (Hardebeck, 1973), are nonetheless valuable sources of evidence when properly gathered. Documents are of very limited value except under very special conditions in which records are systematically maintained.

It is not necessary to elaborate on sources of information that, though commonly used, are of relatively little value in gathering objective evidence about instructional practices. Some of these include gossip in the teachers' lounge, parental opinion at the bridge table, and judgments by the principal based on walks through the halls or eavesdropping via the intercom system.

Of all the sources of evidence mentioned above, the most reliable and fully descriptive are based on direct observations. The more systematic and objective the observations, and the better trained the observer, the richer the array of evidence. Pupil reports gain value from the extensive contact pupils have with the instructional process, but the evidence suffers from lack of systematic procedures. The teacher self-report also gains from the teacher's extensive contact with the instructional process, but the evidence suffers from lack of observer objectivity (Hook and Rosenshine, 1979). Both of these sources suffer in providing reliable evidence because of lack of training in observational techniques (Newfield, 1980). The pupil and the teacher are so actively involved in the events being observed that observational activities tend to be haphazard rather than systematic.

For these reasons, formal systematic, objective, structured observations are regarded as essential to the best understanding of instructional practices (Stake, 1969). Such observations can be undertaken by a variety of trained educators—supervisors, principals, department heads, and teachers. Visiting consultants or accreditation team members are often such observers.

Getting to Know You

One of the specific uses to which systematic classroom observations are applied involves getting to know the teacher. It may be a principal, a supervisor, or a team leader who needs to know. The observer wants to identify strengths, weaknesses, unique procedures, teaching style, and so forth. The results of these observations are learnings for the observer, even though they may in turn affect the observed teacher at some later point in time.

These observations may provide the basis for a variety of staffing decisions. This information may assist in deciding on renewal of contracts, reassignments, promotions, rewards, and, of course, dismissals.

Much attention has been given to the negative aspects of observations utilized in these ways. Unfortunately, like good news, positive uses of observation data get little attention. A conscientious principal observes in every classroom, gathers observation data from other sources, and recommends every teacher for contract renewal—and no one says a word about the usefulness of the activity that supported these decisions. Let that same principal decide *not to renew* one contract in one hundred, and suddenly classroom observations are a menace to the faculty! It may be that the problem here is not in classroom observation practice at all but rather in a situation so full of secure complacency that any rare occurrence questioning the right of an individual to continue shines forth into the consciousness with the annoying sharpness of a streak of sunlight into a dark room.

A distinction must be made between the use of systematic observation techniques for these purposes and the use of traditional annual *rating rituals* generally used by school principals (Ingils, 1970). In the former, systematic procedures are followed to gather a variety of data, with analysis and interpretation processes of evaluation preceding any valuing or decision making. Rating scales in general use call for no such systematic procedures, no evidence is recorded, and therefore no explicit analytical and interpretive procedures are followed. These rating scales will be illustrated later in this chapter. They are generally simple instruments, vaguely suggesting patterns of behaviors or characteristics. Because they are rarely based on research or theory, the unreliable judgments recorded with them have little practical significance. Teachers naturally distrust these pseudo-observations.

Guiding Self-Analysis

A major approach to the use of classroom observation techniques emphasizes self-analysis (Harris and Hill, 1982; Hunter and Amidon, 1966; Newfield, 1980). With audiotape or videotape recordings, it is feasible for the classroom teacher to be his or her own analyst.

The role of the supervisor may become that of trainer as he or she assists teachers in developing analytical skills. Even when a live observer is employed rather than a mechanical device, the teacher may desirably assume major responsibility for self-analysis if properly trained for both analysis and interpretation of raw evidence gathered using one observation system or another (Irvine, 1983).

Some of the strongest advocates of self-analysis have been Borg (1968) and others associated with the Far West Laboratory for Educational Research and Development. Fuller (1969) employed self-analysis with beginning teachers, using 8-mm films, but follow-up interpretation conferences were also involved. Wilhelms (1973) expresses enthusiasm for any supervisory system that makes teachers the fullest possible partners. McGreal (1982) and Harris and Hill (1982) are among recent advocates of teacher self-evaluation programs.

The new and better observation tools now available provide encouragement that the shoddy efforts at teacher self-evaluation in the past need not be repeated. However, cautions should be expressed. Several different observation instruments may have to be used to provide the feedback teachers require, and learning to use such a variety of instruments may be too demanding. Furthermore, the need for interpretative interaction is very real if observational data are to be effective in stimulating change. In fact, computerization of the analyst's role may take much of that away from both teacher and supervisor in the near future, leaving interpretation, valuing, and decision making in the hands of the teacher. He or she might well need assistance in handling these evaluative processes.

Reciprocal Visitations

Intervisitations, along with teaching demonstrations, have long been favored by teachers as an in-service activity. Their effectiveness has generally been limited, however, by the lack of frequency and variety and by the observing teachers' inability to really observe and analyze events to make them useful in transfer. Training of teachers as observer-analysts provides the basis for making intervisitations and demonstrations more effective. The frequency and variety problems tend to remain, however.

Recent efforts at reciprocal observations of several kinds seem quite promising:

1. Joint teacher-supervisor-principal visitation teams have been utilized in Corpus Christi as an approach to comprehensive evaluation of a school. A team is drawn together from throughout the district and trained to observe in classrooms. Team members then spend several days on released time, observing in a designated school. They provide individual teachers with feedback before leaving, but a team leader brings a carefully developed report back to the faculty at a later date.
2. Team members in teaching team situations can develop observation and analysis skills to use on one another on a reciprocal basis. The very fact of a team situation provides at least some possibility of freeing one teacher for observation duty periodically.
3. A continuous plan for teacher observation and feedback was developed in Post, Texas, schools as part of a larger, more complex evaluation system. Substitute teachers, off-periods, teacher aides, parent volunteers, student teachers, and students were organized to relieve teachers for observation duty. The plan calls for every teacher to be trained as observer-analyst over a two-year period, with new observation instruments introduced into the system periodically. The goal is three to five observation-feedback cycles for each teacher each year.

Surveys and Studies

The survey or special study utilizes systematic classroom observations in ways that can be quite important. In-service education program plans based on a survey of classroom practices provide the basis for specifying training objectives more in line with urgent needs. Similarly, curriculum development projects could well be selected on the basis of a survey of current practices. Then, too, new curricula being implemented can be studied, using observational survey techniques to guide modifications. Personnel practices could readily be improved by using observational studies, not for contract renewal purposes, but for identifying staff weaknesses and strengths building by building and program by program, providing the basis for more selective recruitment, assignment, and reassignment of staff.

An illustration of this survey approach to classroom observations was provided in connection with a migrant education project. A team of observers was trained to use a comprehensive observation instrument. Observers included the principal, assistant principal, counselor, home visitor, curriculum coordinator, project director, and a visiting consultant. Over a two-week period, classrooms were observed throughout the project school. While individual teachers were given some feedback to satisfy their interest, the time devoted to this was minimized. Observation records were content analyzed and were combined by grade and subject areas to pinpoint program strengths and weaknesses.

Clinical Analyses

The clinical use of classroom observation holds great promise for improving teaching skills (Adams, 1970). Because it is highly personalized, it tends to be perceived as very relevant by the teacher, but for that same reason it is very time-consuming and hence expensive.

Cogan (1973) and Goldhammer and associates (1981) are but two of many who have developed rather elaborate clinical models. They tend to draw heavily upon microteaching methodology, simply using the reality of the classroom as the vehicle for learning rather than structuring a laboratory situation.

A clinical cycle might involve the following steps or phases (Reavis, 1978):

1. Planning cooperatively
2. Teaching realistically
3. Observing systematically
4. Analyzing
5. Providing for feedback
6. Interpreting cooperatively
7. Valuing
8. Decision making for improvement
9. Replanning cooperatively

This kind of close working relationship can frequently be productive. The logic of the sequence gives a clarity of purpose and responsibility to the teacher-supervisor relationship that is often lacking in other situations (Hunter, 1968).

Since the supervisor works closely with the individual teacher in a clinical setting, the teacher can learn to assume increasing responsibilities for each step in the cycle. As the teacher learns to analyze observational data objectively and to interpret them critically, the clinical approach can undergo a transition toward self-analysis.

A relationship of growing or continuing dependence upon the supervisor is a danger that needs to be carefully dealt with in these situations as in all clinical relationships. The excessive cost of this clinical use of observations is also a serious problem. Observations are costly even without extensive follow-up activities.

SYSTEMATIC PROCEDURES

We have been discussing uses of systematic classroom observations without really being explicit about what it means to observe and to be systematic. Both terms deserve attention.

Looking is not synonymous with *observing*. To be effective, observation activities should be systematic. They should therefore be active endeavors that include preliminary arrangements appropriate to the purpose, a guide developed and skillfully used, and follow-up analysis of data. Good observations for supervisory purposes are not casual affairs. They involve hard work and professional competence (Semmel, 1978).

An Active Procedure

Whatever the purpose for being in the classroom, mere looking and listening are not enough. The observer tends to see what he looks for, and he never sees everything. When the observer is quite sure about what is most important for him to see and hear, he can consciously focus attention on these specific events. However, there is usually too much to be observed. Some choices must be made. All that is important cannot be carefully attended to in any live classroom situation. These choices should be carefully and consciously made by the observer. The purposes for which the observation was scheduled should determine such choices as well as available instruments.

When an observation is not planned with a definite purpose, the observation focus is not clear and the observer is likely to try to see a bit of everything. In doing so, he observes nothing well! When an observer permits himself to observe without clearly identified items to attend to, his attention will drift with events. Those items of interest to the observer will be observed rather than those items that are most pertinent to the situation. The observer's interests and his biases will tend to make unconscious choices for him.

The mechanism whereby the observer consciously selects impressions from the total observed field of events is sometimes called *cognitive tuning*. The professional observer tunes in on the situation with conscious purpose.

Even with purposes clearly determined and with the observation planned for cognitive tuning in upon the most pertinent items, the observer must be active. His eyes and ears must constantly be focused on the teaching-learning situation. His mind must actively be screening that which he sees and hears in order to determine its pertinence. The observer must force his attention on the objective facts being observed and must actively refrain from making judgments. He must keep his eyes and ears moving from one part of the observation field to another, being certain to obtain coverage of all that is pertinent while not allowing some unanticipated event to escape notice.

In addition to all this active looking, listening, and analyzing, the skilled observer must make some kind of a written record for future reference. Despite the need to exercise some precautions in making notes while observing classroom teaching, it is desirable and even essential to do so.

The biases of the observer as well as those built into the instrument itself are not to be ignored or denied. Those who criticize teacher evaluation efforts based heavily upon classroom observations (Ingils, 1970) lose much of their argument when instruments are used that require descriptive evidence to be recorded instead of value judgments. Nonetheless, the best instruments have been structured with some categories of evidence included and others excluded (Johnson et al., 1980). Similarly, each observer views the world of the classroom through a screen of past experiences, preferences, and prejudices that are going to influence the evidence observed and therefore the recording, analyzing, and interpreting processes as well (Capie et al., 1978). There are at least two important differences between systematic observations and subjective watching:

1. The use of a pretested instrument to guide the trained observer, thus making biases explicit, and regularizing their use in the evaluation process.
2. The commitment to gathering and analyzing evidence while withholding one's interpretations and values until later, thus minimizing the effect of personal bias.

Systematic procedures for classroom observations involve selecting or developing an appropriate instrument to guide the observing and recording processes (Furst and Hill, 1971). They also involve being well trained in the specific techniques demanded by any given instrument. Instruments should *not* be used "for real" until they have been thoroughly tested in similar situations. Observers should not trust themselves to make actual use of any instrument until they have checked themselves for interobserver reliability and observer consistency (Capie et al., 1978).

Preobservation Preparations

Making arrangements to observe in the classroom of a given teacher may entail almost no preliminaries, or it may necessitate elaborate plans and clearance procedures. The persons involved, the purpose, and past relationships—all need to be considered.

In general, the arrangements for a classroom observation include the following:

1. Identifying a purpose
2. Getting that purpose accepted by others involved
3. Setting the time
4. Selecting an instrument

5. Reviewing observation procedures
6. Reassuring the teacher
7. Deciding upon follow-up activities

The observer should know his purpose for observing. The purpose should be known and accepted, if at all possible, by the teacher and students and any others involved, such as the principal or even the parents. The time should be set as precisely as is needed to ensure the accomplishment of the purpose. The teacher should know what observation procedures are to be employed so they do not come as a surprise. The teacher should be reassured about consequences so that any fears may be allayed.

Establishing purpose.   When observational data are to be used for getting acquainted or for survey purposes, the teacher and others are not likely to be much concerned with either the procedures or the results. However, observations to facilitate self-analysis must be carefully and cooperatively planned so that the teacher gets the kind of evidence needed to serve his or her needs well. Clinical purposes, on the other hand, require considerable cooperation in identifying purposes and setting of time, but the selection of instruments and planning procedures can largely be left to the observers.

Helping the teacher get ready.   In agreeing on a lesson and a time to be observed, the teacher should be encouraged to proceed as naturally as possible. Designating the time for an observation a day or two in advance allows the teacher an opportunity to do a bit of special planning. Too much advance notification may cause some teachers undue strain and worry. Encouragement and assistance in helping the teacher to overplan the lesson is appropriate. This gives assurance that "things will go well." However, teachers need to be cautioned against presenting a "canned" review or a rehearsed lesson. These are rarely "good" because spontaneity is lacking in both teacher and students. Furthermore, the skilled observer can readily detect the artificialities. As far as possible, prearrangements with the teacher should be planned so that the observer will view one of the better samples of the kind of instruction that is characteristic of normal activity in that particular classroom. The teacher is urged to show the best that she can do; the observer is challenged to accurately gather the evidence presented so that analyses and interpretations will reflect both strengths and needs for improvement.

The emphasis given to making arrangements with the teacher will, of course, vary with the situation (Evertson, 1981). In general, the more threatening the observation is likely to be, the more carefully the arrangements should be made in order to reduce this threat and to maintain normalcy. The more precise and specific the purposes of the observation, the more carefully the arrangements should be made to ensure the accomplishment of those purposes. Above all, perhaps, arrangements should be such that they will avoid creating serious abnormalities in the teaching-learning situation.

Guides required.   All observations should be guided by a specified list of criteria or items to be observed. The items may represent behaviors or conditions. They are selected in terms of the purpose of the observation and should be in a form that facilitates observing, accommodates evidence recording, and is conducive to analysis and interpretation.

When ratings are to follow observations, the guide will specify the descriptive criteria on which ratings will be based. When the purpose is the exploration of a variety of practices, the guide may be a checklist of practices. When the observer is interested in pupil-teacher interaction, a guide that permits the tabulation of specified varieties of interaction may be employed. Purposes involving attempts to analyze the pattern of teaching in progress will employ more complex guides for describing certain events or for tabulating the frequency of various categories of teacher behavior.

Teaching and learning are extremely complex clusters of processes. No observation guide will suffice to do justice to all of these fascinating events, of course, but the use of a variety of guides for a variety of purposes helps to give direction and objectivity to the use of observations as supervisory activity (Good and Brophy, 1978).

The temptation to create "our own instrument" should be resisted until other carefully developed and tested instruments have been fully utilized. No instrument will be entirely satisfactory to a particular unique situation or group of people. However, instrument development is a demanding, technically difficult task. It requires not only special expertise but also long hours of field testing and revising. Local supervisors can and should learn to develop their own instruments, but only with proper appreciation for the complexity of the task after carefully considering available alternatives. Frequently, supervisors who are initially unimpressed with an available instrument find it surprisingly helpful after learning to use it skillfully. At that point, minor revisions often suffice to make an instrument better serve local needs.

Training.   Observing is a complex professional skill. Good observers are trained, not born. They are trained to be active, to be systematic, to control biases, to define purposes, and to use specific techniques. Observer training assumes a certain basic familiarity with teaching, children, subject matter, and their relationships. To expect to make a trained observer out of one who is ignorant of the discipline of education is simply to be unrealistic. But, conversely, knowing about teaching, learning, and subject matter does not of itself produce a professional observer (Semmel, 1978).

There are various training techniques. Two or three observers viewing the same teacher simultaneously can provide opportunities for comparing recordings and relating them to observed events. Discussion among teachers and observers following a class session—to analyze the events as seen by various individuals—is indispensable. Using a given guide in a wide variety of situations is most effective in helping the observer see the full range of events to be observed. Many available instruments include observer manuals, which provide instruments on specific procedures (Flanders, 1970; Harris and Hill, 1982; Lynch and Ames, 1972); these manuals should be studied carefully by those planning to use such instruments to avoid long hours of training by trial and error. Pretraining activities that involve programmed exercises, typescripts, films, or videotapes (Hiatt and Keesling, 1979), and sound recordings are all helpful and economical ways of acquainting observers with an instrument and the skills required for its operation. Such training activities must always be regarded as preliminary, however. Observation practice in actual classroom situations is essential for ensuring that observers can use the instrument under the influence of a full range of conditions.

Training is essential to effective observation, not only because it increases the ability to see and perceive but also because it promotes consistency and reliability. The studies of Cornell and others (1952) more recently (Marshall, 1977; Evertson and Veldman, 1981; Capie et al., 1978) indicate the need for repeated observations of a given situation before two observers can report reliable findings. Similarly, an observer must have repeated experiences with a given observation guide before he can expect it to serve him with consistency. When the situation requires measures of great precision, as in research studies, high levels of interobserver reliability are important. Similarly, major decisions should be based on the most reliable data available. Routine observations are not nearly so demanding, but precision should nevertheless be encouraged to the greatest extent possible.

Complex instruments may require 20–30 hours of carefully planned training activities to obtain high interobserver reliability measures. Simple instruments require much less, but rarely less than 10 hours of training. Poorly designed instruments cannot be used with reliability because they do not adequately guide the observing-recording activities. Most rating scales calling for judgments or descriptions of broad classes of behavior are not reliable without sufficient training.

In-Classroom Practices

Each instrument will be structured to demand special observing activities within the classroom. Certain generally applicable procedures need to be considered, however, along with the specific demands of a selected instrument. For instance, Flanders's (1970) interaction analysis system calls for the observer to record entirely verbal behavior. Accordingly, it is important that the observer be able to hear both teacher and pupils. This may require that the observer move from place to place in the classroom as the teacher moves to work with various individuals or student groups. Generally, such movement by the observer is discouraged—it may even be highly undesirable under crowded or highly teacher-controlled room conditions, and it may be quite unnecessary with nonverbal instrumentation.

On entering the classroom.   The observer should take a seat in a place that provides good opportunities for seeing and hearing without being too much in view. A side location is often preferred to either one in the rear or one in the front of the room. If possible, the observer should arrive during a natural break in the class activities. Intensive preoccupation by the observer with the instrument during the initial minutes of the observation period will help encourage both teacher and students to ignore the "intruder." The observer can use this time to review the instrument, record routine kinds of information, and become familiar with the physical surroundings of the classroom.

Engaging in conversations with pupils or teachers creates a special problem for the observer. Such conversations disrupt the normal flow of events that the observer wishes to study. Such conversations also prevent the observer from systematically observing and recording. Students will normally leave the observer alone if he or she does not interact with the student when first approached. It seems a bit rude, but the professional must be safeguarded. A simple response to an approach usually suffices to convey the message that the observer is busy and cannot converse. If a child asks, "Whatcha doing, mister?" the observer can respond, "Writing." Such a simple answer hardly encourages further interaction. If new approaches are made, the observer may have to be explicit and say with a smile, "I know you have things to do, and I'm very busy. I can't talk with you now."

Teachers who want to talk about their teaching and their students instead of being observed at work are a special problem. Such teachers may be anxious for fear that the observer will not understand. A teacher may not realize the importance of the observer's concentrating on recording evidence. Most of these problems can be prevented by careful preplanning with the teacher. However, sometimes these preplanning precautions do not work. The observer may have to be very firm in asking to be undisturbed. Comments like the following have been used successfully:

> "Don't let me take you away from your lesson. We can talk about these things later."
> "I need to observe what's happening over there. Excuse me."
> "Excuse me! I need to complete my work with the instrument."
> "You just go ahead with your lesson as usual. I'll be busy recording and will try not to interfere."

Instrument inappropriateness can be a frustrating problem for the observer. When cooperative planning has preceded the observation, the appropriate instrument is readily selected. There are times when the selected instrument turns out to be inappropriate, however. If the lesson plan has been changed for some reason, if an emergency develops, or if an unsuitable lesson has been selected for whatever reason, the observer needs to decide on a different course of action. Several alternatives are available. (1) Another instrument may be brought into play if readily at hand. (2) The observer may excuse himself and pursue other activities. (3) The observer may change roles from observer to helping teacher. The first alternative is often the most desirable, since it serves the expectations of both observer and teacher. However, emergencies often suggest the selection of the second alternative.

Supervisors need to be quite cautious about the third alternative. A helping teacher role has value, but the supervisor's time is generally too scarce (and too expensive) to be used for tasks that an aide, an inexperienced teacher, or a student might assume. Of course, the supervisor does often work as an assistant to the teacher when new materials or procedures are being tested. These activities ordinarily need careful planning to be effective, however.

On rare occasions, *teacher abdication* is a problem for the observer. A teacher may wish to abdicate responsibilities for teaching while the observer is present. This takes a variety of forms. The teacher may greet the supervisor this way:

> "Children, we have our supervisor visiting us today. Let's all tell him about our work."

Whereupon the teacher moves to the back of the room, leaving the supervisor to face the children and listen to their stories. Abdication takes the form of a request for a demonstration, too. "Mr(s). _____, I'd like to have you show us how you teach . . ." Another form of the problem is more subtle—the teacher simply gets the supervisor engaged in the discussion.

In the most unusual situation I have encountered, a supervisor reported having had the teacher turn the class over to her on arrival as the teacher announced that she was going to take a break. This drastic circumstance calls for drastic actions by the supervisor. I suggested she beat the teacher to the door with these words: "Good! I need a break too. I'll go with you."

Most of these problems can be handled more normally. The supervisor needs to make clear his or her role as an observer. If this has somehow not been communicated prior to the observer's arrival in the classroom, then it should be explained promptly and firmly, but softly. Responses that have worked with teachers seeking to abdicate include the following:

> "No, thank you. I'm here to observe only. Just ignore me as best you can."
> "I'm sure the lesson you've planned is too important for me to interrupt."
> "I'll have a chance to talk with the students later, perhaps at lunchtime. You just go right ahead with the activities you've planned."

Difficulties in seeing or hearing may face the observer. During the class period, the observer is guided by the instrument design, the physical surroundings, and the flow of events. A group of students may move to a corner of the room and be out of sight. If the instrument requires seeing all students, then the observer must consider moving. A display across the room may be difficult to see in sufficient detail to permit an objective recording, and movement by the observer is called for. Students may be working at tasks that are not clearly understood by the observer without walking up to a student and watching him or her at work. Movements about the room should be carefully timed and cautiously initiated. Interrupting or distracting from classroom events should be avoided. However, classrooms where students have freedom of movement do not pose any problem to the observer, for the latter too can move about without adding or subtracting from the normal flow of events. On the other hand, highly structured, static learning environments are distracted by observer movements, which should be minimized. Fortunately, little is lost in accuracy or fullness of record in these latter classrooms because they tend also to have only a limited array of events to record and the rate of change of events is slower and more predictable. All these conditions facilitate precise observing and recording.

The length of the observation period is normally dictated by the character of the instrument. A more complex instrument requires more time than one having only a few simple categories. Extremely short observation periods of 10 minutes have been reported when survey uses were being made of the data. Ordinarily, a 30-minute observation is minimal, 40 minutes is highly desirable, and a full class period has many advantages. Entering and leaving the classroom during natural breaks reduces the chances of disruption and gives the observer an opportunity to see events that do not often occur at other times. The observer can use preclass time to good advantage to get acquainted with the room, find a good place to sit, and review the instrument. This argues for entering the room during a break, even if the departure must be in the middle of a lesson.

Teachers are often uncomfortable with the idea that the observer is seeing only a fragment of a larger sequence of events. They express fear of having their work misinterpreted. The observer too must be aware that he is sampling a larger body of events and must withhold judgment for just that reason, among others. Obviously, an adequate sample is not provided by a single observation to interpret, let alone judge, teacher performance in any conclusive or universal sense. A single observation can be interpreted with confidence, however, regarding what the character of the instructional program was during that time frame! A single observation can also be used to cautiously raise questions regarding the larger pattern of events.

In approaching the question "What is an adequate number of observations?" the observer and the teacher alike must consider the way the evidence will be used. To provide the teacher with a "mirror of behavior" (Simon and Boyer, 1970), a single observation by a skilled observer can serve quite well. To provide a basis for an exploratory conference on teacher concerns and needs, a single observation is excellent. To provide a bit of evidence to add to many others in surveying a program, the single observation is quite useful. Obviously, clinical and self-analysis uses of observations require an array of observations.

Postobservation Activities

Observations, to have any value, require some kind of follow-up activities. The purpose of the observation will determine the follow-up activities that are most useful. In general, follow-up activity involves some kind of re-recording of data, analysis, a plan for feedback to the teacher, and other appropriate activities growing out of the observation.

Completing the recording of observational data immediately after leaving the classroom is important. Impressions are quickly lost or distorted by intervening experiences and time. Time and solitude should be allotted for recording from memory in considerable detail. When the observation includes in-class recording, additional time will be required for completing the record, filling in details, and clarifying meanings (DeRoche, 1981). Even an observation record that is purely a tabulation sheet should be accompanied by a descriptive record of the situation, which can help with the interpretation of tabulations.

The schedule for the observation should include both preobservation and postobservation plans as well as the actual in-classroom observation. The purposes to be served will dictate some of the events that must follow; the instrument itself will dictate others. Certain follow-up activities should be included in an observation schedule:

1. Postobservational recording and rerecording
2. Analyzing recorded data for better communications to teacher and others
3. Gathering supplementary data related to the classroom situation
4. Using feedback to inform the teacher and others
5. Interpreting, valuing, and decision making
6. Planning for improvement

These six types of activities may or may not be appropriate after every observation. They are each an essential part of making optimum use of observations. Under certain circumstances the teacher might be able to assume major responsibility for each follow-up activity. In other instances only postobservational recording and analysis would need to be completed by the supervisor. Still other teachers might need to be guided through each of these activities. Obviously, the teacher's involvement in all such follow-up activities is highly desirable.

Supplementary information to be used in interpreting, valuing, and decision making is often ignored. Observers are so preoccupied with the evidence they have gathered that they overlook much evidence that is quite relevant (Lamb and Thomas, 1981). Obviously, the most important source of other information is the teacher. He or she knows what happened before, what is planned to follow, and so forth. These are things the observer can rarely know. Lesson plans are a valuable source of supplementary evidence. The teacher's personnel file includes information that may be useful to the supervisor in interpreting or valuing data from observations. Prior observation reports may be more valuable than the current one if a series has already been completed.

Informal Visiting

The position this author has taken on the importance of systematic observation of classroom instruction does not preclude the use of informal visits. The word *observation* is reserved intentionally to refer to planned, purposeful, instrumented, data-gathering activities. However, supervisors and principals have many good reasons for more casual visits to classrooms.

Casual classroom visits that are brief, unannounced, and not structured as observations can be used to get a bit of information, give a message, demonstrate interest in what's going on, keep an eye on a kid, or just to remind the staff that you are still around. Lengthy visits to classrooms hardly seems justifiable for such casual and limited purposes. Ordinarily, these brief visits take only a minute or two to complete. I know one elementary school principal who has a habit of getting to every classroom for a moment once each day.

Prolonged classroom visits that are still not observations are commonly used for both supervisory and special service purposes. Personalized supervision activities often call for the supervisor or principal to demonstrate techniques or to coteach while some new approach is being tried. In such instances the supervisory person is not an observer-analyst. Special service personnel often need to visit classrooms to watch students at work, to gain background on the classroom, lessons, and problems that individual students are experiencing. While such efforts to learn more about students as they function in the classroom setting could become formal observing, it often is quite informal. In any case, it represents something quite different from systematic classroom observation as discussed in this chapter.

A major source of confusion, anxiety, and conflict among principals, supervisors, and teachers is lack of certainty about formal observations and informal visits. Every effort should be made to clearly differentiate one from the other.

Myths, Misconceptions, and Issues

Many views of classroom observation are distorted by myths and misconceptions. These myths and misconceptions continue to be the basis for a series of debates that might be more productive if better informed. Several myths have been referred to previously, but considering them directly may contribute to clarity of understanding.

Some misconceptions relate to the value of observing classrooms in the first place. Others represent concerns about problems believed to be caused by observations. Other misconceptions concern methodology or anticipated outcomes. Nine of these are briefly analyzed below.

1. Teachers just won't accept observations.   Based on long years of malpractice, many, perhaps most, teachers have never been observed in a professionally competent or systematic way. Hence, their fears and concerns are over an unknown process. Experience with thousands of teachers over the past 30 years, using systematic procedures, indicates that teachers, while often a bit anxious at first, do come to accept observations as at least tolerable. Many teachers become quite enthusiastic about the value of observational feedback. Almost unanimous preferences are expressed for systematic observation instead of judgmental rating.

2. Only pupil achievement can tell the story of teacher effectiveness.   The implications here are that teachers can get results almost any way and who cares how they get them so long as kids are learning. The fallacies in this view are abundant. First, it would be nice if we could wait and see, but unfortunately once we find a teacher to be ineffective the damage has been done. Second, the problem of tracing the resulting learning to a particular teacher or even to the school are insurmountable at this point in the development of evaluation technology. Third, the notion that teachers getting good results do not need and do not want a chance to improve their practices is hardly defensible. Fourth, a danger in looking only or even primarily at results rather than practices is the fact that when problems do surface, the supervisor must start from "scratch" at that late point in time to begin uncovering causes and taking remedial steps.

3. Observers disrupt and never see a really "normal" situation.   This criticism is widely expressed as a way of saying either "it's not worth doing" or "the results are suspect." Unfortunately, few studies are available to guide our thinking about this. Those that do exist are reassuring, however. Some evidence indicates that any observer's influence on the situation is largely limited to the first few minutes and to rather extreme events. The stability of patterns of teacher behavior under repeated observations is substantial (Evertson and Veldman, 1981), suggesting that observations must be very consistent in the way they distort normal events, if in fact they do.

Pupil reports often confirm observation reports as much or more than teacher reports do. Basic patterns revealed in teacher self-reports are often very similar to observed patterns (Harris and Hill, 1982; Hardebeck, 1973).

4. *Recording while observing in the classroom is disruptive.*   This is one of the most persistent myths. It has no foundation in fact as far as can be determined. The problem is one of teacher anxiety. The cause is not recording or writing in the classroom, but rather the teacher's uncertainty about the nature of the record and its potential uses. When the teacher knows the instrument, knows what the observational data look like, and has had positive experiences with observers, this problem disappears.

5. *Teachers put on a performance that is unreal unless you observe unannounced.*   This is a persistent concern that indicates lack of faith both in the teacher and in the observer. In fact, logic dispels this myth in part with the simple realization that the teacher cannot possibly "perform" acts for which he or she has no competence. Lack of faith in teachers is exemplified in this myth not only by the concern for "faking" but also by the inference that they are constantly doing less well than they know how! Even if we were to accept the notion that teachers perform well only when observers are around, that would be a strong argument for more observations. Furthermore, acceptance of this assumption of laziness would not argue for surprise observations, but rather for rigorous observation procedures which would set expectations for "performances" beyond levels of current practice.

6. *You do not need all these fancy procedures.*   "I can tell who's a good teacher by just walking down the hall." This reflects such a crude and outmoded concept of teaching that it hardly deserves discussion. It may be sufficient to say that those who still believe that good teaching can be equated or even approximated by using such simple evidences as noise level in the room, neatness of bulletin boards, or conformity with rules and regulations need some help that is more basic than the information in this book.

7. *Just focus on the pupils rather than on the teacher.*   This issue is rarely debated but is commonly raised by supervisor practices. When ostensibly observing, the supervisor concentrates on pupil behaviors, content, and materials, almost ignoring the teacher. This is comforting to both the teacher and the supervisor. The feedback has to focus on the pupil or on materials of instruction as long as all evidence is on these objects rather than on teacher behavior. Unfortunately, it denies the central importance of the teacher in the teaching-learning process. There is no evidence to indicate the teacher's position is a neutral one; it may be positive or it may be negative, but the importance of the teacher, actually and potentially, is hard to deny.

8. Just use a tape recorder.   The fascinating development of electromechanical aids has fostered the misconception that a tape recorder or a videotape recorder or a motion picture camera can observe instruction. Actually, none of these are observation devices. They are recording instruments but have few of the capabilities of a trained observer. They are confronted by the same problem that confronts the live observer, namely, too much to see and record. Unlike the human observer, the camera has no memory. If an event is not in focus when it occurs, it is simply not recorded. The camera operator is in fact a full partner with the camera in securing video or photographic observation records. An untrained technician leaves much to be desired for these reasons. As useful as electromechanical recording devices are as tools for observation and analysis of instruction, they neither replace the professional observer nor do they do many things as well. The human eyes and ears in cooperation with the central nervous system remain the most flexible and comprehensive system for observing classroom events.

9. Just let them view themselves and they will change.   This represents the overly enthusiastic response of those who are impressed by teachers' acceptance of observational feedback. There is reason to believe that awareness is an important step in the process of change. Feedback often provides this awareness. Changes in attitude, understanding, and skill may still have to be generated by follow-up activities (Perrott, 1976; Mills, 1980).

TYPES OF INSTRUMENTS

The preceding ideas about classroom observation have been presented on the assumption that an *observation guide* of some structured kind will be employed (McGreal, 1982). There are many sources of detailed information on some of the better-known observation systems. At least two listings (Simon and Boyer, 1970); Borich and Madden, 1977) of many instruments are available. This chapter will not try to either list or analyze a large number of instruments. Instead, the various types of observation instruments will be reviewed, and some of their unique strengths and weaknesses will be identified.

There are at least four essentially different observation instrument types: a free response, frequency tabulation, checklist, and rating. Some instruments are combinations of these types. The *free-response* instruments are sometimes referred to as *descriptive* or *narrative* types. They are structured with categories of events clearly designated. The observer describes the specific evidence as it relates to any category. The *frequency tabulation* instruments are structured for recording the frequency of occurrence or for counting the number of units of a particular category of event. The *checklist* has designated categories of events but asks only for a simple indication of its presence or absence. Although, in a sense, this is not a unique type of instrument, it is unique in that it supplies a large array of categories to be observed. *Rating* scales provide defined categories of events as do all the others, but they give *quantitative* or *qualitative* estimates of events rather than descriptions or frequencies.

Rating Scales

Since rating scales are generally best known and often of poorest quality, they are worthy of initial consideration. Any observation instrument must provide evidence for analysis and interpretation. Accordingly, a rating scale must clearly define sets of observable events. The *Individualization of Instruction Inventory* by Coody and Harris (1971; Harris et al., 1979, pp. 296–97) illustrates this type of instrument with descriptive scales, such as the following:

Item j: There is freedom of movement within the classroom.

5	4	3	2	1
Pupils are permitted to change work stations as needs arise.		Teacher suggests or approves all changes that are made in work stations.		Pupils remain at work stations for nearly all activities.

The observer circles the one number over the statement that most closely conforms to the events observed. In doing this, the observer is *not* making a value judgment. On the contrary, the number is simply a code designating the estimated extent to which these "freedom of movement" events were observed. Similar instrumentation has been used by Ryans in the *Teacher Characteristics Schedule* (1960).

Instruments that look much like the scale example shown above have deficiencies that are critical. Typical teacher evaluation scales look something like this:

	RATINGS			
	POOR			OUTSTANDING
1. Personal appearance	1	2	3	4	5
2. Room appearance	1	2	3	4	5
3. Daily preparation	1	2	3	4	5
4. Knowledge of subject	1	2	3	4	5

This is a rating instrument, but notice that (1) the events being rated are not clearly specified, and (2) the ratings do not designate different amounts of the events. Which events are being estimated under personal appearance is not clear. In fact, some items do not really refer to clearly observable events (knowledge). How much of what kind of daily preparation does it take to make a rating of 5 or 3 or 1? This type of instrument is virtually useless to the observer and the teacher alike. The ratings are often highly unreliable, and the numbers are uninterpretable to the teacher and everyone else (except, possibly, the observer).

There have been many efforts to try to improve on rating scales. Items in one instrument were carefully defined in observable terms, as shown in the following example:

0 1 2 3 4   32. Teacher seeks and uses the advice and assistance of "specialists" to supplement his own teaching.
Teacher grows in meeting needs of pupils.
Sample Evidence:
Confers with school nurse, attendance officer and guidance counsellor. Students with physical defects given attention such as:____.

In using this instrument, the observer is told to give a rating of 4 when the "practice or condition involves all, or nearly all, pupils and is consistent." Similarly, the rating of 1 is defined as "practice or condition is present but inconsistent, reaches few pupils." A zero stands for "no opportunity to observe."

The defects in this instrument are quite obvious. While the character of the events is fairly clearly defined for each category, the relationship between these events and the numbers on the scale is not made clear. Furthermore, the author has so many kinds of events in a single category that a rating cannot reflect any specific event with clarity.

Where many designers of rating scales make their mistake is in trying to simplify the evaluation of the teaching process. The search for the pot of gold at the end of the rainbow is a search for a nice simple one-page instrument that can be prepared in a few minutes. Such a magic instrument is not to be found. Rating instruments can be reliable and useful only if they clearly describe specific classroom events and provide numerical values for differentiating observable events on a continuum of quantity or quality. Such instruments must provide a single scale for each category of events and must clearly specify the character of the events that should be assigned each numerical value (Capie et al., 1978).

Some rating scales do an excellent job of clearly specifying the events to be observed but fail to employ a suitable scale of estimation of those events. One instrument used by the U.S. Air Force exemplifies this problem:

C. Introduction:
1. Did the instructor state the lesson objective clearly?

On this instrument, space is provided for answering the question *yes* or *no*, but a value judgment is also called for as follows: "Superior (S); Excellent (E);

Good (G); Fair (F); Weak (W) . . ." Aside from the confusing use of letters, which complicates quantification of the data, this is a truly meaningless set of designations. If the teacher did *not* state the lesson objective, there is no point in giving it a value judgment, assuming it is desirable to do so. If the teacher *did* state the objective, what do the valuing symbols mean? *How* does one have to state an objective to be "superior"? Is there some forbidden way to state an objective that warrants a "weak" designation?

The item above has all the descriptive power needed, perhaps, when one of two designations is selected. A *yes* or a *no* tells a fairly clear story about what did or did not happen when such an explicit event is described. If more careful gradations estimating the quality of the event were desired, they could be provided by a rating scale such as the following:

C.   Introduction:
    1.   Did the instructor state the lesson objective clearly?

Did not state the objective.	Hardly. Only implied the character of the objective.	Somewhat. Stated the objective, but not very clearly.	Yes. Stated the objective very clearly.
1	2	3	4

Notice the special utility added to this scale when designed this way. Now a number (1, 2, 3, or 4) not only describes events more precisely than before but makes them less value-loaded. A 2 may well be a *more* desirable event under certain conditions from some points of view. At least there are not the explicit values assigned to these numbers that are implied in words like "superior" and "weak."

Rating scales look deceptively simple. They are, but only when poorly designed. The observer should be cautious in selecting any rating instrument to use as an observation guide and even more cautious in constructing an original one. Any rating scale must be extremely explicit about the observable events being rated. Each narrowly defined category of events must have a separate scale. Each of several points on the scale must be specified as a clearly differentiated subclass of events within the category. Finally, each point described on the scale must logically be on a quantitative continuum.

These conditions for good scale construction are not easy to attain. Even well-designed scales of this types are difficult to use with reliability. Rating instruments, poorly conceived and badly utilized, provide much of the basis for general criticisms of classroom observations by Dunkerton (1981), Eisner (1977), and many others.

Frequency Tabulations and Checklists

Frequency tabulations and checklists come in a variety of forms and are basically much alike. These two types of instruments define a set of categories as observable events. The frequency, sequence, or quantity of the event is then designed in some systematic way.

The *Flanders system of interaction analysis* (1970) is one of the rather simple and very popular observation instruments of the frequency tabulation type. Each of the 10 Flanders categories applies to a defined cluster of events. All events in this system are verbal, and they are sharply specified for the teacher and give little attention to pupil behavior. Each category of events has a distinguishing number:

Teacher

1. Accepts pupil's feelings
2. Praises or encourages
3. Accepts pupil's ideas
4. Asks questions
5. Lectures
6. Gives directions
7. Criticizes or justifies authority

Pupil

8. Responds to teacher
9. Initiates response
10. Silence or confusion

Useful as this category system has been, some of its weaknesses are apparent even to the casual observer. Categories like number 4, "Asks questions," include a great variety of question-asking events. Category number 10, "Silence or confusion," is obviously a catchall category that is hardly useful at all for this very reason. Even with these weaknesses, however, careful, consistent, systematic use of these categories by a trained observer does offer a helpful way of describing verbal interaction in the classroom.

In using Flanders's categories, the instrument used in the classroom is a ruled tablet on which the observer records a category number for every distinctly different event. He also indicates the duration of these events by repeating a category number every three seconds. The record looks like the example that follows:

Start (10:15am)

10	6	8	5	4	5	5	8	4	4	5	1
5	6	4	5	8	4	5	2	8	8	5	5
5	6	8	5	2	8	5	5	5	5	4	5
5	4	4	5	4	4	4	5	5	5	8	5/

Stop (10:18am)

In an observation period of 20 or 30 minutes, the observation record depicting verbal events in the classroom will consist of sheets of paper with columns of numbers. Four to six hundred numbers will be recorded.

Flanders's system, while clearly illustrating the use of a frequency coding or tabulation-type instrument, also illustrates the problem of analyzing a mass of data to give it form that conveys more meaning. In this "raw data" form, the verbal interaction data are not really useful. A matrix analysis technique will be described later to show how analyses can guide the interpretation process.

A *Pupil Enthusiasm Inventory* reported by Harris and associates (1969) is another example of a frequency tabulation-type instrument used to describe events in the classroom. This instrument defines five categories of pupil behavior that are presumed to be evidences of "lack of enthusiasm." The frequency with which these behaviors are observed over time provides a profile of enthusiasm levels in the classroom. Classroom activities are also designated to permit associating enthusiasm estimates with lesson activities.

The observer uses this instrument either continuously or with time-sampling technique. In either case, natural sequences of class activity are described in relation to tabulations. In the example in Figure 7.1 a junior high school class in remedial reading is engaged in vocabulary-building activities using a variety of machines and programmed materials on a highly individualized basis. The steady decline in frequencies of behaviors suggesting lack of enthusiasm provides a pattern for teacher-supervisor interpretation.

This instrument illustrates one that is useful in relating teacher behavior to the direct reactions of pupils. It also suggests an approach to the problem of recording frequencies of events when they are occurring simultaneously. This instrument is designed to *sample* the behaviors of students systematically so that the frequency of tallies is representative of all events even though *all* have not been observed or recorded. The observer in this instance simply rotates his focus about the room in a designated pattern. He or she focuses on each visible student for a second, tallies all designated behaviors that are observable, and moves on to the next student. This continuous (or time-sampled) rotating observation-recording procedure ensures a reasonably accurate record of these events by time period sequence.

A *teacher question tabulation* instrument based on work by Bloom is presented by Sergiovanni (1977, pp. 367–70) as one of many instruments designed in recent years for observing and analyzing teacher questioning behavior. In nearly all these instruments, the questions asked by teachers are categorized in relation to studies on cognitive or affective learning so as to enable the teacher to interpret his or her questioning in terms of probable impact on pupil learning.

The OSCAR *instruments* or Medley and Mitzel (1963) not only were among the very early efforts at instrumentation but have been refined and

PUPIL BEHAVIORS	Class Activity	Time 9:40 — Teacher introduces lesson, gives assignments.	10:00 — Pupils get out materials, wait for Teacher to signal.	10:20 — Pupils work on machines. Teacher circulates to help.
Time Sample				
a. Lack of Attention. (Looking out window, watching visitor, looking in purse, watching student, etc.)		LHt · LHt I ⑪	LHt // ⑦	// ②
b. Poor Posture. ("Slumping" in seat, head on desk, legs in aisle, etc.)		LHt ⑥ · I	//// ④	/// ③
c. Aimless Physical Activity. (Manipulating hair, ring, watch, clothes; playing with materials; swinging arms or legs; jumping or strolling about without apparent purpose, etc.)		LHt /// I ⑨	LHt LHt ⑩	LHt I ⑥
d. Unapproved Purpose. (Reading a comic book, writing personal letter, combing hair, passing note, chatting with another, etc.)		//// ④	// ②	// ②
e. Misconduct (Throwing paper, hitting another, shouting, ignoring teacher probe, etc.)		/// ③	①	⓪
Total: Lack of Enthusiasm		33	24	13

FIGURE 7.1   Pupil Enthusiasm Inventory.

adapted over the years. Initially, the OSCAR was designed to guide the observing and recording of classroom events in a very comprehensive way! Subsequent revisions have emphasized verbal interactions but retained features showing a sequence and origins of events. The system tends to be regarded as too complex for most supervisors. Adaptations of the several generations of OSCARs appear in numerous research reports, however.

Checklist-type instruments differ from frequency tabulation types in that they include many more categories of events. This is possible if only the presence or the absence of the event is recorded. This is a useful kind of recording when a simple survey is being made or when the events are sufficiently unique that evidence of their presence or absence in and of itself is worth recording. Because of these rigid requirements, the checklist is no longer very popular. Common examples of the checklist are those found in evaluative criteria documents of accrediting associations. As observation instruments have been developed to focus on the differentiated roles of teachers, paraprofessionals, and aides, the use of a checklist format has helped observers deal with the large array of event categories included. Studies of physical facilities and playground arrangements obviously make valuable use of a checklist.

Descriptive-Narrative Instruments

The great variety of relevant events going on in the classroom and the complexity of relationships among pupils, teachers, and the physical environment combine to make comprehensive classroom observation almost an impossibility. The era of the teacher-rating scale was one of struggling with the overwhelming complexity of the teaching-learning process in the belief that somehow it could all be analyzed and evaluated in some highly simplistic way. Similarly, teacher characteristics and personality studies of the past have enthusiastically been pursued in the hope of being able to *predict* teacher behavior, hence avoiding the necessity of observing it directly. The recent flurry of interest in various kinds of pupil-teacher interactions has been characterized by a willingness to take a few limited but important categories of events and thoroughly analyze them. Obviously, this latter course of action has been most rewarding but is also very limiting.

The demand that increasingly larger constellations of instructional practice be included in observation instruments persists. Supervisors who become acquainted with verbal interaction analysis nearly always react by saying, "Fine, but what about the nonverbal?" and so Galloway's work on "body language" (1972) became popular. The child-centered supervisor complains that Flanders's categories do not permit careful analysis of pupil responses, so Ober's Reciprocal Category System (1968, 1969) gains acceptance.

Each new experience with a new observation instrument that truly guides the recording of evidence regarding instructional practices tends to generate a new interest in finding a way to objectively describe other aspects of classroom life.

These piecemeal efforts to develop instruments for studying instruction are valuable, even necessary. They fail to come to grips directly, however, with the problem of observing more comprehensively with a focus on broader constellations of events without losing precision or descriptiveness. The descriptive-narrative instruments seem to offer some promise in facing this challenge because they *do not* require the tabulating or coding of minute bits of evidence and can therefore embrace larger categories and larger varieties of events as well.

These descriptive instruments are characterized by a set of well-defined procedures that call for the observer to describe in *narrative* form any observed event that relates to the purpose to be served. Descriptive-narrative instruments are structured and used in two distinctly different forms. One is a *sequential* description of events. The other is a structured category instrument. These categorical-descriptive type instruments were pioneered by Harris and McIntyre in the early 1960s. Coody and Harris later developed and tested the *Descriptive Observation Record for Individualization of Instruction* (1971; Hardebeck, 1973). Other instruments of this kind have been developed to guide observation of science laboratories, school libraries, and curriculum implementation projects. (See Figure 7.2 and case illustrations in Chapter 9.) The ethnographic approaches to analyzing classroom practice are interesting examples using sequential-narrative-descriptive recording techniques in many instances (Berliner and Tikunoff, 1977).

Because the use of such descriptive instruments (sequential and categorical) require extensive writing during the observation period, they call for substantial training of observers in the use of standard procedures, and detailed criteria as well as postobservational rewriting and analysis (Stulac et al., 1982). On the other hand, they produce a record that has much face validity (Evertson and Holley, 1981), and is readily accepted by many teachers.

The *Comprehensive Observation of Performance* instrument (CO-oP) is essentially this same type of descriptive, categorical recording device (Harris and Hill, 1982). Procedures for its use call for producing a written set of descriptions of observed events under each category defined as classroom teacher behaviors. Figure 7.2 illustrates one of the pages from this instrument. The criteria guiding the observers' efforts to describe relevant events using CO-oP are shown on the instrument pages as constant reminders of what is to be observed and where the descriptions should be recorded. A trained observer has in mind a more carefully defined set of criteria than is shown on the instrument. For instance, the manual specifies the criteria for behavior 2a—"Speaks to students in positive, praising, encouraging ways"—as follows:

2a(1) Acknowledges student comments or responses verbally without interrupting or or reducing focus on student.

2a(2) Praises student efforts, using phrases, sentences, and tonal inflections which are meaningful to the student(s) involved.

2a(3) Frees students from embarrassment by . . .

2a(4) Avoids giving negative reactions, criticisms, threats . . .

2a(5) Interacts personally . . .

Performance Area #2 — Friendly
The teacher is warm, empathetic, outgoing, positive, and personal.

No
evidence

___ ___ 2a—Speaks to students in positive, praising, encouraging ways.

–T. jokes with students. "Did you get it right?" "Oh, I'll bet you can!"
referring to an assignment.
–T. repeats several times, "I don't think that is very funny."
–T. often uses "Good", "Excellent", "Oh, very good." And encourages
ss to applaud for each other.
"Please don't bang on your desks, that disturbs people!" To class, not individual

✓ ___ 2b—Expresses interest in individuals as persons over and above being students.

–A boy interrupts. Others respond, "Shut up!" T. says, "That's uncalled
for!" No elaboration or reference to individual concerns.
–Students laugh and giggle as comics are read in newspapers.
T. makes no remark.
–T. says, "...that disturbs people..." (see 2a)

___ ___ 2c—Reflects empathy, concern and warm liking of students as related to both school and other aspects of
life.

–T. reprimands using "...excuse me" in a sarcastic sounding tone.
–T. smiles at one boy. Broad smile, shows teeth and asks about
his work from yesterday.
→ "..that disturbs people..." (see 2a)
–T. reassures a student answering incorrectly. "That's
what you were thinking, wasn't it?"

___ ___ 2d—Demonstrates interest and concern for students nonverbally in a variety of ways.

–T. urges, "Let's give a hand." All applaud, teacher too.
–T. reminds by pointing to assignment on board.
–T. remains up front at all times, strolls back and forth, smiles,
but rarely gets close to any individual.
–T. smiles broadly at one boy. (see 2c)
– Boy comes to T. with question. T. puts arm around his shoulder,
leans down, talks to him.

___ ___ *Other Behaviors* (specify):

Performance Summary:

Observed evidence is:	Behaviors							Perf. Area
	2a	2b	2c	2d		Others		
Highly descriptive	HD	HD	HD	HD	HD	HD	HD	HD
Moderately descriptive	(MD)	MD	MD	(MD)	MD	MD	MD	MD
Not very descriptive	ND	(ND)	(ND)	ND	ND	ND	ND	ND

FIGURE 7.2 Performance Area #2—Friendly. Copyright © 1982 by Ben M. Harris and Jane Hill. All rights reserved. Reprinted by permission of National Educational Laboratory Publishers, Inc., Austin, Texas.

Sequential descriptive observation guides are being utilized in clinical supervision cycles as a way of focusing only on the specific events agreed to in the preconference. In still other circumstances, a free response–type instrumentation employing sequential descriptive recording is used for general supervision purposes. A set of categories must still guide the selection of events to be recorded, however. Selected events are recorded sequentially, as illustrated in Table 7.1.

The narrative descriptions of events are in sequence as they occurred. They were selected from among a larger variety of events for purposes of focus and because everything cannot be included. If we recognize that the agreed-upon focus for this observation session was to describe "businesslike" behaviors ("la. Organizes classroom activities . . . , lb. Informs students of objectives . . . , lc. Delegates responsibilities to students . . . , and ld. Paces activities to assure task accomplishments . . ."), then the analytical coding following the observation period makes sense. However, suppose our focus had been on other criteria of performance? Some of the *same* events could be recorded and coded differently if the focus had been on "friendly" teacher

TABLE 7.1   Illustration of a Ten Minute Classroom Sequence: Dual Focus

TIME (MINUTES)	DESCRIPTION OF EVENTS	CODES FOR ANALYSIS* #1	#2
0	Teacher begins checking the roll as bell rings.	1a	
2 3	Teacher stands erect, waits for students attention. Then says, "Your assignment is on the board." Students search for books, paper, and pencils in desks.	1a 1b 1c	
4	Teacher begins walking up and down aisles, peering over students' shoulders. Teacher does not comment or assist any student, just strolls up and down.	1d (neg)	2d (neg)
7	Teacher says, "Bill, it's time you started." Public announcement to Bill across the room.	1d	
8	Several hands raised in effort to—(get help? permission? information?) Teacher does not go to any student with hand raised. Instead walks over to Bill and looks over his shoulder.	1d	2a (neg) 2d
10	Bill looks up, smiles. Teacher walks away.		2d (neg)

*Codes: #1—Businesslike behaviors.
        #2—Friendly behaviors.

behaviors. If we used the descriptive criteria presented in Figure 7.2, the codes would look like those in the last column of the illustration above and designated "friendly."

This illustration of a 10-minute sequential, descriptive observation record reveals important values *and* limitations of this technique. Potentially, the sequential-descriptive form should make an observation record rich in descriptive detail. However, the observer must be guided in selecting from a vast array of events transpiring simultaneously in any classroom at any time. Such selection can be made consciously or not. A set of carefully prescribed, conscientiously utilized criteria assures maximum reliability in observing and recording (McGreal, 1982). If such criteria are not utilized, then the observer becomes a *victim of events and biases* and the recording becomes highly unreliable.

To illustrate the influence of observational focus using specified criteria, consider the descriptive-narrative-sequential record resulting from the observation of the identical class period presented in Table 7.1 but using an alternative set of criteria, as shown in Table 7.2.

This illustration of sequential descriptive recording has many similarities with the one presented earlier. However, a different set of criteria focused the observers' attention and recording efforts on different events. The focus in this instance included the following criteria:

6a(2) Uses chalkboards, charts, bulletin boards, etc. . . .
6a(3) Makes audio materials . . . a regular part of lessons.
6b(2) Structures discussion groups . . .
6b(3) Encourages students to illustrate in graphic or artistic forms.
6b(4) Utilizes games . . .
6b(5) Provides for out-of-classroom learning . . .
6b(6) Arranges for laboratory experiments, special projects, . . .

The observer's focus on media of instruction gave emphasis to the recording of details about protractors, graph paper, recordings, and games. These specifics *might* have been observed and recorded when the focus was on businesslike and friendly relationships, but, as it happens, they were not recorded. Similarly, events recorded when friendliness is the focal point are readily omitted otherwise.

The crucial considerations for the observer grow out of the reality that teaching is enormously complex. It is not possible to observe or record such complex phenomena in any truly comprehensive way (Evertson and Holley, 1981). Even the videotape recorder with camera attached, despite all of its usefulness (Stulac et al., 1982; Lovell and Wiles, 1983, p. 176), is limited by a single lens and no peripheral vision. Hence, observation purposes must be clear and limited. Instrumentation must be selected that best serves the purposes, and severe limitations in all instruments must be recognized. Finally,

TABLE 7.2   Illustration of Alternate Focus Effects

TIME (MINUTES)	DESCRIPTION OF EVENTS	CODES FOR ANALYSIS*
0	Teacher begins checking roll as the bell rings. Teacher hands completed attendance slip to a girl, saying, "It's your turn to go help in the office. Take this to the Attendance Clerk."	6b(5)
2	Teacher says, "Your assignment is on the board." Students search for materials in their desks. Some get out	6a(2)
3	rulers, protractors, and graph paper. Others go to learning centers to use cassette recordings, games, and reference books.	6b(3) 6a(3), 6a(4)
4	Teacher walks up and down, peering over students' shoulders.	
5	Teacher makes rounds of the classroom, checking (to make sure?) each group as it starts to work.	
7	Teacher says, "Bill, it's time you started." Bill comes up to project corner. Teacher and Bill confer. Teacher demonstrates how the surveyor's instrument is adjusted and angles are recorded.	6b(6)
8	Several hands raised in an effort to (Get help? permission? information?) Teacher does not go to any student with hand raised. Instead, Teacher walks over to his desk, gets a book, returns to the project corner, and hands it to Bill.	
9	Students with hands raised form a discussion group in the library corner around a small table.	
10	Bill looks up as he adjusts the transit and checks the reading. He smiles. Teacher walks away toward newly formed discussion group. Teacher joins the group.	6b(4) 6b(2)

*Code: #6—Multimedia.

observation and recording techniques must be systematized to assure reliability.

ANALYSIS AND DIAGNOSIS

Systematic classroom observations with rating scales, frequency tabulations, checklists, or descriptive instruments provide an array of raw data that can be interpreted as evidence on teaching and learning. Sometimes the instruments are self-analytic and require little if any data manipulation beyond that completed during the observation period. Most instruments—in fact, most of those that seem to have the greatest utility for stimulating instructional improvement—require postobservation analysis.

An example of the self-analytic-type instrument is the *Pupil Enthusiasm Inventory* shown in Figure 7.1. The very popular Flanders system is a striking example of one that produces almost useless data until postobservational analysis has been completed. A problem that confronts all supervisors in using existing instruments or in developing new ones is that of finding analytical procedures that reduce and simplify raw data for easy interpretation. And analytical procedures that will make simple sets of data more intelligible to the teacher need to be developed.

Elaborate statistical treatments of data are rarely very useful for the purposes described above. For the supervisor, analytical treatments of simple graphs and tables will ordinarily be most helpful to teachers and most feasible in the majority of situations.

Graphic Analyses

Graphic analyses of various kinds have proved useful for displaying observational data. Matrices, line graphs, grids, and branching diagrams are some techniques used.

Matrix analysis gives meaning to the mass of numbers produced by an observer using Flanders's (1970) categories. Essentially, each sequential pair of events is tallied in a cell representing that set of events. Frequencies in cells and groups of cells represent the patterns of events observed.

Figure 7.3 illustrates a matrix analysis of a lesson. The trained observer-analyst in collaboration with the classroom teacher can explore a host of interpretations through such a graphic display. Even those not intimately acquainted with the reality of classroom interaction represented can gain some insight by interpreting these data. A few interpretations that can be drawn are:

1. Teacher talk was primarily concerned with presenting information (5s = 24 percent) but also with asking questions (4s = 14.8 percent) and accepting students' ideas (3s).
2. Student responses were almost evenly divided between direct response and self-initiated responses.
3. The most frequent pair of events (cell) involved lecturing (5–5 cell = 32).
4. Other quite frequent sets of events included students responding to teacher questions (4–8 cell = 16) and silence followed by more silence (10–10 cell = 20).
5. Extended indirect teacher talk involving extended (continuous) use of praise and accepting feelings and ideas totaled 11 sets of events.
6. Extended direct teacher talk involving extended (continuous) use of directions or criticisms tallied 6 sets of events.

WORK MATRIX

Teacher __Gwen Hall__ Date __11/7/8-__
Class/Subject __5th Language__
Observer __C. Bell__ Time: __9:05__ to __9:15__
Descriptive Notes:

	1	2	3	4	5	6	7	8	9	10	
1					1					1	
2	1		1		1	1			1	1	
3		1	8	3	3				2	1	
4	1			8	2			16			
5				5	32				4	3	
6						6			5	2	
7											
8		2	6	7				4		1	
9		1	2	1	5	5			8	1	
10		2	1	3		1			3	20	Matrix Total
TOTAL	2	6	18	27	44	13	0	20	23	30	183
%	1.1	3.3	9.8	14.8	24.0	7.1	0.0	10.9	12.6	16.4	100%

FIGURE 7.3   Work Matrix.

7. Teacher responses to student talk tended to emphasize praise and acceptance of student ideas as well as lecturing and directing.
8. The 4–8 cell combined with the 8–4 cell represent a tendency toward recitation, but this does not dominate.
9. The 9–9 cell suggests some tendency for students to verbalize beyond simple responses.

Many other interpretations can be drawn from the thoughtful study of a Flanders-type matrix (Schwanke, 1981). Such insights often lead the teacher and supervisor to question the utility of certain teacher talk patterns of behavior. Speculation about what might have happened can lead to hypothesis formulations that teachers seek to test in their classrooms. For instance, this teacher, Ms. Hall, might test the notion that less use of 8–4s combined with the more use of 8–10s, 4–10s, and 9–10s could be productive in getting students to verbalize their understandings and raise better, more thoughtful questions in class (9–9s and 8–9s). (See Chapter 10, page 232, for a case illustration of Flanders matrix analysis in use.)

Combining data to provide a more useful pattern is illustrated by the analytical scheme for the *Teacher Question–Pupil Response Inventory* (Harris, Bessent, and McIntyre 1969, pp. 163–196). A record of teacher questions is maintained, and the techniques used to elicit the responses are related to each question. Pairs of questions and responses are plotted on a simple two-dimensional grid, as shown in Figure 7-4. In interpreting data on this grid, teachers' behavior can be seen in terms of both *control* and *intellectual* stimulation. Teachers with frequent pairs of events in cell *a* can see themselves as acting as though students cannot use freedom or respond to complex ideas. Teachers with frequent pairs in cell *i* can see themselves as using free expression to encourage responses at higher levels of cognition. On the other hand, teachers emphasizing cell *g* may be frustrating themselves by seeking complex responses without sufficient freedom to make them possible. A variety of interpretations can be elicited from a pattern of events portrayed on a grid such as this.

Diagnostic Analysis

Analytical techniques utilized in conjunction with classroom observational data tend to be descriptive but not diagnostic. Rarely do analyses lead directly to diagnostic conclusions regarding "problems," "needs for improvement," or preferred alternatives. Harris and Hill (1982) have utilized a variety of *data sources*—observer, self-report, and student report—in a diagnostic analysis format that does produce some clear guidelines for action.

Congruence analysis is the technique utilized by Harris and Hill in the DeTEK system to translate descriptive data and observer estimates into diagnostic decisions. Figure 7.5 is an illustration of this data analysis technique. A common set of criteria (indicators) has been utilized by observer, students,

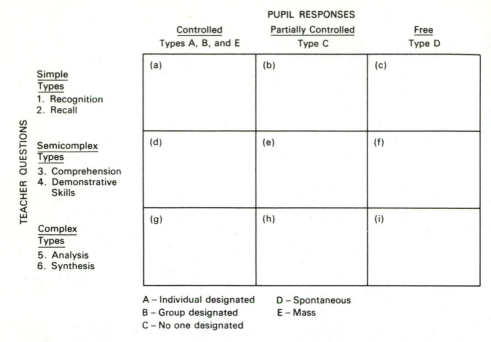

FIGURE 7.4   **Analytical summary of teacher question–pupil response inventory.**

and teacher. The teacher describes his or her teaching practices for each indicator by estimating it as "highly," "moderately," or "not very" descriptive of what would normally be observed in his or her classroom. These teacher self-estimates are recorded in column 2 as HD, MD, or ND (see Figure 7.5). The observer summarizes his or her classroom observation report for each indicator using the same estimates, i.e., the extent to which the criteria are highly, moderately, or not very descriptive of observed events.

These estimates are recorded in column 3. Finally, students are asked to report on the same teaching practices, specifying only the absence or presence of the practices as "something my teacher does." The frequency of positive responses is entered in column 5. Column 4 is utilized simply to record comparisons between teacher self-reported and observer-reported estimates.

When all data are highly congruent across all three sources of data in columns 2, 3, and 5, then a clear diagnostic decision is recorded. When all estimates report "highly" descriptive teaching practices, "Accomplishments" are designated in column 6. Similarly, when all estimates report "not very" descriptive teaching practices, "Needs" are designated in column 7. Incongruent data is interpreted as meaning that the reality regarding such practices is as yet uncertain, and *no diagnosis* is made. Instead, a decision to observe further is made and recorded in column 8.

PERFORMANCE # __4__ — BEHAVIOR # _4b_ – Presents subject matter using a variety

Stimulating   of techniques, styles, and approaches.

(1) Indicators (Write abbreviated description of indicators)	(2) Self-Report II	(3) Observation Report III	(4) Agree or Disagree	(5) Supplemental Student Report IV	(6) Accomplishments (Circle)	(7) NEEDS Yes-Uncertain
4b (1) – Organizes subject matter presentations to show relationships.	HD	MD	Disagree	45	⊛	—
4b (2) – Uses shifts in sensory modes, levels of thinking.	MD	ND	Disagree	31	★	Uncertain
4b (3) – Models and guides	ND	MD	Disagree	34	★	Uncertain
4b (4) – Plans and executes	MD	ND	Disagree	15	★	Need
4b (5) – Sets up and provides resources.	MD	ND	Disagree	22	★	Uncertain

Number of Student Reports = __62__

(8)
If "uncertain" is designated in col. 7, set date for an observation here.

Day _Tues._

Date _11/15_

Time _10:20_

*Based on developmental teacher evaluation system by Ben M. Harris and Jane Hill (1982).
Illustrative data by Jeff Lindzey, Dripping Springs High School, May 1980.

**FIGURE 7.5 DeTEK Instrument V: Data Analysis Worksheet*. Copyright ©
1982, Ben M. Harris and Jane Hill. All rights reserved. Reprinted
by permission of National Educational Laboratory Publishers., Inc.,
Austin, Texas.**

Congruence analysis, as illustrated here, presumes that the criteria being utilized are relevant to the teacher in his or her current teaching assignment. When this is the case, a rather simple analytical process guides collaborative decision making with considerable certainty and ease.

QUALITATIVE ANALYSIS

Eisner (1977; 1982) is one of the more outspoken advocates of "qualitative evaluation" of teaching. His ideas are largely in conflict with the notions presented here about objectivity, description, recording, and analyzing classroom events. One should not take lightly such contrary views, for they are expressed by a variety of scholars and practitioners, and come from several fields of endeavor.

Key points of view expressed regarding "qualitative" approaches include the following:

1. Teaching is an art, not a science, and is not subject to quantitative analysis in any meaningful sense (Eisner, 1982, p. 55).
2. An expert (Eisner, 1977, likes the term *connoisseur*) can determine what is good and not good teaching on the basis of his or her experience and insights (Dunkerton, 1981).

This oversimplifies the argument, of course, but these statements clearly are central to many proposals for qualitative approaches to improving teaching. Each of these points has a kernel of truth that needs to be considered by supervisors in their practices.

Teaching surely is an art to some degree. Potentially, one might argue that teaching should develop increasingly as an expression of human creativity in working with other human beings at complex tasks. Practically, much teaching is anything but artistic, but at its best it is very much a craft. Any craft involves learning to use basic skills, techniques, and tools as a prerequisite to the privilege of a practice (Spady, 1982b). Teaching, to date at least, is practiced mainly as a craft. Fortunately, a scientific basis for the art of teaching is now being established (Gage, 1978; Spady, 1982b). Systematic, rational analysis of objective reality can surely serve as well in understanding most of what now passes for classroom instruction (Lamb and Thomas, 1981). When artistry is discovered to exist, more innovative ways of studying it will undoubtedly be needed.

The use of the expert or "connoisseur" as ultimate determiner of what is and is not "good" teaching is so full of serious implications that it warrants much discussion (Coker et al., 1980). Obviously, the more experienced, educated, sensitive, and open-minded an observer can be, the better (Berliner and Tikunoff, 1977). In fact, one of the strongest arguments for supervisors, administrators, and teachers (Mills, 1980) all observing in classrooms and analyzing teaching together is based on the notion that most of us need much more experience with a broad array of reality about life in classrooms. But "connoisseurship" implies something quite different.

A variety of questions about expertness cry out for answers:

1. On what basis has our expert selected his/her criteria of quality performance?
2. How do we know our expert has really attended to all the relevant criteria?
3. How does our expert qualitatively process the extremely complex array of information being used?
4. What set of values does our expert utilize in assigning worth to the performance?

Now, these are just technical considerations. Practical ones still follow:

5. Suppose we (teacher, administrator, others) don't agree with the values utilized by our expert, what utility is there in the efforts or our expert then?
6. Suppose we do accept the expert (en toto), how can we utilize his/her conclusions?
7. Where do we find (cultivate) a large number of these experts?

Note: Some 2.5 million teachers in the United States are served by 100,000 principals and a third as many more supervisors.

The essential differences in approach advocated by those who favor systematic, objective observations and those favoring "connoisseurship" are less in process than in explicitness:

1. Both approaches ask for knowledgeable, experienced supervisors, but connoisseurs are hard to find.
2. Both approaches call for observing the reality of the classroom, but why not be systematic?
3. Both approaches call for having clearly known criteria of quality, but why not "public" criteria?
4. Both approaches call for gathering information; so, why not *record* it for others to see?
5. Both approaches call for analysis and interpretation of observed information, but why make it an almost mystical and intrapersonal process?
6. Both approaches call for valuing, but must the personal values of the connoisseur be imposed unilaterally?

Qualitative evaluation as discussed and criticized here risks being highly elitist in its orientation as well as highly impractical in many situations.

Another View of Qualitative Analysis

A generally neglected view of qualitative analysis derives from the early work of industrial chemists. Qualitative analysis in the field of chemistry was widely utilized prior to technological developments that made it too costly and inefficient. Such qualitative analysis involves only limited use of measurement techniques, substituting for precise measurements the processes of estimation, categorization, comparison, and logical deduction (Berliner and Brandt, 1982).

The Harris and Hill (1982) adaptation of such qualitative techniques to diagnostic analysis of teaching was described earlier. Observational data, teacher self-report data, and student report data relating to clearly specified observable criteria of performance are reduced to simple *estimates of concordance*. A set of specific indicators of performance are provided, and the three "observers"—supervisor, teacher, and students—each estimate the extent to which observed performance matches the indicators. Diagnostic analysis procedures use these estimates in a simple qualitative way. *Congruence* among estimates is determined by simple comparisons. (See Chapter 9 for a case illustration.)

This application of qualitative analysis techniques is one of a limited variety employed using various observation systems. Flanders's (1970) widely utilized system of coding verbal acts and analyzing them with a matrix technique has also been illustrated above. These are essentially qualitative techniques. Carefully standardized procedures for coding events and preparing the matrix are used, but interaction analysis data must be interpreted with many *qualitative* considerations. The matrix offers any experienced educator numerous opportunities to compare, contrast, and hypothesize about both the objective reality and the underlying meaning. There is some evidence that these techniques are productive in improving teaching too (Adams, 1970).

Unfortunately, many of the published reports on the use of Flanders's categories as observational criteria emphasize data *quantification* for research purposes (Travers, 1978, p. 23). This has led to confusion, for an essentially qualitative approach to observing and analyzing verbal interactions has become widely misunderstood. The preoccupation with i/d ratios and percentages of events overshadows the enlightening possibilities of matrix interpretations.

Persistent Poor Practices

Advocates of both qualitative and quantitative approaches to classroom observation deserve the thoughtful attention of supervisors and principals as they develop their practices. However, the more serious error is not that of choosing between carefully considered approaches, for both will be useful under certain circumstances (Apple, 1978, p. 499). The largest problem is that of avoiding both poor advice and poor practices regardless of source.

Examples of poor advice and practices are reflected in statements such as the following:

There is no way to be objective, so why bother?
Just go in and participate. You learn more that way.

Don't announce observations in advance, just pop in and find out what's really going on.

You can learn all you need to know by just dropping in for a few minutes.

I can tell whether good teaching is going on just by walking down the hall.

Don't write anything while in the classroom; wait until after you leave.

Write everything down; don't omit a thing.

Advocates of traditional varieties of rating scales also continue to prosper despite the fact that most scales have been thoroughly discredited for most purposes. *Descriptive ratings* utilized cautiously as measures of very limited kinds of teaching practices—in the hands of trained raters and used in standardized ways—can of course be useful under certain circumstances (Apple, 1978, p. 499). However, the *judgmental* types of rating scales, still widely used, may be the most common indicator of faulty practice. They are poorly designed instruments in most instances, because their criteria are not clearly defined; they often call for broad generalizations to be made by the raters; they ask for ratings about realities that are often beyond the raters' base of knowledge; and they invite value-laden opinions, not descriptive estimates (Harris et al., 1979, p. 295). Such instruments are not reliable and hence cannot have validity. Even training and standardization of procedures would leave these *judgmental* observation instruments too dangerous to use.

SUMMARY

Classroom observation is a complex activity but indispensable in the work of any supervisor or other person who needs to know about instruction. This chapter is only an introduction to this very important topic.

Observation of instruction is an aspect of the evaluation task, but more than that, it is a vehicle for in-service education, curriculum development, staffing, and public relations as well. Classroom observation involves trained observers, carefully selected purposes, systematic procedures, and disciplined analysis and interpretation of data prior to valuing and decision making.

The new instrumentation has provided supervisors with many guides for observing classrooms. No one instrument will meet all needs, and a variety will be required in any supervisory program. Similarly, technological developments in videotaping, sound recording, photographing, and computerizing are opening up an entirely new era in the analysis of instruction. The supervisor will be the key person in determining whether these aids are used efficiently for improving instruction.

The lively controversy over qualitative versus quantitative approaches to analyzing teaching should stimulate and caution the supervisory practitioner. It is essential that both teachers and those they work with better understand the complexities of classroom life. Systematic observations will be essential for this pursuit of knowledge. More sophisticated analytical techniques will need to be invented and tested against criteria of utility. But cautions cannot be overemphasized if they remind observers of how much knowledge is still lacking and that there are alternative ways of knowing.

Bronowski (1966, p. 65) stresses a dichotomy between scientific and aesthetic knowledge that supervisors and administrators should not neglect: "[A] poem informs us in a mode of knowledge that is many-valued, . . . a scientific paper instructs us in a mode of knowledge that is single-valued." Educational leaders can embrace both ways of knowing but cannot afford to accept that which is clearly neither poetic nor scientific in their ways of working.

A thoughtful social scientist has expressed a similar caution: "Knowledge is only one component that enters into policy." Research provides only one component of knowledge (Weiss, 1980, p. 276). It is a mistake to overstress this one component, especially in its too heavy reliance on measurement and quantification. Yet systematic, rigorous, objective recording or observable evidence is an initial rung on the ladder toward understanding.

Refer to Chapter 10 for case reports on observation techniques applied to real situations.

SUGGESTED READINGS

BEEGLE, CHARLES W., AND RICHARD M. BRANDT,   *Observational Methods in the Classroom*. Washington, D.C.: Association for Supervision and Curriculum Development, 1973.

A brief but useful review of a variety of approaches to classroom observation.

BORICH, GARY D., AND SUSAN K. MADDEN,   *Evaluating Classroom Instruction: A Sourcebook of Instruments*. Reading, Mass.: Addison-Wesley, 1977.

This book is designed to present the numerous instruments that have been developed to study teacher and pupil behavior in the classroom. It provides a comprehensive review of currently available instruments. A descriptive framework of each instrument is given that includes (1) type of measure, (2) description of instrument, (3) psychometric characteristics, and (4) administration and scoring. Instruments are grouped into conceptual categories.

COKER, HOMER, DONALD M. MEDLEY, AND ROBERT S. SOAR,   "How Valid are Expert Opinions About Effective Teaching?" *Phi Delta Kappan, 62* (October 1980): 131–34.

The lack of evidence of the validity of the competency measures often used to determine effective teaching is reviewed. Strategies for defining competencies were tested by gathering data from four existing observation instruments (STARS, OScAR 5V, FLACCS, TPOR). Student gains were also measured. Some of the behaviors positively related to achievement gains were (1) involving students in organizing and planning, (2) listening skillfully and (3) respecting the individual's right to speak.

DUNKERTON, JOHN,   "Should Classroom Observation be Quantitative?" *Educational Research*, 23, no. 2 (February 1981): 144–51.

The author compares unstructured observation practices to systematic observation and determines that, if observation is to become an accepted scientific method, then it must conform to some rules and procedures and be analytic. Unstructured observations are unlikely to yield reliable, objective data on classroom behavior. Several types of systematic observation sampling are explained (natural sampling, static sampling, one-zero sampling, predominant activity sampling). It is suggested that one-zero time sampling methods that record behaviors only once in any time unit should be used cautiously as a means of quantifying behavior.

FLANDERS, NED A.,   *Analyzing Teacher Behavior*. Reading, Mass.: Addison-Wesley, 1970.

A systematic treatment of the use of Flanders's verbal interaction analysis categories. The rationale for the system, studies using the system, and technical information on procedures and techniques are provided.

FRICK, TED, AND MELVYN I. SEMMEL,   "Observer Agreement and Reliabilities of Classroom Observational Measures," *Review of Educational Research*, 48 (Winter 1978): 157–84.

This paper discusses the methods and conditions of measuring observer agreement so that variations can be minimized. It concludes that observers should be trained to reach agreement with a criterion or expert coder on videotaped examples of behavioral categories. Since teachers and students do not always exhibit behaviors that fall neatly into predefined observation categories, perfect agreement cannot be expected.

GOOD, THOMAS, AND JERE BROPHY,   *Looking in Classrooms*, 2nd ed. New York: Harper & Row, 1978.

A primer on observation techniques. Suggests a variety of ways of viewing and recording data. Written more from the teacher's viewpoint than that of an administrator or supervisor, it offers a variety of interesting ideas.

JONES, KEITH, AND ANN SHERMAN,   "Two Approaches to Evaluation," *Educational Leadership*, 37 (April 1980): 553–57.

Eisner's Educational Criticism model is compared to Flanders's Interaction Analysis System. The emphasis in Eisner's model is on context. Predefined instruments are not used. The observer is a seasoned educator who relies on "perceptive skills" sharpened by knowledge and experience. The two approaches are compared according to thick versus thin description, objectivity versus subjectivity, and quantity versus quality. The authors believe that too much emphasis has been placed on quantification of behavior and more should be given to the quality and meaning of events shaping the lives of students.

MCGREAL, THOMAS L.,   "Effective Teacher Evaluation Systems," *Educational Leadership* 39, no. 4 (January 1982): 303–305.

The author identifies nine commonalities to serve as a basis for developing an effective teacher evaluation system within a school district. He emphasizes formative evaluation and the importance of observation in classrooms in such evaluation efforts.

SIMON, ANITA, AND GIL BOYER, ED.,   *Mirrors for Behavior II: An Anthology of Observation Instruments, Volume* A. Philadelphia: Classroom Interaction Newsletter, 1970.

A listing and description of a vast number of observation instruments. While most listed instruments emphasize verbal interaction, a substantial variety are included. Companion volumes provide detailed information on instruments.

CHAPTER EIGHT
EVALUATION
OF INSTRUCTIONAL
PROGRAMS*

Evaulation in education is universally endorsed, widely misunderstood, poorly planned, crudely implemented, haphazardly staffed, and even ignored when the results are in! Nonetheless, supervisors are coming to accept responsibililty for the evaulation task by recognizing that it is essential for guiding the improvement of the instruction process.

Evaluation was once thought of as *testing* when pupil learning was being considered, and as *ratings* when teacher effectiveness was in question. These simple, old-fashioned concepts of evaluation continue to come into prominence in the literature and in practice from time to time (Miller, 1972; Weinheimer, 1980). However, the best practice and research and development activities are all moving slowly but persistently in the direction of viewing evaluation as a way of systematically gathering evidence on instruction-related events and analyzing these data in ways specifically designed to illuminate decision making for improving instruction (Stufflebeam et al., 1971; Anderson and Ball, 1978; Guba and Lincoln, 1981).

Cronbach (1980, p. 12) elaborates on this by defining evaluation as a "systematic examination of events occurring in and consequent of a contemporary program." Accordingly, such "examinations" are intended to assist in

*Revised with the assistance of Pamela Hall.

improving programs. Anderson and Ball (1978, pp. 37–42) detail evaluation purposes of six kinds: (1) deciding about program installation, (2) deciding about program continuation, (3) deciding about program modifications, (4) obtaining evidence in support, (5) obtaining evidence against, and (6) understanding basic processes. The last three of these purposes are really just extensions of the first three.

THE NATURE OF EVALUATION

Evaluation of instruction as discussed here is defined as a set of processes rather than a single act or even a simple set of isolated acts. A useful way of viewing these processes is to place them on a continuum even though they frequently overlap. Seven processes of evaluation can be defined as follows:

1. *Specifying criteria.* In terms of the purpose to be served and the problem in focus, the criteria of performance to be used in guiding decisions are specified.
2. *Instrumentation.* The instruments for gathering data relevant to specified criteria are selected (or developed), and their use is clearly designated.
3. *Data gathering.* The instruments are employed in appropriate ways, with trained personnel, to obtain the data needed with maximum objectivity.
4. *Data analysis.* The raw data provided through proper instrumentation and data-gathering procedures are analyzed in ways that provide the clearest picture of the situation being analyzed. Data analysis involves manipulation of raw data to discern trends, central tendencies, relationships, contrasts, similarities, and patterns. A major need is for data reduction so that many bits of data can be combined to convey meaning.
5. *Interpretation of findings.* The trends, contrasts, patterns, or other meanings suggested by data-analysis procedures are given interpretations that add to these meanings by forming larger configurations with other related events. Interpretation also involves relating the data to the criteria specified.
6. *Valuing.* Values are assigned to the findings as interpreted. This involves judging the seriousness of, and discrepancies between, the criteria specified and the findings as interpreted. It may also involve relating findings to one's own values and biases—implicitly or explicitly (Weiss, 1972; Fathy, 1980).
7. *Decision making.* Values attached to the findings as interpreted are used to guide decisions to change, maintain, or evaluate further.

Some would argue that the evaluation task is completed when interpretation of data has been completed. Certainly valuing and decision making involve personnel beyond those engaged in the other evaluation processes, and the data become relatively unimportant to these users. Distinctions are sometimes drawn between assessing, appraising, and evaluating. Most uses of these terms are consistent with the seven processes listed.

To give the concept of evaluation as a set of processes more concrete meaning, an outlined illustration of a specific evaluation effort may be useful:

Given as a purpose the guiding of teaching practices toward greater individualization of instruction—

1. *Criterion.* Extent of intraclass grouping employed by teachers.
2. *Instrumentation.* The Descriptive Observation Record for Individualization of Instruction (Harris and McIntyre, 1981).
3. *Data gathering.* A series of five observations in each classroom at randomly selected times.
4. *Data analysis.* Estimation of level of intraclass grouping, using a descriptive rating scale applied to observation data (Coody and Harris, 1971).
5. *Interpretation.* Teachers with relatively high and low levels of observed intraclass grouping practice identified. Consistencies and inconsistencies among teachers noted. Contrasts or similarities in findings to those of other studies identified. Relationship of findings to theoretical formulations clarified.
6. *Valuing.* Judgment made regarding the "goodness" of the individualization practices. Judgment made regarding who is doing a "good" job and who is performing inadequately. Judgments made regarding the seriousness of the situation with those not individualizing well. Values include consistent use of practices, use of a full array of practices, and use in a variety of subject fields.
7. *Decision making.* Decisions to reward, dismiss, criticize, reorganize, provide training, or take other corrective actions to improve individualization practices.

PURPOSES TO BE SERVED

The evaluation of instructional programs is a gigantic and bewildering task, at best. Its purpose must be specific, limited, important, and feasible. It would be nice indeed if some magically simple evaluation design could be found to give us answers to all our perplexing problems. The truth is that useful evaluation is never simple, and its usefulness is generally limited to giving new leads, providing better probabilities, and making fewer serious mistakes (Dyer, 1970). With these cautions in mind, a serious analysis of alternative purposes to be served by an evaluation subsystem is in order.

All Things to All People

When an effort at instructional evaluation tries to serve too many purposes, nothing is likely to be well evaluated. The superintendent's wanting to know if the new program is any better than the old one is defensible. The federal project director's wanting to demonstrate to Washington the justifiability of re-funding a special project is understandable. The school board president's wanting to know how much more the program costs the local district is reasonable. The personnel director's wanting to have information on whom to recommend for reemployment is worthy. The parent's wanting to know whether his children will be well prepared for college is understandable. The teacher's wanting to know if it really makes enough difference in pupil learning to justify all the extra time is relevant. The principal's question regarding an alternative such as smaller class size is sound. But answers to questions suggested by any *one* of these "needs" are difficult to provide. As a typical array of evaluative questions, they present too formidable a task for the staff, time, and resources generally available for evaluation purposes.

When we develop new programs or try to assess old ones, it is essential that this comprehensive approach be avoided. Instead, the decisions that *must* be made need to be clearly identified. The criteria upon which such decisions can be made must be specified and given priorities or relative weights. The evaluation design can then focus attention on those data that permit better decisions because they inform the decision makers about their high-priority concerns. Gerhard (1981, p. 9) suggests the need "to combine the programs to be evaluated *and* the evaluative process itself in a single unifying conceptual model" as a way of assuring evaluations that serve well.

Focus on Improvement of Instruction

The supervisor is justifiably involved in evaluation of instruction because of its implications for the improvement process. From this point of emphasis, evaluation endeavors must lead to better decisions regarding ways of improving instruction. As such, the focus tends to be more on the teaching-learning process than on products–pupil learning. Alternatively, the focus might well be on inputs that influence the quality of instruction—curricula, materials, space, organizational arrangements, and so forth.

Some find it difficult to accept an evaluation design that fails to give top priority to product evaluation—achievement, interest, retention rates, college admission rates, jobs secured (Weinheimer, 1980, p. 13). It is not appropriate or necessary even to ignore such data in evaluating with a focus on instructional improvement. However, the identification of weaknesses in product is not particularly useful unless the evaluation process *also* leads to probable causes. Similarly, identification of strengths in the products of the school or classroom is of little worth unless such an evaluation system guides decision makers to probable contributing inputs or processes so they can be *selectively* reinforced or studied in greater detail.

Weinheimer makes the points that "evaluations . . . have focused almost exclusively on outcome measures. . . . Common sense dictates that we should expect the level of program implementation to influence the program's effect. Yet . . . implementation . . . has not received much formal attention from evaluators." It must gain the attention of supervisors.

Failure of evaluation efforts for improvement of instruction purposes to actually associate product strengths and weaknesses with probable contributing factors leads to negative side effects (Gerhard, 1981, p. 13). Those staff members associated with an aspect of instruction that is identified as "weak" are often defensive because they may rightly view themselves as innocent. Their colleagues who may actually be contributing to the weakness can use the same defense unless a substantial array of contributing variables has actually been studied. Furthermore, pinpointing weaknesses in product without offering similar clues for corrective action leads staff members to be overly anxious and to respond irrationally.

Strengths identified through product evaluation have undesirable effects by promoting indiscriminate reinforcement of practices. Grandparents, parents, community leaders, teachers, administrators, and supervisors all take pride in their Rudolph's being a National Merit Scholarship awardee. In fact, all or none may have made any real contribution to this event. Principals and teaching staffs alike at the secondary level are all too eager to retain pupils in the same grade and encourage dropouts as a reaction to product evaluation that provides these staff members with rewards for having a high percentage of their "graduates" (not all of the students) attend college.

Operational Decision Making

Operational decision making is a kind of evaluation for improvement, too. Instead of focusing on the teaching-learning process, evaluation for operational decision-making purposes is primarily concerned with the context and inputs for instruction. This focus for evaluation is resorted to when the teaching-learning process is presumed to be quite adequate, when it is not feasible to gather reliable data about it, or when it is perceived as relatively impervious to direct influences for improvement.

Most surveys of school programs and accreditation studies focus on the context and inputs of the classroom, school, or district. Class size, room size, library book collection, staff qualifications, pupil characteristics, curricula, community relations, and financial support data are of importance in such evaluations. Decisions from this kind of evaluation are limited to those having to do with organizational change, physical change, and rule change as defined in Chapter 2. Little guidance on functional or personnel change is offered by such a focus on evaluation.

Evaluation that focuses on organizational decision making without concern for the teaching-learning process is forced to make assumptions that can be misleading. For instance, the accreditation study that looks at teacher qualifications as an input (degrees, grades, certification, experience, letters of recommendation) is likely to err in identifying *both* strengths and weaknesses. Certain assumptions about the relationship between these teacher qualification inputs and actual teacher performance have to be made, and they are likely to be faulty. Similarly, seemingly logical assumptions about homogeneous grouping of students and the influence of these arrangements on teacher performance have generally been discredited.

Go, No-Go Decision Making

Go, no-go decision making is a unique focus for evaluation of instruction. Most instructional program elements are basically continuous (Eichelberger, 1974). That is to say, they are going to continue to exist and be supported by the system within wide ranges of efficiency and effectiveness. Under certain conditions some aspects of the instructional program can be discontinued if they have no firm lease on continuity. It is with such elements in the school operation that go, no-go decisions need to be guided by evaluation efforts. Alkin and associates (1979, p. 230) describe the elimination of an experimental music program based on a specific evaluative effort. This is fairly common when *special* or innovative efforts are being evaluated.

To illustrate the continuous versus the discontinuous program elements, the new course offering may be a case in point. If the course is something not normally offered, not required by law or regulation, precariously valued by some and suspect by others, it is almost certain to be potentially discontinuous. On the other hand, a course that is widely offered in other schools, has been well received by students, faculty, and community, or is required by law illustrates a condition of probable continuity. Most pilot programs and major changes fall into the class of instructional elements that are potentially discontinuous and hence subject to go, no-go evaluation. Even so, the negative decisions relating to such programs may lead only to resource reallocations, and hence the evaluation problem is not as simple as it might seem (Weinheimer, 1980, p. 15).

This kind of evaluation focuses on products primarily. Since decisions to be guided are concerned with the life or death of a program or a practice, it is the end results that get attention. Reasons for failure to produce results may be interesting to the social scientist and the educational researcher, but to the administrator and the supervisor they are not crucial *when* the time to make a stop-go decision arrives.

The dangers inherent in evaluation systems of this go, no-go variety are in the inappropriate preoccupation with, and timing of, such decisions. An evaluation plan that is initially designed to serve only this kind of decision fails to provide the information needed for corrective actions, as previously discussed. As a result, we may have a self-defeating system. Since it does not guide corrective decisions, they are made inefficiently or not at all, so the results are likely to be unsatisfactory. The evaluation results guide the decision to abandon the program when it may well have prevented such actions.

The judicial model has been advocated for use in educational evaluation (Nadler and Shore, 1979). While rarely used, it might well be most appropriate when go, no-go decisions of real consequence are being contemplated.

Dismissal or reduction in force decisions involve evaluation processes of the go, no-go type. Reductions of positions under conditions of declining enrollments or severe budget limitations, tend to be dominated by seniority considerations (Harris et al., 1979, p. 228). Ethnic or sex balance considerations may also enter into the evaluation process. Dismissal decisions are also full of complications for evaluators. Pressures from organized teacher groups, parents, and the courts make go, no-go decisions very sensitive. Hence, they are rarely the simple product-centered evaluation efforts that some evaluators (and officials) would like to believe they are.

SYSTEMS ANALYSIS

Nearly all current thought and increasing amounts of practice adopt a systems view of the evaluation task. Vast differences eixst among those who are concerned with product, process, or input evaluation; but there is agreement that a systems analysis approach to instructional evaluation is most promising.

The systems view of evaluation was introduced to the reader in Chapter 3. A review of this chapter may be helpful, as more specific applications to evaluation are presented here.

Instructional evaluation is concerned with a vast array of events influencing what is learned. Research theorists classify these events slightly differently, but they generally fall into one of four groups (Stufflebeam et al., 1971).

1. Surrounding conditions (context variables)
2. Basic operating resources (input variables)
3. Essential operations (process variables)
4. Resulting outcomes (product variables)

In systems analysis approaches, these four sets of variables are studied to see if resulting outcomes are as expected—and if not, why not. Simple as that seems, it gets very complex when so many variables with so many possible interrelationships are involved Cronbach and associates describe four main approaches to evaluation efforts they refer to as "systematic inquiry." The four approaches are deliberate trial, diversity of evidence, comparison, and controlled assignment (1980, p. 269–318). Pilot programs often represent deliberate trials. Comparisons among two or more existing programs offer an approach to evaluation. Controlled assignment, while ideal in some ways, offers serious problems for evaluators and supervisors alike in most school settings.

Several models for approaching this complex evaluation task have been developed. Accountability models tend to focus only on product evaluation

(Klein and Alkin, 1972; Weinheimer, 1980). Other models emphasize evaluation on inputs as the variable that can, perhaps, be most readily manipulated. Still others are primarily concerned with process as the crucial variable where truly significant changes must be generated. Only in recent years has there been a concerted effort to develop evaluation systems for realistically emphasizing a full range of variables where cause-and-effect relationships become primary concerns.

A Variety of Models

Gerhard describes the need for models "that are complex enough to reveal the impact of decisions, yet simple enough to be readily understood. . . . The result is clarification . . . such that fear of change does not prevent change and the glamour of change does not accelerate it . . ." (1981, p. 11). He also warns against "random tinkering" in lieu of systematic evaluation activities. Guba and Lincoln (1981) describe and compare a variety of models that are well known.

Katz and Morgan present a "holistic" model for formative evaluation that draws on various earlier works (1974, pp. 210–31). These authors identify eight basic components and utilize three analyses in a series. Congruence analyses are utilized to compare desired and actual products, but expediency and process effect analyses are also called for, hence decisions are guided for program modification purposes.

Ralph W. Tyler's evaluation model (Guba and Lincoln, 1981, pp. 1–22) has been most influential in educational circles. His process is based on the concepts of objectives and was developed primarily with a focus on curriculum evaluations. Tyler maintained that "the process of evaluation is essentially the process of determining to what extent the educational objectives are actually being realized" (Tyler, 1949, p. 69). His process consisted of nine basic components or steps largely concerned with the formulation of objectives in clear and relevant form. However influential, the Tyler model has many shortcomings. The process focuses on the strengths and weaknesses in outcomes. But it provides little guidance on the actual processes of analyzing and interpreting data (Guba and Lincoln, 1981, p. 6). The important questions about how to modify the program or curriculum for better results are not answered. This is, of course, the crucial question from a supervisory point of view.

Many evaluation models distinguish between *formative* and *summative* evaluation. Guba and Lincoln (1981, p. 49) distinguish the two evaluations according to purposes: "The aim of formative evaluation is refinement and improvement. . . . The aim of summative evaluation is to determine impact or outcomes." Various researchers view these two approaches to evaluation slightly differently. Bloom and associates (1971) differentiated between formative and summative evaluation but also referred to "diagnostic evaluation."

The work of Stufflebeam and associates (1971) is unique in conceptualizing an evaluation model that is clearly compatible with the concepts of systems. The CIPP model is concerned less with objectives-product relationships and more with the nature of the system in operation and the decisions that can influence that operation. Hence, C = context evaluation addresses questions about the influences playing upon the program from the outside. I = input evaluation addresses questions about the appropriateness and need for inputs for use in the program operations. P = process evaluation addresses questions about the quality of operating events. Finally, P = product evaluation addresses questions about intended outcomes in comparison with actual outcomes.

Project Evaluations

Grand evaluation schemes, useful as they may be, rarely assist local evaluation efforts with more than a few general guidelines for action. A better understanding of the role that evaluation may play in the local educational setting may be gained from projects or proposed projects utilizing sophisticated evaluation techniques. While such project evaluations may not be directly transferable, they suggest approaches.

Evaluating a training program in development is illustrated in Flanagan's description of a project of the American Institutes for Research in Palo Alto (1969, p. 225). The objective of this project was the development of a $7\frac{1}{2}$-hour first-aid course to give Red Cross certification in basic first aid. First, an analysis of thousands of accidents yielded 500 items of specified information judged to be essential knowledge for such a course. A test based on these items was administered to groups of individuals who had and who had not recently completed a previously developed first-aid course. Information from this test led to the elimination of items of general knowledge. The remaining items were grouped into topical units, and a standard lesson format to cover these was developed. This consisted of a short instructional film, a period of skill practice, and a workbook study session. Preliminary units were tried out on small groups, with immediate achievement testing always following. Then came revision—motion pictures were edited or filmed over again where necessary and workbooks were rewritten. Evaluation followed each step, and the development of earlier units led to greater efficiency in the preparation of later units. The final course required $7\frac{1}{2}$ hours to complete, and achievement on test items was around 81 percent, where test scores of the sample group that had been enrolled in the previous course had averaged only between 40 and 50 percent; by including time as one of its fundamental criteria, a program was developed that conserved the time of its students.

Supervisors might use approaches similar to that described above, for example, in the development of in-service training programs. There, too, the time criterion is often all-important.

Comparing schools on reading productivity (Dyer, 1970, p. 97) is illustrated in a proposal for the evaluation of reading programs in grades four, five, and six for 91 schools of one state. Actual reading achievement score means at grade four are used to calculate predicted score means for grade six. These predicted means take into account both the input and the surrounding school conditions. When actual grade-six means are available, they are plotted on a graph with predicted means for this grade level. Some schools within systems that have similar predicted means will nevertheless differ on actual reading achievement. One will be high, another low. At this point, discrepancies may be investigated in terms of *process* variables—what did the school with higher means than predicted provide in reading activities that the others did not?

Such evaluation is designed to sharpen the focus of evaluation on discrepancies from expectations and hence stimulate hypotheses about the causes of high and low performance. Provided with some concrete hypotheses, supervisors are in a much better position to recommend innovative programs that will probably lead to program improvement on a consistent basis.

Evaluation as actions for change is described by Diederich and Link (1967, p. 181) in a report on the attempt of one school system to assess its contribution toward one major ideal of most English programs: the creation of a lifelong love for reading. The particular evaluation described here arose out of the initiation of a cooperative evaluation program in the junior high schools of the system involved. That program began with the organization of a districtwide evaluation committee that consisted of department heads and was directed by the coordinator of secondary education. A consultant gave assistance on measurement problems. Also, advisers were appointed; these were responsible for about 20–30 students. The advisers maintained record folders and were responsible for reporting to or advising students and parents. Students had a voice in the selection of their advisers. The evaluation committee was responsible for specifying or approving departmental goals and for deciding upon measurement instruments. Measurements for permanent records were made on a systemwide basis. Any measure recorded in a student's folder had to represent the independent judgment of two individuals. Tests were limited in number, and systemwide preparation and analysis promoted greater validity and reliability of measurements. Folders contained, in addition to achievement records, sociometric ratings, records of behavior problems, records of independent reading done in the library, a self-scored academic interest measure, and various other types of information.

The evaluation committee's concern with reading started with the general recognition that independent reading begins to show a sharp decline at about the eighth-grade level. Yet, a goal of most secondary English programs—including the one of this system—has been to increase independent reading. The evaluation data gathered by the committee revealed that the same phenomenon of a drop in reading in junior high had occurred in these schools. Analysis of the school program indicated several possible causes. First, homework increased greatly at about that level, and students became involved in more social activities. Second, students at this stage were being asked to make the transition from juvenile to adult reading. Many seemed unable to make the leap.

With those interpretations, the departments involved began valuing the situation to ascertain what changes might be made. Decisions followed. Scheduling was adjusted to provide independent study periods allowing some work previously done as homework to be completed during school hours when teachers were available for assistance. Specific periods for independent reading were allotted. Independent reading rooms with only fiction were set up; the physical setting was designed to encourage such reading. Paperback book sale racks were installed in or near cafeterias to encourage book buying. The course of study in English was analyzed to determine where it failed to meet students' needs. It was found that materials were not chosen by realistic standards in terms of student reading abilities. Adjustments in the curriculum were made. Instruction in specific reading analysis skills was introduced. More use was made of discussions that were based on student questions, and these questions were in turn analyzed by classes for their appropriateness.

In this school system continuous evaluation promised to lead to continuous change.

Process Evaluation

In process evaluation it is important to determine which variables should be studied as components of the teaching-learning process and which variables may more properly be considered context, input, or product variables. For example, teachers' educational qualifications would be considered input variables, but teachers' classroom verbal behaviors are process variables. The number of overhead projectors in the school is an input variable, but the frequency of use of the projector in a teachers' lesson is a process variable. The teachers' salary schedule is a context element, as is the number of new teachers employed; how well those better-paid, newly recruited teachers verbalize in positively reinforcing ways is a process variable. How their students respond may be a product variable.

Even when viewed restrictively, the number of process variables to be considered is overwhelmingly large. One possible division of these variables would consist of teacher variables, student variables, curriculum variables, instructional method variables, and material variables. These categories are broadly inclusive of many lesser variables. The teacher group might include, for example, such variables as teacher-aide behaviors, discipline styles, or responsiveness to student ideas.

In process evaluation, not only is it necessary to consider the individual categories of variables, but equally important are the interactions between variables. Traditional measures of teacher effectiveness, for example, yielded little research data to support one teacher behavior over others. Only when a system was developed that allowed the analysis of simultaneous student-teacher behavior were some significant relationships with output identified.

Both traditional research and evaluation of the teaching-learning situation tended to look at one factor, or a few at a time, hence not evaluating the full range of complexity in the teaching-learning process. Instruments and techniques to allow such an approach are being devised. Computer technology can and will play an important role in future evaluations and make possible the analysis of the more extensive data required.

It is well to note here that the greatest problem with process evaluation at the moment is the lack of supportive evidence relating most measures to student achievement or affective outcomes. However, Flanders (1969), Gage (1978), Medley (1977), and Dunkin and Biddle (1974), and others are providing increasing evidence of significant relationships between student achievement and teacher behavior. The dynamic measures in general seem to promise more than the static measures, many of which have repeatedly been shown to lack any significant correlations with product measures.

MULTIFACTOR EVALUATION

Emphasis on only a single factor or one type or cluster of factors continues to prevent evaluation findings from being fully utilized and leads to faulty conclusions too often when they are utilized. State testing programs, studies of scholastic aptitudes, National Assessment Center reports, and even regional accreditation studies fail to provide either the kind or variety of data most often needed by program directors.

Several quite different efforts to address these concerns seem to offer some promising departures. Bessent and Bessent (1979) are now making rather extensive use of *data envelopment analysis* techniques to study school efficiency and effectiveness. Wolfensberger and Glenn (1975) have developed and tested elaborate techniques for analyzing program services in human delivery systems. Branching diagram analysis techniques have been utilized by Harris (1981) to adapt CIPP model concepts to discontinuous program operations.

Each of these is briefly described here.

A Branching Diagram Analytic Technique

In an effort to associate input, process, and outcome measures with each other, we must draw upon multivariate analysis techniques. However, it is essential to keep data analysis techniques and data displays simple and easily understandable by laymen and classroom teachers. Several preliminary studies have indicated some promise on both counts for a *branching analysis* technique different from, but not unlike, the path analysis approach used in the behavioral sciences (Duncan, 1966).

In brief, branching analysis involves (1) selecting measures to be related to each other; (2) "splitting" the cases into high and low subgroups, and (3) showing relationships as highs or lows for logically related measures.

An illustration of this technique is shown in Table 8.1. This is the simplest application of the technique in that only two measures are used. The diagram employs arrows to show the assumed direction of causality. Obviously, a causal relationship has not been established, but for guiding operational decisions, the assumption is entertained that individualization of

TABLE 8.1 Basic Data and Branching Analysis Diagram for Relating Process to Outcome

TEACHER	PROCESS MEASURE RAW SCORE	RANK	OUTCOME MEASURE RAW SCORE	RANK	BRANCHING CATEGORY
1	79	1	+3	6	Hi Hi
2	76	2	+4	4 1/2	Hi Hi
3	70	3	−9	13	Hi Lo
4	69	4	+5	3	Hi Hi
5	65	5	+6	2	Hi Hi
6	63	6 1/2	+19	1	Hi Hi
7	63	6 1/2	+4	4 1/2	Hi Hi
8	57	8	−6	12	Lo Lo
9	54	9	0	7	Lo Lo
10	46	10	−4	10	Lo Lo
11	39	11	−3	8 1/2	Lo Lo
12	39	12	−5	4	Lo Lo
13	36	13	−3	8 1/2	Lo Lo

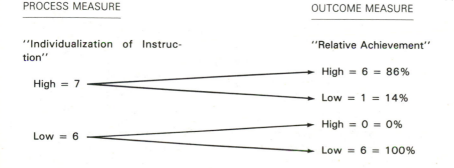

PROCESS MEASURE

"Individualization of Instruction"

High = 7

Low = 6

OUTCOME MEASURE

"Relative Achievement"

High = 6 = 86%

Low = 1 = 14%

High = 0 = 0%

Low = 6 = 100%

instructional practices is likely to be causally related to pupil achievement. The "process measure" was a mean score derived from several classroom observations.

Another example of the use of branching analysis diagrams is shown in Figure 8.1, where three measures are related. Here a measure of teacher self-perception is classified as an input to the instructional system. The relation-

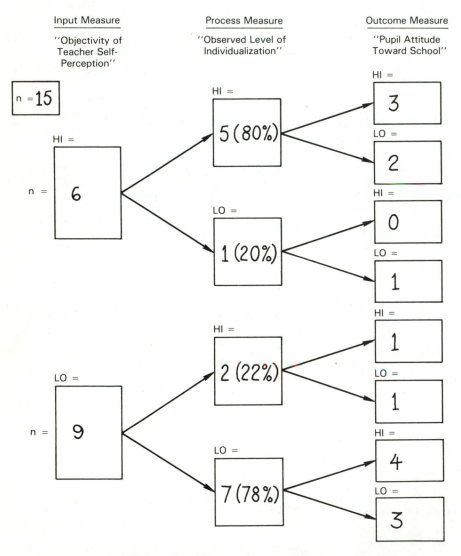

FIGURE 8.1   **Branching analysis diagram for 15 elementary school teachers, relating input, process, and outcome measures.**

ships between this measure (input), individualization of instruction (process), and pupil attitudes toward school (outcome) are diagramed. Again, assumptions of directionality are made in interpreting the diagram for decision-making purposes.

Interpreting these diagrams involves using the data to answer selected evaluation questions of relevant kinds. Figure 8.1 provides the basis for clearly answering the question:

> Do our teachers who individualize *most* tend to get more measured pupil achievement than those who individualize least?

The answer is a rather strong *yes* in the context of this situation with these specific teachers and pupils. Decision making directed toward maintaining and increasing these specific practices logically seems to follow.

Figure 8.2, on the other hand, presents a more complex, less conclusive picture for interpretation. It addresses the following questions:

> Do teachers with more objective perceptions of self individualize more?
>
> Do more objective, more individualizing teachers stimulate more positive responses toward school among their pupils?

The answer to the first question is distinctly *yes* in this situation with these teachers! However, *no* is the best answer to the second question. Hence, decision making can logically be directed toward the problem of less-objective teachers individualizing their teaching less. However, other analyses are called for to explain variations in attitudes toward school.

A *new team-teaching* program was studied with the branching diagram technique in a single school to provide guidance on several aspects of operations. Teachers on each team were observed, pupils' enthusiasm and their expressed attitudes were measured, and certain organizational characteristics of the program were studied. These several kinds of data were diagramed as shown in Figure 8.2

This diagram offers guidance for decisions about departmentalized organizational arrangements in this school if high levels of pupil enthusiasm are desired in response to individualized practices. The most consistent pattern is with low levels of departmentalization combined with individualized practices, since all these teachers seemed to produce enthusiastic students. Departmentalization also seems to be stimulating of pupil enthusiasm when individualized practices are low. Generally speaking, neither high departmentalization nor low individualization seems to produce consistent patterns of pupil enthusiasm. When a combination of enthusiasm and pupil verbal self-initiated behavior is used as a product measure, the importance of individualization is seen as very great. Policy decisions based on these analyses would be very cautious about departmental organization while encouraging

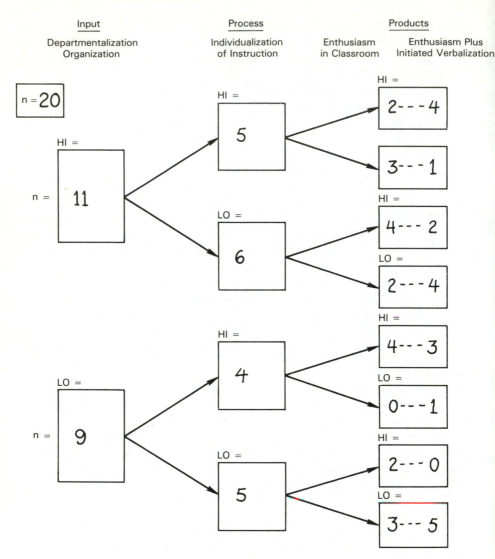

FIGURE 8.2 Relationships between departmentalization, individualization, and pupil enthusiasm.

individualization without it. Departmentalization would have to be justified on the basis of very high individualizing practice levels.

The *Taba training program* in one city school system was studied by Carthel (1973) using this branching analytic technique. The achievement and interest data on students were secured as product variables. Teachers' use of the Taba strategies in their classrooms as promoted by intensive in-service

TABLE 8.2   Branching Diagram Analysis for Selected Relationships in an In-Service Training Program

VOLUNTARINESS	INDIVIDUAL HELP PLUS TRAINING	USE OF TABA STRATEGIES

```
                                         High = 9        High = 8
                                                         Low = 1
         High = 16
                                         Low = 7         High = 3
                                                         Low = 4

                                         High = 10       High = 5
                                                         Low = 5
         Low = 16
                                         Low = 6         High = 0
                                                         Low = 6
```

training was measured as a process variable. Voluntariness of participation in the program was used as an input variable. Table 8.2 shows the branching diagram relating these variables to each other. This is a striking example of an analysis leading to clear interpretations about the impact of voluntariness, training, and individual consultative assistance producing desired practices.

Branching Product Analyses

A variation on the branching analysis technique involves analysis of two or more product measures when the *product* falls short of expectations and a "discrepancy" is said to exist. However, the problem remaining, locating the cause of the discrepancy, may well be quite bewildering. What the supervisor needs is a way of analysing *product* data to reveal the discrepancy *and also* to indicate the probable cause or causes. Without such clues, the resources expended to confirm suspicions might better have been spent on direct remedial efforts.

A *simple example* of branching product analysis involves the evaluation of a new instructional package or module.* Two product measures are utilized to determine the cognitive outcomes and the pupils' interest in, or enthusiasm for, the activity. These measures are then analyzed as shown in

*This technique for assessing new curricula was developed by Dr. Robert Randall, Southwest Educational Development Laboratory, Austin, Texas.

TABLE 8.3   A Simple Two-Product Branching Analysis

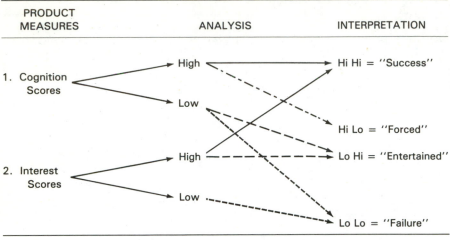

PRODUCT MEASURES	ANALYSIS	INTERPRETATION

Table 8.3. If a large percentage of pupils score high on both measures, "success" is indicated. However, when large percentages of pupils are found with other combinations of measures, alternate diagnoses are *inferred*. High cognitive scores along with low interest scores are diagnosed as "bored" or "forced learning" and lead to inferences that the activity was needlessly lengthy, or the content was too simple, or the activity was not stimulating. Conversely, low cognitive scores along with high interest scores are diagnosed as "entertainment," indicating that the activity was stimulating but not well designed to promote specified learning outcomes. Finally, low scores on both measures indicate serious deficiencies that require more rigorous evaluation.

While product measures alone are often not as informative as measures of input, process, and product combined, they can still be analyzed to guide decisions. The key to using these *branching product analyses* is having multiple measures rather than only a single one. Multivariate analysis provides opportunities for making logical inferences about possible cause-and-effect relationships that are not available with traditional analyses.

Branching diagrams require no sophisticated statistical treatments. Spady (1970) has devised a comparable analytical technique that can be used to add sophistication to the conclusions. Maher's synoptic evaluation technique or framework is closely related to branching diagram analysis. He defines and illustrates a variety of variables under each category—input, process, and outcome as well (1978).

Data Envelopment Analysis

This evaluation technique utilizes the individual school as a focus and provides answers to three key questions:

1. How efficiently are schools using their resources (inputs) to produce selected outcomes? That is, "What is the productivity of a given school in terms of its measured outputs in relation to its resources when compared to the outputs of schools with similar resources?" (Bessent and Bessent, 1979)
2. Which resources are most clearly contributing to outcome production?
3. Which resources are "slack" and might be more productively utilized?

An elaborate computer program is utilized to provide printouts for school personnel that can be readily interpreted in terms of the questions above. An analytical procedure has been developed to take into account factors such as socioeconomic status of the students' families and the mobility/stability of the school. Presently a centralized computer-based analytical system serves a consortium of school systems organized as a "Productivity Council" (Bessent and Bessent, 1979). Representatives of each district in the council meet, decide on outcomes to be studied, input factors that are to be utilized, and the instruments to be administered. Each district gathers and provides the data. The computer data base and the analyses are provided to all council participants on a shared-cost basis. Workshops are provided for principals, supervisors, teachers, and others to assure their ability to interpret the computer printouts, which are relatively simple scattergrams with accompanying tables. A micro-computer-based version of this system will soon be available.

Data envelopment analysis *does not* give close attention to intraschool or intraclassroom variations in productivity. It focuses instead on the status of the school unit. However, it goes well beyond most evaluation models using outcome data in providing each school faculty with a report on its relative efficiency and resource utilization. Hence, there is provided a basis for decisions and actions within each school to improve instruction.

Figure 8.3 reports on over 300 schools in a Productivity Council. The principal and faculty of the circled school can see the status with respect to reading test scores in comparison with all other council schools. The circled school has a productivity (efficiency) index of 92 percent, with a mean reading score of 76 percent of test items correct. If the faculty is concerned, it needs to investigate "sources of inefficiency" provided in the computer printout tables not shown here. The arrow extending from the illustrative school indicates the position this school could be expected to hold on the scattergram if it succeeded in becoming 99 percent productive.

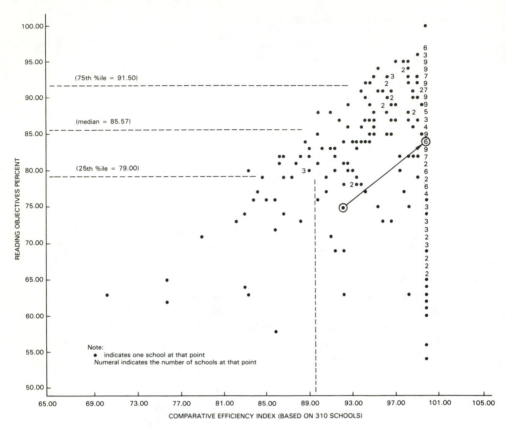

FIGURE 8.3   DEA efficiency diagram for third-grade reading. Copyright © 1982 by E. W. Bessent. Reprinted by permission. All rights reserved.

Other supervisory personnel might be especially interested in the Figure 8.3 scattergram for identifying and working with the faculty representatives of the 17 low-achieving, low-efficiency schools to find causes and eradicate them.

Program Analysis of Service Systems (PASS)

The PASS system calls for a team of carefully trained "raters" to study and analyze an organization, using an elaborately detailed set of 50 operational criteria. The team of evaluators consists of three or more persons who have undergone five days of training plus guided practice. The visting team observes, interviews, studies documents, and studies facilities. Individual ratings are completed and then compiled to provide a profile of "quality of service" for the entire organization.

Wolfensberger and Glenn (1975) developed and tested the PASS evaluation materials with hospitals, nursing homes, and prisons. An effort has been made to specify criteria of quality operations that are relatively generic to human services of various kinds. It is doubtful how well they would serve in school or college settings. What is interesting about this system for evaluation is the attention to operating processes, the use of descriptive rather than judgmental ratings, the validation of weightings for profile interpretation, and the use of trained evaluators.

While the PASS approach to program evaluation has much resemblance to the best of the procedures utilized by regional school accrediting associations, there are many differences. A similar approach might well be considered for use in school accreditation efforts.

SUMMARY

Evaluation of instructional programs is rapidly emerging as a supervisory task that almost ranks with in-service education in importance for improving instruction. The need for and commitment to instructional change by our society has been spawning a variety of movements, such as grand federal projects, state-mandated testing programs, and others still to come. Useful as these may be as motivators for change, they are not the highly developed steering systems needed.

Evaluation systems must be focused clearly on the improvement process rather than on accountability for end product. These systems must be operated close to the points of intervention for change. They must guide operational decisions first, but enlighten policy making as well. They must prevent the need for "no-go"-type decisions.

Systems analysis approaches to instructional evaluation are being developed that hold great promise of meeting the needs of schools and colleges. The complexities of the evaluation problems faced in education must be dealt with so that multivariate analyses can be provided to guide supervisors' efforts in change. Traditional research approaches, while useful in other ways, cannot be expected to serve the decision-making requirements of instructional program development activities. On the contrary, some fairly sophisticated, yet adaptable and easily communicable, analysis and feedback systems must be developed. Branching diagram data envelopment analyses presented in this chapter illustrate at least two approaches to meeting such requirements for supervisors. Data-gathering and analysis techniques that emphasize multifactor evaluation and speak to operational decision making are becoming available and need to be tested for feasibililty and utility by practitioners.

SUGGESTED READINGS

BORICH, GARY D., AND RON P. JEMELKA,   *Programs and Systems: Evaluation Perspective.* New York: Academic Press, 1981.

A thought-provoking book about values in evaluation that goes much further and conceptualizes evaluation as part of the program planning and design process. Chapter 3 argues for value-oriented evaluation and clearly distinguishes this from notions of "subjectivity." A "modeling approach" to evaluation is described in Chapter 7, followed by chapters on systems-oriented and holistic evaluation.

CRONBACK, LEE J., ET AL.,   *Toward Reform of Program Evaluation.* San Francisco: Jossey-Bass, 1980, Chapters 1 and 5, pp. 12–75 and 269–318.

Chapter 1, "Where Evaluation Stands Today," examines the concept of program evaluation. The authors define evaluation as a systematic examination of events occurring in and consequent to a contemporary program. The examination is conducted to assist in improving the program and others having the same general purpose. They define program as a standing arrangement that provides for social service. The discussion deals basically with complex organized programs—those that affect many persons in many places. The authors describe program evaluations that contribute to the discussion of alternative plans, and not quantitative-statistical methods. In Chapter 5, "The Shape of the Field Study," the authors describe systematic evaluative research. Four main themes of systematic inquiry are given: deliberate trial, diversity of evidence, comparison, and controlled assignment. The authors discuss the trial of social interventions, the strategy of diversifying evidence, and the use of comparisons. The disadvantage of comparison is the division of resources that it entails.

FATHY, SHADIA H.,   "The Role An Evaluator's Values Should Play in Program Evaluation," *Adult Education, 30* (Spring, 1980): 166–72.

This article describes the role the evaluator's values play in program evaluation and the important competencies needed by an evaluator. The author considers three main questions: 1. What are values? 2. How can values help the individual relate intelligently to his world? 3. What is evaluation and how does it relate to values? Ms. Fathy suggests that for an evaluator's values to play a constructive role in the program evaluation the evaluator should draw upon both logical and conceptual framework and empirical measurements. To accomplish this the evaluator must have competence relating to developing sound values, syllogistic reasoning and logical deduction, and communicating effectively.

GUBA, EGON G., AND YVONNE S. LINCOLN,   *Effective Evaluation.* San Francisco: Jossey-Bass, 1981, Chapters 1 and 3, pp. 1–22 and 39–52.

Chapter 1, "Comparing Evaluation Models," compares several evaluation models. The Tyler rationale is described. Tyler insists that the curriculum needs to be organized around certain objectives. His evaluation process is based on the concept of objectives. The authors give the nine components of Tyler's process. The Countenance Model is also described using two data matrices, description matrix and judgment matrix. The Context-Input-Process-Product model takes a closer look at organizers of the process. The Goal-Free model is described. The last model describes the Connoisseurship model. Two basic characteristics of the model are: A judgmental emphasis on the human being as a measurement instrument, and metaphoric analysis; and the use of the metaphor of the art critic for the generation of its basic concepts. Chapter 3, "Determining Merit and Worth," relates the terms *merit* and *worth* to formative and summative evaluation. The authors contend that the purpose of summative developmental (or merit) evaluations is to modify and improve the design of an innovative program or curriculum while it is still under development. The purpose of summative evaluation adoptive (or worth) evaluation is to certify or warrant the adapted program or curriculum for permanent local use.

KATZ, DOUGLAS S., AND ROBERT L. MORGAN,   "A Holistic Strategy for the Formative Evaluation of Educational Programs," in *Evaluating Educational Programs and Products*, ed. Gary D. Borich. Englewood Cliffs, N.J.: Educational Technology Publications, 1974, Chapter 8.

The chapter presents a general model for formative evaluations of educational programs. The model can be applied to summative evaluation upon completion of the formative stage. The model has eight basic components: mission, desired products, desired processes, observed processes, observed products, throughput entities, environment, and decision makers. The authors give a detailed description of each component and how it functions in the entire process. The authors rely on Goodwin Watson to explain how to reduce resistance to change.

LIGHT, RICHARD J.,   "Evaluation Methodology for Education Programs with Diffuse Goals," *Education and Urban Society*, 13 (November 1980): 109–134.

This article discusses current practices and procedures in evaluation research as they influence studies of programs being done retrospectively. He poses two questions: What positive impacts, if any, do these various extension programs have on their intended beneficiaries? and How can such studies be systematically organized and carried out? Mr. Light gives a review of alternative evaluation designs, some specific suggestions for interpreting past evaluation studies, and a way of thinking about how to proceed with extensive evaluation in the future.

NADLER, BARBARA, AND KENNETH STONE (1979),   "Evaluating Educational Programs with the Judicial Evaluation Model," *Education*, 99 (Summer 1979): 387–91.

This article describes the Judicial Evaluation Model; illustrates how it functions, using a program component of Public Law 94–142, the Individualized Education Program; and gives the limitations of the model. This model provides a means of evaluating educational programs using a format analogous to a jury trial: two advocates, designated as case analysts, defend opposing views of a program or policy.

WEBSTER, WILLIAM J.,   *The Evaluation of Instructional Materials.* Washington D.C.: Association for Educational Communications and Technology, 1976.

This booklet consists of a paper on the evaluation of instructional materials. The objectives of the paper are: to synthesize, through a selective review of the literature, a brief description of the state of the art of evaluation; to present a working model demonstrating the functions of various forms of evaluations; and to provide an annotated bibliography of sources for readers seeking further information on evaluation.

He gives a description of four evaluation frameworks: the CIPP model, Scriven, Stake, and Provus. The author presents a model for instructional materials evaluation; using a flowchart to explain the process in terms of: needs assessment, input evaluations, determinations of resources, program planning, program implementation, product evaluation, applied research, nonempirical information, and determination of program fate.

CHAPTER NINE
SUPERVISORS
AT WORK

The reports that follow reflect the work of a variety of supervisors in a variety of situations. The series of vignettes reported by the small-city supervisor trying to "cover" demands in 40 elementary schools gives a glimpse of the diversity of role expectations faced and underscores the need to approach supervisory staffing in rather different ways.

A typical day in the life of the general supervisor is interesting for its minute-by-minute descriptions of events. This report reveals the tendency of the supervisor to become an extension of the principalship when assigned within the school building. Contrasting ways of working are suggested in the reports on curriculum planning and the whirlwind schedule of a visiting consultant.

The work of the bilingual consultant is described for a period of several days. As a visiting consultant working intensively, but intermittently, with teachers and other local school and district staff, many of the realities of tactical versus strategic supervisory planning are brought into focus as discussed in Chapter 2.

A job description for a director of secondary education suggests the use of task and activity descriptions presented in Chapters 1 and 4 for analyzing a person's work in a position.

LIFE AND PROBLEMS AS A NEW SUPERVISOR*

The Oak Hills Public School District has operated for a number of years with only two general supervisors for all of its forty elementary schools. In addition to these general supervisors, there were five special supervisors in physical education, music, art, library, and instrumental music.

I was added to the staff as a general supervisor at the same time that the physical education supervisor resigned and a director for elementary curriculum was appointed.

I was asked to work in the areas of physical education, science, social studies, and mathematics for all grades in the elementary schools. My work was to cover forty schools.

In the pages that follow, I have tried to report a bit of my experience in this position. Log notes form the basis for vignettes of specific incidents which should help you understand my life as a new supervisor.

Vignette Number 1:
The Grammarian

I was visiting classes selected by the principal of the school. The principal was especially interested in my visiting and observing one of the teachers new to the school. The only class that I had time to visit was one in language arts. This is not one of the areas specified in my assignment, but I have a background in the area, since I helped write the teaching guide and have taught language arts.

When I entered the room, the fifth grade was discussing adjectives. The discussion lasted for some five to ten minutes. At the conclusion of the discussion, the teacher passed out two sheets of commercial ditto practice exercises concerning parts of speech. These involved filling in blanks. I could see no real relationship between the discussion and the practice. I could not even see how the discussion had arisen, since we do not teach parts of speech as such in the elementary grades.

I was unable to stay after my observation for a conference with the teacher, since I was due in another school. I did talk briefly to the principal to see if his school had decided to teach formal grammar in the intermediate grades. He told me that they followed the district guide. I explained my concern about the lesson that I had heard. I asked if I might come back the next day for a conference with the teacher. He agreed and asked me to go over the guide with the teacher and explain how we use it.

On the following day I met with the teacher. I opened the discussion by asking her what type of activity had led up to the lesson I had observed.

---

*These accounts were taken from the daily log of this supervisor during his first year on the job in a city school system. The city schools enrolled about 30,000 pupils in the elementary and secondary grades combined.

She said that it was just a routine lesson on grammar. She explained that she had taught freshman college English before coming to this school this year. I tried to give her a background concerning the functional type of English taught here and how we try to make it very practical. She appeared to be very eager to learn how it could be done, so I went into detail, telling her ways in which she could use language arts effectively. I also explained that we would have drill with this type of program, but it would be drill based on real needs and problems of communication.

Just as we were finishing our conference, she asked me some questions about science. I went with her to her classroom to help her identify some rocks and minerals.

This conference was quite satisfying to me, since the teacher seemed to want the help I offered and was eager for more. I had not approached the conference with the aim of disapproving the way in which she taught her lesson, but I approached it with the aim of trying to find out why she was teaching it. She responded well to this approach.

Vignette Number 2:
The Policy Maker

I arrived at the Pine Crest School at 1:00 P.M. for my first visit and was met at the door by the teacher of the combination first-second grade. She said that her pupils had gone home for the day. We discussed the problems that she was finding in this year's work.

At 2:00 P.M. I went into the combination third-fourth grade to observe a lesson in science. At the conclusion of the lesson, I talked with the teacher for a short time and expressed my pleasure with the good lesson I had seen.

When I returned to my office, I started working on my report concerning my visit. As I was writing, I realized that there should have been second-grade children still at school in the first room I visited! At that portion of the school year first-graders go home at 12:00 noon, but all other grades remain for a full school day. I tried to recall the conversation that I had with the teacher. I could recall nothing that led me to think any pupils stayed for classes after lunch. I reported this to the elementary director.

Later the director told me that my findings were correct—no pupils stayed after noon during the first six weeks. The teacher said that she had never kept the second grade as long as she'd been teaching!

Vignette Number 3:
A-V Education

The principal had arranged a schedule for me, so I was following it when I went to Mrs. B's room. When I arrived she was preparing to show a filmstrip. She had great difficulty in threading the strip into the machine. She was going to show it on a bulletin board that was covered with black paper. The picture from the filmstrip would not show up on the surface. After trying vainly to find another place on which to show the picture in the back of the room, the teacher finally decided to use the green chalkboard as a screen. It would not work, either. All of the time that this was taking place, two little boys were trying to cover the glass in the door with a piece of butcher paper. Mrs. B kept cautioning them not to use too much tape in fastening the paper to the door.

I had seen a sheet of tagboard on Mrs. B's desk, so I finally fastened that to the board to be used as a screen. We started looking at the filmstrip on transportation. Mrs. B started asking the class to tell *me* about the trains that we were seeing. No one could. Mrs. B was getting more upset by the minute. When she finished showing the filmstrip, she said that she had to send the projector to another teacher. As she started to lift the projector, the shield over the lamp came off. She jammed that on again. Then she could not get the legs on the projector down. She pulled those out. Finally, I got up and loosened the screw that released the legs so that they would go back into the machine. Mrs. B was so nervous that I did not know just how to help her without making matters worse.

We next heard a record on transportation. Mrs. B started the record on the wrong side and at the wrong speed. She finally got things going correctly. When the record was over, she could not turn off the record player, so she just jerked out the cord.

I left the room rather hastily! I felt that I could no longer be sure that I could keep from laughing if another blunder appeared. I felt that the best thing for me to do was to leave before I committed a blunder myself.

Vignette Number 4:
The Fall Guy

I had known Principal Bill Kurton for a number of years. I have a great deal of respect for him, but I have not liked the ways in which I have had to work in his Jefferson School.

When I made my first visit to his school, he asked me during our conference to make a special point of visiting his primary grades to observe their physical education program. He also asked me to tell the primary teachers that I did not want them to make their children walk with their arms folded. I really could not understand why he asked me to do this, but I decided to let it go and try to see for myself. I did get a natural opportunity to express my own dislike of this procedure. I could see that the teacher responsible for the practice was displeased by my saying that I did not like it. When I was ready to leave the school, the principal asked me to write a report back to him concerning the things I did not like. He wanted to use my report as a weapon to make his teachers do a better job. I did write one, but I am not sure that he ever used it.

On my second visit, Mr. K was displeased with the first grade teachers' teaching their pupils to square dance. He asked me to tell them that square dancing was not appropriate for the first grade. It is not, but the teachers in this school have done it for years. Again, I was fortunate in getting a natural opening for expressing my opinion.

Mr. K's requests have made my effectiveness in his school very doubtful. I feel that I have been made a scapegoat for him. I have been asked to do things for him that he recognized as wrong and yet that he had not taken care of himself. I still am not sure why he did not do these things for himself. If it were designed to maintain his own popularity with the teachers, the evidence that I have would lead me to believe that he has failed.

ELEMENTARY SUPERVISOR—A TYPICAL DAY*

The Southern Plains Elementary School is located in an old remodeled building in the downtown section of Plainville. It serves children mainly from impoverished homes, with many coming from migrant families. Mrs. Helen Robertson is of Mexican-American descent, as are most of the children and about one-half of the teachers. The principal, Rudolfo de Galvez, has been a local resident for many years.

In addition to twenty-eight classroom teachers, there is a nurse, a school social worker, an assistant principal, a counselor, and about twenty teacher aides on the staff. Special teachers include a librarian, two art teachers, and one music teacher. All staff members participate in a program of elective course offerings for upper-grade children.

A bilingual program has been developed and implemented in all primary-grade classrooms to emphasize the development and use of the Spanish language right along with the development of English as a second language for most pupils. The aural-oral approach is being stressed in this program, with consultative assistance from the state department of education and a regional education laboratory.

Mrs. Robertson is officed in the Southern Plains Elementary School and spends most of her time there with primary-grade teachers. Other supervisors, consultants, and the principal work with the program and staff in the middle and upper grades.

Log notes recorded by Mrs. Robertson on February 9, describing activities exactly as they happened, follow.

*Adapted from log notes prepared by the supervisor herself.

Time	Activity
7:45	(1) Mrs. Spain, art teacher, left a note on my desk to go by her room. She wanted to know how to use puppets in her class. I went there; we discussed puppets and went over her schedule.
7:55	(2) Mrs. Spain and Mrs. Anderson are sharing a room. Mrs. Anderson wanted to know how to encourage regular teachers to display art projects the students make even though they weren't pretty or what the regular teacher "likes." I suggested that she take advantage of a time when classroom teachers were in the room to discuss some of these pictures and praise the students' work by calling attention to good art principles the students had carried out in their pictures. Soon teachers would see their value and start displaying them.
8:00	(3) Stopped by Mrs. Ortega's room to discuss lessons which her children were to work on in the bilingual program.
8:05	(4) Mrs. Trevino, music teacher, came to the office to discuss songs she is teaching in both Spanish and English.
8:30	(5) Mrs. Oliphant, second-grade teacher, came by the office to discuss her bilingual lessons. She complained that evaluation activities for Level 1-Science are too elementary for her children. We decided to skip them and go on to Level 2.
8:45	(6) Went to Mr. de Galvez's office to talk about assignments of elective teachers. Met two visitors from Primrose School in his office.
9:00	(7) Mrs. Conroe and Mrs. Lorenz (district supervisors) came to the office to discuss developments at Southern Plains School.
9:15	(8) Had a conference with Mr. Halford (program director), Miss Reinhold (curriculum consultant), Mrs. Conroe, and Mrs. Lorenz in my office.
10:45	(9) Observed Miss Pena, third-grade teacher, present a lesson on Indians to three combined classes.
11:15	(10) Visited with Mrs. Ortega, Miss Valdez, and Mrs. Salas in Miss Valdez's room. I needed to talk to Mrs. Ortega to find out what Mrs. Ortega's children had worked on in Spanish lessons so that I can begin teaching them on Monday. The discussion led on to what each one of them was doing and how to cope with some of the problems they are encountering.
11:50	(11) Lunch in lounge with Mr. Halford and Miss Reinhold.
12:25	(12) Mr. Alderson, seventh-grade teacher, came by the office to discuss art elective class and some of his pupils. He needed ideas for art projects and how to get all of his pupils interested in helping themselves.
12:45	(13) Mrs. Smith, seventh-grade teacher, came to discuss SRA reading materials and the plans for her Daily Living class. She has found it difficult to communicate with the girls in this class. We are both thinking about a change in what she could best teach as an elective class next semester.
1:05	(14) Discussed elective classes with Mrs. Henderson, seventh-grade teacher, Mrs. Knowles, eighth grade, and Mr. Garcia, sixth grade, in the lounge. They said that what we were offering this semester were good subjects and that a journalism class should be started. Mrs. Henderson volunteered to teach it.
1:30	(15) Mrs. Walsh, Scholastic representative, came to show new books and records that are being sold now.

1:55	(16) Went to Miss Murphy's sixth-grade room and Mr. King's seventh-grade room and asked them to think about what they would like to teach as an elective class next semester. Mr. King immediately said, "Chess."
2:00	(17) Went to Mr. de Galvez's office to discuss journalism and chess classes. He thought these were good ideas.
2:10	(18) Met with four third-grade teachers to discuss the observation guide I was planning to use, and also to discuss field trips and other activities in which one of the classes could be included. This one class is on the first floor and is usually excluded from the other third-grade activities. They will divide into two groups and go on a field trip next week.
2:40	(19) Went to Mr. Verdugo's study hall class to ask him to think about what he would like to teach during elective class. He will let me know next week what he would like to teach. We discussed purposes and procedures followed in elective classes.
2:50	(20) Next week I will begin teaching the Spanish lessons for Mrs. Ortega's class. I read the lessons for science on self-concept.
3:10	(21) Went to materials center and made thirty-four picture cards for the science lesson and name-and-address tags for the self-concept lesson.
4:20 to 4:30	(22) Returned to office, cleared desk, and left for home.

CURRICULUM PLANNING IN A BOOM TOWN*

"Sprawling, brawling, ranching, hauling"—these are among the adjectives poet Reatha Thorpe uses to describe Colstrip, a coal and cattle town in Southeastern Montana. As billions of tons of coal buried under the land were mined, the Colstrip schools faced all the problems typically associated with boom towns—rapidly expanding population (from less than 100 in the 1960s to over 8,000 today), sizable school building construction projects ($25 million) and a burgeoning teaching staff (from 12 to more than 160 certified staff by the 1982–83 school year).

School trustees felt that despite these problems, they wanted quality education for the children in Colstrip, and to a large extent, the best way to accomplish this was through curriculum development. The trustees hired Tom Everett as assistant superintendent and set curriculum development as his primary responsibility.

Everett outlined four critical concerns to be addressed at the outset:

Commitment on the part of trustees, administrators, and teachers to ensure project completion;

Teacher involvement from the beginning to ensure teacher ownership;

*By Harold Tokerud and Thomas Everett, *The School Administrator*, 39 (June 1982): 8. Reprinted by permission, American Association of School Administrators.

Professional teacher-administrator relationships to ensure a free exchange of ideas;

Mutual trust between teachers and administrators to ensure that the criterion-referenced tests critical to the project were regarded as a measure of student progress rather than teacher performance.

The curriculum development method we used involved "flow charting." We started with a generic heading such as a course name or a job title. Each generic heading was subdivided into its major components until no more subdivisions were possible.

For example, starting with the job title, "Elementary Principal," we identified ten major components of the position, e.g., attendance, discipline, etc. Next, we listed performance responsibilities for each component. We cross-referenced each flow chart with existing job descriptions. Each administrator proceeded in like fashion with his or her own job, comparing results with immediate superiors to ensure agreement concerning expectations for the position.

By the time this operation was completed, each administrator had experience with the process and had shared expectations with supervisors.

The administrative cabinet picked mathematics as the first area for curriculum development. During teacher orientation in the fall of 1980, we began working with teachers. After the first month of school, we scheduled meetings with all the kindergarten teachers and used a process similar to that described above. Each program, beginning with kindergarten mathematics, was broken down into its components and learner outcomes. When writing learner outcomes, we asked teachers, "What is it you expect these students to do after instruction that they could not do before instruction?" We also asked teachers to code learner outcomes with either an "M" for mastery or a "D" for developmental.

This process was continued for each grade level, and as we met with subsequent grade level teachers, we shared charts developed by other teachers. Principals attended these meetings to help determine desired outcomes. The communication aspect of this process was fantastic to watch. The process opened communication between what might otherwise have been isolated groups of teachers operating in a vacuum. Flow charts were shared from grade to grade, and junior high mathematics charts were shared with the entire high school mathematics department.

As we developed the curriculum, we contracted with the Institute of Educational Research in Illinois to develop criterion-referenced tests (CRT's) based upon the learner outcomes developed for grades three, six and eight. We also use an annual norm-referenced testing program which will give us a cross-check on our CRT's. Periodically, teachers are also asked to share flow charts with the trustees during regular board meetings. Since evaluation is an essential part of the process, meetings are scheduled in the spring with groups of teachers to revise learner outcomes.

To assure that flow charts are used in the classroom, we tied our evaluation procedures to the process. In each meeting scheduled before a classroom evaluation, teachers are asked how lessons are related to the flow charts.

Careful, shared planning has made effective curriculum development possible even in a rural boom town.

VISITING CONSULTANT FOR BILINGUAL EDUCATION*

Sunday, March 19

Met with the supervisor acting as project coordinator from Bay View Schools to finalize the schedule for the week's staff development activities. Established priorities for supervision, according to the most urgent needs in staff development.

Monday, March 20

8:30 A.M. Made plans and prepared a first-grade demonstration lesson in English at Bay View Elementary School.

10:00 A.M. Conducted the demonstration lesson specifically for some teachers who were having difficulty developing the concept of *movement*. A discussion was held immediately following the lesson.

1:10 P.M. Observed first-grade teacher giving an oral language lesson in Spanish.

2:30 P.M. Had a staff development in-service meeting with all first- and second-grade teachers from the several schools conducting Follow Through classes.

Tuesday, March 21

Observed in second-grade classrooms. After each observation, I had a short individual conference with the teacher to discuss the lesson and to find out if she had any concerns pertaining to the SEDL (Southwest Educational Development Laboratory Curriculum) curriculum.

*Adapted from log notes of the consultant, Ms. Hercilia Toscano, Southwest Educational Development Laboratory, Austin, Texas.

I conducted another demonstration lesson at the request of one of the teachers. As usual, a discussion of the lesson followed the demonstration.

1:30 P.M.   A meeting with the Spanish-language consultant, the Spanish-language teachers, and the aides. The emphasis of this meeting was on the Spanish materials, especially on the Spanish reading program. The district's reading consultant attended this meeting.

Wednesday, March 22

8:30–11:30 A.M.   Observed several teachers at Del Valle School. Every observation was followed by a conference to discuss the lesson, curriculum materials, or any concerns the teacher might have.

12:30 P.M.   Presented a classroom demonstration in reading in Spanish, second grade. All the Spanish teachers and assistant teacher aides attended. A short conference to discuss the classroom demonstration followed.
A luncheon meeting with the Spanish-language coordinator and her assistant followed.

3:00 P.M.   Had a meeting with the district superintendent, the project coordinator, and the Spanish-language consultant.

Thursday, March 23

Spent this day at M. L. King School in nearby Southside School District. All of the first-and- second-grade teachers were observed teaching some segment of the new curriculum.
I had a luncheon meeting with the project coordinator and the principal of the school, and we discussed the progress of the Follow Through project.
The afternoon was spent with the project coordinator discussing areas where she needs to further supervise her teachers. We planned for my next visit.

8:30–9:00 A.M.   Met with the site coordinator and the principal of the school and checked the schedule. We discussed some of the problems observed by the coordinator when she visited the teachers.

9:00–9:30 A.M.   Observed Helen Bown's first-grade oral language lesson.

9:30–10:00 A.M.   Observed Idalia Buzani teaching a first-grade lesson in social studies.

10:00–10:30 A.M.   Observed Irene Toscano teaching a first-grade oral language lesson.

10:30–11:00 A.M.   Observed Alice Miel teaching a second-grade lesson, "The Desert."

11:00–11:30 A.M.   Observed Henrietta Ruiz teaching a first-grade oral language lesson on animals.

11:30–1:00 P.M.   Had luncheon meeting with site coordinator.

1:00–1:30 P.M.   Observed Bill Johnston teaching a social studies lesson in second grade. The unit was entitled "Just for Fun."

2:00–4:00 P.M.   Had in-service meeting with the principal of the school, the site coordinator for Follow Through, the parent coordinator, and the first-, second-, and third-grade teachers.

4:00–5:00 P.M.   Had conference with site coordinator to make plans for my next visit.

7:30–9:30 P.M.   Attended and addressed a parent meeting at the Bay View Community Center. Presented the oral language and reading materials, and discussed parent participation in the classroom.

Friday, March 24

Returned to Bay View School District and spent the day observing more teachers in these schools.

Conferences were held with each teacher.

Part of the afternoon was spent with the project coordinator, making plans and developing a schedule for the next visit in April.

4:10 P.M.   Headed for air terminal to catch my plane.

JOB-DESCRIPTION ANALYSIS: DIRECTOR OF SECONDARY EDUCATION*

Jefferson Township includes the villages of Jefferson and Cedar Park and a large unincorporated area of suburbia. The township has a rather stable population of 27,700 residents. Most of Jefferson's working people commute to the city for employment. It is a middle-class and upper-middle-class community with little poverty but much delinquency.

*Based on a school district simulation project under the auspices of the University Council for Educational Administration. The author is indebted to Jerry M. Gideon for much of the work in developing this job-description analysis.

The Jefferson Township School District is organized into four elementary schools (grades 1–6), one junior high school (grades 7–9), and one senior high school (grades 10–12). Approximately four thousand children attend the public schools, and approximately one thousand children attend private schools in or near the district.

To operate its schools, the Jefferson school system employs a professional staff of 260, which consists of classroom teachers, special teachers, librarians, nurse-teachers, supervisors, counselors, principals, and central administrators. The professional staff is very stable, having less than 10 percent turnover each year. Staff members' training and experience rank them well above the average.

The central administration includes the superintendent, assistant superintendent for business management, assistant superintendent for instructional services, director of secondary education, and director of elementary education.

In this study, an attempt was made to describe in precise detail the job of the director of secondary education in the Jefferson Township School District. This job description was also analyzed using as a framework the tasks of supervision and activities as defined by Harris.

The job descriptions were written using the following guidelines for information to be specified.

1. A task area should be clearly implied.
2. The type(s) of activities employed should be indicated.
3. The person(s), if any, toward which the action is directed should be made clear.
4. The person(s), if any, with whom the action is undertaken should be indicated.

The degree of responsibility for getting different jobs done by any public school supervisor might vary considerably. Therefore, only 24 of 82 jobs are listed here as the primary or sole responsibility of the director of secondary education.

Job Descriptions

Each job described in this section is grouped according to the task area into which it seems to fit best. The numbers in parentheses following each description refer to the supervisory activities involved (see Chapter 4).

DEVELOPING CURRICULUM

1. Works in committees with teachers and other selected personnel in establishing teaching objectives consistent with the school's philosophy of education, in cooperation with superintendent (12, 22).
2. Works in committees with selected professional personnel to develop and implement pilot projects, in cooperation with superintendent of schools (13, 12).

3. Edits and publishes curriculum bulletins, guides, courses of study, pamphlets, etc., and gives demonstrations for using these materials for the instructional staff, in cooperation with secondary principals and assistant superintendent for instruction (8, 22).

ORGANIZING FOR INSTRUCTION

4. Selects committees of science teachers and principals and works cooperatively with them to design instructional program and the development of projects in relation to the science fair, in cooperation with assistant superintendent for instruction (6, 12, 22).
5. Assumes responsibility for implementing new and revised curriculum practices as decided by the faculty steering committee, in cooperation with secondary principals.
6. Studies personnel needs, teacher-pupil ratios, etc., and makes recommendations to principals on better staff working conditions, in cooperation with supervisory staff (9, 13).

STAFFING

7. Interviews teacher applicants, to screen and recommend to principals, in cooperation with assistant superintendent for instruction (9).
8. Works cooperatively with assistant superintendent for instruction and recommends to principals any personnel assignment changes needed in the instructional program (9, 11).

PROVIDING FACILITIES

9. Arranges and directs meetings with instructional staff and principals to obtain information regarding equipment design and specifications for superintendent and assistant superintendent for instruction (12, 15, 18).
10. Makes regular classroom visitations to gain ideas on equipment specifications, facility utilization, etc., and advises central supervisory staff, in cooperation with instructional staff and principals (7, 9).

PROVIDING MATERIALS

11. Works with instructional staff, individually and in groups, to explain, demonstrate, exhibit, or direct practice in the use of new materials, along with appropriate special consultants (1, 6, 8, 9).
12. Works with instructional staff in directed practice to gain skills in the use of various instructional media, in cooperation with secondary principals (9, 11, 23).

ARRANGING FOR IN-SERVICE EDUCATION

13. Plans and arranges for demonstration teachings by local teachers and special consultants to show instructional staff various teaching techniques (7, 13).
14. Surveys, plans, and directs in-service programs designed for specific areas in the instructional program, in cooperation with supervisory staff and principals (1, 7, 13, 15, 18).

15. Plans and directs meetings to show films and give lectures on new and revised teaching procedures for instructional staff, along with appropriate special consultants (1, 4, 7, 13).

ORIENTING NEW STAFF MEMBERS

16. Plans for and directs programs, meetings, and social gatherings prior to the opening of school to acquaint new secondary personnel with the local school district, in cooperation with superintendent of schools (1, 12).
17. Plans and directs meetings designed to inform new personnel of the health, recreational, and other facilities of the community, in cooperation with secondary principals.

RELATING SPECIAL SERVICES

18. Prepares memoranda and reports orally to instructional staff on a continuous program to coordinate special services and the major instructional goals of the school, in cooperation with principals and supervisory staff (1, 13, 22).

DEVELOPING PUBLIC RELATIONS

19. Works cooperatively with all administrative and supervisory personnel through publications and public speaking in defining and interpreting the instructional program for the community (1, 22).

EVALUATING INSTRUCTION

20. Works in committees with other supervisory personnel in developing and revising long-range policies for a systemwide evaluation program involving all school personnel (12, 22).
21. Orders and distributes to principals and counselors the materials needed for administering the student testing programs for achievement, aptitude, etc., in cooperation with assistant superintendent for instruction (22).
22. Makes studies and does research to make recommendations to principals and teachers concerning the value of specific teaching techniques, such as field trips and lectures, in cooperation with assistant superintendent for instruction (9, 13).
23. Selects, organizes, and directs committees of secondary staff personnel and principals to evaluate entire instructional program in accordance with Southern Association Accreditation Standards, in cooperation with superintendent for instruction (7, 12, 13, 15, 18).

PERFORMING ADMINISTRATIVE AND OTHER TASKS

24. Works in committees with the administrative staff to administer the budget allotment for curriculum and instruction most efficiently, in cooperation with superintendent of schools (12, 13, 15).

CHAPTER TEN
OBSERVATION
APPLICATIONS

A substantial variety of observation instruments and their uses are described in Chapter 7. Case material and project reports are presented here to reflect supervisory uses of classroom observation activities. The initial case reports describe individual teacher-supervisor relationships. The John Carroll case suggests a diagnostic-analytical scheme for relating observations to the improvement process.

Observation instruments of the descriptive kinds are presented to give readers a bit more information on these instruments in practice. Flanders's interaction matrix analysis is also illustrated in these cases.

Throughout these case reports, problems associated with feedback and resistance to change are illustrated. The classic but rare problems of passive resistance, evasiveness, and direct confrontation are dramatized in these cases. The reader, of course, will be aware of a persistent point of view in this chapter, namely, that interaction about objective events over which teachers have direct control should dominate in preference to concerns for feeling per se.

THE CASE OF JOHN CARROLL

John Carroll is a young, energetic teacher of the fifth grade in the Elsworth School. Elsworth is a small town, and John's class is largely composed of a cross-section of the age group of the community. A substantial number of the children in John's class are of Mexican-American background and come from homes with rather low incomes.

John has not taught very long and is still working hard to develop himself as a teacher. He has a strong interest in teaching and works hard at it. John's principal has observed him several times and sees both his strengths and his weaknesses:

> He works at the job of teaching probably more than any other teacher I have. He spends more energy. He goes from desk to desk and deals directly with the child. He seems to be very versatile in several subject-matter areas. I think he can do a creditable job. I say creditable as a beginning teacher—in that sense. When he first started, he was the autocrat of the room. He felt that the job of the teacher was to be talking all the time. In fact, he thought learning could not take place unless the teacher was talking. Later, though, he began to get the idea that it would be fun if he could develop a situation in which children could share in the learning process. He began to let the children talk. I think he is developing quite well toward this concept of teaching. I think he has grown in his compassion toward children. In the beginning, he was very quick to condemn children for every act that seemed to him to be the least bit out of line. And he did it vocally. He was loud about it. Lately he has begun to understand that he contributes to their misbehavior as much as anyone. His whole attitude toward them has changed. He has become kinder and more considerate of what they are interested in. John has grown in his courage, too.
>
> I don't think he will ever develop into a creative teacher. He will take suggestions readily and try anything if someone offers suggestions, but if change depends upon his own initiative, I'd say that he is very inflexible. He changes very little of his own accord. He is slow to catch a change in the direction of interest of the students. He still doesn't work effectively with individuals. Now he tries. His work with individuals isn't personal.

A Class Session

As we walked into the classroom, John Carroll was in the midst of explaining something at the chalkboard. His classroom furniture was composed of seven or eight tables, with five or six children clustered around some of them. John was saying, "When you are adding . . . now these numbers don't have the same common denominator. . . . The easy way to do this until you get used to it is to multiply one denominator by another." At this point John demonstrated what he had said by doing a couple of addition-of-fraction problems on the board. He explained to the class what he was doing and why he was doing it as he went along. Following this demonstration the pupils returned to doing their own arithmetic problems individually at their tables. A pupil at one of the tables asked the teacher how to do the problem.

John: "All right, give me an example."

The pupil gave him an example, and the teacher went to the board to demonstrate how to do it. Most of the pupils watched attentively while he was demonstrating this problem on the board. A few of them continued to work on their own problems at their table, and two or three were fidgeting around and not paying very much attention.

When the demonstration was over, the children returned again to doing their own problems. There was an occasional question here and there. Pupils would raise their hands, and the teacher would go over to help them. John gave a sharp glance every now and then over across the room to one table of pupils who were fidgeting around and making some noise. As he finished helping the pupils at one of the tables, he turned around to the noisy table and said, "Remember, Mary Elizabeth, you and Carmen are in charge of the table." As that table quieted down, the teacher returned to helping various individuals with their problems. A few minutes later he turned his attention to another table and said, "Bobby Anderson, your table's getting noisy." A few moments later a girl got up and went over to one of the other tables, leaned down, and began to whisper to a girl at that table.

John called out across the room, "Mary, what are you doing up?"

Mary responded, "Carmen was going to tell me something."

The teacher replied, "It's not the time to be telling things. Sit back down at your table." He said this quietly but firmly.

As John stood surveying the group at work, one boy went over to him. He said, "I'm stuck on a problem. Can you help me?" John responded, "Go back to your seat and raise your hand and then maybe I'll help you." The boy went back to his seat at the table and raised his hand. John went over to help some other pupils individually and after a few minutes went back to the boy who had asked for help.

A boy at one of the tables seemed to be dozing. John went over and put his hand on the boy's head and said, "Hey, fellow, you're sleeping on me again." The boy came to with a start and grinningly said, "I'm tired." John smiled at the boy and turned and walked up to the front of the room. He faced the class and said, "All right, let's put our arithmetic books away and let's be quiet about it. The quietest table today has been the one over there," and he pointed to the table in the corner. The pupils at this table grinned and looked very pleased that they had been singled out as the quietest table.

John now walked over to one of the tables at the front of the room where the pupils were beginning to get rather noisy. He said to two of the girls, "Carmen, Mary Elizabeth, if you don't quiet down over there and change, I'm going to have to report you." Again his tone was quiet but firm.

Then turning to the class he said, "OK, we're going to go over the test that we took yesterday in geography. Now the first question was an easy one. What is the largest island in Japan?" Most of the pupils had their hands up, wanting to answer the question. He called on one of them, and she said, "Honshu." John responded, "Honshu, I'll bet we've repeated that word a hundred times in here. Now, what is the large and famous mountain near the city of Tokyo? I want the full name—no nicknames for this." A pupil responded as John nodded at him, "Mount Fujiyama." Teacher: "That's right. Fine. Now what continent is Japan a part of? Now I want not only the name of this continent but I want you to know the names of all the other continents in the world." Eight or ten pupils raised their hands to answer. John called on one and the pupil answered his question, giving the name of not only the continent of Asia but also all the other continents in the world. At this point the bell rang. John asked the children to put their materials away, and they proceeded to go out for recess.

Comprehensive Lesson Analysis

The observer in John Carroll's classroom during the period of time described above finds much to be analyzed. "The Profile" for the *Comprehensive Observation of Performance** instrument shows the observer's estimates of evidence regarding 22 behaviors (see Figure 10.1). A very complex pattern is revealed as progress in two performance areas but with very little strength in either verbal interaction or individualization.

In a conference with John Carroll, some of the specific behaviors are discussed. John is perplexed about the observer's report on his verbal interaction. He thinks of himself as relatively strong in this performance area:

JOHN CARROLL: I feel I really am very verbal in my work with the children!
    OBSERVER: Let's look at our criteria, the behaviors that I was using as I observed, and see what evidence was recorded.

The two turn to the observation guide to see what was recorded by the observer.

    OBSERVER: Now this behavior, 3a—*Communicates clearly and concisely.* I recorded your careful explanation on the chalkboard, but notice also that I recorded, "Interrupts class to respond to individual student's question." Clear, concise communication is defined as more than just giving explanations.
JOHN CARROLL: Well, what about these other behaviors?
    OBSERVER: Well, let's look at the recorded evidence under 3b—*Encourages and guides student responses and interactions.* Notations include the following: "Gives information . . . does not ask for suggestions. . . . No probing for understanding. . . . No rephrasing."

*Ben M. Harris and Jane Hill, *Developmental Teacher Evaluation Kit* (Austin, Tex.: National Educational Laboratory Publishers, 1982).

Teacher __John Carroll_____ Grade __5<u>th</u>___ Subject __Math and Soc. Stud.__

School__Elsworth Elem. School_____Observer__Harris_____Date__Jan. 22____

Lesson and Topic __Mathematics (addition of fractions) and_____ Time __1__:__20__ to __2__:__00__
_____Social Studies (The cities, mountains and other
_____geographic features of the islands of Japan).___

THE PROFILE

Performance	Behaviors: Summary of Observed Evidence				
	a	b	c	d	Other
1. Businesslike	(H)	(H)	(M)	(N)	(—)
2. Friendly	(M)	(H)	(M)	(M)	(—)
3. Verbally Interactive........................	(N)	(N)	(N)		(—)
4. Stimulating	(H)	(N)	(N)	(N)	(—)
5. Individual Oriented.......................	(M)	(N)	(M)	(N)	(—)
6. Multi-Media Integrative................	(N)	(N)	(M)		(—)
Other_____	(—)	(—)	(—)	(—)	(—)

OBSERVED ACCOMPLISHMENTS: Performance areas ____ None ____

SUGGESTED FOR FURTHER ANALYSIS: Performance Areas: __#3__ or 5 ____

Behaviors: # __3a__ # <u>or</u> # __5b__ # __5d__ # ____

Comments:
     Much progress apparent in #2 Friendly. Area #1 also shows progress, especially 1a and 1c.
     Verbal interaction (#3) <u>and</u> individualization need much attention. Consider best starting points.

FIGURE 10.1   A DeTEK Instrument: Comprehensive Observation of Performance. Copyright © 1982. Ben M. Harris and Jane Hill. All rights reserved. Reprinted by permission of National Educational Laboratory Publishers, Inc., Austin, Texas.

JOHN CARROLL: Gosh, that doesn't sound very good!
    OBSERVER: Well, these are complex behaviors. It's not easy to learn to interact skillfully in the classroom.

Carroll and the observer continue to discuss the observation report as it relates to improving John's practices in verbal interaction and individualization.

JOHN CARROLL: What do you suggest for me to do now? I feel a bit down. I've been trying things and thought I'd really been doing fine.
    OBSERVER: Perhaps you've been trying too much. You have made real progress in the Businesslike and the Friendly areas. Why not focus now on your verbal interaction skills? We can use Flander's interaction categories to assist you in trying some new technqiues.
JOHN CARROLL: Ok! I'm willing.
    OBSERVER: I'll bring you some material describing the Flanders categories. We can meet and talk about using different verbal techniques and then I'll observe you and we can analyze your efforts together.

The conference ends with some target dates set.

Flanders Analysis

In February John Carroll planned a lesson especially for being observed using the Flanders categories. John selected a mathematics lesson, feeling most comfortable in that subject area. The lesson was taught, observed, and tape recorded on February 18. John and the observer met and prepared the matrix (see Figure 10.2) together.

Once the work matrix was completed, there was lots to talk and to think about. The observer brought along the tape recording of the lesson to encourage John to listen to himself after the conference. But the conference itself focused primarily on being sure John was able to *interpret* the interaction patterns and consider possible changes to produce in subsequent lessons.

Some of the interpretations discussed included the following:

1. *Column total interpretations.* a. Limited but not insignificant use of 1s—accepts feelings and 2s—praises. b. Almost no emphasis on 3s—using students' ideas. c. Nearly half of teacher talk in 4s—questions, 5s—lectures, and 6s—gives directions. d. Heavy use of criticizing. e. Student responses largely 8s—direct response. f. Very limited self-initiated student responses—9s.

WORK MATRIX

Class 5th Elsworth Elem. School — No. of Pupils 27 — Date Feb. 18

Teacher Carroll, John — Time of Obs. 8:48 to 9:00 — Observer ______

Topic and Subject Mathematics (add. of fractions) and Special Projects

	1	2	3	4	5	6	7	8	9	10	
1											
2		1							1	3	
3											
4	1			7	11	2		18		12	
5				2	12	8	3			3	
6	1	2		4	9	12	6	5		7	
7						6	16			5	
8	1	6		3	3			4			
9			1	2	4	2					
10	2	1			6		3		2	3	Matrix Total
TOTAL	5	10	1	18	45	30	28	27	3	33	200
%	2	5	1	9	23	15	14	13	2	16	

I/D Ratio = 34/103 = 1/3

Revised I/D Ratio = 16/103 = 1/6

Extended Indirect = 1/103 = 1%

Extended Direct = 40/103 = 40%

Extended I/D = 1/40

3-3 Cell = 0

9-9 Cell = 0

FIGURE 10.2 Work Matrix.

2. *Cell interpretations.* a. 4-5, 5-5, 6-6, and 4-8 are all among the most frequent sets of events. These represent question followed by lecture, lecture followed by more lecture, directions followed by more directions and questions followed by answers. b. Cell 7-7 is most frequent of all. It represents criticism followed by more criticism. c. Nine cells in upper-left corner (1-1, 1-2, 2-1, etc.) show a total of only 1 set of events. This represents almost no use of extended positive reinforcement.

3. *Some possible changes to consider:*
   Reduce 7s, replace with 10s or nonverbal acts.
   Increase 2-2s and 3s.
   Increase 9s with more 8-10s, 2-10s, and 10-10s.

CONTRASTING WAYS OF WORKING*

I was assigned to work cooperatively with one of the more experienced consultants in a specific school that was part of a special project. After visiting the school, we had a conference to decide upon my role. I was assigned to be in three classrooms, one hour each every week, in addition to participating in the once-a-week, after-school, three-hour-long in-service session. The guidelines within which the field consultant suggested that I work could be paraphrased as follows:

> Be a friend to the teacher.
> Become indispensable to the teacher by helping her in little things that take up much of her time.
> Provide a variety of materials and suggest that she use them in the room.
> Make materials for the teacher during the time spent in the classroom.
> Tutor difficult students for her and, using demonstration techniques, urge the teacher to change some of the things that are either wrong or not working.
> Refrain from any *evaluation,* as we are in the classroom to help the teacher change and evaluation will only make her guarded and resentful.

I did not like the guidelines. I felt they were contrary to common sense. Everyone who goes into a teacher's classroom makes an evaluation—even if only a casual visitor who merely looks at the bulletin boards. However, I bowed to the consultant's experience. I do not like confrontation. I felt that I wanted to go along for a while and get my feet on the ground. I also thought that I might be able to change things gradually.

I worked in the school for one month following those guidelines. I brought materials to the teachers. I helped rearrange their rooms. I tutored children and made materials. I tried to talk to the teachers about things that I thought needed changing. I sat through in-service meetings that sometimes did and sometimes did not meet what I thought were the needs of the teach-

*Based on a project report by Helen P. Almanza.

ers. But I couldn't really support my ideas about necessary changes or my ideas about the kinds of needs that should be met by in-service training. All I had were my "feelings" about the situation.

The final straw came one day when one classroom teacher had me take over her entire class while she tutored one child in the rear, another classroom teacher asked me to make multiplication strips by laboriously copying them (it would have taken five minutes on a spirit master), and I sat through a three-hour in-service session that, if properly planned, would have taken 35 minutes.

I decided to confront!

The consultant in charge knew I was upset, and she wanted to know what was wrong. That gave me the opening I needed. I explained that I had decided to change my strategy. I was no longer going to function as a helper to the teacher, at least not in that manner. I was going to use data-gathering instruments such as the Flanders and the *New Comprehensive Observation Guide** to evaluate the teaching-learning process. I explained that I intended to confer with the teachers concerning the data gathered and to plan our in-service meetings according to what I felt the observations indicated. I made it clear that I intended to work from a base of systematic evaluation. The consultant in charge was upset! She objected furiously and warned of serious consequences. But I wasn't going to make one more multiplication strip, much less waste a whole semester's opportunity—even if it was only one of the schools to which I was assigned.

I began doing exactly what I had intended, and I found that the teachers were delighted. Not only did they seem relieved at not having to find something for me to do in their classrooms, but they soon became intrigued with the Flanders and the New COG. With the Flanders they wanted to try to fill in previously vacant squares, and with the New COG they were anxious to either fill in blanks or else change the notation from "lack of evidence." The teachers also seemed relieved because now they knew what I was looking for and what I was "evaluating" when I stepped into their rooms.

The conferences that I held with the teachers ranged from one that was completely disastrous to some that were quite well done. The disastrous one was an absolute nightmare . . . with the teacher in complete hysterics! I didn't think it was funny at the time. I had butterflies in my stomach. It was the first time I had used the Flanders in anything but a practice situation. I was very serious when I entered into the conference. I was prepared. The matrix was filled out. Pertinent comments were firmly established in my mind (I had practiced a little in the washroom). I sat down and couldn't remember what any of the numbers stood for or what any combination meant! I couldn't interpret the matrix, much less remember any of the pertinent comments!

---

*Ben M. Harris et al., *A Manual of Observing with the New Comprehensive Observation Guide* (Austin, Tex.: Instructional Leadership Training Materials, 1975).

It was one of the worst moments of my life. My mind had completely blanked out. I was finally able to pull myself together and struggle through the interpretation. It was terrible! That teacher always wanted me to do a Flanders of her from that moment on, and I was never quite sure if it was because she wanted to change her verbal behavior or because she was hoping I would blank out again! The two of us have laughed many times about it.

I conferred individually with the teachers after each data-gathering session and designed the few remaining in-service sessions around what I thought the two instruments (Flanders and the New COG) indicated was needed. We worked on appearance of the room, rearrangement of learning centers, necessity for coordination of activities, and arrangement of instruction by level of skill on the part of the individual child. We worked on teacher expectations and how to make content decisions on the basis of those expectations. We tried to decide how to increase indirect teacher influence verbally and how to change less desirable verbal interaction patterns. We also tried to think of ways in which recognition of social and ethnic differences could be made in positive ways.

The teachers reacted in a very positive manner to the use of the data-gathering instruments. They actually did the evaluating themselves. I explained the results of the data gathering and then guided them in *their* evaluation. They were not guarded, nor were they resentful. They tried to make changes that they identified based on logic rather than on emotion.

OBSERVATION RECORD—WORLD HISTORY

THE NEW COMPREHENSIVE OBSERVATION GUIDE
Teacher   Miss Ray   *Grade* 10th   *Subject*   World History
Time: 8:00 A.M. to 9:00 A.M.   *Date*   March 22, 19—
Observer Dr. Geneva Gay.

Instructions

This instrument is designed for use as a diagnostic tool. The observer should be thoroughly familiar with each item in the guide before trying to use it.

The general procedures can be summarized as follows:

Systematically look for evidence relating to each question in this guide. Don't trust your memory. Review every question during the observation period.

If notations can appropriately be made on the guide *while in the classroom*, keep them brief.

Immediately after leaving the classroom, record evidences observed under each question. If nothing pertinent has been observed concerning a particular question, leave the space blank; but be sure to look for evidence on each question.

Avoid discussing the lesson with anyone until *after* you have recorded all observed evidences.

Do not allow any other events to occupy your attention until all evidences are recorded.

Prepare the Observation Summary after you have studied your completed guide, thought about the total situation, and discussed it with the teacher.

Room Diagram

Draw a sketch of the floor plan of the instructional space being observed. Show the location of groups and the number in each group. Show seating arrangements, displays, equipment, etc.

A. THE CLASSROOM

_____ 1.   How is the physical environment conducive to learning insofar as it is under the teacher's control?

2 chalkboards; room divided into two sections—large aisle in center; girls sat on left side facing front of room—boys on left facing side of room (≡||||); seats neatly arranged in straight rows; one file cabinet; two bookcases; one filled with paperback books and supplementary texts; one overhead projector; table with work supplies (student notebooks, books, papers) in front.

_____ 2.   How is the classroom made attractive?

Blinds uneven; seats arranged in neat rows; no papers on floor; bulletin boards had sketches of students' work; smaller bulletin board bare, covered only with white paper.

_____ 3.   How functional are the seating arrangements and what evidences in the room illustrate orderliness, good taste, and systematic procedures?

Boys and girls separated. Chairs arranged to give teacher room to move freely about among students. Room free of papers and other trash; storage cabinet; bulletin board not orderly arranged—no letters or captions or drawings on display; one other bulletin board bare.

_____ 4.   What evidences show that materials, equipment, and facilities are well cared for?

Books neatly arranged in bookcases; reference books in use stacked neatly on teacher's desk; student notebooks not in use remained in a box.

_____ 5.   What indicates that the teacher makes available a sufficient supply of materials, supplementary materials, and instructional aids?

1 globe; 1 dictionary; 1 overhead projector; 4 wall maps; 1 chart visible; student notebooks.

_____ 6.   What evidences are there of a connection between materials seen about the room and what has been or is being taught?

Dictionary used in lesson (discussion) of the day by students to look up definitions of words; notebooks kept by students used to write new words and meanings down and to refer to previous notes.

_____ 7.   What are the evidences of instructional and display materials that are

_____   a) pupil-made?

—Drawings (sketches) on bulletin board; notebooks of notes from class discussion.

✔ ✔   b) teacher-made?

No evidence.

_____   c) commercially-produced?

Chart of Southeast Asia; 4 wall maps.

_____ 8.   What evidences of long-range and short-range planning suggest good preparation and adequate use of chalkboards, bulletin boards, tables, or other display areas?

Words for the day's discussion were on chalkboard when the class entered; also future assignments written on chalkboards; student notebooks of previous work.

_____ 9.   What evidences show that the teacher evaluates and returns work that the pupils are required to hand in?

Student notebooks were in a box on table in front—when they entered they picked up these to continue keeping notes on meaning of new words; previous work in notebooks had been graded by teacher, using only letter grades—no comments.

__✔____10.   How are materials arranged to stimulate pupils' curiosity to seek new understandings?

Only one dictionary available—otherwise no evidence.

B. THE TEACHER

_____11.   How does the teacher's appearance set a good example for the pupils?

Well-groomed, neat appearance—wore gray dress with light gray hose and darker gray shoes.

_____12.   What shows that the teacher has a warm, friendly relationship with pupils?

Moved about among the students—did not remain "up front"—never laughed—patient with students—never raised her voice or criticized students (even when she asked one student to return to his seat and sit down)—very businesslike.

_____13.   How does the teacher show enthusiasm for the ongoing activities?

Proceeded in a businesslike manner—voice indicated neither enthusiasm nor excitement—reflection always about the same level.

_____14.   What indicates that the teacher is sensitive to the well-being of pupils and frees them from embarrassment or feelings of insecurity?

One of overhead lights had burned out; introduced visitor (me) to students; when student refused to answer or comment when called upon, the teacher did not insist but moved on to another student.

✔ ✔ 15.   What indicates that the teacher tries to gain as much knowledge about the pupils as possible in order to understand them better and guide them more effectively?

No evidence.

✔ ✔ 16.   How does the teacher attempt to enhance the development of the group as a social unit?

No evidence.

_____17.   How does the teacher recognize the contributions of pupils?

Teacher seemed interested in student answers, examples, and illustrations; asked students to expand on their feelings and attitudes on "violence" and "marriage" as values in our society. Encouraged students to explain why they thought these were fallacies or myths for some people (questions directed to those students who took exception).

✔ ✔ 18. How does the teacher illustrate an understanding and acceptance of the ethnic differences and differences in socioeconomic levels represented in the class?

No evidence.

_____19. How does the teacher recognize and provide for individual differences in levels of achievement, ability, and interest?

Accepted questions and student-initiated comments; teacher decided which student would look up the word in the dictionary. Teacher usually reacted to student answers with "all right"—said "That's a good example" a number of times.

✔ ✔ 20. How does the teacher maintain harmonious and constructive work in several small groups at the same time?

No evidence.

✔ 21. How does the teacher employ democratic principles such as pupil participation in classroom decisions and in planning assignments?

Encouraged students to express differences of opinions.

_____22. How does the teacher arrange and guide efficient management of activities in the classroom?

Teachers personally passed dictionary from one student to the next as it was needed; listed words on chalkboard that were to be discussed that day.

_____23. What shows the teacher's ability to *use* various types of instructional materials and aids effectively?

Room contained overhead projector, supplementary textbooks, but only dictionary was used during the lesson; word list on chalkboard served as guide for discussion.

_____24. What indicates that the teacher has a satisfactory background of knowledge in the subject being taught and keeps informed on new developments?

She appeared confident; used a variety of examples and illustrations; compared our "cultural traits," "mores," etc., with other countries'.

✔ ✔ 25. What indicates that the teacher uses new ideas and develops imaginative approaches to teaching?

No evidence.

THE PUPIL

————26. What indicates that the pupils' participation in the lesson is enthusiastic, eager, and active rather than passive?

7 students, especially one girl more than any other, participated in discussion frequently; 8 students didn't say anything for the entire class
period; ideas and examples to illustrate meanings of words often given
from their own personal experiences.

————27. What indicates that pupils know what they are doing and why they are
doing it?

Students usually waited for teacher to direct discussion—i.e., indicating when to move from one term to the next. Student examples of
different words and/or terms usually accepted by teacher as being appropriate.

✔ ✔28. What shows that pupils engage in creative activities?

No evidence.

————29. How do pupils show signs of self-discipline?

Group remained rather quiet and passive; two boys talked out frequently, making nonsubstantive statements in response to a teacher
and/or student comment, such as "well, all right then!" Five students
came in late, all at different intervals. (19 students—all black; 9 boys,
10 girls)

✔ ✔30. What types of behaviors indicate that pupils are developing positive
self-concepts?

No evidence.

✔ ✔31. What evidence is there of pupils' working together, sharing responsibilities, and tutoring and assisting each other?

No evidence.

D. THE LESSON

————32. What experiences are provided for pupils to *put to use* the degree of
skill gained in a particular area, thereby refining and further extending
the skill?

Drill on knowledge of definitions of words followed by examples and
illustrations—students could give examples to illustrate words. Students give examples of word meanings from their own experiences.

_____33.   What indicates the lesson's relationship to other lessons and to the general development of the subject?

Review of words previously discussed.

_____34.   How is class discussion developed by appropriate and effective questioning rather than being limited to the recitation of isolated facts?

Teacher asked for definitions of words. Students also asked to give examples or illustrations of the terms once they were defined. Students asked to make up and write down sentences using certain terms.

_____35.   What practices show that the teacher probes beneath verbalisms to see if understanding is present?

Asked for illustrations of word meanings; comparisons of "what we say" with "what we do" in our society.

_____36.   What evidences are there that assignments are worthwhile, appropriate, and logically developed?

Students had defined some terms in notebook previous to the day's lesson. Each student required to keep a notebook and to write down notes on the discussion. Students required to keep notebooks as stated above in items 8 and 9. Plenty of time given for students to write down definitions—some definitions were repeated as many as four times by the teacher.

_____37.   How is the work of the class constantly directed toward certain objectives, while maintaining sufficient flexibility to allow the teacher to capitalize on situations as they arise?

Questions directed toward getting an understanding of meaning of words and terms designated by teacher, yet students encouraged to give examples from their own experience and to explain in greater detail when they talked about certain mores which deviated from the norm of our culture.

_____38.   How is a convincing connection made between subject matter and pupil needs and interests?

"Will you give examples of mores, folkways, etc." "Why do you say that some people value marriage and others don't?" "Is violence right or wrong?—then is it a more?"

_____39.   How are pupils encouraged to go beyond the textbook, seeking information through people and source materials?

Used dictionary in class. Students were asked to give examples and situations from their daily life experience.

——————40. How does the teacher give direct, specific help to pupils in developing effective study habits?

No student said he didn't understand; one student told a girl she was reading the definition too fast; students asked teacher for help in spelling difficult words; some students neither participated verbally in class nor took notes on the discussion. "Write these definitions down in your notebooks." "Write a sentence using this word."

✔ ✔ 41. What methods are used to diagnose individual or group difficulties?

No evidence.

——————42. What efforts are made to involve pupils in objectively analyzing and evlauating their own performance?

Teacher encouraged some students to explain and analyze their feelings; other students were not called on during the class.

✔ ✔ 43. What practices indicate an effort to keep parents well informed on pupils' progress?

No evidence.

SUPERVISORY STRATEGY CASE:
A MATTER OF VALUES

Supervisor Harry Ransom is the middle school supervisor for Hartley Public Schools, a young, handsome man, full of enthusiasm and expressiveness in his way of relating to people. Despite being fairly young, he's been a supervisor for some five years and had substantial teaching experience prior to that. He works with approximately a hundred teachers of science, social studies, and other subjects across 20 different schools in a metropolitan community.

We were discussing classroom observation techniques and the use of descriptive observation records in the feedback conference with the teacher. Supervisor Ransom said, "You know, most of our teachers are so cooperative and they're so eager to get feedback and to discuss their ideas and open to my ideas, too. But, what do you do when the teacher agrees with everything that is in the observation record as to its accuracy, but is unwilling to acknowledge any needs for improvement?"

I asked for clarification: "In what way does he or she refuse to acknowledge any needs for improvement?"

"Well," Harry said, "I see a lot of things that are absent from the classroom situation as I observe it. I see some things that are persistently not there, and I even see negative evidence."

"Are you referring to a particular teacher, Harry?"

"Well, yes I am, but this is not an isolated case!"

"Tell me about the teacher!"

"Well, she simply, in a variety of ways, not in every way by any means, because she is a good teacher in many ways, but in a variety of ways there's lots of room for improvement and finally she'll acknowledge it and when I point out the possibility for trying something new or changing her approach she simply will not accept any such ideas."

"Tell me again how she indicates to you that she does not accept your notions or your concern about the lack of certain practices or the use of undesirable practices."

"Well, she just says, 'I've been doing these things for years and I think it's good teaching and I don't want to change it.' That's her position."

"So I hear you saying," I commented, "that you and this teacher agree on the facts, data that you record as an observer, and she even agrees on your analysis of that data—what really is going on. But when it comes to interpreting and valuing, she assigns all positive values to everything she's doing and you see some need for improvement."

"Yeah, I guess that's right, that's what's happening."

"And you try to make it very clear," I asked, "that there is specific need for improvement?"

"Yes, I . . ." he pauses. "Of course, I try to get her to acknowledge these needs herself. But, then after I see the same problem over and over again, I feel it's my obligation to say that these things seem like they need to be changed! And then she simply says, 'Well, I think they're all right. I don't want to change them.'"

"Have you confronted her with the reality of the situation? Have you discussed with her where you think you and she are with regard to each other?"

"What do you mean?" Harry Ransom asked, a bit startled.

"Well, have you said, 'Look, here's where we are in working with each other. You agree with me on what's going on in your classroom, but we differ in our assessment of your teaching. You say you think it's good and needs no improving. I see some things that are not good enough!'" I paused to let Harry react to this idea for confronting the situation.

"I think she knows that's the situation."

"Well, perhaps it's time to move on then to the next step in the evaluation process. That is, if she clearly understands that you've agreed to disagree regarding the quality of the teaching performance, perhaps you should move to the point of making decisions. Of course, you can let her make the decision, and her decision will probably be to do nothing."

"Well, but some of these problems," supervisor Ransom exclaimed, almost in desperation, "some of these problems are really quite serious! We can't afford to allow children to suffer without making some effort to improve the situation."

"Well," I countered, "if that is your assessment of the situation, that is, if you have arrived at a carefully considered judgment that this is not only inappropriate teaching behavior in a variety of ways, but that it is seriously deficient, then the question is 'What kind of professionally responsible supervisory decision alternatives are available?' One alternative is, of course as I suggested, to let this teacher make the decision, which in a sense you will do if you don't propose alternatives."

Harry Ransom was shaking his head and frowning as I spoke.

"Another alternative, of course, is for you to take decision making away from the teacher and prescribe a course of action. For instance, you could mandate some kind of specific corrective behavior."

Supervisor Ransom frowned more deeply and said, "I hate to do that because you know she'll get angry. She'll go through the motions and we're not likely to get any real improved performance that way."

"Well, that's quite true," I agreed. "That kind of unilateral mandate or prescription is not likely to be very effective. What other alternatives are there?"

Harry did not respond. He waited.

"Well, another decision might be agreeable to both of you. The two of you could negotiate a decision to work toward resolving your disagreements—your agreement to disagree, your differences in the way you value the teaching performance in question. That may be an approach."

"I don't quite understand what you mean."

"Well," I said, "you can confront the teacher with the fact that you have quite different points of view, one from the other, and reminding her that you're both professionally responsible, intelligent people with obligations. Then, you can outline those obligations. Hers include being the best teacher she can be, becoming better every year, and being open-minded about the questions professionally responsible colleagues are raising about her teaching practices."

"Your obligations on the other hand involve using your professional experience and technical skills in working with teachers to see to it that boys and girls get the best teaching they can. Above all, you are obligated to generate improvements in teaching whether deficiencies exist or not."

"Well," said Harry, "I don't see where that would lead us."

"I'm not sure either, but it might lead to a course of action that would be acceptable to both of you."

"Let me suggest, for instance, some of the action-oriented decisions that might follow: the two of you would agree, for instance, to resort to outside sources in resolving the two points of view."

"What would that involve doing?" Harry asked.

"You might propose a series of actions. (1) Both of you could visit some other teachers who are known as good teachers. And see if these things which you are valuing and she is not are present in those teachers' classrooms, (2) Both of you do some reading provided by the other persons. You could put it to her this way: 'I'll read one or two or three articles or monographs, or chapters of books—whatever you think that you can provide to support your position. And you in turn will read some things that I provide to support my position.' "

Harry Ransom interrupted, "Boy, this is getting to involve a lot of work. I'm just not sure I can afford this much time with this teacher."

"Well, I'm not sure you can either," I responded. "I think that's a decision that you need to make. You have several options, and we've discussed three. There may be others, of course."

NOT-SO-EAGER HELEN BEAVER*

It was nearly the end of October and I was getting pretty well acquainted with the Manhattan Beach Elementary faculty and school as the new assistant principal. Henry Danforth, my principal, and I were chatting about my work over the past two months and agreed it might be a good idea for me to see what teachers were doing in the classrooms. I had met all of the faculty, supervised bus arrivals and departures, handled supply distributions, clerked on the attendance desk, substituted in kindergarten, third, and fifth grades, and "handled" dozens of behavior problems. Now it was time to see what the instructional program was like.

Danforth suggested that I begin by observing Helen Beaver and Larry Neiman, both sixth-grade teachers. "You've had more experience in the upper grades and secondary school, so why not start with these?" I agreed, eager to get a chance at some real supervision.

Tuesday, October 21:   Entered Ms. Beaver's classroom to observe. She was involved in teaching a social studies lesson when I arrived. The topic was the recognition of physical features—mountains, rivers, plains, etc. About 15 minutes after my arrival, the lesson came to a close and her students lined up for lunch. I apologized for coming in at the end of the lesson, and she urged me to come back.

Wednesday, October 22:   Chastened by my errors yesterday, I stopped by to ask Larry Neiman about a good time to visit and observe in his class. He asked several questions about why I wanted to visit and expressed reluctance about being observed at all.

*Adapted from a case report by David Lee Moore.

I shared these two experiences with Henry Danforth this afternoon. "Well, I'm not surprised by Neiman's response. You can wait on him for a while. What's your plan with Helen?" I told him we were having a chat on Thursday after school.

Thursday, October 23:   I met with Ms. Beaver in her classroom at 3:30 P.M. We talked about her class and her 14 years as an elementary school teacher. She shared her ideas on grading and lesson planning.

When I finally raised the question about observing her teaching, it was 4:47. She responded a bit startled: "Did Mr. Danforth send you to me?" I replied that he had suggested her but that I planned to observe in many classrooms during the coming months. This seemed to be an acceptable explanation to her. "OK," she said, "How about coming in on Monday morning?" "Great," I replied, relieved at her willingness.

Monday, October 27:   On my arrival this morning I found Helen Beaver absent due to illness. I called her. It was just hay fever, she said. We agreed to reschedule for Wednesday morning.

These delays gave me a chance to plan more carefully. I reviewed the handbook for the *Developmental Teacher Evaluation Kit* and decided to use the comprehensive observation instrument included in that system and to ask Ms. Beaver if she would use the self-assessment inventory also provided.

Wednesday, October 29:.   I met Helen Beaver at 10:35 A.M. in her classroom. We had a chance to talk briefly before her students returned from their P.E. class. I tried to reassure her saying: "I really need this more than you! It doesn't have anything to do with your annual evaluation." She replied, "This morning I could care less!"

I provided Ms. Beaver with a copy of the DeTEK Instrument I for teacher self-analysis, and asked her to bring it to our conference. She was familiar with both the observation and the self-assessment instruments from discussions about them in our pre-school faculty meetings.

I observed, from 10:50 to 11:35, a social studies lesson, and departed at the end of the lesson with a wave of my hand.

Monday, November 3:.   Met in Ms. Beaver's room at 8:00 A.M. to review my observation record with her and compare it with her self-report. I had a xerox copy of my report to give her. I wanted this to be a really effective feedback session.

As we talked, Ms. Beaver kept changing the focus. She commented on how much she "like[s] to teach sixth grade." She talked of frustrations with two boys who "won't behave, no matter what." Her day-to-day alterations in lesson plans and how she handled the problems of discipline seemed to dominate, no matter what I said about the observation of her self-analysis.

Finally, almost in desperation, for our time was running out, I took control!

"Helen! Look here. We've only a few minutes before your class begins. Now, I'm not going to solve your problems for you—especially not this morning with only one observation. But at least let's look at *our data* (I stressed the word *our*). It may be a starting point, at least."

Ms. Beaver looked startled, but stopped rambling on. "OK," she said.

I briefly compared the profile from the observation report with her self-assessment profile.

"Your assessment shows two strong areas. #2—Friendly and #4—Stimulating. Areas #3, #5, and #6 are reported as relatively low on your self-analysis. Now, if we compare that with my observation summary, there are both similarities and differences. Do you see what I mean?"

Helen looked at the profile sheets which I had placed before us side-by-side [see Figures 10.3 and 10.4]. She frowned a bit. "You didn't give me many high marks!"

"That's true," I replied, trying to sound as matter-of-fact as I could. I wondered if I was going to get some kind of outburst from her. But I pushed on: "It would be unrealistic to expect a large number of behaviors at the 'highly descriptive' level in only a single observation. Let's consider some similarities in *our* reports on your teaching." I emphasized *our* again as sharply as I could.

Helen looked at the profiles again. "We agree on 1b, and 4a, but you observed me as more verbally interactive. That really surprises me!"

"What about area #5—Individual Oriented? Notice that we both see that as a low-performance area."

"Yes, I see that," she agreed. "And you didn't think I was very businesslike!"

"The data is rather inconsistent on both of our profiles." I tried to remain neutral about it all.

Helen Beaver sat up straight, looked me in the eye for the first time, and said: "I'm really organized but I know I don't look that way!" Then, with a pause she added: "And, you know, I'm probably as businesslike as I'll ever be and I don't have time to be more individual with the kids. I'll be that way no matter what."

I didn't know what to say. She was so determined in her tone of voice. I gambled with a comment: "You just don't think those are areas you can consider for further improvement."

"You can see my desk," she answered. "See what I have to take home now? And then there's that Vietnamese boy who hardly speaks a word of English. . . . I have to plan special lessons for him each day. . . . And more would be almost impossible!"

I sensed that she was clearly closing the door on that performance area. I had the good sense to say nothing. I just sat there, looking at her, sympathetically, I hoped.

Teacher __Helen Beaver__   School __Manhattan Beach Elem.__   Date __October 30, 198-__

Teaching Assignment: Grade __6th__   Subject(s) __Self-Contained (Except for Art and P.E.)__

DIRECTIONS:

After completion of sections A and B

A. TALLY choices from Section A to column A below.
B. Transfer check marks (✓) from Section B to column B below.
C. Check HIGH Performance clusters.
   (4 or 5 choices and 3 or 4 checks)
D. Check LOW performance clusters.
   (0, 1, or 2 choices and 0 or 1 check)
E. SELECT a performance and one or more of its behaviors for study.

	A. Performance Choices	B. Behaviors a b c d				Performance Clusters C. High	D. Low
1. Businesslike	1 1	(✓)	(✓)	(✓)	( )	X	
2. Friendly	₩₩ 5	(✓)	(✓)	(✓)	(✓)		X
3. Verbally Interactive	11 2	( )	( )	(✓)	( )		
4. Stimulating	1111 4	(✓)	(✓)	(✓)	( )	X	
5. Individual Oriented	1 1	( )	(✓)	( )	(✓)		
6. Multi-Media Integrative	11 2	(✓)	( )	( )	( )		X
7. Other	- -	( )	( )	( )	( )		
8. Other	- -	( )	( )	( )	( )		

Comments:

E. SUMMARY

Selected Performance (1 only):   (3)
Selected Behaviors (1, 2 or 3):   __3a__   __3b__ _____

FIGURE 10.3   DeTEK Instrument I: Teacher Performance Screening Inventory.

Teacher _Helen Beaver_____ Grade _6th___ Subject _All(except art
and P.E.)
School _Manhattan Beach Elem._____ Observer _Moore_____ Date _October 29, 198-_

Lesson and Topic _Social Studies, geography — maps, time zones_____ Time _10:50_ to _11:35_
____around the world. Review._____

THE PROFILE

Performance	Behaviors: Summary of Observed Evidence				
	a	b	c	d	Other
1. Businesslike	(M)	(H)	(N)	(N)	(−)
2. Friendly	(M)	(N)	(M)	(M)	(−)
3. Verbally Interactive	(H)	(H)	(M)		(−)
4. Stimulating	(H)	(M)	(M)	(N)	(−)
5. Individual Oriented	(N)	(N)	(N)	(N)	(−)
6. Multi-Media Integrative	(M)	(M)	(N)		(−)
Other_____	(−)	(−)	(−)	(−)	(−)

OBSERVED ACCOMPLISHMENTS: Performance areas ___ ___ ___

SUGGESTED FOR FURTHER ANALYSIS: Performance Areas: _# 1_ _# 5_ _____

Behaviors: #_1 c_ #_1 d_ #_5 a_ #_5 b_ #_5 c_

Comments:

FIGURE 10.4   A DeTEK Instrument: Comprehensive Observation of Performance. Copyright © 1982. Ben M. Harris and Jane Hill. All rights reserved. Reprinted by permission of National Educational Laboratory Publishers, Inc., Austin, Texas.

After fourteen years of teaching in elementary schools she knew something substantial about her strengths and weaknesses and she knew how to shy away from the latter. We both sat there, staring at the profile sheets. She broke the silence after what seemed an eternity, because I didn't know what to say next.

"I'd really like to look at this Verbally Interactive area," she said, rather matter-of-factly.

I was relieved but confused. From the very start of my work with Ms. Beaver I found no lack of ability in this area. Behavior 3c—"Utilizes a variety of questioning techniques . . ." was estimated as moderately descriptive on my observation report. She had checked this same behavior as one of her strengths.

Behaviors 3a and 3b were not checked as strengths in her self-analysis but were observed as highly descriptive by me. It seemed less than fully rational to select the verbally interactive performance area, but she was willing to work on these behaviors and I decided to go along. The other needs would have to wait. We agreed to focus on these two behaviors for further diagnostic analysis.

Friday, November 7:   Met with Helen Beaver to discuss use of diagnostic instruments. I went over procedures carefully with her to be sure she was with me. I reminded her of the steps (self-analysis, focused observation, student reports, and diagnostic conference, followed by growth planning). Her response pleased and surprised me: "You know, I really think that this might help me."

Tuesday, November 11:   Arrived at Beaver's classroom at 8:32 A.M. She had two students at her desk. She had them distribute the student report forms for behaviors 3a and 3b, which had been prepared according to plan.

When these forms had been collected, Helen went on with her planned lesson and I observed as agreed, using focused observation guides.

At the end of the lesson the students left for P.E. class. Helen Beaver picked up the stack of student reports on the table. Before looking at them she said, "I'll bet I know one thing they've marked me down on—that I spend too much time giving directions." She was correct.

Thursday, November 13:   We met to complete the diagnostic analysis step. Two clear needs for improvement were identified as follows:

3a(2)—"Avoids directions or
          comments which disrupt . . . and
          waste . . . time."
3b(3)—"Prompts, reflects, accepts
          disagreements, and waits for
          student thoughts . . ."

Real accomplishments were also clearly identified as: 3a(1), "gives directions . . . to assure progress"; 3a(3), "uses . . . language students . . . understand"; and 3b(1), "gives and asks for information . . ." and several others.

Tuesday, November 18:   Met with Helen to develop a Growth Plan. This went very well. Helen was in a good frame of mind.

"This is good. I can see that I spend too much time giving directions . . . so much so that a lot of kids get bored. I have been to workshops where they talked about the importance of the time you wait after asking a question. I know these are things I can work on."

Monday, November 24:   Dropped by to give Ms. Beaver a book on questioning techniques. She volunteered, "What you're doing is a lot more helpful to me than what I've had. . . . You're helping me where I need to improve. . . . It takes more time, but I think it's helped me already. I like it."

A SURVEY FOR CURRICULUM REVISION AND IN-SERVICE PLANNING*

Your name is Carlos Tristan. You are the principal of the Happy Days Early Childhood Center, located in a large metropolitan area of Santa Rosa, Texas. Your center is located in the deep "East Side" of the city, which comprises approximately 92 percent Mexican-Americans, 5 percent Black Americans, and 3 percent Anglo-Americans. Eighty-nine percent of the parents are employed as unskilled laborers, 10 percent are skilled laborers, one-half of one percent have managerial positions, and one-half of one percent are professionals. Average annual family income is well below the "poverty" level.

The Happy Days Early Childhood Center is a modern, new facility, constructed with federal funds this past year. Because of the innovative features in architecture, several types of teaching arrangements are feasible: team teaching, demonstration classes, self-contained classrooms, or semiopened rooms. The rooms contain carpeted "pupil pits," sinks, drinking fountains, and bathrooms. Half of each room is carpeted; the other half is in tile, suitable as a "wet area" and for art and lunch activities, which occur in the room.

The school's playground, intended to lead to creative play, is extremely dangerous because of the cement structures erected there. Although the area is completely fenced in, it is littered with broken bottles, old cans, and pieces of rusty wire thrown in by mischievous youngsters who live in the low-rent courts across from the center. This is an every-weekend occurrence.

*Adapted from a report by Teresa Dent.

The faculty consists of seventeen teachers, seventeen assistant teachers, one nurse, one supervisor, and one social worker. Two curriculum writers also work within the center, coming from the regional education laboratory. Ten of the seventeen teachers have elementary teaching certificates, and four of these have also earned the kindergarten endorsement. Two of the class units consist of totally migrant pupils; these children enter late and leave early in the year.

There are approximately four hundred pupils, ages three and four, enrolled at the center. The majority of the pupils are Mexican-American, with only six black pupils and four Anglos. The pupils are bused from their neighborhood elementary schools every morning and are returned to their neighborhood schools at 2:30 in the afternoon. The assistant teachers serve as bus monitors and supervise the children before and after the bus trip to the center.

For the past four years, your district has entered into a contract with the regional laboratory, the Southwest Early Learning Systems, to cooperatively develop and pilot–field test a bilingual, bicultural curriculum for the target population.

For this purpose, you have established a feedback system which includes data from the end-of-unit and mastery criterion-referenced tests, teacher lesson evaluation sheets, and age-level meetings to gather formative evaluation data on which you can then base curriculum revisions and in-service education activities.

You are not completely convinced that the problems are likely to be found solely in the curriculum materials, so you have embarked on a series of classroom observations to determine what other factors, if any, impede successful performance of objectives, and what implications these may have in designing an in-service program for your teachers.

Observation 1

Assistant Teacher: Susan Ochoa
Class: Four-year-olds   *Date:*   4/2
Component: English   *Time:*   9:15–:35 A.M.

Room Diagram

I.   Interclass Grouping

Teacher had predetermined list for involving pupils in group based on proficiency in English.
Teacher exchanged groups in twenty minutes.
Groups varied in size from three to five children.
Group was called for a specific presentation on English lesson.

Pupils not with the teacher or assistant teacher moved about freely choosing from among the various options for independent activity, i.e., blocks, puzzles, design cards, role playing.

II. Variety of Materials

A library stand with several books in English and Spanish was available in the room.

No teacher-made materials evident.

A variety of commercial manipulative materials was available.

Materials varied in difficulty, number of puzzle pieces, and complexity of design cards for pegs, colored inch cubes, and parquetry.

III. Pupil Autonomy

Pupils were carrying on a variety of self-directed, but not self-disciplined, activities.

Pupils were engaged in leadership roles in the block area, directing building.

Pupils working on puzzles and design cards were self-evaluated.

Pupils in the manipulative and block areas offered assistance to their peers.

IV. Differentiated Assignments

Pupils working in subgroups were noisy, unsure of boundaries.

Pupils working with teacher were easily distracted by the following:
a. Activities occurring in another classroom directly opposite them
b. Hallway traffic
c. Children playing in the coatrack directly behind the teacher
d. Child playing with toy truck near them
e. Pupils constantly reaching for books on the table behind them

V. Teacher Use of Curriculum Materials

Teacher had prepared pictures for lesson.

Teacher had not adequately studied manual, as evidenced by the following:
a. Kept manual on lap; referred to it often.
b. Was unfamiliar with questions and the sequence of the lesson; jumped ahead and had to regress to previous action word.

VI. General Concerns

Flow of lesson seemed awkward; not keeping children's attention.

VII. Other problems:
a. Area chosen to give lesson was too close to hall, other class, table with books. Position of children was in straight line, facing hall, other room, rather than centered around her in a quiet area.
b. Area chosen was too distracting. Areas for other children should be defined so that child with truck does not interfere with lesson; children do not play in coatrack.

Suggestions to Consider

LESSON PREPARATION

1. Role-playing lesson with other teachers to become more confident in the presentation.
2. Study lesson sufficiently to be able to present without use of manual on lap; a reminder "cue card" may be an appropriate intermediate step. Practice writing cue cards.

CLASSROOM ARRANGEMENTS

1. Using cutouts, assist the teacher in establising well-defined area or center. Half of the room should be fairly quiet for lessons, while the other half can be used for "active" experiences. Art, library, and science centers can be used as buffers between the zones.
2. Materials appropriate for each center should be kept together, i.e., blocks, library books, manipulative equipment.

CLASSROOM MANAGEMENT

1. Noise level should be kept at a reasonable volume so pupils will not be distracted.
2. Children need training in the following:
   a. Keeping materials within a designated area
   b. Playing away from lesson area
   c. Attending to task, providing distractions are removed and lesson is more motivating

Observation 2

Assistant Teacher: Mary Rueben
Class: Four-year-olds   *Date:* 4/84
Component: Visual   *Time:* 10:00–10:15 A.M.

Room Diagram
Self-Contained

I. Interclass Grouping

Teacher had grouped for specific skill desired.

Teacher exchanged groups in twelve minutes.

Groups varied in size from two to seven pupils.

Students not in assigned lessons moved about in the housekeeping, manipulative, and block areas only. One child at art easel completed painting and joined in housekeeping activity.

Children moved about quietly and orderly in exchanging puzzles, cards, and materials.

II. Variety of Materials

Library stand with books available.

Teacher had made a three-box sorter of small milk cartons stapled together into which a child was sorting geometric shapes first by color (red, blue, yellow) and then by shape (square, circle, triangle).

A variety of commercial manipulative materials was also available.

Materials varied in difficulty from simple to complex.

An E.F.I. (Electronic Future, Inc., similar to a Language Master) was being used independently by a child using earphones.

III. Pupil Autonomy

Pupils very self-directed and self-disciplined.

Activity in housekeeping area showed leadership role of mother preparing for children.

Cooperative planning in block area.

IV. Differentiated Assignments

Pupils working in subgroups were gainfully engaged in a variety of learning activities.

Pupils working with teacher and assistant teacher were attending to tasks.

V. Teacher Use of Curriculum Materials

Teacher was prepared, as evidenced by the following:
a. Cards for building 3-D block designs from 2-D picture in perspective were readily at hand and appropriately colored as indicated by lesson plan.
b. Color cubes for building designs sufficient for each child in appropriate number and color for each design card were positioned in front of each child.
c. Teacher did not have to keep referring to manual, indicating she knew steps in procedure to follow.
d. Teacher had failed to check out (usually by role play) *each* of the four designs called for in the lesson.

VI. General Concerns

Lesson followed; teacher initiated lesson demonstrating task expectation.

Children attentive and involved in making the block design from the cards.

After completing three designs, children experienced difficulty with the fourth card. It was incorrect, since this lesson calls for the design to be erected upright, translating the 2-D pattern card into a 3-D structure made of colored inch cubes. Since there was no cube to sustain the topmost blue cube, this design was impossible.

The teacher merely stated that this design was not possible and that the children were very alert in finding the error ("I almost tricked you"). She turned an awkward situation into an evaluation activity, testing to see if the children would try an impossible design.

Suggestions to consider—Recommend the design card be corrected.

Set up a series of situations that include incorrect media and role play, and let participants find error in materials. Discuss ways of dealing with the same type of situation; ways to turn a "boo-boo" into a learning or an evaluation activity. Praise children for being alert to error and for being independent thinkers confident enough to challenge teacher directions to complete design.

SUGGESTIONS FOR DEALING WITH THE UNOBSERVABLE

New Principal

What do you do when you have a teacher you know is an excellent teacher, probably tops in every way, but who just does not want to be observed? What do you do? I've preached from day one that being observed is going to help to improve. "You have no worry. You don't have to be uptight about all this," I keep saying. But at the same time, this person feels . . . I have one or two persons who have just asked me "I'll do anything, but just don't bother me in class." How can I change that?

Experienced Principal

Well, I think you must recognize that this is an unusual case. I think you need to deal with it as a very individual problem and be as sympathetic with these anxieties and concerns as you can. So I wouldn't push this teacher into the DeTEK* sequence too hastily or too quickly. As you move ahead with other teachers, peer influences will help him (her) to feel a little more at ease about it. But ultimately, and by that I don't know when, within a year or two, you have to bite the bullet.

I'd bite that bullet in a very sympathetic way. I'd say, "You know, you've a job to do and it's called teaching. And it goes on mostly in that classroom. I understand you're an excellent teacher, but I really don't know much about it. I hope you don't want me to rely entirely on rumor and gossip and innuendo. My way of really knowing how good you are and being able to help you and support you in what you're doing, is to be in your classroom enough to really know what you do and how you do it."

"Furthermore, we're on a team around here. And if you're as great at doing some things as I hear you are, I want to know more about that because I want to be able to share some of those great techniques with other people. I can't do my job as it relates to improving instruction in the school, unless you and I work together. Part of that working together means my being in your classroom."

"As a result, I expect that we will understand each other better, and we will surely find some things that I can certify as *accomplishments* for you.

*Ben M. Harris and Jane Hill, *Developmental Teacher Evaluation Kit* (Austin, Tex: National Educational Laboratory Publishers, 1982).

We may also find some things that require growth planning. It is just possible that there are a few places where you could become a much better teacher! I want to help you with that if I can!"

Experienced Principal Continues

We want everybody to have the privilege of becoming a better teacher, no matter how good they are at the moment. Now, if the teacher isn't responsive to that logic, that rational empathetic view, then there may come a time when you would have to say, "Look, you are interfering with *my* professional performance. Legally and professionally I must know what's going on."

PASSIVE RESISTANCE?

Last summer, supervisor Marge Landford asked to talk with me about a "problem teacher" that she had been working with intensively throughout the spring semester. I arranged a conference time with her, and we sat down to talk.

"This is the most peculiar case I've run into in years," Ms. Landford exclaimed—a past-middle-aged reading consultant who has had many years of both teaching and supervision experience in a medium-sized industrial city, working with rather high-quality teachers.

"Tell me more about what makes this teacher so 'peculiar,'" I asked.

"Well, she just doesn't seem to respond to anything I try to do with her." I asked her to clarify.

Ms. Landford responded, "Well, I spent over seventeen hours with her this past spring alone. I have done everything that you ordinarily tell us we ought to be doing."

"Tell me what the sequence of events has been in your work with her."

"Well, I've observed her several times."

"What did you find?" I asked.

"Well, it was just terrible!" Ms. Landford shook her head from side to side to emphasize her feelings.

"What do you mean by terrible?" I asked.

"Well, the kids were not paying attention; she was screaming and hollering at them to be quiet! She had to shout in order to give directions so that they could hear! They didn't seem to be able to do the things that she assigned them to do. Once she got them down to work, she didn't follow up to see how they were doing or to give them any assistance. She just sat there in front or stood in the back with her arms folded across her chest, glaring at them."

"Did you find this to be true just in one instance or did you have more than one observation that showed this pattern of lack of control, shouting, poor organization, etc.?" I asked.

"Well, it's very much that way almost every time I go in to observe; and I've been in there several times now."

"Tell me what you have been doing in working with this teacher other than observing in her classroom?" I queried.

"Well, we sit down and we talk after every observation; I talk to her about the situation I see. She agrees with me about everything. She admits it's terrible, that she needs to improve, and then she starts talking about this student and that student and how much trouble they give her; and I try to point out to her that the things she is doing are not helping and may be causing the problem; and she just shakes her head and looks at me with those big brown eyes of hers, but it doesn't seem to sink in!"

"Tell me what you mean when you say it doesn't seem to 'sink in'. Does she argue with you?"

"Oh, no. She doesn't argue. She agrees! She's very responsive in that she agrees with everything I say. She asks me for suggestions. I make suggestions to her, but nothing seems to happen."

"Tell me more about how she responds to your suggestions and your impression that nothing seems to happen."

"Well, of course, I began to work on just the simple matter of organization and control in the classroom. So I told her to try just a few simple things, like having the assignment written on the board, giving very brief, short directions the minute the bell rings, not raising her voice, and keeping it low, waiting for attention before she speaks. You know, those *standard* procedures. But I go back into the classroom and I observe and she isn't doing any of these things."

"Well, that really is a strange case. What does she say when you confront her with her failure to do the kinds of things you have suggested? Does she argue that she doesn't know how or does she say she's tried them and they don't work? How does she respond?"

"Well, she does both of those things," Landford responded. "Sometimes she says, 'Well, I've been trying it, but it doesn't work and then I lose my patience,' or she says, 'I'm trying.' Frankly, I'm not sure that she really understands what I'm talking about."

"Well," I said, "it isn't unreasonable to begin to wonder whether this teacher really understands what you're talking about."

"I think you're right, but what do I do now?" Landford pleaded.

"Several diagnoses have come to your mind, I'm sure," I said. "On the one hand, it may be that she doesn't really know what you're talking about. On the other hand, she may be aware of what it is you want her to do, but really cannot perform, simply because she doesn't have the skill, the understanding, the self-control that it takes to do these things. And then, of course, it is possible that she is just not sufficiently concerned. She may be responding in an agreeable way, and placating you, and yet may not really be willing to put forth effort. Or she may not be convinced that what you see is really a problem for her. Can we rule out any one of these diagnoses?"

Ms. Landford knitted her brow so as to wrinkle her nose and tapped her pencil on the desk. "Well, I really don't know. She looks at me with those big brown eyes when I discuss these things. She seems to understand what it is I'm talking about. She even uses some of the same words that I use. So I guess I've assumed that she is aware of what I'm talking about. She certainly indicates a willingness to try, and she gives recognition that there is a problem, although I must admit she doesn't seem to be overly worried or anxious. It seems almost as if she has learned to tolerate the situation."

I asked her if she'd like to consider some other alternatives? "Perhaps some of them you've already utilized. Let me mention some approaches that you may already have exhausted or ruled out. But I'll mention them anyway and see what you think.

"For one, it seems to me that *intervisitation* is worth considering. You would make arrangements for her to go with you to see a particularly well-organized classroom situation; and by going with her, you could point out and later discuss some of the specific things that this other teacher is doing, and she would once again be made aware of what a normal healthy classroom situation under control is like. She may have forgotten that there are such things.

"Number two. I wonder if you have actually sat down and planned a lesson including a set of fairly carefully prescribed procedures with her? And then perhaps, actually gone into the classroom to watch as she makes an effort to implement those techniques?

"Finally, I wonder if you've used some very highly focused observation procedures such as Flanders's interaction analysis or the Pupil Response Inventory? With these you can help her see more explicitly what she is doing in relation to the youngsters' activities and their lack of responsiveness."

I paused to see how supervisor Landford would respond to these alternatives. She commented that in fact she had done some of these things. She had planned lessons with her and sent her back into the classroom with very detailed understandings about how to proceed, but admitted she had not actually had time to go into the classroom with the teacher to watch the implementation of the plan.

"I'm spending much of my time with this one teacher as it is," she said. "I'm not sure how much more time I can give."

"What about the intervisitation?" I asked.

"Well, we did send her to see two different teachers. I wasn't able to go along with her, so I'm afraid she didn't get very much out of that."

"That's very likely," I said. "Unfortunately, a teacher like this isn't going to gain much out of an intervisitation by herself, because if she had those kinds of analytical capabilities she would be more thoroughly analyzing her own situation."

"You said 'we' sent her to see two different teachers. Who else has worked with this teacher?"

"Oh, the principal has been more or less involved all along!"

"I see, but he did not go with her on these visits, either?"

"No," she admitted, matter-of-factly.

"What about using the focused observation technique?"

"Well no," Landford admitted, "I haven't tried any focused observations. I've been working on such very simple things. My God! Surely she can understand these things without formal recording and analyzing." Reading consultant Marge Landford just shook her head again and again.

CHAPTER ELEVEN
PROGRAMS
IN ACTION

Examples of in-service education programs are documented in this chapter. They range from a typescript of an interview with a new teacher to descriptions of several elaborate programs and to simple session plans and evaluation efforts. The variety presented in these case materials serves to emphasize the many sides of instructional supervision in action.

The supervisory interview with a beginning teacher illustrates a rather directive approach to helping the teacher analyze his or her own practices. The supervisor is rather persistent in asking questions about objective-activity relationships.

The several in-service training programs dealing with a task force, reading disabilities, the professional improvement center, and human relations range from a single session to elaborate programs. They illustrate many of the activities described in Chapter 4.

Several of the case reports focus on evaluation of in-service efforts. While the ways of viewing in-service education activities are quite simple, they are also reasonably useful in sharpening planning. The crucial character of the in-service education task combines with the low quality of many programs in action to demand better planning as well as better evaluation.

SUPERVISOR INTERVIEW WITH NEW TEACHER

SUPERVISOR: Let me ask you just how did you feel about it? How do you feel about the way the lesson went?

TEACHER: I feel very pleased so far with the whole unit. I've been pleased . . . some days more than others, of course. I was enthusiastic to begin with. They asked more questions than I had anticipated. That was good to me. That's why I didn't get through the second filmstrip. I just hadn't anticipated their questions. We had seen the first one before . . . yesterday we saw it. . . .

SUPERVISOR: Yes, I know.

TEACHER: They saw it again to take notes and draw out the major emphasis of the film and then the second one. . . . I didn't think it was coming in. . . . It was due either today or tomorrow. I did have another one Monday and had to send it back, . . . so that's what happened.

SUPERVISOR: Did you have a chance to preview it? The second filmstrip . . .

TEACHER: I didn't remember it was so long! It was a review for them. Some parts could have been left out. . . . It was a bit repetitious. The part with Lincoln on his deathbed—everyone knows he died. Some things were important but we did know others. . . . And with the time so short, we could have gone over them. . . .

I was trying to get through it. I was just very pleased, though, with their enthusiasm. I wasn't sure it would go over. It was review to a large extent.

SUPERVISOR: Attention was good, too, even though it was review and they were there over an hour. . . . It was evident that they didn't seem to be losing interest.

[*Teacher and supervisor exchange comments about the mechanics of using the projector more easily. Then the supervisor initiates a transition.*]

SUPERVISOR: Another question. . . . Interest was there, you were well organized, you knew what you were moving to, your timing was off, and you had to rush on through the second filmstrip. As you think back about the lesson, what had you wanted them to learn from this lesson? I'm talking about objectives again. What had you wanted as learning? What did you want them to leave the room with, today?

TEACHER: The idea of the black in America. . . . The concept of slavery today in the United States. . . . To narrow the area. . . . How slaves came, where they lived, what part of the country. . . . And then the idea of being accepted! I chose the first filmstrip because it startled them with the idea of the black first being accepted after the Civil War. He joined the Union Army and gained his first acceptance in the United States as a black. I wanted to introduce this concept. Monday I start modern acceptance and contributions. This is a good follow-through after spending a whole week getting slaves to America from Africa.

SUPERVISOR: You spent time on the past. You were trying to zero in on the notion of the Civil War as a departure . . . you spent time showing how they got here; now for some follow-through on what happened here? How they came here? The notion of the Civil War as a departure could demonstrate their contributions to war through participation?

TEACHER: The second half of the filmstrip starts with Negroes going home. Then it starts immediately with the contributions of George Washington Carver, etc. It's to be shown Monday. . . .

SUPERVISOR: I'm talking about this lesson though—not Monday's. . . .

TEACHER: My reason for showing the filmstrip was . . . the Civil War was the beginning of the acceptance of the black. That's the reason for this major emphasis. The goal today was really review to see if they had picked up the major ideas discussed this week—where they settled, how they were treated, and what they did. . . .

SUPERVISOR: I see. You were hoping to depart to that other objective next week. Now, trying to fix on some learnings, were there four or five key ideas you were trying to review?

TEACHER: In trying to review, there could have been hundreds. How the black was treated and accepted or wasn't. I think most important was the role he was beginning to play in society after the Civil War; his admittance into the Union Army, and probably . . . I don't know. . . . You can get very specific; you have a lot of them [objectives].

* * * * * *

SUPERVISOR: I see. You say your objective was primarily to review, since the second film covered the same ground that had been presented previously. As you think back, what would you estimate (all you can do is estimate) to be the ratio of your talking to their talking?

TEACHER: [*Frowns. Not sure she understands at first.*] Actually, I felt it was fairly good. I was talking when reading; but not counting my talking during the filmstrip, I would say it was forty-sixty, with me being the sixty. It was fairly close today.

SUPERVISOR: You got much response to the filmstrips, especially with the second one. Without a record, it would seem fairly close. It would be interesting to find out. Usually you talk more than you think. I do, anyway! [*Laughs*]. Let me read you some of my comments from the observation guide I used. You are familiar with it? See what you think. What I try to do is exclude opinions and judgments if possible and instead raise critical questions. But you remember the guide. It asks some big questions about what's happening here. [*Reading from guide:*]
What shows the teacher has warm, friendly relationships?
  Smiles. "Yes, we're going to talk about it now." "Thank you." Uses "please."

How does teacher show enthusiasm?
Facial expressions frequent.

What indicates that teacher tries to gain as much knowledge as possible about the students?
Black boy utilized well? Seemed to know a lot about slave ships. Did he?

How does the teacher attempt to enhance the development of groups as social unit?
No real discussion of ideas. All work was individual. . . . "I'll come back to that if you are interested."

How does teacher recognize contributions of pupils?
"I don't want an answer—just want to see that it's clear." Boy raises hand, gives answer. Teacher says "Wasn't that wonderful" to class. Another boy volunteers—ignored as teacher passes on.

How does teacher show an understanding of the socioeconomic levels?
Have any of the kids picked cotton? Idea of whole families picking in the fields—do they get the meaning of manual labor? Experiences of students not related. . . .

How does teacher provide for individual differences in levels of achievements and abilities?
One youngster didn't understand. Teacher explains. Melanie and other children are answering ahead of seeing strip.

[*Supervisor stops reading from his observation notes.*]

SUPERVISOR: Well, you can see my notes. How do you react to my reactions? Does it tell you anything about yourself? Anything new or different?

TEACHER: I know there are a lot of little things to pick up. I shouldn't have handed out guides so soon. I would have saved time and questions. Others could have been working.

I accomplished what I wanted to today. I feel pleased because of their contributions. I expected some, but didn't expect as many as I got. It makes me feel as if they were interested . . . the class comments, etc.

SUPERVISOR: What about improvements? If you could do it all over again? Of course, you could change the mechanics. . . . I am trying to urge you to move the unit beyond the factual.

TEACHER: I have a film next week . . . excellent! It begins after the Civil War with the Emancipation Proclamation. It begins right away with different people and with the black—what's he going to do now? It shows G. W. Carver, who was the son of a slave. Now, this is second generation. Some were even slaves. My film is good in that. Slave at one time—he is now developed. So I'm still going back to slavery. It's not forgotten. It's still here and has developed through generations.

SUPERVISOR: When you get through giving serious attention to, say, G. W.

Carver, how are you going to tie it back to ideas about slavery? Is it enough to say, "Look, he was a slave and see what he did"?

TEACHER: I'd like to bring connection. He had been a slave . . . look what he did. He would not have been recognized had not the Emancipation Proclamation taken place. Times progressed . . . opportunities presented themselves for him to get an education, one time not allowed.

SUPERVISOR: Suppose you pursue that line of reasoning—"one hundred years later and still many haven't gotten an education"! [*mock reply*] . . . How do you explain this to students? This is going around in their minds. Suppose I'm Clifford and I say, "Look at all those ignorant colored people all over the country and this is one hundred years later." What are you going to say?

TEACHER: Something to the effect, "Many places and people still hold prejudices against blacks as if they were still slaves. Many blacks are being held back and can't make contributions. Contributions have been made that haven't been recognized, too. He was a slave."

SUPERVISOR: [*Mock student question*] "He made it, Miss Holt. Why couldn't others make it if they really wanted to?"

TEACHER: It might have been just something in G. W. Carver. His own drive and enthusiasm and education to help his people as well as the entire world. . . .

SUPERVISOR: [*Mock student question*] "Aren't they really inferior? Only a few are like G. W. Carver. Most are inferior people and never will amount to anything like white people."

TEACHER: Many people have ideas of the black person. He was held back from the beginning, looking back to when slaves were brought over. No opportunity to learn . . . held back many years. A lot of people have the attitude that he is inferior because he doesn't have the background of the whites—learning, education, culture. He is just beginning to get this background. His inferiority is becoming less prominent today. At last, he is getting a chance.

SUPERVISOR: [*Mock student question*] "But Miss Holt, my daddy says they will always be inferior . . . and he is going to vote for _____in the coming election for that very reason."

I am raising the kind of questions that youngsters will raise—even though not on a verbal level because they know it's not nice to say these things. Notice what your responses were to my pretty fundamental questions. Kids ask very fundamental sets of questions. Remember the little boy? "Why didn't they let them read and write?" You gave him a logical but simple explanation because you were moving along. "Why are changes in laws needed?" If I were you, I would spend a whole lesson on why this law and why other laws are making it difficult for the black, because these are fundamental questions. He is not satisfied as you are not with your answers. [*Pause.*] What role were you playing with me?

TEACHER: I was giving fairly general answers. Relatively the same.

SUPERVISOR: You were playing the role of answer-giver, weren't you?

TEACHER: . . . and not drawing from the students.

Insights! The end (of interview) and a beginning too!

DISSEMINATING RESEARCH
ON CLASSROOM MANAGEMENT*

The following case study describes a North Carolina school district's success in implementing research findings. It illustrates how researchers, along with state and local education agencies, can work together to bridge the gap between research and practice.

How It Worked in Currituck County

After hearing of the Research on Classroom Learning and Teaching (RCLT) Program's classroom management studies at a conference sponsored by the Appalachia Educational Laboratory, members of the North Carolina Department of Public Instruction saw the potential usefulness of this work for their schools. A Title 11-B grant was used to obtain the training and materials on classroom management for regional educational centers and local school districts in the state. An intensive, two-day workshop, conducted by RCLT staff member Barbara Clements, was presented in Raleigh in June, 1981. Over 100 persons attended. RCLT findings were presented and the manual, *Organizing and Managing the Elementary School Classroom,* and related activities were introduced.

Jane Cross, General Supervisor of Currituck County Schools, was one of those in attendance. Following the workshop, Cross met with the principals of the five schools in her district. They decided to implement a districtwide classroom management inservice program for all 100 of their K-8 teachers.

"Before this program, teachers here had a sense of frustration, being trained for one job and doing another. They were policing instead of teaching. We were losing many teachers to technical jobs. Not necessarily for the money, either. The attitude was simply 'why bother' to try to teach," Cross said.

"We had a psychologist conduct a stress management series—five two-hour workshops. We rented a day camp for the workshops to get the teachers away from the schools so they could relax and blow off steam. But this was just a temporary measure. We were treating the symptoms."

Some teachers viewed this new attempt (management workshops based on RCLT research) with some disbelief, Cross explained. "I had to persuade them to promise to try the program by the book this first time," she said.

*Adapted from "Case Study: North Carolina School District Success with R and DCTE," *R and DCTE Review,* Vol. 1, No. 1. (January 1983):6-7. A publication of the Research and Development Center for Teacher Education, The University of Texas at Austin.

The Workshops

During the first workshop, teachers were grouped according to grade level taught (K–3, 4–6, 7–8) and method or area of teaching. "Resource people were grouped with resource people, team teachers with team teachers, which normally doesn't happen in our school district," Cross said. "There is not much communication between peers, except for meetings, and then you have a full agenda."

District personnel, trained in using RCLT materials, served as facilitators for small group discussion. These group leaders had taught successfully at various grade levels within the county. "This helped legitimize the program," she said.

The workshop included a discussion of organizing classroom space and supplies for the beginning of school. Another area covered was the establishment of appropriate rules, procedures, and consequences for all classroom activities. Several related exercises were conducted.

The following day, principals from each school conducted their own inhouse schoolwide workshop. All school staff members, including teachers, aides, custodians, cafeteria personnel and bus drivers—everyone except the person answering the phone—met together to choose a set of rules for the school, the buses, the cafeteria, and the outdoor areas. "The core of rules that is always present in a school was defined in a better way," she said.

Despite some initial reluctance on the staff's part to participate in the inservice training, most teachers were enthusiastic about the program. "The workshops went beautifully," Cross reported. "They can be completed on a shoe string. We did it for $5 per teacher for materials plus initial training. The workshops were conducted during teacher work days, so there were no expenses for substitutes. It's the most cost-effective program we've ever had." And, she says, "the effects have been amazing."

The Benefits

"The biggest change has been in teacher morale. And instruction is better." There are not the same behavioral distractions to deal with, so there is more time to devote to teaching. "Stress among our teachers is down," said Cross, "and their perception of their jobs is better now because they're teaching and not policing.

"People who come into our schools now say 'the kids are different.' But they're the same kids who used to drive some teachers up the wall. It's the method of classroom management that's different. Without us saying anything, people have noticed how quiet the school is now, and how everyone is smiling," Cross continued.

The benefits of the program were most readily apparent in the junior high school. Previously, there had been high levels of teacher frustration and discontent because of frequent disciplinary problems. Discipline referrals in the school have decreased dramatically. In October, 1980, before the classroom management program was implemented, there were 129 referrals to the principal. In October, 1981, after the program, referrals dropped to 28.

"The effects of the program have snowballed," says Cross. She reports three unexpected benefits of the program in her county. First, the teachers have been pleased with how well their classes are progressing and have communicated this pleasure to their students. Students, in turn, are far happier in school, more willing to cooperate, and have expressed these feelings to their parents. Finally, parents are more positive about the schools. "Parent participation is different now, because the kids are going home with much more positive information about their school," Cross explained.

District staff members continue to evaluate the effects of the program. In addition, they are surveying teachers to obtain suggestions for a refresher session for experienced staff in the fall and an inservice program for all staff new to the district.

"Before we discovered this material, our staff development programs were hit or miss affairs. You don't know how much energy—time, money, personal—could have been saved if we'd known about this material sooner," says Cross.

While the program results reported here are subjective, they parallel those observed in studies where the materials were field-tested. The preceding case study illustrated how one school district took the initiative to put useful research products to effective use in their schools.

THE CONSULTANT TASK FORCE
IN INTENSIVE TEAM SUPERVISION*

Background

This case study describes a special program in a relatively small urban elementary school. The school is located in a low socioeconomic neighborhood near the industrial area of a medium-sized city. The school has predominantly black-American, some 20 percent Mexican-American, and very few Anglo-American, students. In an attempt to meet the unique educational needs of youngsters in this area, the school district has implemented a special program in reading and mathematics. The program utilizes a diagnostic teacher and an aide who work with children individually and in small groups to supplement the regular classroom program. A supervisor was assigned half-time to this school to assist in the operation of the special program. The roles of this supervisor were to function as a consultant to teaching team members and to plan cooperatively with the teachers and principal for a team effort

---

*Warren Alexander is responsible for initially assembling the information upon which this case narrative is based.

to improve the reading skills of the students. With minimum emphasis upon mathematics, high priority was being given to improvement in reading.

The reading program selected for use in this school is Scott, Foresman's *Open Highways,* especially designed for the child who lacks English language skills. The program assumes that many of these children must be introduced to reading skills in a program that first builds oral language and related concepts. It employs multisensory resource materials to help the child learn to read in whatever ways are most natural—seeing, hearing, tracing, writing, and manipulating. The child is introduced to decoding skills when he demonstrates readiness for the task. He then proceeds at his own rate of speed.

Our Problem

During the previous year only the first grade had participated in this program. At the time the writer arrived at the school, the program was being expanded to include the second grade. None of the three second-grade teachers had prior experience in the program, nor had two of the first-grade teachers, who were first-year teachers.

Initially, the principal, supervisor, diagnostic teacher, and aide focused attention on the participation of two first-grade teachers. During the third week of school sufficient materials became available to expand the program to include two second-grade teachers, one a beginning teacher and the other an experienced teacher who was somewhat predisposed against the program. A fifth primary teacher had a split section and was not asked to participate.

For the next three weeks the principal and supervisor devoted virtually exclusive attention to the second-grade teachers. The diagnostic teacher and aide were apparently functioning quite effectively with the first-grade classes. The picture was somewhat less rosy in the second grade. The experienced teacher, who was an extremely hard-working and capable person, was not completely sold on the program. The beginning teacher was experiencing a multitude of difficulties, running the gamut from problems of control of pupil behavior to problems of planning and organization for instruction.

At the time these second-grade teachers were to be brought into the program the principal scheduled a meeting with them and the supervisor. In this meeting the commitment of the school district to the program was cited, fundamentals of the program were explained, and teaching materials and guides were presented to the teachers with time allowed for their examination and a discussion of their use.

The supervisor met with these teachers frequently (daily at first) to assist in planning following the initial meeting. She also worked with them in the classroom daily as an assistant or helping teacher. To further aid the teacher experiencing the most difficulty, the supervisor gave demonstration lessons to her class. The principal conferred privately with this teacher to suggest ways to organize and to maintain discipline. He arranged a small group meeting in which the other second-grade teachers shared their "trade secrets" with this teacher in order to give her ideas for her own classroom. He visited her classroom often and talked with her children on several occasions about why we have rules of conduct in schools, letting students suggest rules and reasons for them.

During this time the principal was required to administer punishment to and counsel with more children from this classroom than from all other classrooms in the school combined.

At the beginning of the second six-week period, an additional primary teacher was added to the staff. She was assigned to first grade, and the teacher who had been teaching the split section was assigned to second grade. This made it possible to include all primary students and teachers in the special reading program.

The principal met with first-grade teachers to assist in assigning students to the incoming teacher. It was decided that she would receive the first-graders from the split section, who were the top students in terms of readiness scores, plus the best of the "repeating students" from the other two first-grade classes. In order to equalize classes and to give the second-grade teacher who had been experiencing great difficulty a "fresh chance," the second-grade teachers and the principal liberally reassigned second-grade students, being certain to create a heterogeneous group in terms of ability, to assign students with behavioral problems to best advantage, and to maintain a suitable ethnic balance.

Once again instructional leadership requirements had to be reassessed. There were now three first-grade teachers participating in the program. One was an experienced teacher who had participated the previous year, one was a beginning teacher who had participated since the opening of school, and one was a beginning teacher. Of second-grade teachers, one was a capable, experienced teacher who was predisposed against the program, one was a beginning teacher who was experiencing difficulty in almost every phase of her assignment, and the other was an experienced teacher who was brand-new to the program. This is the stuff of which ulcers are made. Clearly, the problem was to develop a leadership approach that was general enough to provide assistance in understanding the total problem yet specific enough to concentrate attention on the needs of individual teachers. Finally, there was no time for a long-range program of in-service education. Immediate results were required.

Solution?

In this context, the supervisor and the principal met with members of the central office consultant staff to seek approaches. As a result of these conferences, the principal proposed the creation of a consultant task force to visit the school. The group would be composed of six consultants, including the coordinator of the district's elementary reading program and the district's director of planning and evaluation. The task force idea developed into the following plan:

November 10 (2:45–4:00).   The district's director of planning and evaluation would present a report on the evaluation of the first year of the program, with special emphasis on results in this school. His presentation would allow time for a question-and-answer session. Purposes of this activity would include:

1. Orienting teachers to the objectives of the program,
2. Familiarizing teachers with the methods of evaluation of the success of the program, and
3. Effecting positive attitudes toward the program by displaying measures of success in its initial year.

November 11 (2:45–4:00).   The coordinator responsible for the reading program in the district's elementary schools would make a presentation to the teachers on the topic "Characteristics of a Good Primary Reading Program," offering general suggestions for the teaching of reading. Discussion of the ideas presented would follow.

November 16 (1:00–4:00).   On a one-to-one basis, all six consultants would visit classrooms of the teachers in the program for the purpose of observing a reading lesson. During the planning sessions that would follow the class, the consultant and the teacher would do a critique of the presentation. On the basis of this experience, and with the help of a preliminary list provided by the teacher and information provided by the principal and supervisor prior to the date of the visit concerning the specific teacher's needs, the consultant would assist the teacher in formulating objectives for the improvement of the teacher's performance.

November 17 (1:00–4:00).   Each consultant would return to the same room in which she worked in the previous day and teach a lesson in which she would exemplify good technique and attempt to demonstrate some skill or procedure in which the teacher has recognized a need for improvement. During the planning period that would follow, the teacher and consultant would critique this lesson. They would continue the development of the teacher's objectives for self-improvement.

Implementation

Ten days prior to the beginning of the program, the principal met with the primary teachers and explained the planned visit of the Consultant Task Force in terms of what we could reasonably hope to accomplish. At this time

teachers were asked to begin preparation of preliminary lists of self-improvement objectives. (This assignment was given to all teachers in the school, but
primary teachers were given the additional assistance of the consultants.)

The program was implemented exactly as planned. Attending the two
general meetings (November 10 and 11) were all six consultant members of
the task force, all six primary teachers in the school, the two third-grade
teachers (who are to be involved in the expanded program next year), the
diagnostic teacher and her aide, the supervisor, and the principal. The other
meetings were, of course, between a consultant and a teacher.

Evaluation

A combined subjective and objective evaluation was conducted. The
objective evaluation was by means of an evaluation instrument given to
teachers at the conclusion of the final day of the program and returned to
the principal the following day.

One measure of the success of the program was teacher enthusiasm.
Their remarks and participation indicated that the teachers considered the
first two meetings quite successful. And teacher enthusiasm continued to grow
throughout the program, as indicated by attitudes toward the final two days'
activities. The following table shows how the teachers ranked the four days'
activities.

			TEACHER				
DATE	#1	#2	#3	#4	#5	#6	MEAN
Nov. 10	4	4	4	3	4	4	3.8
Nov. 11	3	3	3	4	3	3	3.2
Nov. 16	2	1	2	2	2	2	1.8
Nov. 17	1	2	1	1	1	1	1.2

1 = most helpful, 4 = least helpful

The teachers were also asked to rate the program on a scale from 1
(least effective) to 7 (most effective) in comparison to other in-service programs with which they were personally familiar. This program got no mark
below 5, and the average rating was 5.8.

Still one more measure of teacher acceptance of the program was obtained through the open-ended responses on the evaluation questionnaire.
Four of the six teachers suggested that useful follow-up activities would call
for the same consultant to visit with the teacher later in the year to observe
the teacher and to make additional suggestions to the teacher that might help
her to accomplish her objectives for improvement.

The ultimate effect upon teaching in these classrooms was not determined, but the program appears to have been very successful in meeting two of its objectives:

1. Teachers were given a broad orientation to the purposes, objectives, and operation of the special reading and mathematics program.
2. Teachers seem to be more positive in their attitudes toward the program.

And, at least superficially, it appears to have spoken to the specific needs of individual teachers.

The participating consultants were also quite positive about the experience, although they were anxious to see whether there would be any noticeable changes in teacher behavior.

The cost in extra consultant time was substantial. With planning and preparation time the six consultants invested approximately two days each or a total of twelve consultant days. Since they worked with only six teachers, this is two days per teacher. Extending this to a working year of two-hundred days, such service would require one consultant per hundred teachers. This is a realistic ratio, perhaps.

IN-SERVICE PLAN FOR TRAINING
IN READING DISABILITY*

Program goal.   To provide an in-service program for nine teachers of grades K through 4, one physical education teacher, and one music teacher in perceptual aspects of reading disabilities and the perceptual examination report for the purpose of helping them improve their ability to identify pupils with perceptual difficulties.

Immediate objective.   Given a pupil who has previously been identified as having perceptual difficulties to observe, the teacher will use the perceptual examination report according to the criteria provided in the in-service program for observing the pupil, identifying the kinds of perceptual difficulties, and prescribing remediation of the pupil's difficulties at a level of performance judged satisfactory by a remedial reading specialist.

Long-range objective.   In his own classroom situation the teacher will use the procedure mastered in the in-service sessions to test, to evaluate test results, to prescribe remediation, and to implement remediation for perceptual difficulties according to the criteria established in the in-service program at a satisfactory level as evidenced by increased consultation with and referral to the remedial reading specialist and the principal.

*Excerpts from a training packet developed by Donald D. Eilerts.

PROGRAM AGENDA

THURSDAY, AUGUST 26

TIME	SESSIONS	TOPIC	LOCATION
9:00 A.M.	1. A Rationale for Perceptual Aspects of Reading Disability		Library
10:30 A.M.	(Coffee break)		Cafeteria
11:00 A.M.	2. Analysis of Reading Disabilities: Observation of Perceptual Difficulties Kinds of Perceptual Difficulties		Library
12:00 noon	Adjourn		

FRIDAY, AUGUST 27

TIME	SESSIONS	TOPIC	LOCATION
9:30 A.M.	3. Selection and Prescription of Remediation Alternatives		Library
10:30 A.M.	(Coffee break)		Cafeteria
11:00 A.M.	4. Implementation and Evaluation of Remediation		Library
12:00 noon	Adjourn		

A Rationale for Perceptual Aspects of Reading Disability — Session 1

Session objective. Given fifteen minutes to observe five pupils who are engaging individually in specified activities, the teacher will differentiate the one pupil who has previously been identified as having perceptual difficulties from four pupils who have no marked evidence of perceptual handicap.

Enabling objectives. During the session, the teacher will complete practice frames giving evidence that he can:

1. Recognize the definition of *learning disabilities*;
2. List the three types of disability;
3. Name the five most common areas of perceptual deficit;
4. List four characteristics usually observable in a child having the syndrome of "minimal cerebral dysfunction;"
5. Recognize the definition of *perceptual handicap*;
6. List three possible causes of perceptual handicap;
7. List four other mental processes that may be impaired if a child is perceptually handicapped;

8. List four kinds of perceptual handicaps, and state the way each may cause a pupil to malfunction in the classroom.

Outline of Learning Activities and Materials

PURPOSE OR OBJECTIVE	LEARNING ACTIVITY	TEACHER ACTIVITY AND MATERIALS
Establish atmosphere	Participating in perceptual exercises	Supervising exercises: 1. Write name on folded paper held on forehead 2. Touch index finger—psycho-motor exercise
Pretest	Selecting one pupil who has perceptual difficulties	Arrange to have five pupils individually perform specified activities: balance-beam exercises, walking board, eye-movement using Marsden ball, beanbag catching
Overview and 1, 2, 3, 4	Reading objectives (HO 1) Doing frames 1–4 (HO 2) Reading introduction (HO 3) Reading Frostig test (HO 4)	Explaining handouts using transparencies: 1. Three types (disclosure) 2–6. Perceptual defects
5, 6, 7, 8	Reprint (HO 5) Doing frames 5–8	Discussing handout (optional method—learning cells)
Review	Questioning, discussing	Answering questions, guiding discussion
Posttest	Selecting one pupil who has perceptual difficulties	Same as pretest, using different pupils
Evaluation	Providing feedback (HO 6)	Quick check sheet

Summary of Other Sessions

Session 2. The remedial reading specialist will administer the "Perceptual Examination Report" in a demonstration situation while the in-service participants observe in a darkened section of the room and fill out their own reports. At the end of the 30-minute demonstration, participants will compare their observations with those of the specialist and discuss the results.

Session 3.   Following explanation and discussion of a handout concerning remediation alternatives for various kinds of perceptual difficulties, participants will complete the recommendation section of the report for which they observed in Session 2. Their recommendations will be compared with those of the specialist. At the end of Session 3, participants will be asked to hand in written questions on issues that they would like to see discussed at the next session.

Session 4.   Discussion of implementation of the procedures in the individual classroom will be followed by discussion of the questions handed in at the preceding session.

Continuation.   Each participant will be asked to select a pupil from his classroom whom he has identified as having perceptual difficulties and follow the procedures learned in these sessions in identifying, perscribing for, and remediating the pupil's perceptual difficulties. The teacher will establish a target date (approximately three weeks) for going over the report with the remedial reading specialist and the principal.

HUMAN RELATIONS WORKSHOP*

When I first came to work as consultant in Big City's area office I was apprised of the school-community conflict at Foster Jones Elementary School. My deputy superintendent was concerned about the alleged insensitivity of some teachers to the needs of children. Jones Elementary is the largest school in the city, with over 1200 pupils, mostly blacks, with a few of Puerto Rican extraction. The teaching staff, on the other hand, is only 35 percent black.

At the suggestion of my superintendent, I contacted the principal at Jones Elementary to explore ways of helping. We discussed a *human relations workshop* as a beginning effort with the faculty. He was quite enthusiastic. A committee of seven teachers was appointed, and we began planning.

Preliminaries

The bell for school dismissal was rung at 2:25 P.M. It immediately became self-evident that we would not start the workshop promptly at 2:30. Indeed, it was 2:40 before most teachers were seated. The remarks by principal and deputy superintendent lasted ten minutes, five more minutes than I had allocated for them. This time was well used by the superintendent's reading a recent newspaper article concerning adults' understanding of children. It was well received by the teachers and helped to create an informal

---

*Adapted from a report by Ruben Saenz, Principal, Rio Grande City High School.

atmosphere. My remarks were mainly confined to the rationale of human relations in education and the importance of human relations above and beyond race relations.

Vignette for Role Playing

Some students complain to their teacher, Miss Jones, that they are becoming confused, tired, and frustrated with her class because she does not take time to go over the subject matter even when the students tell her they do not understand what is being presented. They tell her they realize they are not the brightest students around, but if she would only slow down and explain the subject matter more thoroughly they would do better. Miss Jones reacts by telling the students that they have faulty listening habits. If they would only listen to what is being presented in class, instead of daydreaming and playing, they would understand. She tells them that because of their behavior they are really to blame if no learning is taking place. She accuses some of being lazy and rude and of not really wanting to learn. The students tell her that she really does not understand them as individuals. They threaten to report her to the principal.

A. Do students have the right to question teaching methodologies used in the classroom?
B. How should teachers react to such questioning?
C. Is there a danger in becoming subject matter–oriented?
D. How can teachers better understand students in a deparmentalized setting?

Role Playing

The cast, four females, carried out the assignment rather well and followed the major theme throughout. The "students" could probably have been more forceful in presenting their allegations against the teacher. They concluded the skit by threatening to report the teacher to the principal. At this point I stepped in and signaled that the role-playing situation was over, and the cast received a good round of applause from fellow teachers.

Buzz Groups

The instruction to the buzz groups was brief—to assemble at the predesignated tables, select a group leader, buzz about any or all of the situational questions, and reassemble at the semicircle at my signal.

Report from Buzz-Group Leaders

Buzz-group leaders were each given a maximum of one minute to report their group's main responses to the situational questions. The following are characteristic responses:

A. To the question "Do students have the right to question teaching methodologies used in the classroom?" all agreed that students indeed have the inherent right to question their teachers' methodologies. However, all cautioned that the student should use tact and diplomacy in communicating with the teacher. Teachers should create a classroom atmosphere where students feel free to make suggestions or comments about what they are learning without fear of repercussions from the teacher.

B. To the question "How should teachers react to such questioning?" most agreed that teachers should understand that students are partners in the learning process, the prime partners at that, and teachers must not react defensively when questioned but should listen to the students.

C. All leaders agreed that there was great danger of becoming subject matter–oriented. They felt that teachers should understand that they were dealing first with human beings and second with subject matter.

D. Only four groups addressed themselves to this question. They felt that every teacher must strive and take time to get to know and to understand the students in a departmentalized setting. All stated how easy it was for a teacher to fall into the subject matter–oriented trap in a departmentalized setting.

Closing Thoughts

Probably no other profession has as much opportunity to collectively and individually practice sound human relations daily as do persons engaged in the art of teaching. Every individual worth being singled out as a successful teacher has attained this status on three rudimentary principles—subject-matter expertise, sound teaching strategies, and healthy human relations with students, other school personnel, and community patrons.

Evaluation

A reactionnaire was distributed and completed as the meeting ended. Forty-five of the forty-eight participants indicated strong positive reactions to the session.

DIAGNOSTIC EVALUATION
OF A STAFF DEVELOPMENT WORKSHOP

Background

A regional service center was responding to new state legislation requiring a substantial increase in the amount of in-service education offered to teachers. The center contracted with three consultants to plan and present a full-day workshop for administrative and supervisory personnel on "Planning In-Service Education Programs." A preliminary planning conference indicated that an interested group might number between 50 and 70 participants consisting mainly of principals and instructional supervisors plus a few teachers and superintendents. On this information base, the consultants proceeded to plan a series of sessions extending from 9:30 A.M. through 3:30 P.M.

As shown in the following agenda, the basic idea guiding session planning was that of providing demonstrations of new and hopefully useful approaches. Emphasis was to be placed upon the planning of in-service education programs, but demonstrations of planning approaches were to include illustrations of activities that would also be useful in the implementation of such programs (brainstorming, buzz groups, etc.). Plans were developed to ensure a great deal of involvement by participants in order to hold their interest.

Agenda

May 12, 19—

Topic: *Planning In-Service Education Programs*

9:30   *Introduction:* Center staff member.

9:40   *Brainstorming Session:* Develop list of problem statements using the case "Changing the Curriculum at Southside" as "Situation."

10:10   *Lecturette:* An introduction of the structure and technique of force-field analysis. What is it? How to use it? Illustrate the technique of identifying forces, using a hypothetical problem.

10:20   *Break*

10:40   *Task Groups:* Three groups applying force-field analysis technique to the problem statement evolved in brainstorming session. Consultant works with each task group to guide its use of f.f.a.

11:45–

1:00   *Lunch*

1:00   *Buzz-Group Discussion:* Buzz groups of six or eight people discuss the in-service problems of their local districts' local needs. Three consultants circulate and pick up those items that emerge as identifiable group concerns and record them. Buzz-group recorder asked to get consensus from group on one or two problems of most concern.

1:30   *Panel:* Conceptualizing in-service education in broad perspective. Presentation of overall concepts and strategies to consider in planning in-service education programs or implementing them.

2:45   *Discussion:* General wrap-up to consider direction setting, next steps, alternatives open in the future, etc. How does the center fit into the picture? Has your view of the problem changed? *Evaluation instruments* distributed, completed, and collected.

3:20   Adjourn.

Liabilities

From the beginning, consultants were a bit anxious about the assignment for several reasons: (1) very little time was available for planning; (2) consultants had not worked with prospective participants in any previous workshop and knew little about them; (3) consultants were given no opportunity to plan directly with representatives of the participant group; (4) service center personnel responsible for coordinating the workshop were changed shortly before the designated date, and this brought to the consultant some new perceptions of the needs of the participants; and (5) participants with various administrative and supervisory positions would have diverse responsibilities related to in-service planning.

Workshop Sessions

To attend the workshop, which began 30 minutes late on the designated day, more than 50 participants had to drive from various towns of the region to the centrally located motel in a small city. The late start was the result of a time change, which some had heard about but others had not. Tables and chairs had been arranged for participants' use to facilitate buzz groups and other interaction activities. As they came into the large meeting room, an inventory checklist was handed to each participant as well as a printed case 11 pages long. Participants were asked to prepare the following inventory and to study the case while waiting for others to come in.

Inventory Checklist of Problems

Your Code:_____

Directions: The list of statements below suggests many possible outcomes from this day of activities. *Please check* those that best fit you and your school situation.

____1. We need more time for effective in-service activities.

____2. We need more money for elaborate programs.

____3. We need outside consultants who can lead in-service programs.

____4. We need to involve teachers more fully in identifying needs.

____5. We need to arrange for more grade-level or special subject groups.

____6. We need to find ways to systematically evaluate our in-service efforts.

____7. We need to assist teachers in running their own in-service programs.

____8. We need to learn how to work with teachers in force-field analysis.

____9. We need to sharpen our ways of using a wider variety of in-service activities.

__10. We need to learn to more carefully design in-service programs for continuity and experience impact.

__11. We need to learn to use brainstorming and other group involvement techniques for planning in-service programs.

__12. We need to see what in-service programs the ESC can offer to our teachers for next year.

__13. We need to evolve better modes of working with the ESC to bring about continuing in-service programs.

__14. We need to learn how to work effectively with small groups of teachers.

__15. We need to develop individualized modes of in-service as one alternative strategy.

The inventory was designed as a problem census. It was planned to be used both before and after the day's events to provide a comparison of responses which might indicate the insights into the problem of in-service program planning that had developed during the day. The case material that participants were asked to read was to be the simulated reality upon which laboratory activities for the morning session were to be based.

During the morning session, especially during the coffee break, some comments were heard indicating a certain amount of dissatisfaction with the beginning activities as some participants interpreted them. In opening the session, a representative of the sponsoring service center staff tried to clarify misunderstandings which had apparently developed previously. Some participants had gained the impression from correspondence or announcements that this workshop was going to *make decisions* regarding in-service programs the center was to plan for the local schools. The center had apparently been under pressure to provide in-service programs for the schools of the region. The policy the center had recently adopted was to concentrate on assisting local personnel in planning their local efforts. This policy was clarified in the introductory statement, but apparently some participants were still concerned about it.

Before the luncheon break, a reactionnaire was distributed to obtain a session rating indicating general interest in the morning session. No formal luncheon arrangements had been made, so participants went in groups to various restaurants, both within the motel and nearby. At the resumption of the program in the afternoon, the group was greatly reduced in size. Only 25 of the original 51 participants returned for the afternoon session.

At the end of the afternoon session, interest reactionnaires were once again distributed so each remaining participant could express his level of interest in the ideas and activities. The copy of the inventory checklist of problems was also distributed, and each participant indicated again the problems of planning and implementing in-service programs as he or she viewed them.

Evaluation Design

Based on the two primary types of participant response data, an evaluation effort was undertaken immediately after the workshop. The rationale of this design can be summarized as follows: A successful in-service experience is one in which interest and enthusiasm of participants is rather high, and in which participants tend to learn those things for which the experience was designed. Ratings of general interest in the sessions—one administered at the end of the morning session, the other at the end of the afternoon session—were combined and used as an interest measure. The *Inventory Checklist of Problems* was scored to produce a measure of learning. A weighted scoring system was used that assigned positive, zero, or negative values to those items that were checked by participants. Participants who attained a relatively high score on the postinventory checklist or who had substantially increased their score from preadministration to postadministration were presumed to be those who had learned to perceive the problems of in-service planning and implementation more realistically and to recognize some of the necessities for such planning. In this sense the central objective of the workshop was to develop an awareness of the kinds of problems and the necessary approaches to such problems required for good in-service planning.

Data from the interest ratings and the preinventory-postinventory scores were analyzed using designated scores for high and low subgroups. Participants were designated as high in interest when their combined ratings averaged 7 or better on a 9-point scale. Similarly, each participant was rated high on achievement of objectives either on the basis of terminal score on the checklist of 5 or more or on the basis of a prechange and postchange score of 4 or more. Those in attendance both morning and afternoon were included in this analysis. Obviously, those who had left at lunchtime could not be included. Hence, the meaning of their participation had to be inferred from other kinds of analyses.

Analysis of Reactions

A quick view of the interest and checklist measured learning is shown in Table 11.1. Only 25 sets of matching scores were available for participants. Those who left early are listed as "indeterminate." Nearly half of those who remained were high on both interest and learning measures. Thirteen participants fall into the other three categories. Seventeen of the twenty-six participants who left early rated the morning session as low in interest.

The presence of 12 high-interest, high-learning participants is reassuring, but an analysis of who they are and what force-field analysis groups they participated in could give leads to the reason for this success.

Table 11.2 shows strongest interest and learning by superintendents

TABLE 11.1   Distribution of Participants by Interest and Learning

INTEREST ON REACTIONNAIRE	LEARNING ON CHECKLIST			TOTAL
	HIGH	LOW	INDETERMINATE	
High	12	5	9	26
Low	3	5	17	25
Total	15	10	26	51

TABLE 11.2   Participant Positions by Interest-Learning Categories

PROFESSIONAL POSITION	HIGH INTEREST– HIGH LEARNING		LOW IN EITHER INTEREST OR LEARNING, OR BOTH		TOTAL
	NO.	%	NO.	%	NO.
Superintendent	5	42	7	58	12
Principal (elementary)	1	12	7	88	8
Principal (secondary)	3	60	2	40	5
Supervisor	3	27	8	73	11
Other	0	0	5	100	5
Total— All positions	12	29	29	71	41

and secondary principals. Least success seems to have been experienced by elementary school principals and others. Supervisors as a group seemed to profit less than superintendents and secondary principals, though not so little as elementary principals.

Table 11.3 shows that 50 percent of those in Task Group Z during the session on force-field analysis technique were in the high-success subgroup. Substantially smaller portions of Task Groups were in the high-success category. Hence, it may well be that the influence of Task Group Z activities was of special value.

TABLE 11.3   Participant Task-Group Assignments by Interest-Learning Categories

TASK GROUP	HIGH INTEREST– HIGH LEARNING		LOW IN EITHER INTEREST OR LEARNING, OR BOTH		TOTAL
	NO.	%	NO.	%	NO.
X	2	13	13	87	15
Y	3	25	9	75	12
Z	7	50	7	50	14
Total— All groups	12	29	29	71	41

Summary

This workshop involved special problems from the very beginning. Poor communications, misunderstandings, and mixed interests were all part of the problem faced by the consultants. An evaluation effort to determine what effect the activities had on participants was inconclusive, but not without useful outcomes. Apparently, a fairly large portion of the participants who left early were not much interested in the morning activities. An analysis of the last activity of the morning where three subgroups were utilized suggests that only one of these was effective in overcoming the confusion of the early part of the day.

THE PROFESSIONAL DEVELOPMENT CENTER*

The Professional Development Center (PDC) is a highly structured organizational pattern for delivery of in-service education that features direct modeling of individualized teaching. The Professional Development Center is defined in a participants' orientation publication as a "commitment to develop and directly model real world operational teaching designs which facilitate changing the teacher's behavior toward individualizing and personalizing instruction for each student."

The Professional Development Center, then, is a structured system designed to develop the skills required for individualizing instruction. Thirteen skill areas are taught as separate independent study units (ISUs). Individual study units concern (1) purposes for individualizing, (2) continuous progress learning, (3) failure and the child, (4) team teaching, (5) writing and using objectives, (6) diagnosing student learning needs, (7) prescribing learning activities, (8) grouping for individualized instruction, (9) recording progress of pupils, (10) grading and reporting progress, (11) individualizing with learning centers, (12) organizing materials for learning centers, and (13) flexible scheduling.

This Professional Development Center was first operationalized at Woodridge Elementary School in San Antonio, Texas, and accepted its first group of participants in 1974. Established as a pilot project in September 1972, the system was first tested on faculty members in nine different schools. The pilot testing enabled the system developers to refine their materials for use in an areawide delivery system.

This case study is based on a review of documents, interviews with staff, and the researcher's personal Professional Development Center experience.

*Adapted from Nancy Joyce Hagen, "A Comparative Analysis of Selected Inservice Education Delivery Systems" (dissertation, The University of Texas at Austin, 1981). The PDC described is operated by Education Service Center, Region 20, San Antonio, Texas.

The Professional Development Center is unlike many others in that a single overarching design for training is utilized. It is this overall design that is the core of the system.

The Model

The delivery system emphasizes training for individualized instruction incorporating the following:

First, the training is presented in modular form with a linear core of required experiences and a series of branched programmed options. The core experiences required of all teachers present skills, information, and attitudes important to any teaching strategy. However, one-third of the training is in branching options, or self-selected modules, offering a variety of instructional procedures aimed at providing optimal learning opportunities for all trainees.

Secondly, the complete set of core materials, experiences, and branching options is divided into three phases or components: (1) Orientation Kit, (2) Individual Study Units, and (3) Classroom Planning and Implementation. These three components correspond to three separate time periods—before, during, and after teachers' training activities at the Professional Development Center site.

Operating Plans

The following sequence of events describes participation in the Professional Development Center.

1. Participants receive the Orientation Kit about three weeks before their first visit to the Professional Development Center campus.
2. Participants begin a two-, three-, or five-day training sequence at the Center campus in a modeled, structured training program for individualizing instruction. Table 11.4 describes six work centers utilized for this on-site training.
3. Participants return to their classroom the following Monday. Staff consultants contact them to see what assistance they will be needing in implementing concepts acquired during the on-site training period.

Before leaving the Professional Development Center campus, staff members will gather to discuss decisions about the performance objectives participants have chosen to implement and will then schedule times to meet with them and their principals to help iron out any problems and answer questions related to the objectives.

The last step is participants' continuing efforts at careful planning in the implementation of individualized and personalized instruction.

Once participants have been nominated for training by the school principal, they complete and turn in the Orientation Kit materials. This material consists of taking a pre-test on the 13 concepts of individualized instruction, based on readings about individualized learning theory. The participant is then ready to engage in the intensive training activities (phase b). These activities are guided by individual study units.

The individual study units involve the trainee in individualized simulation exercises designed to provide realistic experiences under instructor control. Each ISU is directed toward shaping new teacher behavior. The trainee's acquisition of these new teaching skills within the Center proceeds through a three-step process;

b-1   The instructor models the skills, attitudes, and knowledge necessary.
b-2   The teachers engage in simulated activities.
b-3   The instructor provides audio and visual feedback concerning the teacher's approximation to the skills, attitudes, and knowledge.

The above sequence is followed for each concept selected for each individual participant.

The individual study units are especially designed to actively involve the teacher in the acquisition of new skills, attitudes, and knowledge. The teacher is permitted to feel and see the effects of each teaching innovation from the perspectives offered by being a teacher and learner involved in a wide range of classroom teaching strategies.

Five management systems are presented to participants though the use of the 13 individual study units. In addition to the core concepts of individualizing instruction that every PDC participant is expected to master, he or she is having experience as a learner with each of these five different management systems for individualized instruction: (1) large-group instruction, (2) timed scheduling through work centers, (3) individual prescriptions with direct teach sessions based on diagnostic placement, (4) individual prescriptions with no required direct teach sessions, and (5) independent study.

Thus, the PDC participant is exposed twice to the skills of managing individualized instruction, directly through ISU materials and again through the modeling experiences built into the design for training.

Learning rates and needs vary for individuals in the PDC. Participants of full-cycle training who do not demonstrate mastery on any posttest are recycled into other learning experiences that address the same objectives. ISUs produce mastery at levels varying from 99 percent for ISU-B to only 85 percent for ISU-I. Participants are free to choose ISU activities from among J, K, L, and M.

ISUs J through M are the most "hands-on" modules; A through I consist largely of cognitive knowledge acquisition. Objectives for ISUs J through M include "to design an appropriate learning center for your classroom" (ISU-K), "to develop schedule cards" (ISU-M), and "to design an individualized reporting system" (ISU-J).

Participants can and do "pretest" out of some ISUs. The ISU that most participants (316 of 384) had to master through completing ISU activities as opposed to pretesting out was ISU-G, "Prescribing Appropriate Learning Activities for an Individual."

During the training sessions, clients are grouped by need (as determined by pretest), grouped by choice (as for games), and grouped by skill (as for direct teach).

PDC's Organization

Planning with school districts entering the Professional Development Center program is constrained by the fact that both the district and the campus must be committed to individualization prior to participant entry. Planning is collaborative in nature, as it represents shared interests and local education agency commitments to support the program.

Involvement of participants is of course extensive and is best illustrated by the fact that whole faculties or teams from a school sometimes take the training together, and these groups are reassembled after the formal training experience for assistance to each other as follow-up in classrooms proceeds. The commitment to the use of school classrooms is necessitated by the nature of the training. Teachers are expected to individualize their own classrooms, hence all follow-up activities are conducted in the home classrooms of participants. Clients sometimes include administrators. Entry into the PDC is by district decision, represented by a written contract with each district involved.

TABLE 11.4   Seven Work Centers of the PDC

TITLE	PURPOSE
1. Direct Instruction Center	• whole and small-group instruction • day begins and ends here • participants gather here
2. Reading Center	• contains current literature on each PDC module • participants read here
3. Audio Center	• contains current cassette tapes on PDC modules • participants listen
4. 16-mm Center	• contains current films on PDC modules • participants review here
5. Games Center	• contains individual and group oriented games related to each PDC module • participants play alone or in groups
6. Filmstrip Center	• contains current filmstrips on PDC modules • participants view here
7. Problem Solving Center	• contains culminating activity for each ISU • participants apply skills here

APPENDIX A
COMPETENCY
STATEMENTS
FOR SUPERVISORY
PERFORMANCE*

A. DEVELOPING CURRICULUM

Setting Instructional Goals—A-1

Given a mandate to clarify major goals of instruction, the supervisor can lead groups of parents, citizens, specialized personnel, teachers, and pupils through a series of discussions, presentations, training sessions, and other experiences to produce a report showing some of the most important instructional goals on which there is agreement.

Designing Instructional Units—A-2

The supervisor can design instructional units which specify performance objectives, instructional sequences, a variety of appropriate teaching/learning activities, materials, and evaluative procedures.

Developing and Adapting Curricula—A-3

Having secured innovative curricula developed outside the school or district, the supervisor can adapt the curricula to meet the needs of a student

*Source: *The Developmental Supervisory Competency Assessment System (DeSCAS)* 3rd Edition by Ben M. Harris. Copyright © 1979, 1982. All rights reserved.

289

or student group, and make them available to local personnel for use in guiding instructional planning.

B. PROVIDING MATERIALS

Evaluating and Selecting Learning Materials—B-1

Given expressed needs for learning materials, the supervisor can develop a set of evaluative criteria and procedures to determine the quality, utility, and availability of learning materials, and can organize and conduct review sessions where teachers and other personnel can apply the criteria to new materials and make recommendations for acquisitions in needed areas.

Producing Learning Materials—B-2

Given learning needs and a curricular design to meet those needs, the supervisor can arrange for the production of the necessary learning materials to complement, fulfill, and/or enhance the aims of the curriculum.

Evaluating the Utilization of Learning Resources— B-3

Given an array of learning resources currently available for use, the supervisor can design and conduct a study to determine the extent and appropriateness of their utilization, and, based on the results of that study, can make recommendations for the improved utilization of specific learning resources in specific ways.

C. PROVIDING STAFF FOR INSTRUCTION

Developing a Staffing Plan—C-1

Given a new project proposal which specifies budget, general objectives, and operational procedures, the supervisor can describe essential staff positions to be filled, develop job descriptions for each, and specify the competencies required of the individuals who will fill the positions.

Recruiting and Selecting Personnel—C-2

Given a description of several staff positions to be filled, the supervisor, by engaging in a variety of selective recruitment activities, can secure a list of several possible applicants from various sources, can systematically secure and validate relevant information on the applicants by conducting personal interviews, by checking with previous employers, and by using other selection procedures, and can prepare a set of recommendations for filling the vacancies with the applicants who will best fulfill job requirements.

Assigning Personnel—C–3

Given the task of assigning new personnel and reassigning currently employed personnel to achieve instructional improvements, the supervisor can analyze the needs, expectations, and composition of existing staff groups in various units, and, based on that analysis, can prepare and justify recommendations for assigning and reassigning staff members to positions for optimum educational opportunity.

D. ORGANIZING FOR INSTRUCTION

Revising Existing Structures—D–1

Having determined the strengths and weaknesses of an existing organizational structure, the supervisor can propose carefully reasoned or research supported changes, which may include the alteration of assignments, of the use of staff time, of the required reporting patterns, or of the allocation of resources to improve efficiency, productivity, and morale, and, in so doing, improve the instructional process.

Assimilating Programs—D–2

Given a successful instructional program operating within a center, school, classroom, or other unit, the supervisor can design a plan for the smooth integration of the entire program or selected components thereof into a larger system, prepare a timetable and assignments for the transferring of responsibilities, and assure that the instructional improvement evidenced in the program is continued in the system to which it is transferred.

Monitoring New Arrangements—D–3

Given the task of implementing a new organizational arrangement, the supervisor can determine reporting procedures, compare actual operations with planned developments, and when necessary, make recommendations to modify operations to bring them into agreement with formulated plans.

E. RELATING SPECIAL PUBLIC SERVICES

Analyzing and Securing Services—E–1

Given a need for supporting services, the supervisor can develop a list of sources from which to secure such services, and can develop a proposal for adding such services to the system with efficiency and effectiveness.

Orienting and Utilizing Specialized Personnel—E-2

Given a need for specialized assistance, the supervisor can secure the services of a variety of resource persons and can make arrangements for these persons to contribute their unique expertise to assist staff in serving student needs.

Scheduling Services—E-3

Given diagnoses of pupils' needs and regular instructional personnel, the supervisor can propose a set of schedules to distribute services appropriately, to balance the loads of the staff members who provide the services, and to provide an opportunity for recipients of the services to maintain maximum integration with regular school programs.

Evaluation of the Utilization of Services—E-4

Given a plan for providing better supporting services within a district, the supervisor can compare that plan with the current operation by utilizing objective data gathered in accordance with previously identified criteria and can propose recommendations that would increase the effectiveness and quality of the support system.

F. ARRANGING FOR IN-SERVICE EDUCATION

Supervising in a Clinical Mode—F-1

Given a teacher experiencing difficulties within a classroom, the supervisor can lead the teacher through a clinical cycle using classroom observation data, non-directive feedback techniques, and various planning and in-service experiences to produce significantly improved teacher behavior.

Planning for Individual Growth—F-2

Given a teacher and data concerning various facets of his/her on-the-job performance, the supervisor can assist the teacher in establishing individual professional growth plans which include objectives for change in classroom practices, a schedule of experiences sequenced for continuous stimulation and growth, criteria specified for interim and terminal evaluation, and a specified period for accomplishing the objectives.

Designing In-Service Training Sessions—F-3

Given a description of a specific staff group, including description of their needs for training, the supervisor can design or adapt a training session plan specifying objectives, activities, procedures, materials, and methods for evaluation to assure participant interest, involvement, and learning.

Conducting In-Service Training Sessions—F-4

Given a description of a specific staff group, the supervisor can select an appropriate training plan, make arrangements, and lead participants through a sequence of meaningful learning activities.

Training for Leadership Roles—F-5

Given individuals who have demonstrated both a high level of competence in a specific area and emergent leadership capabilities, the supervisor can train these people to conduct in-service sessions and to provide follow-up activities that result in the improvement of instructional skills.

Assessing Needs—F-6

Given a client group, the supervisor can produce an assessment of needs for in-service education which results in a set of priorities in terms of individuals, programs and organizations.

Developing a Master Plan—F-7

Given a diverse client group and an array of programs in operation, the supervisor can develop a master plan for in-service education of all personnel which provides clear guidelines for specific programs, identifies resources required and available, and designates strategies and relationships among in-service program plans.

Writing a Project Proposal—F-8

Given a specific set of training priorities and a client group, the supervisor can write a program or project proposal for in-service education which details goals and objectives, describes activity sequences, displays schedules, costs, staffing arrangements, and materials; but also defines evaluative criteria.

Designing a Self-Instructional Packet—F-9

Given a specific kind of training that is needed recurrently, the supervisor can produce a self-instructional training packet which employs multimedia, carefully sequenced content, and outcome measures built in to provide feedback to users.

Designing a Training Program Series—F-10

Given a clearly defined goal for in-service education, the supervisor can lead a group in planning and designing a series of sessions, all of which relate to the same goal but differentiated objectives, provide for active participation, and assure opportunities for freedom of choice.

G. DEVELOPING PUBLIC RELATIONS

Informing the Public—G-1

The supervisor can establish, promote and maintain favorable impressions of public school programs among community members by disseminating school information through the public media, by speaking to public and school groups, by conferring with parents and other interested individuals, and by meeting, as necessary, with community groups and leaders.

Involving the Public—G-2

Given any kind of community, the supervisor can plan and organize for parents and other interested individuals in great variety and representing diverse segments of the community, can become productively involved in and trained to assist with various educational programs.

Utilizing Public Opinion—G-3

Given public opinion data regarding an educational matter, the supervisor can establish the urgency of the topic, determine the facts involved, and as appropriate, utilize the information guiding the decision-making process for modification of current programs or practices.

H. PROVIDING FACILITIES FOR INSTRUCTION

Developing Educational Specifications—H-1

Given a school, district or program requiring new facilities, the supervisor can identify instructional programs that need to be improved, develop educational specifications clearly indicating anticipated instructional operations and suggesting departures from present practices related to facilities.

Planning for Remodeling—H-2

Given a facility which no longer serves instructional purposes well, the supervisor can develop a detailed analysis of discrepancies between desired instructional activities and the physical characteristics of the facility.

Outfitting a Facility—H-3

Given a new or remodeled facility to be outfitted, the supervisor can produce a list of all essential and desirable instructional equipment, specifying educational requirements and justifying high priority items.

I. EVALUATING INSTRUCTION

Observing and Analyzing Teaching—I-1

Given a teacher or program to be evaluated, the supervisor can utilize systematic procedures and objective instruments for observing in classroom(s) to produce reliable data with useful analyses and interpretations of teacher performance.

Designing a Questionnaire—I-2

Given a staff group or program to be served, the supervisor can construct a questionnaire which elicits objective, reliable, discriminating information for use in evaluating materials, instructional activities, or program outcomes.

Interviewing In-Depth—I-3

Given the need for in-depth information from individuals, the supervisor can conduct an interview, using a structured schedule which will gather reliable and discriminating data of greater "depth" than that generally produced by questionnaires.

Analyzing and Interpreting Data—I-4

Given an evaluation problem and an array of raw data from various sources, the supervisor can analyze and draw useful interpretations, using several tabular, graphic and statistical techniques.

APPENDIX B
SPECIFIC
PERFORMANCES
BY COMPETENCY
FOR THE INSERVICE
TASK AREA*

F–1   *Supervising in a clinical mode:*

        Leads a teacher (or other client) through a complete *clinical cycle* leading to improved classroom practice.

        Observes systematically in a classroom, using a selected observation instrument, producing highly reliable, objective data.

        Conducts a supervisory interview with a teacher (or other client) using non-directive techniques and shared decision-making procedures.

F–2   *Planning for individual growth:*

        Interprets data on teacher performance using collaborative procedures which encourage the client to question, contribute, choose and accept without coercion.

        Assists the teacher (or client) *in selecting* and carefully specifying objectives for his/her change in classroom practices.

*Source: Ben M. Harris, *Developmental Supervisory Competency Assessment System* 3rd ed. (Round Rock, Tex.: Ben M. Harris Associates, 1982). © Copyright. All rights reserved.

Develops a schedule of experiences to be arranged for, stimulating individual teacher (client) growth, including specifying target dates and responsibilities.

F–3   *Designing training sessions:*

Specifies objectives for an in-service training session that clearly relate to needs of participants in ways that are realistic for accomplishment yet important to improving instruction.

Plans a training session to include a variety of stimulating, involving activities, with materials and procedures for their use clearly developed.

Develops evaluation procedures and materials for providing feedback on an in-service training session that clearly assists with future planning.

F–4   *Conducting training:*

Selects a training plan or strategy for a specific group which is clearly appropriate to their needs.

Arranges for an *in-service* training session with thoroughness; providing for advanced information, physical arrangements, and all essential resources.

Leads participants in a session through a sequence of meaningful activities, maintaining task orientation, promoting involvement, and respecting participant needs.

F–5   *Training leadership personnel:*

Identifies highly competent teachers (or others) with potential leadership ability and promotes their interest in in-service education.

Provides training for teachers and other clients who are given responsibilities for planning and implementing in-service education activities.

Organizes "debriefing" sessions or other forms of feedback for teachers (or other clients) who have assumed leadership responsibilities for in-service education sessions.

F–6   *Assessing needs:*

Analyzes needs assessment data in ways that assist decision-makers to fully understand the variety, intensity, and complexity of needs.

Consults with decision-makers and planners in prioritizing needs and relating them to long-, short-, and intermediate-range in-service plans.

F–7   *Developing a master plan:*

Describes an array of distinct inservice programs, showing their relationships to priority needs and their relationships to each other within a master plan for in-service education.

Designates strategies for use in in-service programs, matching strategies to needs and constraints for efficiency and effectiveness.

Identifies resource needs and their sources in relation to specific programs of in-service education.

F–8   *Writing project proposals:*

Selects and adapts (or constructs) needs assessment *instruments* and procedures for gathering data on in-service training needs as reflected by individuals, programs, and institutions.

Writes project or program proposals which clearly convey ideas about the problem, goals, and objectives.

Constructs displays for program and project proposals that clearly communicate activity schedules, cost estimates, and staffing arrangements.

Coordinates the work of various individuals in preparing program or project proposal that conforms to expectations and gets attention.

F–9   *Designing self-instructional module:*

Sequences the content and objectives for a self-instructional training packet so as to be easily and logically followed.

Selects or develops media for inclusion in a self-instructional packet that provides for stimulating and trouble-free progress by users.

Programs self-instructional activity sequences with "progress tests" or other provisions for feedback to users.

F–10   *Designing training programs:*

Guides planning of an in-service education program or series to assure that activities will offer active, meaningful, practical involvement for participants.

Designs in-service education programs to assure responsiveness to individual differences and freedom of choice for participants.

Leads a group in systematic planning of a series of in-service education sessions to assume that each session is related to the others.

REFERENCES

Achilles, Charles M., and Russell L. French, ed., *Inside Classrooms: Studies in Verbal and Nonverbal Communication.* A report of the University of Tennessee, IDER Studies (1970–1975). Danville, Illinois: The Interstate Printers and Publishers, Inc., 1977.

Adams, Warren, "A Comparative Analysis of Three Approaches to ISE Designed to Change the Behavior of Classroom Teachers in Social Studies (K–12)." Ph.D. dissertation, University of Oregon, 1970.

Advisory Commission for the Study of the Intermediate Unit, *Study of Intermediate Unit in Texas.* Austin, Texas: Texas Education Agency, June 1956.

Alfonso, Robert J., and L. Goldsberry, "Colleagueship in Supervision," Chapter 7 in *Supervision of Teaching,* ed. T. J. Serfiovonni. Alexandria, Va.: Association for Supervision and Curriculum Development, 1982.

Alioto, Robert F., and J. A. Jungheur, *Operational P.P.B.S. for Education: A Practical Approach to Effective Decision Making.* New York: Harper & Row, 1971.

Alkin, Marvin C., "Accountability Defined," *Evaluation Comment,* 3 (May 1972): 1–5.

Alkin, Marvin C., Richard Daillals, and Peter White, *Using Evaluations: Does Evaluation Make a Difference?* Volume 76, Sage Library of Social Research. Beverly Hills, Calif.: Sage Publications, 1979.

Allen, Dwight M., *MicroTeaching.* Menlo Park, Calif.: Addison-Wesley, 1969.

Almanza, Helen K., "A Study of Inservice Education Programming Associated with Highly Innovative Programs in Selected Elementary Schools," Ph.D. dissertation, University of Texas at Austin, 1980.

Alpert, Judith L., *Psychological Consultation in Educational Settings*. San Francisco: Jossey-Bass, 1982.

Anderson, Robert H., ed., *Improving Classroom Practice Through Supervision*. Dallas: Texas Association for Supervision and Curriculum Development, November 1981.

Anderson, Scarvia B., and Samual Ball, *The Profession and Practice of Program Evaluation*. San Francisco: Jossey-Bass, 1978.

Apple, Michael W., "Ideology and Form in Curriculum Evaluation," in *Qualitative Evaluation: Concepts and Cases in Curriculum Criticism*, ed. George Willis. Berkeley, Calif.: McCutchan Publishing Corp., 1978.

Arends, Richard I., and Jane H. Arends, *Systems Change Strategies in Educational Settings*. New York: Human Science Press, 1977.

Argyris, Chris, *Reasoning, Learning, and Action: Individual and Organizational*. San Francisco: Jossey-Bass, 1982.

Authier, Jerry, and Kay Gustafson, "Microtraining: Focusing on Specific Skills," in *Interpersonal Helping Skills* by E. K. Marshall et al. San Francisco: Jossey-Bass, 1982.

Babb, Adrienne M., "Pittsburgh's Potemkin Village—The Team Project: 1960–1969," unpublished paper, Chatham College, Pittsburgh, Pa., 1969.

Bagin, Donald, Frank Grazian, and Charles H. Harrison, *School Communications Ideas That Work*. Chicago: McGraw-Hill, 1974.

Bailey, Edwin, et al., "The Contributions of Instructional Laboratory Centers (ILC) in Promoting Professional Education and Facilitating the Development of Specialized Career Education," in *Remaking the World of the Career Teacher*. Washington, D.C.: National Commission on Teacher Education and Professional Standards, N.E.A., 1966.

Bailey, George W., "Management and Change" in *Schools Conflict and Change*, ed. Mike M. Milstein. New York: Teachers College, Columbia University, 1980.

Baker, George A., "The National Institute: A Partnership for Development," in *New Directions for Community Colleges: Organization Development—Change Strategies*, No. 37. San Francisco: Jossey-Bass, 1982.

Bales, Robert F., *Interaction Process Analysis—A Method for the Study of Small Groups*. Cambridge, Mass.: Addison-Wesley, 1950.

Ban, John R., and John R. Soudah, "A New Model for Professionalizing Teacher Evaluation," *Peabody Journal of Education*, 56 (October 1978): 25–33.

Banathy, Bela H., *Developing a Systems View of Education: The Systems-Model Approach*. Belmont, Calif.: Lear Siegler/Fearon Publishers, 1973.

Banathy, Bela H., *Instructional Systems*. Palo Alto, Calif.: Fearon Publishers, 1968.

Bandura, Albert, *Social Learning Theory*. Englewood Cliffs, N.J.: Prentice-Hall, 1977.

Bassin, Marc, and Thomas Gross, "Turning on Big Schools: Pragmatic, Participatory, Problem Solving," in *Schools, Conflict and Change*, ed. Mike M. Milstein. New York: Teachers College, Columbia University, 1980.

Beegle, Charles W., and Richard M. Brandt, *Observational Methods in the Classroom*. Washington, D.C.: Association for Supervision and Curriculum Development, 1973.

Beisser, Frederick, G., "On Strategic Planning," *Air University Review*, 32 (March–April 1981): 79.

Belton, John R., "Wisconsin's New District Educational Service Agencies," *Journal of State School Systems Development*, 1 (Winter 1968): 203–222.

Bender, Robert H., "Team Building: Watch Out for the Syndicate," *The School Administrator*, 39 (June 1982): 16–17.

Benjamin, Robert, *Making Schools Work: A Reporter's Journey Through Some of Amer-*

ica's Most Remarkable Classrooms. New York: Continuum Publishing Corp., 1981.

Berliner, David, and Ron Brandt, "On Improving Teacher Effectiveness: A Conversation with David Berliner," *Educational Leadership, 40* (October 1982): 12–15.

Berliner, David C., and William Tikunoff, "Ethnography in the Classroom," in *The Appraisal of Teaching: Concepts and Process* by Gary D. Borich and Kathleen S. Fenton. Reading, Mass.: Addison-Wesley, 1977.

Berman, Paul, and M. W. McLaughlin, "Federal Programs Supporting Educational Change, Volume I," *A Model of Educational Change.* Santa Monica, Calif.: Rand Corporation, 1974.

Berman, Paul, and M. W. McLaughlin, "Factors Affecting the Process of Change," in *Schools, Conflict and Change,* ed. Mike M. Milstein. New York: Teachers College, Columbia University, 1980.

Bessent, Authella, and E. W. Bessent, *Determining the Comparative Efficiency of Schools Through Data Envelopment Analysis.* Austin: Center for Cybernetic Studies, University of Texas, Research Report CCS 361, December 1979.

Bessent, E. W., Ben M. Harris, and M. P. Thomas, Jr., *Adoption and Utilization of Instructional Television,* Bureau of Laboratory Schools Monograph No. 20. Austin: University of Texas, 1968.

Bishop, Leslee J., "Implementing a Curricular or Instructional Change: Tasks, Functions and Processes" (mineographed). Athens: Center for Curriculum Improvement and Staff Development, University of Georgia, 1970.

Bishop, Leslee, J., *Staff Development and Instructional Improvement: Plans and Procedures,* Boston: Allyn & Bacon, 1976.

Bishop, Lloyd K., *Individualizing Educational Systems.* New York: Harper & Row, 1971.

Blake, Robert R., and Jane S. Mouton, "OD Technology for the Future," *Training and Development Journal, 33* (November 1979): 54–64.

Bloom, Benjamin S., "The New Direction in Educational Research: Alterable Variables," *Phi Delta Kappan, 61* (February 1980): 382–85.

Bloom, Benjamin S., et al., *Handbook on Formative and Summative Evaluation of Student Learning.* New York: McGraw-Hill, 1971.

Blumberg, Arthur, *Supervisors and Teachers: A Private Cold War,* 2nd ed. Berkeley, Calif.: McCutchan Publishing Corp., 1980.

Boles, Harold W., "An Administrative Team?" *Journal of Educational Administration, 13* (October 1975): 73–80.

Bolton, Dale L., *Selection and Evaluation of Teachers.* Berkeley, Calif.: McCutchan Publishing Corp., 1973.

Borg, Walter, et al., "Videotape Feedback and Microteaching in a Teacher Training Model." Berkeley, California: Far West Laboratory for Educational Research and Development (mimeographed), 1968.

Borich, Gary D., ed., *Evaluation of Educational Programs and Products.* Englewood Cliffs, N.J.: Educational Technology Publications, 1974.

Borich, Gary D., and R. P. Jemelka, *Programs and Systems: An Evaluation Perspective.* New York: Academic Press, 1981.

Borich, Gary P., and Susan K. Madden, *Evaluating Classroom Instruction: A Sourcebook of Instruments.* Reading, Mass.: Addison-Wesley, 1977.

Bortner, Doyle M., *Public Relations for Public Schools.* Cambridge, Mass.: Schenkman Publishing Co., 1972.

Boyan, Norman J., and Willis D. Copeland, *Instructional Supervision Training Program.* Columbus, Ohio: Charles E. Merrill, 1978.

Bronowski, Jacob, *The Identity of Man.* New York: The Natural History Press, 1966.

Brookover, Wilbur B., et al., *Measuring and Attaining the Goals of Education.* Alexandria, Va.: Association for Supervision and Curriculum Development, 1980.

Brown, Wayne, et al., *Consultation: Strategy for Improving Education.* Boston: Allyn & Bacon, 1979.

Bruschi, Philip, "Listening: The Neglected Communication Skill," *Journal of Communication Management,* 11: 17–18.

Burch, Barbara G., and W. Elzie Danley, Sr., "The Instructional Leadership Role of Central Office Supervisors," *Educational Leadership,* 37 (May 1980): 636–37.

Burton, Barry, and T. A. Petri, "Levels of Leader Development," *Educational Leadership,* 37 (May 1980): 628–31.

Butler, Martha, and Lavern McMillan, *The Role of the Department Director in the Port Arthur Independent School District.* Port Arthur, Tex.: Board of Education, 1968.

Butler, Matilda, and William Paisley, *Factors Determining Roles and Functions of Educational Linking Agents With Implications for Training and Support Systems.* San Francisco: Far West Laboratory, January 1978.

Caldwell, Bruce G., *Differentiated Staffing: The Key to Effective School Organization.* New York: Center for Applied Research in Education, 1973.

Caldwell, David F., and Charles A. O'Reilly, "Boundary Spanning and Individual Performance: The Impact of Self-Monitoring," *Journal of Applied Psychology,* 67 (February, 1982): 124–127.

California State Legislature, "The School Principal: Recommendations for Effective Leadership," Education Committee Task Force Report on Elementary and Secondary Principals. Sacramento, Calif.: September 1978, ERIC ED 115–325.

California Teachers Association, *Six Areas of Teaching Competence.* Burlingame: California Teachers Association, 1964.

Cantor, Nathaniel, *Learning Through Discussion.* Buffalo, N.Y.: Human Relations for Industry, 1951.

Capie, William et al., "The Objectivity of Classroom Observation Scales," a paper presented at the Southeastern Association for the Education of Teachers of Science, New Orleans, 1978, ERIC ED 182–306.

Carthel, James T., "An Application of a Systems Analysis Model to the Evaluation of an Instructional Improvement Program," Ph.D. dissertation, University of Texas at Austin, 1973.

Cawelti, Gordon, "Focusing Instructional Leadership on Improved Student Achievement." A paper presented at the annual meeting of the American Association of School Administrators, Anaheim, Calif., February 15–18, 1980, ERIC ED 184–241.

Champagne, David W., and R. Craig Hogan, *Consultant Supervision: Theory and Skill Development.* Wheaton, Ill.: CH Publications, 1981.

Coccia, Joseph A., "Point Principals: Not Middle Management," *NASSP Bulletin,* 61 (January 1977): 79–84.

Cogan, Morris, *Clinical Supervision.* Boston: Houghton Mifflin, 1973.

Cohen, Michael, "Removing the Road Blocks: Effective Principals," *The School Administrator,* 39 (November 1982): 14–16.

Coker, Homer, et al., "How Valid Are Expert Opinions About Effective Teaching?" *Phi Delta Kappan,* 62 (October 1980): 131–34.

Coles, Gary J., and A. B. Chalupsky, "Evaluation of Innovations," in *Educational Environments and Effects,* ed. Herbert J. Walberg. Berkeley, Calif.: McCutchan Publishing Corp., 1979.

Comstock, V. Nora, "Staff Development in Community/Junior Colleges: Practitioners' Perceptions of Ideal Concepts, Institutional Expectations, and Current Practice," Ph.D. dissertation, University of Texas at Austin, 1982.

Comstock, Vivian C., and G. E. Swartz, "One Firm's Experience with Quality Circles," *Quality Progress, 12* (September 1979): 14–16.

Coody, Betty, and Ben M. Harris, *Individualization of Instruction Inventory, Revised.* Austin, Tex.: Instructional Leadership Training Materials, University of Texas, 1971.

Cooper, Bruce S. et al., "Incentives That Work: An Administrative Innovation in the Dade County Schools," *Phi Delta Kappan, 61* (April 1980): 523–24.

Corbett, H. Dickson, "Principals' Contributions to Maintaining Change," *Phi Delta Kappan, 64* (November 1982): 190–200.

Cornell, Francis G., Carl M. Lindvall, and Joel Saupe, *An Exploratory Measurement of Individualities of Schools and Classrooms.* Urbana, Ill.: Bureau of Educational Research, University of Illinois, 1952.

Coughlan, Robert J., and G. Zaltman, "Implementing the Change Team Concept." Paper presented at the Symposium on Change Process in Education, American Educational Research Association, Chicago, 1972.

Crandall, David, "Training Supportive Linking Agents," in *Linking Processes in Educational Improvement,* eds. N. Nash and J. Culbertson. Columbus, Ohio: University Council for Educational Administration, 1977.

Crane, A. R., "Anxiety in Organizations: Explorations of an Idea," *The Journal of Educational Administration, 18* (October 1980): 202–212.

Crapo, Ray, "Is There a Catalyst in the House?" *Training and Development Journal, 35* (January 1981): 66–69.

Crawford, George J., Cecil Miskel, and Claradine Johnson, "An Urban School Renewal Program—A Case Analysis," *The Urban Review, 12* (Winter 1980): 195–200.

Creekmur, Jimmie L., "A Descriptive Analysis of In-service Education Programs of Selected Texas School Systems Utilizing Operational Criteria," Ph.D. dissertation, The University of Texas at Austin, 1977.

Cronbach, Lee J., et al., *Toward Reform of Program Evaluation.* San Francisco: Jossey-Bass, 1980.

Cuban, Larry, "Persistent Instruction: The High School Classroom, 1900–1980," *Phi Delta Kappan, 64* (October 1982): 113–118.

Cunningham, Luvern L., and Joseph T. Henges, *The American School Superintendency, 1982: A Summary Report.* Arlington, Va.: American Association of School Administrators, 1982.

Cunningham, William, "Research-Based Strategies for Fighting Teacher Burnout," *Education Digest, 47* (May 1982a): 230–33.

Cunningham, William G., *Systematic Planning for Educational Change.* Palo Alto, Calif.: Mayfield Publishing Co., 1982b.

Cuthbertson, Joseph Wesley, "Decision Making Structures and Environmental Uncertainty," unpublished Ph.D. dissertation. Austin, Tex.: The University of Texas at Austin, May 1982.

Davies, Ivor K., *Objectives in Curriculum Design.* Maidenhood, Berkshire, England: McGraw-Hill Co. Ltd., 1976.

Department of Elementary School Principals, *The Elementary School Principalship in 1968: A Research Study.* Washington, D.C.: National Education Association, 1968.

DeRoche, Edward F., *An Administrator's Guide for Evaluating Programs and Personnel.* Boston: Allyn & Bacon, 1981.

Dewar, Donald L., *Quality Circle: Leader Manual and Instructional Guide.* Red Bluff, Calif.: Quality Circle Institute, 1980.

Dewar, Donald L., *Implementing Quality Circles in Your Organization.* Red Bluff, Calif.: Quality Circle Institute, 1982.

Dillon, Elizabeth A., "Staff Development: Bright Hope or Empty Promise?" *Educational Leadership,* 34 (December 1976): 165–70.

Donoughue, Carol, ed., *In-Service: The Teacher and the School.* London: Kozan Page, Ltd., 1981.

Drucker, Peter F., *Managing in Turbulent Times.* New York: Harper & Row, 1980.

Dull, Lloyd W., *Supervision: School Leadership Handbook.* Columbus, Ohio: Charles E. Merrill, 1981.

Duncan, O. D., "Path Analysis, Sociological Examples," *American Journal of Sociology,* 72 (July 1966): 1–16.

Duncan, Robert B., "Criteria for Type of Change Agent in Changing Educational Organizations." A paper presented at the Symposium on Change Process in Education, American Educational Research Association, Chicago, 1972.

Dunkerton, John, "Should Classroom Observation Be Quantitative?" *Educational Researcher,* 23 (February 1981): 144–51.

Dunkin, M. J., and B. J. Biddle, *The Study of Teaching.* New York: Holt, Rinehart & Winston, 1974.

Dyer, Henry S., "Toward Objective Criteria of Professional Accountability in the Schools of New York City," *Phi Delta Kappan,* 52 (December 1970): 206–11.

Edelfelt, Roy A., and E. B. Smith, *Breakaway and Multidimensional Approaches: Integrating Curriculum Development and Inservice Education.* Washington, D.C.: Association of Teacher Educators.

"Education Amendments of 1976, Intent to Issue Regulations," *Federal Register,* 41 (November 22, 1976): 51550–52.

Edwards, A. D., and V. J. Furlong, *The Language of Teaching: Meaning in Classroom Interaction.* London: Heinemann Educational Books Ltd., 1978.

Eichelberger, Tony, "Evaluating Ongoing Instructional Programs," in *Evaluating Educational Programs and Products,* ed. Gary D. Borich. Englewood Cliffs, N.J.: Educational Technology Publications.

Eisner, Elliott, "An Artistic Approach to Supervision," in *Supervision of Teaching,* ed. T. J. Sergiovanni. Alexandria, Va.: Association for Supervision and Curriculum Development, 1982.

Eisner, Elliot W., *Cognition and Curriculum, A Basis for Deciding What to Teach.* N.Y.: Longman, 1982.

Eisner, Elliot, "Educational Connoisseurship and Educational Criticism: Their Form and Functions in Educational Evaluation," *The Journal of Aesthetic Education,* 10 (July/October 1976): 135–50.

Eisner, Elliot, "Emerging Models for Educational Evaluation," *School Review,* 80 (August 1972): 573–90.

Eisner, Elliot, "On the Uses of Educational Connoisseurship and Criticism for Evaluating Classroom Life," *Teachers College Record,* 78 (February 1977): 345–58.

Eisner, Elliot W., "Some Alternatives to Quantitative Forms of Educational Evaluation," *Thrust for Education Leadership,* 5 (November 1975): 13–15.

Enos, Donald F., "A Cost-Effectiveness Analysis of Competency-Based and Non-Competency-Based Teacher Education at San Diego State University." Ph.D. dissertation, The University of Texas at Austin, 1976.

Esposito, James P., et al., "A Delineation of the Supervisory Role," *Education,* 96 (Fall 1975): 63–67.

Evertson, Carolyn M., and Freda M. Holley, "Classroom Observation," in *Handbook of Teacher Evaluation,* ed. Jason Millman. Beverly Hills, Calif.: Sage Publications, 1981.

Evertson, Carolyn M., and Donald J. Veldman, "Changes over Time in Process Measures of Classroom Behavior," *Journal of Educational Psychology,* 73 (April 1981): 156–63.

Fathy, Shadia H., "The Role an Evaluator's Values Should Play in Program Evaluation," *Adult Education, 30* (Spring 1980): 166–72.

Feuerberg, Linda, "Communication: Key to the Productivity Doorway," *Journal of Organizational Communication, 10* (1981): 3–5.

Feyereisen, K. Y., et al., *Supervision and Curriculum Renewal: A Systems Approach.* New York: Appleton-Century-Crofts, 1970.

Firester, Lee, and Joan Firester, "Differentiated Staffing: Some Reflections," *New York State Education, 57* (March 1970): 7–28.

Firth, Gerald R., and K. P. Eiken, "Impact of the Schools' Bureaucratic Structure on Supervision" in *Supervision of Teaching,* ed. T. J. Sergiovanni. Alexandria, Va.: Association for Supervision and Curriculum Development, 1982.

Flanagan, John C., "The Use of Educational Evaluation in the Development of Programs, Courses, Instructional Materials and Equipment, Instructional and Learning Procedures and Administrative Arrangements," in *Educational Evaluation: New Roles, New Means,* ed. Ralph W. Tyler. 68th Yearbook, National Society for the Study of Education. Chicago: University of Chicago Press, 1969.

Flanders, Ned A., *Analyzing Teaching Behavior.* Reading, Mass.: Addison-Wesley, 1970.

Flanders, Ned A., and Anita Simon, "Teacher Effectiveness," in *Encyclopedia of Educational Research,* 4th edition, ed. R. L. Ebel. New York: The Macmillan Co., 1969, pp. 1423–37.

Floden, R. E., et al., "Responses to Curriculum Pressures: A Policy-Capturing Study of Teacher Decisions About Content," *Journal of Educational Psychology, 73* (1981): 129–41.

Foster, Garrett, and Peter Easton, "Updating the Model and Goals of an Educational Change Program: A Third Dimension of Formative Evaluation," *CEBR Quarterly, 13* (Summer 1980): 22–8.

Frank, John Jr., *School Principal's Handbook of Evaluation Guidelines.* West Nyack, N.Y.: Parker Publishing, 1979.

Fuller, Frances F., "Concerns of Teachers," *American Educational Research Journal, 6* (March, 1969): 207–226.

Furst, Norma, and Russell A. Hill, "Classroom Observation Systematic," in *The Encyclopedia of Education.* ed. Lee C. Deighton, Vol. 2. New York: Macmillan Company, 1971, pp. 168–83.

Gage, N. L., *The Scientific Basis of the Art of Teaching.* New York: Columbia University, Teachers College Press, 1978.

Gall, Meredith, D., and Joyce Gall, "The Discussion Method," in *The Psychology of Teaching Methods,* ed. N. L. Gage. 75th Yearbook, Part I. Chicago: National Society for the Study of Education, 1976.

Gallessich, June, *The Profession and Practice of Consultation.* San Francisco: Jossey-Bass, 1982.

Galloway, Charles G., "Body Language," *Today's Education, 61* (December 1972): 46–67.

Gerhard, Ronald J., "The Organizational Imperative," in *Evaluation of Complex Systems,* ed. Ronald J. Wooldridge. Number 10 in New Directions for Program Evaluation. San Francisco: Jossey-Bass, 1981.

Giacquinta, Joseph B., "The Process of Organizational Change in Schools," in *Review of Research in Education,* ed. Fred N. Kerlinger. Itasca, Ill.: F. E. Peacock Publishers, 1973.

Glickman, Carl D., "The Developmental Approach to Supervision," *Educational Leadership, 38* (November 1980): 179–80.

Glickman, Carl D., *Developmental Supervision.* Alexandria, Va.: Association for Supervision and Curriculum Development, 1981.

Goldhammer, Robert, R. H. Anderson, and Robert Krajewski, *Clinical Supervision,* 2nd ed. New York: Holt, Rinehart & Winston, 1981.

Goldstein, William, *Supervision Made Simple,* Fastback 180. Bloomington, Ind.: Phi Delta Kappa Educational Foundation, 1982.

Good, Thomas, and Jere Brophy, *Looking in Classrooms,* 2nd ed. New York: Harper & Row, 1978.

Goodlad, John I., *The Dynamics of Educational Change: Toward Responsive Schools.* New York: McGraw-Hill, 1975.

Goodman, Paul S., et al., *Change in Organizations.* San Francisco: Jossey-Bass, 1982.

Goodson, Max R., and W. O. Hagstrom, "Using Teams of Change Agents," in *Organization Development in Schools,* eds. Richard A. Schmuck and Matthew B. Miles. Palo Alto, Calif.: National Press Books, 1971.

Grant, W. Vance, and Leo J. Eiden, *Digest of Education Statistics.* Washington, D.C.: U.S. Department of Education Statistics, U.S. Government Printing Office, 1981.

Grant, W. Vance, and Leo J. Eiden, *Digest of Education Statistics–1982.* Washington, D.C.: National Center for Education Statistics, May 1982.

Greenblatt, Cathy S., and Richard D. Duke, *Principles and Practices of Gaming-Simulation.* Berkeley, Calif.: Sage Publications, 1981.

Griffin, Gary A., ed., *Staff Development,* Part II, 82nd Yearbook of the National Society for the Study of Education. Chicago: The University of Chicago Press, 1983.

Gryna, Frank M., Jr., *Quality Circles: A Team Approach to Problem Solving.* New York: AMACOM, A Division of American Management Association, 1981.

Guba, Egon G., and Yvonna S. Lincoln, *Effective Evaluation.* San Francisco: Jossey-Bass, 1981.

Hagen, Nancy Joyce, "A Comparative Analysis of Selected Inservice Education Delivery Systems," unpublished doctoral dissertation, University of Texas at Austin, 1981.

Hall, Gene, "Induction: The Missing Link," *Journal of Teacher Education,* 33 (May–June 1982): 53–55.

Hall, G. E. et al., "A Developmental Conceptualization of the Adoption Process within Educational Institutions." Austin: Research and Development Center for Teacher Education, University of Texas, 1973.

Hall, Gene E., Susan Loucks, "Teacher Concerns as a Basis for Facilitating and Personalizing Staff Development," *Teachers College Record,* 80 (September 1978): 36–53.

Hardebeck, Richard J., "A Comparison of Observed and Self-Reported Individualization of Teaching by Vocational, Academic and Special Education Teachers in Texas," unpublished doctoral dissertation, The University of Texas at Austin, 1973.

Hare, A. Paul, *Creativity in Small Groups.* Beverly Hills, Calif.: Sage Publications, 1982.

Harris, Ben M., "The Case of John Carroll—5th Grade Teacher." Austin: Instructional Leadership Training Materials, Department of Educational Administration, University of Texas, October 1972. (Mimeographed.)

Harris, Ben M., *Developmental Supervisory Assessment System* (DeSCAS), 3rd ed. Round Rock, Tex.: Ben M. Harris Associates, 1982.

Harris, Ben M., "Evaluation of Inservice Education: A Harder, More Revealing Look." A paper presented at the Renewal Conference, Ohio State Department of Education, Columbus, Ohio, (May 6, 1981), ERIC ED 206-593.

Harris, Ben M., *Improving Staff Performance Through In-service Education.* Boston: Allyn & Bacon 1980.

Harris, Ben M., E. W. Bessent, and Kenneth E. McIntyre, *In-service Education: A Guide to Better Practice*. Englewood Cliffs, N.J.: Prentice-Hall, 1969.

Harris, Ben M., Louisa Goodlet, and Cynthia M. Sloan, A *Manual for Observing with the New Comprehensive Observation Guide*. Austin: Instructional Leadership Training Materials, University of Texas, 1975.

Harris, Ben M., and Jane Hill, *Developmental Teacher Evaluation Kit*. Austin, Tex.: National Educational Laboratory Publishers, 1982.

Harris, Ben M., and B. Lightsey, eds., *Professional Supervisory Competencies*, Document #7 revised. Austin: Special Education Supervisor Training Project, The University of Texas, 1975.

Harris, Ben M., and Kenneth E. McIntyre, *Descriptive Observation Record for Individualization of Instruction* (DORII). Austin: Instructional Leadership Training Materials, Department of Educational Administration, University of Texas, 1971.

Harris, Ben M., Kenneth E. McIntyre, Vance Littleton, and Dan Long, *Personnel Administration in Education*. Boston: Allyn & Bacon, 1979.

Havelock, Ronald G., *Planning for Innovation Through Dissemination and Utilization of Knowledge*. Ann Arbor: Center for Research on Utilization of Scientific Knowledge, Institute for Social Research, University of Michigan, 1971.

Heller, Jack F., *Increasing Faculty and Administrative Effectiveness*. San Francisco: Jossey-Bass, 1982.

Hering, William M., Jr., "Student Learnings from Sociology Project Materials According to Teacher Preparation in Sociology," *Educational Leadership*, 61 (October 1972): 46–54.

Herriott, Robert E., and Neal Gross, *The Dynamics of Planned Educational Change: Case Studies and Analyses*. Berkeley, Calif.: McCutchan, 1979.

Hersey, Paul W., "The NASSP Assessment Center Develops Leadership Talent," *Educational Leadership*, 39 (February 1982): 370–71.

Hersey, Paul, and Kenneth H. Blanchard, *Management of Organizational Behavior: Utilizing Human Resources*, 3rd ed. Englewood Cliffs, N.J.: Prentice-Hall, 1977.

Hiatt, Diana B., and J. Ward Keesling, "The Dependability of Classroom Observations." A paper presented to the American Educational Research Association, San Francisco, (April 1979), ERIC ED 175–929.

Hillson, Maurie, and Ronald T. Hyman, *Innovation in Elementary and Secondary Organization*. New York: Holt, Rinehart & Winston, 1977.

Hollinshead, Betty, and Mantz Yorke, *Perspectives on Academic Gaming and Simulation*. Simulation and Games: The Real and the Ideal. The proceedings of the 1980 conference of the Society for Academic Gaming and Simulation in Education and Training. London: Kogan Page Ltd., 1981.

Hood, Paul, and Carolyn Cates, *Alternative Approaches to Analyzing Dissemination and Linkage Roles*. San Francisco: Far West Laboratory, ERIC ED 166–810.

Hook, Collin M., and B. V. Rosenshine, "Accuracy of Teacher Reports of Their Classroom Behavior," *Review of Educational Research*, 49 (Winter 1979): 1–12.

Horn, Robert E., and Anne Cleaves, *The Guide to Simulations/Games for Education and Training*, 4th ed. Beverly Hills, Calif.: Sage Publications, 1980.

Hunter, Elizabeth, and Edmund J. Amidon, *Improving Teaching: The Analysis of Classroom Verbal Interaction*. New York: Holt, Rinehart & Winston, 1966.

Hunter, Madeline, "Six Types of Supervisory Conferences," *Educational Leadership*, 37 (February 1980): 408–12.

Hunter, Madeline, "When the Supervisor Innovates," *Instructor*, 77 (March 1968): 31, 42.

Illich, Ivan, *Toward a History of Needs*. New York: Pantheon Books, 1977.

Ingils, Chester R., "Let's Do Away with Teacher Evaluation," *Clearing House,* 44 (April 1970): 451–56.

Irvine, Jacqueline J., "The Accuracy of Pre-Service Teachers' Assessments of Their Classroom Behaviors," *Journal of Research and Development in Education* (in press).

Ivey, Allen E., and J. R. Moreland, *Micro-Counseling: Innovations in Interviewing Training.* Springfield, Ill.: Charles C. Thomas, 1971.

Jackson, Shirley A., "The Curriculum Council: New Hope, New Promise," *Educational Leadership,* 29 (May 1972): 690–94.

Johnson, Charles E., et al., "An Introduction to the Teacher Performance Assessment Instruments: Their Uses and Limitations." Athens, Ga.: College of Education, Division of Program and Staff Development, January 1980.

Jones, Linda, and Andrew Hayes, "How Valid Are Surveys of Teacher's Needs?" *Educational Leadership,* (February 1980).

Joyce, Bruce R., and Beverly Showers, *Power in Staff Development Through Research on Training.* Alexandria, Va.: Association for Supervision and Curriculum Development, 1983.

Kahle, Lynn R., ed., *Methods for Studying Person-Situation Interactions,* Number 2, New Directions for Methodology of Behavioral Science. San Francisco: Jossey-Bass, 1979.

Kane, Rosalie A., *Interprofessional Teamwork.* Syracuse, N.Y.: Syracuse University School of Social Work, 1975.

Katz, Daniel et al., eds., *The Study of Organizations.* San Francisco: Jossey-Bass, 1980.

Katz, Douglas S., and Robert L. Morgan, "A Holistic Strategy for the Formative Evaluation of Educational Programs," in *Evaluating Educational Programs and Products,* ed. Gary D. Borich. Englewood Cliffs, N.J.: Educational Technology Publications, 1974.

Kaufman, Roger A., *Educational System Planning.* Englewood Cliffs, N.J.: Prentice-Hall, 1972.

Kearsley, Greg, and Terry Compton, "Assessing Costs, Benefits and Productivity in Training Systems," *Training and Development Journal,* 35 (January 1981): 52–61.

Kersh, Bert Y., *Faculty Development for Inservice Education in the Schools.* Washington, D.C.: American Association of Colleges for Teacher Education (September 1978).

Kerr, Donna H., "The Structure of Quality in Teaching," in *Philosophy and Education,* ed. Jonas F. Soltis. 80th Yearbook, Part I, National Society for the Study of Education. Chicago: The National Society, 1981.

Killough, Don, "A Descriptive Analysis of the Roles of Education Service Centers in Providing Inservice Training Programs for Public School Staffs of Texas During the 1975–76 School Year," Ph.D. dissertation, University of Texas at Austin, 1977.

Kindsvatter, Richard, and William W. Wilen, "A Systematic Approach to Improving Conferencing Skills," *Educational Leadership,* 38 (April 1981): 525–28.

King, J. D., *Training Manual for a Competency-Guided, Individualized Program for Special Education Supervisors, 1972–1975* (Document No. 13). Austin: Special Education Supervisor Training Project, The University of Texas, 1976.

Klein, Stephen P., and Marvin Alkin, "Evaluating Teachers for Outcome Accountability," *Evaluation Comment,* 3 (May 1972): 5–11. Los Angeles: Center for the Study of Evaluation, University of California at Los Angeles, 1972.

Klugman, Edgar, "Can the Teacher Education Institution Respond Through the

Teacher Education Center to the Changing Needs and Expectations in This Field?" Wheelock College, June 1974.

Korda, Michael, "How to Be a Leader," *Newsweek*, January 5, 1981.

Krajewski, Robert J., "Clinical Supervision: A Conceptual Framework," *Journal of Research and Development in Education*, 15 (Winter 1982): 38–43.

Krantz, Lavern L., *Staffing New Programs, A Research Study*. Athens: Center for Educational Research and Service, College of Education, Ohio University, 1966.

Lamb, Morris L., and Kevin J. Swick, "A Historical Overview of Classroom Teacher Observation," *Education Digest* (April 1975): 39–42.

Lamb, Ronald W., and M. Donald Thomas, "The Art and Science of Teacher Evaluation," *National Elementary Principal*, 61 (September 1981): 45–47.

Lane, Carolyn A., "Using the Tools of Philosophy: Metaphor in Action" in *Field Assessments of Innovative Evaluation Methods*, ed. Nick L. Smith. San Francisco: Jossey-Bass, 1982.

Lawrence, Gordon, Dennis Baker, Patricia Elzie, and Barbara Hansen, *Patterns of Effective Inservice Education*. Gainesville, Fla.: University of Florida, College of Education, December 1974.

Lewey, Arieh, ed., *Handbook of Curriculum Evaluation*. New York: Longman, 1977.

Lieberman, Ann, "Practice Makes Policy: The Tensions of School Improvement" in *Policy Making in Education*, eds. Ann Lieberman and M. W. McLaughlin. Eighty-first Yearbook of the National Society for the Study of Education, Part I. Chicago: University of Chicago Press, 1982.

Lieberman, Ann, and Lynn Miller, "Synthesis of Research on Improving Schools," *Educational Leadership*, 38 (April 1981): 583–86.

Lieberman, Myron, "Suggestion: Let's Stamp Out Innovations," *The American School Board Journal*, 167 (February 1980): 27.

Light, Richard J., "Evaluation Methodology for Education Programs with Diffuse Goals," *Education and Urban Society*, 13 (November 1980): 109–34.

Littleton, Vance G., "A Study of Factors Contributing to the Predisposition of Elementary Principals to Try Selected Innovations," Ph.D. dissertation, University of Texas at Austin, 1971.

Lovell, John T., and Kimball Wiles, *Supervision for Better Schools*, 5th ed. Englewood Cliffs, N.J.: Prentice-Hall, 1983.

Lozano, Judith A., "*Relationships Between Characteristics of Planning Documents and Selected Indicators of Quality Operations for Inservice Education Programs in Public School Systems*," unpublished doctoral dissertation, The University of Texas at Austin, May 1980.

Lucio, J., William H. and John D. McNeil, *Supervision in Thought and Action*, 3rd ed. New York: McGraw-Hill, 1979.

Lynch, William W., Jr., and Carol Ames, *Individual Cognitive Demand Schedule: ICDA Training Booklet*. Bloomington: Center for Innovation in Teaching the Handicapped, Indiana University, 1972.

Maher, Charles, "A Synoptic Framework for School Program Evaluation," *Journal of School Psychology*, 16 (Winter 1978): 322–33.

Marks, James R., Emery Stoops, and Joyce King-Stoops, *Handbook of Educational Supervision: A Guide for the Practitioner*. Boston: Allyn & Bacon, 1978.

Marshall, Eldon K., et al., *Interpersonal Helping Skills: A Guide to Training Methods, Programs, and Resources*. San Francisco: Jossey-Bass, 1982.

Marshall, Hermine H., "Stability of Classroom Variables as Measured by a Broad Range Observational System," *The Journal of Educational Research*, 70 (July–August 1977): 304–11.

Maryland University, "Teacher Education Center Self-Study: A Preliminary Report of and to the Partners." College Park, Maryland: University of Maryland, College of Education (January).

McCleary, Lloyd E., "Model of Competency Based Curriculum," paper presented at the 1971 National Conference of Professors of Educational Administration (mimeographed), University of Utah, Salt Lake City, 1971.

McGreal, Thomas L., "Effective Teacher Evaluation Systems," *Educational Leadership*, 39 (January 1982): 303–05.

McIntire, Ron, "Expectations for the Teacher Assessment Program," draft paper, Houston Independent School District, Houston, Tex.: 1982. (Mimeographed).

McLendon, Dan P., "A Delphi Study of Agreement and Consensus Among Selected Educator Groups in Texas Regarding Principles Underlying Effective Inservice Education," unpublished dissertation, The University of Texas at Austin, August 1977.

Medley, Donald, *Teacher Competence and Teacher Effectiveness: A Review of Process-Product Research.* Washington, D.C.: American Association of Colleges for Teacher Education, 1977.

Medley, Donald M., and H. E. Mitzel, "Measuring Classroom Behavior by Systematic Observation," in *Handbook of Research on Teaching*, ed. N. L. Gage. Chicago: Rand McNally and Company.

Meisgeier, Charles, Don Boney, and George G. Garver, *Memorandum Announcing Plans to Use DAI Laboratory for Inservice Training.* Houston, Texas: Center for Human Resources Development and Educational Renewal, Houston Independent School District, October 19, 1972.

Merton, Robert K., and P. L. Kendall, "The Focused Interview," *American Journal of Sociology*, 51 (1946): 541–57.

Miller, Richard I., *Evaluating Faculty Performance.* San Francisco: Jossey-Bass, 1972.

Mills, Johnnie Ruth, "A Guide for Teaching Systematic Observation to Student Teachers," *Journal of Teacher Education*, 31, (November–December 1980): 5–9.

Mills, Theodore M., *The Sociology of Small Groups.* Englewood Cliffs, N.J.: Prentice-Hall, 1967.

Milroy, Ellice, *Role-Play: A Practical Guide.* Aberdeen: Aberdeen University Press, 1982.

Molyneaux, Dorothy, and Vera W. Lane, *Effective Interviewing: Techniques and Analysis.* Boston: Allyn & Bacon, 1982.

Monte, Rudeen, "The Productivity Environment," *The Quality Circles Journal*, 4 (August 1981): 13–15.

Moxley, Russ S., Jr., *Interacting.* Dallas: Interact, Inc., 1977.

Murphy, Jerome T., *Grease the Squeaky Wheel.* Cambridge, Mass.: Center for Educational Policy Research, Harvard Graduate School of Education, February 1973.

Nadler, Barbara, and Kenneth Shore, "Evaluating Educational Programs with the Judicial Evaluation Model," *Education*, 99 (Summer 1979): 387–94.

Nadler, Leonard, "Implications of HRD Concept," *Training and Development Journal*, 28 (May 1974): 3–13.

National Study of School Evaluation, *Elementary School Evaluative Criteria.* Arlington, Va.: National Study of School Evaluation, 1973.

Nelson, David E., "Investigative Journalism Methods in Educational Evaluation," in *Field Assessments of Innovative Evaluation Methods*, ed. Nick L. Smith. San Francisco: Jossey-Bass, 1982.

Netzer, Lanore A., Glen G. Eye, Dwight M. Stevens, and Wayne W. Benson, *Strategies for Instructional Management.* Boston, Mass.: Allyn & Bacon, 1979.

Newfield, John, "Accuracy of Teacher Reports: Reports and Observations of Specific Classroom Behaviors," *Journal of Educational Research,* 74 (November–December 1980): 78–82.

Nicholson, Alexander, et al., *The Literature on Inservice Teacher Education,* Palo Alto, Calif.: Stanford Center for Research and Development in Teaching, 1975.

Northwest Educational Cooperative, "Quality Circles in Education Facilitator Training." An illustrated brochure. Arlington Heights, Ill.: Northwest Educational Cooperative, 1982.

Ober, Richard, "The Nature of Interaction Analysis," *High School Journal,* 51 (October 1969): 7–16.

Olsen, Hans C., C. Barbour, and D. C. Michalak, *The Teaching Clinic: A Team Approach to Improved Teaching.* Washington, D.C.: Association of Teacher Educators, 1971.

Organization for Economic Cooperation and Development, *Participatory Planning in Education.* Paris, France: OECD, 1974.

Ostlund, Leonard A., "Case Discussion Learning in Human Relations," *Journal of Human Relations,* 16 (1968): 213.

Ouchi, William G., *Theory Z: How American Business Can Meet the Japanese Challenge.* Reading, Mass: Addison-Wesley, 1981.

Owens, J. G., "Strategies of Curriculum Innovation," *Journal of Curriculum Studies,* 1 (November 1968): 19–25.

Owens, Robert G., and Carl R. Steinhoff, *Administering Change in Schools.* Englewood Cliffs, N.J.: Prentice-Hall, 1976.

Paris, Norman M., "T-Grouping: A Helping Movement," *Phi Delta Kappan,* 49 (April 1968): 460–63.

Patchin, Robert, *Remarks on Quality Circles, Northrop's Experience.* A presentation before the Committee on Ways and Means, Subcommittee on Trade. San Diego: Aircraft Division, Northrop Corporation, October 14, 1980.

Paul, Douglas A., "Change Processes at the Elementary, Secondary, and Post-Secondary Levels of Education," in *Linking Processes in Educational Improvement: Concepts and Applications,* eds. Nicholas Nash and Jack Culbertson. Columbus, Ohio: University Council for Educational Administration, 1977.

Perez, Roberto, "A Comparison of Centralized and Decentralized Inservice Education Programs: Teacher Involvement, Program Characteristics and Job Statisfaction," Ph.D. dissertation, University of Texas at Austin, 1979.

Perrott, Elizabeth, "Changes in Teaching Behavior After Participating in a Self-Instructional Micro-teaching Course," *Educational Media International,* (March 1976): 16–25.

Pfeiffer, J. William, and John E. Jones, *Reference Guide to Handbooks and Annuals,* 2nd ed. La Jolla, Calif.: University Associates, Publishers and Consultants, 1977.

Pino, R. F., and R. E. Emory, *Group Process Skills.* Portland, Oreg.: Commercial Educational Distributing Services, 1976.

Popham, W. James, *Educational Evaluation.* Englewood Cliffs, N.J.: Prentice-Hall, 1975.

Provus, Malcolm, *Discrepancy Evaluation for Program Improvement and Assessment.* Berkeley, Calif.: McCutchan Publishing Corp., 1971.

Reavis, Charles A., *Teacher Improvement Through Clinical Supervision.* Bloomington, Ind.: Phi Delta Kappan Educational Foundation, 1978.

Reavis, Charles A., "Weighty, Precise Supervision: A Report of Beginnings," in *Improving Classroom Practice Through Supervision,* ed. R. H. Anderson. Dallas: Texas Association for Supervision and Curriculum Development, 1982, pp. 3–18.

Redfern, George B., *Evaluating Teachers and Administrators: A Performance Objectives Approach.* Boulder, Colo.: Westview Press, 1980.

Rogers, Carl R., "Significant Learning: In Therapy and in Education," *Educational Leadership,* 16 (January 1959): 232–42.

Rogers, Everett M., and F. F. Shoemaker, *Communication of Innovations: A Cross Cultural Approach,* 2nd ed. New York: The Free Press, 1971.

Rossi, Peter H., Sonica R. Wright, and Howard E. Freeman, *Evaluation: A Systematic Approach.* Beverly Hills, Calif.: Sage Publications, 1979.

Rubin, Louis, *Curriculum Handbook. Volume 1, The Disciplines.* Boston: Allyn & Bacon, 1977.

Rubin, Louis, *The In-Service Education of Teachers: Trends, Processes and Prescriptions.* Boston: Allyn & Bacon, 1978.

Rubin, Louis J., "A Study on the Continuing Education of Teachers," Part III, *Instructor Development,* 1 (May 1970): 5.

Ruch, Charles P., et al., "Training for Planning: Organizational Consultation to Design and Install Constituency-Based Planning," *Planning and Changing,* 13 (Winter 1982): 234–44.

Russell, Bertrand, *An Outline of Philosophy.* Cleveland: The World Publishing Company, 1960.

Ryans, David G., *Characteristics of Teachers.* Washington, D.C.: American Council on Education, 1960.

Sarason, Seymour B., *The Culture of the School and the Problem of Change.* Boston: Allyn & Bacon, 1971.

Schmuck, Richard A., Donald Murray, Mary Ann Smith, Mitchell Schwarts, and Margaret Runkel, *Consultation for Innovative Schools: O. D. For Multiunit Structure.* Eugene: University of Oregon Press, 1975.

Schmuck, Richard A., Phillip J. Runkel, and Daniel Langmeyer, *Improving Organizational Problem-Solving in a School Faculty.* A Preliminary Report. Eugene: Center for the Advanced Study of Educational Administration, University of Oregon, July 1969.

Schwanke, Dean, "Classroom Interaction Research: A Survey of Recent Literature," *Journal of Classroom Interaction,* 16 (Summer 1981): 8–10.

Schwartz, M., N. Steefel, and R. A. Schmuck, *The Development of Educational Teams.* Eugene, Oreg.: Center for Educational Policy and Management, 1976.

Scobey, Mary Margaret, and A. John Fiorino, eds., *Differentiated Staffing.* Washington, D.C.: Association for Supervision and Curriculum Development, 1973.

Semmel, Melvyn I., "Observer Agreement and Reliabilities of Classroom Observational Measures," *Review of Educational Research,* 48 (Winter 1978): 57–84.

Sealey, Leonard, and Elizabeth Dillon, *Staff Development: A Study of Six School Systems,* A Report to the Ford Foundation. New York: The Ford Foundation, 1976.

Sergiovanni, Thomas, *Handbook for Effective Department Leadership: Concepts and Practices in Today's Secondary Schools.* Boston, Mass.: Allyn & Bacon, 1977.

Sergiovanni, Thomas J., ed., *Supervision of Teaching,* ASCD Yearbook. Alexandria, Va.: Association for Supervision and Curriculum Development, 1982a.

Sergiovanni, Thomas J., "Toward a Theory of Supervisory Practice: Integrating Scientific, Clinical and Altistic Views," in *Supervision of Teaching,* ed. T. J. Sergiovanni. Alexandria, Va.: Association for Supervision and Curriculum Development.

Sergiovanni, Thomas J., and Robert J. Starratt, *Emerging Patterns of Supervision: Human Perspectives.* New York: McGraw-Hill, 1971.

Sergiovanni, Thomas J., and Robert J. Starratt, *Supervision: Human Perspectives,* 2nd ed. New York: McGraw-Hill, 1979.

Shane, Harold, and Roy A. Weaver, "Educational Developments Anticipating the 21st Century and the Future of Clinical Supervision," *Journal of Research and Development in Education*, 9 (Winter 1976): 90–97.

Shaplin, Judson T., and Henry F. Olds, eds., *Team Teaching*. New York: Harper & Row, 1964.

Showers, Beverly, *Transfer of Training: The Contribution of Coaching*. Eugene: The University of Oregon Center for Educational Policy and Management, 1983.

Silverblank, Fran, "Analyzing the Decision-Making Process in Curriculum Projects," *Education*, 99 (Summer 1979): 414–18.

Simon, Anita, and E. Gil Boyer, eds., *Mirrors for Behavior II: An Anthology of Observation Instruments, Volume A*. Philadelphia: Classroom Interaction Newsletter, 1970.

Smith, Alfred G., *Communication Status: The Dynamics of a Research Center*. Eugene: Center for the Advanced Study of Educational Administration, University of Oregon, 1966.

Smith, Nick L., ed., *Field Assessments of Innovative Evaluation Methods*, Number 13 of New Directions for Program Evaluation, ed.-in-chief Scarvia B. Anderson. San Francisco: Jossey-Bass, 1982.

Smith, Peter B., *Group Processes and Personal Change*. London: Harper & Row Ltd., 1980.

Smith, Philip D., Jr., *A Comparison Study of the Effectiveness of the Traditional and Audiolingual Approaches to Foreign Language Instruction Utilizing Laboratory Equipment*. Synopsis of the final reports of Project No. 7–0133, Grant No. OEC–1–7–070133–0445. Harrisburg, Pa.: Bureau of Research Administration, Department of Public Instruction, February 1968.

Snyder, Karolyn J., "Clinical Supervision: A Coaching Technology," in *Improving Classroom Practice Through Supervision*, ed. K. J. Snyder. Dallas: Texas Association for Supervision and Curriculum Development, November 1981.

Soar, Robert S., *An Integrative Approach to Classroom Learning*. NIMH Project Nos. 5–R11, MH01096, to the University of South Carolina, and 7R11, MHO2045, to Temple University, Philadelphia, 1966.

Southern Association of Colleges and Schools, *Guide to Evaluation and Accreditation of Schools*. Atlanta: Commission on Elementary Schools, Southern Association of Colleges and Schools, 1975.

Spady, William G., "The Illusion of School Improvement," *The School Administrator*, 39, no. 5 (May 1982a).

Spady, William G., "Keys to Effective Instruction: A Response to Williams," *The Schools Administrator*, 37 (November 1982b): 35–36.

Spady, William G., "Simple Techniques for Multi-Variate Analysis—or How to Amaze Your Colleagues Without the Aid of a Computer," *Interchange*, 1 (1970): 3–20.

Stake, Robert E., "Language, Rationality and Assessment," in *Improving Educational Assessment* ed. Walcott H. Beatty. Washington, D.C.: Association for Supervision and Curriculum Development, 1969.

Stallings, Jane A., "Effective Strategies for Teaching Basic Skills," in *Developing Basic Skills Programs in Secondary Schools*, ed. Daisy G. Wallace. Alexandria, Va.: Association for Supervision and Curriculum Development, 1981.

Stenzel, Norman K., "Committee Hearings as an Evaluation Format," in *Field Assessments of Innovative Evaluation Methods*, ed. Nick L. Smith. San Francisco: Jossey-Bass, 1982.

Stringer, L. A., "Sensitivity Training, An Alternative to T-Group Method," *Teachers College Record*, 71 (May 1970): 633–40.

Stufflebeam, Daniel L., et al., *Educational Evaluation and Decision Making*, Phi Delta

National Study Committee on Evaluation. Itasca, Ill.: F. E. Peacock Publishers, 1971.

Stulac, Josef F., II, et al., *Assessments of Performance in Teaching: Observation Instrument*. Columbia, South Carolina: South Carolina Educator Improvement Task Force, 1982.

Sullivan, Cheryl G., *Clinical Supervision: A State of the Art Review*. Alexandria, Va.: Association for Supervision and Curriculum Development, 1980.

Sullivan, Cheryl G., "Supervisory Expectations and Work Realities: The Great Gulf," a research paper, Emory University, 1982. (Mimeographed.)

Terpstra, David E., "The Organization Development Evaluation Process: Some Problems and Proposals," *Human Resource Management*, 2 (Spring 1981): 24–29.

Texas Cooperative Committee on Teacher Evaluation, *Principles and Guidelines for Teacher Evaluation Systems*. Austin: Texas Classroom Teachers' Association, 1979.

Thomas, Don R., "Preliminary Findings on Self-Monitoring for Modifying Teaching Behaviors," in *A New Direction for Education: Behavior Analysis*, Vol. 1, eds. Eugene A. Ramp and Bill I. Hopkins. Topeka: University of Kansas, Support and Development Center for Follow-through, Department of Human Development, 1971.

Thompson, James D., *Organizations in Action*. New York: McGraw-Hill, 1967.

Travers, Robert M. W., "Some Comments on Qualitative Approaches to the Development of Scientific Knowledge and the Use of Constructs Derived from Phenomenal Experience," in *Qualitative Evaluation*, ed. George Willis. Berkeley, Calif.: McCutchan Publishing Corp., 1978.

Tropman, John E., *Effective Meetings: Improving Group Decision-Making*, A Sage Human Services Guide 17. Beverley Hills, Calif.: Sage Publications, 1980.

Trump, Lloyd J., and Gordon F. Vars. "How Should Learning Be Organized?" in *Issues in Secondary Education*, 75th Yearbook, Part II, ed. William Van Til. Chicago: The National Society for the Study of Education, 1976.

Tyler, R. W., *Basic Principles of Curriculum and Instruction: Syllabus for Education 360*. Chicago: University of Chicago Press, 1949.

U.S. Department of Health, Education, and Welfare, *Statistical Summary*. Washington, D.C.: U. S. Government Printing Office, 1970.

U.S. Department of Health, Education, and Welfare, *Statistics of Elementary and Secondary Day Schools*, HEW Publication No. (OE) 73–11402. Washington, D.C.: Government Printing Office, 1972.

Vak, Stephen M., "The Relationship of Instructional Supervision to Student Achievement," in *Phi Delta Kappan*, 64 (September 1982): 68.

Van Fleet, Alanson A., and F. E. Salzillo, "Teacher Centers in Florida: A Case Study," *School Review*, 85 (May 1977): 412–24.

Wahle, Roy P., ed., *Toward Professional Maturity for Supervisors and Curriculum Workers*, ASCD Commission on Problems of Supervisors and Curriculum Workers, Harold T. Shafer, Chairman. Washington, D.C.: Association for Supervision and Curriculum Development, 1967.

Walker, William L., and Russell L. Hamm, *Twelve-Year Follow-Up Study: Role and Status of Curriculum Workers in Indiana*. Terre Haute: Curriculum Research and Development Center, School of Education, Indiana State University, 1981.

Webster, William J., *The Evaluation of Instructional Materials*. Washington D.C.: Association for Educational Communications and Technology, 1976.

Weick, K., "Educational Organizations as Loosely Coupled Systems," *Administrative Science Quarterly*, 21 (March 1976): 1–19.

Weick, Karl E., "Systematic Observational Methods," in *Handbook of Social Psy-*

chology, 2nd ed., Vol. II, eds. Gardner Lindzey and E. Aronson. Reading, Mass.: Addison-Wesley, 1968.

Weinheimer, Anne, "Implementation Evaluation Vs. Outcome Evaluation," *Evaluation Comment, 6* (December 1980): 13–15. Los Angeles, California: Center for the Study of Evaluation, UCLA Graduate School of Education.

Weiss, Carol H., *Evaluation Research: Methods for Assessing Program Effectiveness.* Englewood Cliffs, N.J.: Prentice-Hall, 1972.

Weiss, Carol H., and Michael J. Bucuvalas, *Social Science Research and Decision-Making.* N.Y.: Columbia University Press, 1980.

Weller, Richard H., *Verbal Communication in Instructional Supervision.* New York: Teachers College Press, Columbia University, 1971.

Wiens, John, "Differences Between Influential and Non-Influential Administrators," *The Alberta Journal of Educational Research, 16* (June 1970): 103–110.

Wiley, Jerold W., "One-on-One Training: A Solid Bet for Skills," *Training* 18 (August 1981): 102–104.

Wilhelms, Fred T., *Supervision in a New Key.* Washington, D.C.: Association for Supervision and Curriculum Development, 1973.

Williams, Jack E., "They Train Lions, Don't They?" *Journal of Teacher Education, 33* (May–June): 31–34.

Williams R. C., "An Organizational Perspective on Instructional Management," *The School Administrator, 39* (November 1982): 33–34. Arlington, Va.: American Association of School Administrators, 1982.

Willis, George, ed., *Qualitative Evaluation: Concepts and Cases in Curriculum Criticism.* Berkeley, Calif.: McCutchan Publishing Corp., 1978.

Wolfensberger, Wolf, and Linda Glenn, *Program Analysis of Service Systems: A Method for the Quantitative Evaluation of Human Services*, 3rd ed. Toronto: National Institute on Mental Retardation, 1975.

Wooldridge, Ronald J., ed., *Evaluation of Complex Systems*, Number 10 in New Directions for Program Evaluating. San Francisco: Jossey-Bass, 1981.

Wright, David McCord, "The Administrative Fallacy," *Harvard Business Review, 38* (July–August 1960): 113–14.

Yinger, Robert J., "A Study of Teacher Planning: Description and Theory Development Using Ethnographic and Information Processing Methods," Ph.D. dissertation, Michigan State University, 1977.

Young, James M., and R. L. Heichberger, "Teachers' Perceptions of an Effective School Supervision and Evaluation Program," *Education, 96* (Fall 1975): 10–19.

Zander, Alvin, *Making Groups Effective.* San Francisco: Jossey-Bass, 1982.

Zenke, Larry, "Quality Control Circles: Cure-All or Cover-Up?" *The School Administrator, 39* (November 1982): 37.

Ziegler, Warren L., "Stasis and Kinesis," paper presented at the First General Assembly of the World Future Society, Washington, D.C., 1971.

INDEX

A

Abdication, teacher, 158
Access, freedom of, 121–22
Accountability:
    analysis and calculation activities
        and, 80
    models, 195–96
Achievement, pupil, 162
Activities, 17–20, 63–89. *See also*
        Strategies
    analyzing and calculating, 79–80
    brainstorming, 80–81
        rules for, 80
        structured, 105
    buzz sessions, 82–83
        as discussion activity, 78–79
        in human relations workshop,
            278–79
        value of, 82

    for change, 68–70
    critical tasks, 63–65
    defined, 17, 63
    demonstration, 75, 94
    discussion, 78–79
    field trips, 83
    film or TV viewing, 73
    group, 31–35, 78–79
    guided practice, 86–87
    instrumentation and testing,
        81–82
    interviewing, 75–78
        focused, 76–77
        nondirective, 77–78
        of new teacher, 263–67
        structured, 75–76
    intervisitation, 83–84, 149–50
    lecturing, 71–72
    listening to tape, radio or record-
        ings, 73–74

material and equipment exhibition, 74
motivation for change and, 65–68
observation of classroom. *See* Observation of classroom
panel presentation, 72–73
planning of, 17
postobservation, 160–61
reading, 79
for staffing, 19–20
for task accomplishment, 17–19
training, 155–56
    designing, 92–98, 297, 298
    role playing for, 85
videotaping and photography, 81
writing, 86, 298
Adams, W., 68, 151, 184
Adequacy Index, 134
Adequacy of staff, numerical, 130–34
Administration:
    as functional area of school operations, 6
    tasks, 226
Administrative fallacy, 36
Agencies, supervising, 118–20
Agentry, change, 135–36, 137
Alioto, R.F., 135
Alkin, M., 194, 196
Allocation of resources, 14, 127–28
Almanza, H.K., 64
Alpert, J.L., 103
Alternate focus effects, 175, 176
American Institutes for Research, 197
Ames, C., 156
Amidon, E.J., 149
Amplified Project Team (APT), 136–43
    basic assumptions underlying, 142–43
    characteristics of, 136–37
    dismantling, 141
    organization of, 138–39
    process sequence for, 139–41
Analysis:
    activities, 79–80
    branching diagram, 200–205
    branching product, 205–6
    competency, 128–29
    congruence, 179–82
    data, 176–85
        envelopment, 207–8
        for evaluation, 190, 191
    fishbone cause-effect, 106
    Flanders system of interaction, 94, 156, 168–69, 232–34
    job-description, 223–26
    matrix, 177–79
    observational, 176–85
        clinical, 151
        diagnostic, 179–82
        graphic, 177–79
        qualitative, 182–85
    pareto, 106
    PASS system, 208–9
    process cause-effect, 106
    self-, 149
    systems:
        of evaluation, 195–200
        flowcharting for, 46–49
        of individualization of instruction, 44–47
Anderson, R.H., 53, 151
Anderson, S.B., 189, 190
Apple, M.W., 184
Argyris, C., 28, 34, 138
Assessment, process of, 13–14
Assignment. *See also* Staff, staffing
    to Amplified Project Team, 139–41
    differentiated staff and, 115–16
    temporary, 126
Athletics, 9
Audio-visual education, 215–16

Authier, J., 81, 86
Awareness through feedback, 164

B

Babb, A.M., 137
Bailey, E., 117
Bailey, G.W., 136
Baker, D., 64
Baker, G.A., 103
Balance, concept of, 129–30
Bales, R.F., 79
Ball, S., 189, 190
Ban, J.R., 111
Banathy, B.H., 44, 46
Bandura, A., 27
"Bandwagon" effect, 60
Barbour, C., 99
Bassin, M., 124
Behavioral goals, 71
Beisser, F.G., 91, 135
Bender, R.H., 123
Berliner, D., 172, 182, 184
Berman, P., 111, 119
Bessent, A., 200, 203
Bessent, E.W., 65, 79, 86, 94, 98,
        169, 179, 200, 203
Bias, observer, 153
Biddle, B.J., 200
Bilingual education, 221–23
Bishop, L.J., 119
Bishop, L.K., 137
Blake, R.R., 54, 103
Blanchard, K.H., 34
Bloom, B.S., 64, 169, 196
Blumberg, A., 111
Body language, 171
Boney, D., 98
Borg, W., 74, 98, 99, 149
Borich, G.P., 82, 164
Bottom, 11
Boyan, N.J., 44, 53, 96
Boyer, E.G., 147, 159–60, 164

Brainstorming activities, 80–81
    rules for, 80
    structured, 105
Branching diagram analysis,
        200–205
Branching product analysis, 205–6
Brandt, R., 184
Bronowski, J., 186
Brophy, J., 155
Brown, W., 92, 102
Bucuvalas, M.J., 186, 190
Burch, B.G., 112
Burton, B., 26
Butler, Martha, 114
Butler, Matilda, 119
Buzz sessions:
    activity of, 82–83
    group discussion compared to,
        78–79
    in human relations workshop,
        278–79
    value of, 82

C

Calculation activities, 79–80
Caldwell, D.F., 34
California Teachers Association,
    5
Cantor, N., 78
Capie, W., 153, 156, 165, 166
Carthel, J.T., 201
Case studies. *See under* In-service
        education; Observation of
        classroom
Cause-effect analysis, 106
Categorical-descriptive instruments,
        172
Cates, C., 102
Cawelti, G., 111
CBAM, 54
Chairpersons, department, 114–15
Champagne, D.W., 86, 102

Change:
  activities for, 68–70
  agentry, requirements of, 135–36,
      137
  approaches to, 29–31
  attitude toward, 39–40
  conflict between maintenance
      and, 142–43
  conservation and, 40–41
  designing for complex, 93–94
  dynamic supervision for, 21–23
  engineering, 26
  evaluation as actions for, 198–99
  fallacy of peaceful, 36–37
  improving teaching through,
      27–31
  motivation for, 65–68
  orientation toward, 20–23
  as precarious value, 38–39
  process dynamics, 33–35
  resistance to, 35–40
    dealing with, 37–38
    as normal, 37
    passive, 258–61
    team supervision and, 135
  strategies, 52–60, 91–109
    basic, 98–103
    in designing for training, 92–98
    diffusion innovations, 55–56
    information processing and
        feedback, 53–55
    local development, 56–57
    organization development,
        103–4
    quality control circles, 104–7
    three-stage, 57–60
  types of, 30–31
Charisma, 34
Checklists, 164–65, 167–71
CIPP model, 197
Classroom:
  arrangements, 255
  management, 255, 267–69
  experience, 96

observations. *See* Observation of
    classroom
Cleaves, A., 98
Clinical analysis of classroom obser-
    vation, 151
Clinical approaches to in-service ed-
    ucation, 98–101
Clinical mode, 296
Clinical supervision:
  as change strategy, 53–54
  in-service education and, 98–99
Cogan, M., 44, 53, 86, 96, 98, 151
Cognitive dissonance, creation of,
    65–68
Cognitive tuning, 152
Cohen, M., 111
Coker, H., 182
Communication theory, 2
Competency(ies), 15–19
  analysis, 128–29
  defining, 15–16
  profile, 129–30
  special, 123
  staffing and, 20, 128–30
  statements, 289–95
Comprehensive lesson analysis,
    230–32
Comprehensive Observation of Per-
    formance (CO-oP), 172,
    230–31, 250
Computer(s):
  -assisted instruction, 98
  data envelopment analysis and,
    207
Concerns based adoption model
    (CBAM), 54
Concordance, estimates of, 184
Conferred status, 123–24
Confrontation method, case study
    of, 235
Congruence:
  among estimates of concordance,
    184
  analysis, 179–82

"Connoisseurship," 182
Conservation, wisdom of, 40–41
Consideration in leadership, 34
Consultant:
   for bilingual education, 221–23
   roles, 102, 103
   task force, 269–74
   strategies for, 102–3
Continuity, orientation toward,
      20–23
Control, quality. *See* Quality control
   circles
Conversations, classroom observa-
      tion and, 157
Coody, B., 172, 191
Cooper, B.S., 66
Coordination, process of, 14
Copeland, W.D., 44, 53, 96
Corbett, H.D., 114
Core group, Amplified Project,
      138–41
Cornell, F.G., 156
Coughlan, R.J., 138
Crandall, D., 118
Crawford, G.J., 91
Critical tasks, 63–65
Cronbach, L.J., 189, 195
Cunningham, L.I., 115
Cunningham, W., 54
Curriculum:
   developing, 18, 19, 224–25, 289–90
   and materials development sub-
      system, 51–52
   planning, experiences of, 219–21
   revision, case report of, 252–57
   study. *See* In-service education
Custodial function, 8–9
Cuthbertson, J.W., 34

D

Danley, W.E., Sr., 112
Data. *See also* Observation of class-
      room
   analysis of, 176–85

envelopment, 207–8
   for evaluation, 190–191
   gathering, 106, 190, 191
Davies, I.K., 68, 71
Deans of instruction, 114
Decision-making. *See also* Leader-
      ship
   for change, 29
   in evaluation, 190, 191
   go, no-go, 194–95
   operational, 193
Demonstration activities, 75–94
Departmentalization of instruction,
      30–31
Department chairpersons, 114–15
DeRoche, E.F., 160
Descriptive-narrative instruments,
      171–76
   categorical, 172
   sequential, 174
*Descriptive Observation Record for
      Individualization of Instruc-
      tion* (Hardbebeck), 172
Design:
   for group processes, 101–2
   process of, 14
   training, 92–93
      for complex change, 93–94
      in current practice, 94–96
      programs, 298
      reality simulation, 96–98
      sessions, 297
DeTEK instrument, 47–49, 101,
      179, 181, 231, 247, 249–50
Development:
   of curriculum, 18, 19, 224–25,
      289–90
   evaluation of, 101
   of instruments, 155
   local, 56–57
   organizational, 54, 103–4
   staff, 59, 65
      workshop for, 279–85
   systems, 49–52
   of tasks, 10

Developmental Supervisory Competency Assessment System (Harris), 129

Developmental Teacher Evaluation Kit (DeTEK), 47–49, 101, 179, 181, 231, 247, 249–50

Dewar, D.L., 104, 105

Diagnostic analysis, 179–82

Diedrich, 198

Differentiated staffing, 7, 115–16, 142

Diffusion of innovations, 55–56

Directing, process of, 15

Discussion:
  activity, 78–79
  buzz sessions for, 78–79, 82–83, 278–79
  as quality circle technique, 105

Dissonance, cognitive, 65–68

Drucker, P.F., 37, 50

Duke, R.D., 79, 98

Dull, L.W., 111, 118

Duncan, R.B., 135, 136, 137, 201

Dunkerton, J., 167, 182

Dunkin, M.J., 200

Dyer, H.S., 191, 198

Dynamic orientation, 26

Dynamic supervision, 21–23, 26–42
  for change, 21–23
  improvement of teaching through, 27–31
  interests, leadership and implementation in, 31–35
  resistance to change and, 35–40
  wisdom of conversation and, 40–41

E

Easton, P., 56

Edelfelt, R.A., 91, 92

Education:
  audio-visual, 215–16
  bilingual, 221–23

Educational Curriculum Resource and Research Center, 117

Education Amendments of 1976, 118

Efficiency:
  criterion, 121–24
  data envelopment analysis of, 207–8
  of group discussion, 79

Eichelberger, T., 194

Eiden, L.J., 113, 114

Eiken, K.P., 22

Eisner, E., 167, 182

Electromechanical recording devices, 164

Elementary and Secondary Education Act of 1965, 117

Elementary supervisor, 217–19

Elzie, P., 64

Emory, R.E., 78

Energy, supervisory functions and, 121

Enos, D.F., 15

Entertainment function, 9

Equipment, exhibition of, 74

Esposito, J.P., 112

Estimates of concordance, 184

Evaluation, 189–212
  as actions for change, 198–99
  in Amplified Project Team, 140
  competency for, 18, 19, 295
  defined, 189–90
  developmental, 101
  focused interview and, 76–77
  focus on instructional improvement of, 192–93
  formative vs. summative, 196–97
  importance of, 64
  job description analysis of, 226
  models, 196–97
  multifactor, 200–209
    branching diagram analysis, 200–205
    branching product analysis, 205–6

Evaluation (*cont.*)
  data envelopment analysis,
    207–8
  PASS system, 208–9
  nature of, 190–91
  product, 192–93
  project, 197–99
  puposes served by, 191–95
  of staff development program,
    282–85
  subsystem, 50–51
  systems analysis of, 195–200
  task, 12
  values in, 190, 191, 243–46
Evertson, C.M., 154, 156, 162, 172,
    175
Expectations, role, 122
Experience:
  classroom, for in-service educa-
    tion, 96
  impact, 68–70
Expert role of consultant, 102, 103

F

Facilities, provision of, 11, 12, 18,
    225, 294
Fallacy of peaceful change, 36–37
Far West Laboratory for Educa-
    tional Research and Develop-
    ment, 96, 99, 119, 149
Fathy, S.H., 191
Fear as motivation for change, 67
Feedback:
  awareness through, 164
  in change strategy, 53–55
  in laboratory design, 96–97
  sessions, case study of, 246–52
Feyereisen, K.Y., 46
Field trips, 83
Film presentation, 73
Fiorino, A.J., 115
Firester, J., 124

Firester, L., 124
Firth, G.R., 22
Fishbone cause-effect analysis, 106
Flanagan, J.C., 197
Flanders, N.A., 2, 67, 156, 168, 177,
    184, 200
Flanders system of interaction anal-
    ysis, 94, 156, 168–69, 232–34
Flexibility, supervisory responsibili-
    ties and, 122
Floden, R.E., 67
Flowcharting:
  in curriculum planning, 220–21
  for systems analysis and planning,
    46–49
Focused interviewing, 76–77
Foresman, 270
Formative evaluation, 196–197
Foster, G., 56
Freedom of access, 121–22
Free-response instruments, 164
Frequency tabulation instruments,
    164, 167–71
Fuller, F.F., 149
Functional criteria, 120–24
Functional changes, 30–31
Furst, N., 153

G

Gage, N.L., 41, 200
Gall, J., 102
Gall, M.D., 102
Galloway, C.G., 171
Games, instructional, 98
Garver, G.G., 98
Gerhard, R.J., 192, 196
Giacquinta, J.B., 135
Glenn, L., 200, 209
Glickman, C.D., 53
Go, no-go decision-making, 194–95
Goals, behavioral and organization,
    71

Goldhammer, R., 53, 151
Goldstein, W., 2
Good, T., 155
Goodland, J.E., 114, 137
Goodson, M.R., 136, 138
Grant, W.V., 113, 114
Graphic analysis, 177–79
Greenblatt, C.S., 79, 98
Gross, N., 79
Gross, T., 124
Group(s). *See also* Buzz sessions
    activities, 31–35, 78–79
    characteristics of supervisor staff,
        136–38
    processes, designing for, 101–2
    size, 68, 69–70
Gryna, F.M., Jr., 105, 106
Guba, E.G., 189, 196
Guides, observation. *See* Instru-
        ments
Guided-practice activities, 86–87
Gustafson, K., 81, 86

H

Hagen, N.J., 64
Hagstrom, W.O., 136, 138
Hall, G., 54
Hamm, R.S., 112, 114, 125
Hansen, B., 64
Hardebeck, R.J., 147, 163, 172
Hare, A.P., 82
Harris, B.M., 5, 11, 16, 34, 47, 49,
        53, 65, 68–69, 79, 80, 82, 86,
        92, 94, 96, 98, 99, 101, 102,
        114, 118, 128–30, 149, 156,
        163, 165, 169, 172, 179, 184,
        185, 191, 195, 200
Harvard-Newton program, 96
Havelock, R.G., 28
Hayes, A., 147
Heller, J.F., 33
Helping teacher role, 158

Hering, W.M., Jr., 27
Herriott, R.E., 79
Hersey, P., 34
Hiatt, D.B., 156
Hill, J., 47, 53, 80, 101, 114, 149,
        156, 163, 172, 179, 184
Hill, R.A., 153
Hillson, M., 115, 116
Hogan, R.C., 86, 102
Holley, F.M., 154, 172, 175
Hood, P., 102
Hook, C.M., 148
Horn, R.E., 98
Human relations workshop, 277–79
Hunter, E., 149
Hunter, M., 151
Hyman, R.T., 115, 116

I

Implementation:
    in APT, 140
    interest and leadership and,
        33–35
    phases of program, 31–33
    of research, 267–69
    strategies, 90–109
        basic approaches for, 98–103
        designing for training, 92–98,
            297, 298
        organizational development, 54,
            103–4
        quality control circles, 54,
            104–7
Improvement, instructional:
    case study of, 228–34
    through dynamic supervision,
        27–31
    evaluation focus on, 192–93
Incentives for change, 66–67
In-classroom practices, observation
        and, 156–60

Individual growth, planning for, 296–97
Individualization of instruction:
  branching diagram analysis of, 201–4
  systems analysis of, 44–47
Individualization of Instruction Inventory (Harris), 165
Individual study units in PDC, 287–88
Ineffectiveness area, 69, 70
Inefficiency area, 69, 70
Informal visiting, 161. *See also* Intervisitation
Information processing and feedback strategy, 53–55
Ingils, C.R., 146, 148, 153
Initiation:
  in leadership, 34
  program phase, 32
Innovations. *See also* Change
  corruption of, 60
  diffusion of, 55–56
  of in-service education, 94–96
In-service education:
  arranging for, 11, 18, 19, 225–26, 292–93
  case studies, 262–88
    human relations workshop, 277–79
    interview with new teacher, 263–67
    profesional development center, 285–88
    research implementation in classroom management, 267–69
    staff development workshop, 279–85
    task force in team supervision, 269–74
    training in reading disability, 274–77
  clinical approaches to, 98–101

  importance of, 64–65
  innovative practices for, 94–96
  planning model for illustrative, 47
  subsystem, staffing and, 51
In-service planning, 252–57, 274–77
Instruction:
  computer-assisted, 98
  Deans of, 114
  departmentalization of, 30–31
  improvement of:
    case study of, 228–34
    through dynamic supervision, 27–31
    evaluation focus on, 192–93
  organizing for, 11, 18, 225, 291
  -relatedness, 3–5, 6
Instructional development system, 50–52
Instructional supervisor. *See* Supervisor(s)
Instrumentation:
  activities, 81–82
  for evaluation, 190, 191
Instruments, 164–76
  bias of, 153
  descriptive-narrative, 171–76
    categorical, 172
    sequential, 174
  development of, 155
  frequency tabulation and checklists, 164, 167–71
  inapropriateness of, 157–58
  rating scales, 149, 165–67, 185
  recording, 164
  reliability of, 156
Interaction analysis system, 94, 156, 168–69, 232–34
Interest, leadership and, 33–35
Interviewing activities, 75–78
  focused, 76–77
  nondirective, 77–78
  of new teacher, 263–67
  structured, 75–76

Intervisitation:
    activity, 83–84, 149–50
    for passive resistance problem,
        260–61
Irvine, J.J., 149
Ivey, A.E., 99

J

Job-description analysis, 223–26
Johnson, C., 91
Johnson, C.E., 153
Jones, J.E., 98, 102
Jones, L., 147
Judicial model, 194
Jungheur, J.A., 135

K

Kane, R.A., 112, 135, 136
Katz, Daniel, 28
Katz, Douglas S., 196
Keesling, J.W., 156
Kendall, P.L., 76
Kerr, D.H., 27
Killough, D., 118
Kindsvatter, R., 77
King, J.D., 15
King-Stoops, J., 116, 119, 125
Klein, S.P., 196
Klugman, E., 118
Korda, M., 34
Krajewski, R., 53, 151
Krantz, L.L., 117

L

Laboratories, regional, 119
Laboratory design, for reality simu-
        lation, 96–98
Lamb, M.L., 146

Lamb, R.W., 161, 182
Lane, V.W., 76
Langmeyer, D., 103
Lawrence, G., 64
Leadership:
    competencies, 123
    components of, 34
    freedom of access and, 121–22
    in group discussions, 78–79
    interest and, 33–35
    processes, 12–15
    team, 123
    time and energy requirements of,
        121
    training, 297
Lead teachers, 115
Learning, supporting functions and,
        6, 7
Lecturing activity, 71–72
Lesson:
    analysis, comprehensive, 230–32
    preparation, 255
Lewey, A., 10
Lewin, K., 37
Lieberman, A., 91
Lieberman, M., 135
Lightsey, B., 16
Lincoln, Y.S., 189, 196
Lindvall, C.M., 156
Link, 198
Littleton, V., 5, 11, 49, 55, 82, 92,
        128–30, 165, 185, 195
Local development, 56–57
Local district staff, 113–16
Long, D., 5, 11, 49, 82, 92, 128–30,
        165, 185, 195
Lovell, J.T., 2, 84, 175
Lynch, W.W., Jr., 156

M

McCleary, L.E., 15, 94
McGreal, T.L., 149, 164, 175

McIntire, R., 94
McIntyre, K.E., 5, 11, 49, 65, 79,
    82, 86, 92, 94, 98, 128–30,
    165, 169, 179, 172, 185, 191,
    195
McLaughlin, M.W., 111, 119
McMillan, L., 114
Madden, S.K., 82, 164
Maher, C., 202
Maintenance, conflict between
    change and, 142–43
Management:
  -by-objectives (MBO), 101
  classroom, 255, 267–69
  in school operation, 5
  stress, 267, 268
  systems in PDC, 287
Marks, J.R., 116, 119, 125
Marshall, E.K., 102
Maslow's hierarchy of needs theory,
    45–46
Master plan, developing, 298
Materials:
  development subsystem, curricu-
    lum and, 51–52
  exhibition of, 74
  functional relationships in im-
    proving utilization of, 8
  provision of, 11, 18, 19, 225, 290
Matrix analysis, 177–79
Medley, D., 169, 200
Meisgeier, C., 98
Merton, R.K., 76
Michalak, D.C., 99
Microlab teaching, 98
Microteaching, 98–99
Miller, L., 91
Miller, R.I., 189
Mills, J.R., 164, 182
Mills, T.M., 78, 137
Milroy, E., 84–85
Miskel, C., 91
Mitzel, H.E., 169

Models:
  accountability, 195–96
  concerns based adoption, 54
  evaluation, 196–97
  judicial, 194
  motivation for change and, 67–68
  social interaction, 56
  systems, 44–49
  utility of, 44–46
Molyneaux, D., 76
Momentum phase of program, 32
Morale-building fallacy, 36–37
Moreland, J.R., 99
Moreno, 84
Morgan, R.L., 196
Motivation for change, 65–68
Mouton, J.S., 54, 103
Moxley, R.S., Jr., 79
Multifactor evaluation, 200–209
  branching diagram analysis,
    200–205
  branching product analysis, 205–6
  data envelopment analysis, 207–8
  PASS system of, 208–9
Multimedia presentations, 72
Murphy, J.T., 125, 137
Murray, D., 53, 92, 103
Myths of classroom observation,
    162–64

N

Nadler, B., 194
Needs:
  assessing, 297
  cultivation of, 67
  for supervisors, estimating,
    131–32
  theory, Maslow's hierarchy of,
    45–46
*New Comprehensive Observation
    Guide*, 235, 236–43

New England School Development
Council, 117
Newfield, J., 148, 149
Nondirective interviewing, 77–78
Northwest Educational Coopera-
tive, 104
Northwest Regional Educational
Laboratory, 119
Numerical adequacy of staff,
130–34

O

Ober, R., 171
Objectives of change activities, 68,
69–70
for training designs, 94
Observation of classroom, 146–76
activity of, 74–75
analysis of, 176–85
clinical, 151
diagnostic, 179–82
graphic, 177–79
qualitative, 182–85
bias in, 153
case studies, 227–61
confrontation method, 234–36
curriculum revision and in-service planning, 252–57
dealing with unobservable,
257–58
feedback problems, 246–52
improvement process, 228–34
New Comprehensive Observation Guide, 236–43
passive resistance, 258–61
supervisory strategy case,
243–46
focused interviews and, 76
instruments, 164–76
descriptive-narrative, 171–76
development of, 155
frequency tabulations and
checklists, 164, 167–71
inappropriateness of, 157–58
rating scales, 149, 165–67, 185
recoding, 164
reliability of, 156
length of periods of, 159–60
systematic procedures, 152–64
active, 152–53
in-classroom practices, 156–60
informal visiting, 161
myths, misconceptions and issues, 162–64
postobservation activities,
160–61
preobservation preparations,
153–56
uses of, 147–51
Olds, H.F., 115
Olsen, H.C., 99
Open Highways (Foresman), 270
Operating system, 49–50
Operation, school, 1–10
functions, 4, 5–10
supervision in, 2–3, 6
two-dimensional framework of, 3
Operational decision-making, 193
Operationalization, systems for,
43–62
in Amplified Project Team, 140,
141
change strategies and, 52–60
diffusion of innovations, 55–56
information processing and
feedback, 53–55
local development, 56–57
three-stage, 57–60
for developmental tasks, 49–52
models for, 44–49
O'Reilly, A., 34
Organizational changes, 30
Organizational development (OD),
54, 103–4

Organizational goals, 71
Organizing for instruction, 11, 18, 225, 291. *See also* Staff, staffing
Orientation:
  dynamic, 26
  toward continuity versus change, 20–23
  of staff, 11, 226
Osborne, A.S., 80
OSCAR instruments, 169–70
Ostlund, L.A., 79
Ouchi, W.G., 53, 104, 136
Overspecialization, problems of, 125, 126
Owens, R.G., 27, 55–56

P

Paisley, W., 119
Panel presentation, 72–73
Pareto analysis, 106
Paris, N.M., 101
PASS, 208–9
Passive resistance to change, 258–61
Patchin, R., 106
Paul, D.A., 56
PDC, 285–88
Pennsylvania State University, 98
"Perceptual Examination Report," 176
Performance, competency statements for, 289–95
Perrott, E., 99, 164
Personnel, supervisory. *See* Staff, staffing
Petri, T.A., 26
Pfeiffer, J.W., 98, 102
Phillips, J.D., 82
Photographic activities, 81
Physical changes, 30

Pino, R.F., 78
Planning:
  of activities, 17
  for Amplified Project Team, 140
  curriculum, experiences of, 219–21
  flowcharting for, 46–49, 220–21
  for individual growth, 296–97
  in-service, 252–57, 274–77
  phase of program, 32
  strategic, 30–31, 91
Policy-regulatory subsystem, 52
Positions, supervisory, 111–13
Postobservation activities, 160–61
Practice activities, 86–87
Preobservation preparations, 153–56
Presentation techniques, 72–74, 106
Principal:
  dealing with unobservable, 227–28
  as instructional supervisor, 114
Prioritizing, process of, 14
Private organizations, as supervisory agencies, 119–20
Problems phase of program, 32–33
Process:
  cause-effect analysis, 106
  change, 33–35
  specialist, 102, 103
  evaluation, 199–200
Product:
  analysis, branching, 205–6
  evaluation, 192–93
"Productivity Council," 207
Professional associations, 119
Professional Development Center (PDC), 285–88
Profiles of competence, 129–30
Program(s):
  evaluation. *See* Evaluation
  implementation strategies, 90–109
    basic approaches for, 98–103
    designing for training, 92–98, 297, 298

organizational development, 54, 103–4
  quality control circles, 54, 104–7
  phases of, 31–33
Program Anaysis of Service Systems (PASS), 208–9
Project. *See also* Amplified Project Team (APT)
  evaluation, 197–99
  -program paradox, 143–44
  proposals, writing of, 298
Psychiatric theories, 2
Public relations:
  development of, 11–12, 18, 226, 294
  as distinct from in-service education, 65
  focused interview and, 77
Public services, relating, 291–92
Pupil:
  achievement, 162
  -relatedness, 3–5, 6
  report, 147, 148
Pupil Enthusiasm Inventory (Harris), 169, 170, 177
Purpose, establishing observational, 154

Q

Qualitative analysis, 182–85
Quality control circles, 104–7
  as change strategy, 54
  characteristics, 104–5
  key elements, 106–7
  techniques, 105–6

R

Radio, presentation through, 73–74
Rating scales, 149, 165–67, 185

RCLT, 267
Reading:
  activities, 79
  disabilities, in-service planning for, 274–77
Reality simulation, 96–98
Reality structure, motivation for change and, 67
Reavis, C.A., 151
Reciprocal Category System, 171
Reciprocal visitations. *See* Intervisitation
Recordings:
  electromechanical devices, 164
  presentation through, 73–74
Redfern, G.B., 53, 101
Regional laboratories, 119
Relevance criterion, 120
Reliability, interobserver, 156
Remedial reading program, 274–77
Reports, pupil and self-, 147, 148
Research, implementation of, 267–69
Research on Classroom Learning and Teaching (RCLT), 267
Resistance to change, 35–40
  dealing with, 37–38
  as normal, 37
  passive, 258–61
  team supervision and, 135
Resource(s):
  allocations, 14, 127–28
  planned diminution of, 126–27
  specialist, 102, 103
  teachers, 115
Responsibilities, supervisory, 120–24
Rogers, E.M., 28, 55, 57, 92
Role(s):
  of consultant, 102, 103
  expectations, 122
  helping teacher, 158
  playing, 84–85, 278
Rosenshine, B.V., 148
Rubin, L., 10, 27

Ruch, C.P., 102
Rules changes, 30
Runkel, P.J., 103
Ryans, D.G., 67, 165

S

Salzillo, F.E., 118
Sarason, S.B., 26
Saupe, J., 156
Schmuck, R.A., 53, 92, 103, 136
School operation, 1–10
    functions, 4, 5–10
    supervision in, 2–3, 6
    two-dimensional framework of, 3
Schwanke, D., 179
Schwartz, M., 136
Scobey, M.M., 115
Secondary education director,
    223–26
Self-analysis, guiding, 149
Self-instructional module, 298
Self-reports, teacher, 147, 148
Semmel, M.I., 152, 155
Sequential descriptive instruments,
    174
Sergiovanni, T.J., 114, 169, 124, 125
Service centers, 116–17
Shadow functions, 8–10
Shane, H., 144
Shaplin, J.T., 115
Shared functions, 6–8. *See also*
    Team supervision
Shoemaker, F.F., 28, 55, 57, 92
Shore, K., 194
Silverblank, F., 102
Simon, A., 147, 159–60, 164
Simulation, reality, 96–98
Skill-building activity, 86–87. *See
    also* Training
Smith, E.B., 91, 92
Smith, M.A., 53, 92, 103
Smith, P.B., 28, 78, 102

Smith, P.D., Jr., 137
Snyder, K.J., 44, 46
Social interaction models, 56
Social-psychological theory, 2
Social systems theory, 2
Sociodrama, 84–85, 278
Southern Regional Education
    Board, 117
Southwest Educational Develop-
    ment Laboratory, 119
Spady, W.G., 50, 91, 182, 202
Special Education Supervisor Train-
    ing Project, 15
Specialists, resource, 102, 103
Specialization, 124–27
Special services:
    as functional area of school
        operation, 5
    function of, 127
    personnel, 127–28, 161
    relating, 11, 18, 226
Staff, staffing, 110–45
    activities for, 19–20
    competencies and, 20, 128–30
    considerations in, 124–28
    current patterns in, 110–20
        intermediate units and service
            centers, 116–17
        local district staff, 113–16
        other supervising agencies,
            118–20
        supervisors and supervisory
            personnel, 111–13
        teacher centers, 118
    development of, 59, 65
        workshop for, 279–85
    differentiated, 7, 115–16, 142
    functional criteria for, 120–24
    and in-service education subsys-
        tem, 51
    job description analysis of, 225
    numerical adequacy, 130–34
    orientation of, 11, 226
    provision of, 11, 18, 290–91

shadow functions of, 8–10
shared functions, 6–8
team supervision. *See* Team supervision
Stake, R.E., 148
Stallings, J.A., 27
Starratt, R.J., 124, 125
State departments of education, 118–19
Statistical check sheet, 106
Status, conferred, 123–24
Steefel, N., 136
Steinhoff, 27, 55–56
Stoops, E., 116, 119, 125
Strategic planning, 30–31, 91
Strategy. *See under* Change
Strategy teams, 138
Stress management, 267, 268
Stringer, L.A., 101
Structured interviewing, 75–76
Studies for classroom observations, 150–51
Stufflebeam, D.L., 189, 195, 197
Stulac, J.F., II, 172, 175
Sullivan, C.H., 2, 17, 44, 90, 112
Summative evaluation, 196–97
Superintendent, 115
Supervision. *See also* Team supervision
   clinical, 98–99
   as change strategy, 53–54
   defined, 10
   dynamic, 26–42
      for continuity and change, 20–23
      instructional improvement through, 27–31
      interests, leadership and implementation in, 31–35
      resistance to change and, 35–40
      wisdom of conversation and, 40–41
   functional criteria of, 120–24

operations of, 10–20
   leadership processes for, 12–15
   special versus general, 124–27
   theoretical perspectives on, 1–2
   tractive, 21, 22–23
   within total school operation, 2–3, 6
Supervisor(s):
   defined, 112
   elementary, typical day of, 217–19
   estimating needs for, 131–32
   group characteristics of, 136–38
   increase in, 113–16
   life and problems as new, 214–17
   organizing, 126
Supplementary Educational Centers and Services, 117
Surveys for classroom observations, 150–51
Swick, K.J., 146
Symposium, 73
Systematic inquiry, 195
Systems:
   concept, 44–46
   development, 49–52
   models, 44–49
   for operationalization. *See* Operationalization, systems for
Systems analysis:
   of evaluation, 195–200
   flowcharting for, 46–49
   of individualization of instruction, 44–47

T

Taba training program, 204–5
Tabulation instruments, frequency, 164, 167–71
Tape:
   of nondirective interviewing, 77–78
   presentation through, 73–74

Tasks(s):
  accomplishment, activities for,
    17–19
  administration, 226
  critical, 63–65
  developmental, 49–52
  force, consultant, 269–74
  types of supervisory, 10–12, 13
Teacher(s):
  abdication, 158
  centers, 118
  during classroom observations,
    157–59
  interview with new, 263–67
  intervisitations by, 83–84, 149–50
  lead and resource, 115
  observations and misconceptions
    about, 162–64
  preobservation preparation and,
    154–55
  self-report by, 147, 148
Teacher Characteristics Schedule
  (Ryan), 65
Teacher Performance Screening Inventory, 249
*Teacher Question-Pupil Response In-
  ventory* (Harris, Bessent, and
  McIntyre), 179, 180
Teacher question tabulation instrument, 169
Teaching. *See also* Instruction
  art of, 182
  as functional area of school oper-
    ation, 5
  supporting functions and, 6, 7
Team supervision, 134–44
  Amplified Project Team, 136–43
    basic assumptions underlying,
      142–43
    characteristics of, 136–37
    dismantling, 141
    organization of, 138–39
    process sequence for, 139–41

consultant task force in intensive,
    269–74
  leadership and, 123
  strategy in, 135
Team-teaching program, branching
    analysis of, 203–4
Television, presentation through, 73
Temporary assignments, 126
Tennessee Valley Education Center
    (TVEC), 117
Termination phase of program, 33
Terpstra, D.E., 103
Testing activities, 81–82
T-groups, competency necessary
    for, 16–17
Thomas, M.D., 161, 182
Tikunoff, W., 172, 182
Time, supervisory functions and,
    121
Tolerance for turbulence, 39–40
Tractive supervision, 21, 22–23
Training:
  activity, 85, 155–56
  conducting, 297
  designing for, 92–98
    for complex change, 93–94
    currently practiced, 94–96
    programs for, 298
    reality simulation, 96–98
    sessions for, 297
  in leadership, 297
  at PDC, 286–88
  preobservation, 155–56
  in reading disability, in-service
    plan for, 274–77
  strategies, 98–103
  Taba program, 204–5
Travers, R.M.W., 184
Tropman, J.E., 79
Trump, L.J., 11
Tuning, cognitive, 152
Turning point phase, 33–34
Tyler, R.W., 196

U

Uniqueness criterion, 121
University Council on Educational
   Administration, 98
University of Pittsburgh, 119

V

Value(s):
   change as precarious, 38–39
   in evaluation, 190, 191, 243–46
Van Fleet, A.A., 118
Vars, G.F., 11
Veldman, D.J., 156, 162
Videotaping activities, 81
Visiting, informal, 151. *See also* In-
   tervisitation
Visualized lecturing, 71–72
Voting, as quality circle technique,
   105

W

Walker, W.L., 112, 114, 125
Weaver, R.A., 144

Weick, K., 135
Weinheimer, A., 189, 191, 194, 196
Weiss, C.H., 186, 190
White-hat fallacy, 36
Wiens, J., 114
Wilen, W.W., 77
Wiles, K., 2, 84, 175
Wilhelms, F.T., 118, 119, 149
Williams, R.C., 112
Wolfensberger, W., 200, 209
Workshops:
   for classroom management, 268
   human relations, 277–79
   staff development, 279–85
      diagnostic evaluation of,
         282–85
Wright, D.McC., 36
Writing activities, 86, 298

Z

Zaltman, G., 138
Zander, A., 37, 78
Zenke, L., 54